THE LANGUAGE OF FAMILY THERAPY

A SYSTEMIC VOCABULARY AND SOURCEBOOK

Fritz B. Simon
Helm Stierlin
Lyman C. Wynne

1985
FAMILY PROCESS PRESS
New York

LIBRARY OF CONGRESS CATALOGING-IN-PUBLICATION DATA

Simon, Fritz B.
    The language of family therapy.
    (The Family Process Press monograph series)
    Includes bibliographies and index.
    Translation of: Die Sprache der Familientherapie.
    1. Family psychotherapy—Language.   2. Family psychotherapy—Terminology.
I. Stierlin, Helm.   II. Wynne, Lyman C., 1923–   .   III. Title.
[DNLM: 1. Family Therapy.   2. Family Therapy—terminology. WM 430.5.F2 S594s]
RC488.5.S5413   1985   616.89′156′014   85-25270

ISBN 0-9615519-0-9

PUBLISHER'S INTRODUCTION

For a number of years the Editorial Board of *Family Process* has considered supplementing publication of its journal with a monograph series. We are delighted to introduce this series of book–length publications with *The Language of Family Therapy: A Systemic Vocabulary and Sourcebook*. As an independent, nonprofit organization, and as the publisher of the first (1962) and perhaps best–established journal in the family therapy field, Family Process, Inc. has regarded itself as having a responsibility to the family therapy field to publish writings of the highest possible quality and interest, and to extend and deepen the scope of the ideas in this field. We have become concerned that there are increasing difficulties for the publication of valuable materials that are too long for journal articles and often are too specialized for consideration as commercial ventures. Additionally, many authors of monograph–length publications want and deserve more rapid publication than is currently possible with commercial publishers, and to achieve wider distribution than is likely for specialized publications at increasingly higher prices. In the *Family Process Press Monograph Series,* we expect that there will be publications on such topics as recommendations for research on efficacy of family therapy, on family therapy training, and on other special topics in family theory. In this new venture, we follow a precedent of monograph supplements to journals, a well–established practice in child development, psychology, and other fields.

The present volume is somewhat different in scope from what we expect will be found in future offerings of Family Process Press. First, the material is not specialized and will be of broad interest to most family therapists. Second, a German version has already been published. (Ordinarily the monographs in this series will be original.) Nevertheless, because of the unavailability of the German version to English–speaking readers and because we thought that it would be a mistake to have the usual long delay before commercial publication in English would be possible, we are pleased to inaugurate the series with this important volume.

In their Preface, Fritz Simon and Helm Stierlin, the authors of the German version, have described how the material in the volume has been conceptualized, selected, and organized. The result is unusual and perhaps unique. The volume is not a glossary in the usual sense of a selection of definitions, nor is it an encyclopedia, with each article written by an authority on that particular topic. While the references usually provide reasonably comprehensive access to most topics, many of the concepts are too complex for discussion of all the major views that have been published. Therefore, we expect that readers will believe that some of their favorite topics have not been considered in an evenhanded manner. Rather, the systemic, philosophic, and psychodynamic orientations of the authors explicitly shaped the selection and discussion of the material. Clearly, the volume is not intended to be a textbook of family therapy in the sense of providing a step–by–step introduction to the field. The volume is not a dictionary because many important terms in use in the family therapy field have not been listed as key words. On the other hand, with the use of the Subject Index, a reasonable approximation to dictionary usage is achieved. Because of the distinctive interweaving and cross-referencing of terms, the volume somewhat resembles a traditional thesaurus—with the addition of critical commentary. The extensive lists of references and historical notes give this volume the quality of a sourcebook. No doubt the unclassifiable quality of the volume results from the effort to use circular, systemic principles in the organization of the material, in a form that is isomorphic to systemic theory itself.

In editing and revising the volume for publication in English, we have hoped to achieve a creative transformation in which the conceptual thrust of the original has been retained, but with an Americanization of some aspects of its content and style. Fritz Simon and Helm Stierlin have trustingly and generously encouraged our stylistic emendations, as well as revisions and additions to the content. In our changes, we have emphasized a number of recent trends and included references pertinent to these trends. The German version, for those of our readers who are interested in the history of the field, is still highly valuable in that it includes the first date of publication for each reference. We have not always followed this practice in the present edition. Also, we have preferred to provide those references more accessible in English, especially those volumes in which there are collections of important articles on specific topics.

In summary, we join Fritz Simon and Helm Stierlin in taking responsibility for idiosyncratic commissions and omissions. In working intensively with the material, as the American editors, we wish to thank Fritz Simon and Helm Stierlin for the opportunity to learn much that was new to us and for the stimulation to re–think much that was familiar. The breadth of their knowledge and scholarship is truly impressive.

Lyman C. Wynne
President of the Board, Family Process, Inc.
Issue Editor, Family Process Press

Margaret L. Toohey
Associate Issue Editor, Family Process Press

PREFACE
Directions for Use of This Book

The way we think, feel, behave, and what we see or overlook, hear or ignore, are largely determined by our language. Our perception is organized according to the structure of the language we speak. We attribute meanings to certain concepts, thereby excluding other possible meanings; we apply different words for the same subject matter. Our convictions about what is right or wrong, logical or illogical, dubious or certain, are molded by the structure of our language. This has far–reaching psychological, social, and political consequences. Our language helps determine whether a certain type of behavior is to be considered sick or immoral, or if a person is to be held liable for his or her deeds. This applies in particular to scientific jargon and to theories that support them. Clarity of concepts allows us to reduce the complexity of the world and to impose a certain order upon that complexity. Without a common language all discussion about theory is impossible.

These issues are painfully relevant to the field of family therapy. Since its advent in the early 1950s, family therapy has developed by leaps and bounds. The Western world now has dozens of family therapy journals, and the flood of publications on the subject shows no signs of abating. Hundreds of universities and institutions are offering courses in family therapy, while many members of the helping professions regard themselves primarily as family or marriage therapists.

The rapid growth in the field of family therapy is comparable to the development of psychoanalysis at the turn of the century. Then too there existed a growing demand for an integration of available information and the plethora of psychoanalytic concepts, and for the collection, categorization, and more precise definition of essential ideas. That is, a reduction of complexity was desired that nonetheless would not prevent access to the complexity of the subject matter. In psychoanalysis it was difficult enough for the practitioner to define his or her concepts clearly and exactly; the scattered and growing amount of knowledge made redefinition and reformulation of concepts a constant necessity.

The task of finding a common language for family therapy is even more difficult. Its conceptualization is not chiefly due to one man's genius. It is far more comparable to a great river whose tributaries were and are a number of innovative therapists and researchers, many of whom were and are in close contact with one another. This resulted in the concurrent (or almost concurrent) development of concepts, frequently meaning much the same thing but called by different names. To add to the confusion, the founding mothers and fathers of family therapy were often representatives of differing theoretical and practical fields of endeavor; psychoanalysts, sociologists, social workers, psychiatrists, psychologists, and anthropologists brought not only their different realms of experience into the discussion, but also their different ways of speaking about this experience. These diverse theoretical backgrounds included communication theory, information theory, general systems theory, and cybernetics, not to mention linguistics, biology, psychoanalysis, psychopathology, and so on.

In this volume we have attempted an integration of these various traditions and methods. We have elected to do this in the form of a lexicon that allows for the "cross–illumination" of concepts. Nevertheless, despite or because of the interdependence of the various keywords and the knowledge contained in them, we were forced to be selective. In the final analysis, the decision as to which keywords we considered important enough to include was ours and ours alone. We do not expect general agreement on the choices we have made because each selection implies a value judgment. Our endeavor is to provide the reader with what we consider to be the current state of the art in family therapy and systems therapy via their vocabulary. During the process of writing this book, it repeatedly became apparent to us how much is in a state of flux and how much is still left to be done, a fact that makes such an endeavor both acutely necessary and dauntingly formidable.

This volume is a reflection of our theoretical and practical backgrounds, which are mirrored in our selection of keywords, in our attempt at integration, as well as in the form of our critique. As psychiatrists and psychoanalysts who have opened themselves to cybernetic thought, we have attempted an evaluation of family therapy models from a largely cybernetic and systemic vantage. Further, we have attempted to extend the discussion to include relatively "soft" concepts such as "power" and "justice," and to elucidate them critically. So far, most of these concepts have been either ignored in the discussion of family therapy or else treated in greatly differing ways.

It became apparent to us in the course of writing this lexicon that many of the terms and concepts we have included are better understood as analogues to or, loosely speaking, metaphors of their usage in other scientific disciplines. When concepts from the natural sciences or mathematics are removed from their original context and placed in the realm of the social sciences, they inevitably change their meaning. Seen from the perspective of a natural scientist or mathematician, these concepts are being used incorrectly, or at least not quite properly. An example of this is the keyword "entropy," which found its way from thermodynamics into the language of family therapy via information theory.

In our opinion, the appropriation of these concepts is justifiable. Scientific language is sometimes derived from common, everyday language, with definitions modified to suit its special usage; it also is often derived directly from Greek or Latin and only slowly makes its way into the vernacular. Thus, the development of family therapy theory is an evolutionary process, determined as much by coincidence as by the necessities of therapeutic experience. Unlike a car or a house, family therapy theory has not been developed from an engineer's blueprint, but rather along the lines of the tinkering of an inspired jack–of–all–trades. François Jacob (1981), a theorist of evolution, has noted that the endless combination of existing mosaic pieces is the principle of the natural history of evolution. All sorts of "junk" are kept in a "junkbox" only to be (re–)discovered as usable, indeed, actively useful at a later date. This systemic vocabulary of family therapy is indeed a product of sorting through the junkboxes of other sciences. Some of the nuts and bolts, wires, and parts that we discovered in the process have been employed differently from the way their inventor perhaps intended. This, however, does not affect their usefulness for family therapy.

Given a cybernetic perspective, our modification of a dictionary format makes particularly good sense. It reflects an aspect of the ambiguity inherent in family therapy. The systemic sciences have shown that the consideration of individuals or isolated objects of study detached from the context must necessarily lead to misperception and fallacy. All of us are caught up in a network of reciprocal relationships and effects. Furthermore, because our thinking is language bound, and because it is in the nature of language to order things sequentially, we find ourselves disassembling and rearranging what naturally occurs into orderly but deceptive sequences.

A textbook espousing a sequential (or lineal) line of argumentation may suggest to the reader that the processes of cognition, in the development of theory and practice, could, might, or even must have been sequential (lineal) as well. This is not the case. Deductive and inductive thought, intuition and methodical examination, genius and just plain hard work were and are involved in the development of family therapy. This kind of interplay is, we believe, reflected in the network of concepts we have brought together, and the form we have chosen, which allows each reader to follow his or her own lines of inquiry.

To guide this process, we have provided nodal points by clustering certain key concepts. Under a number of headings we have placed concepts that tend to be used synonymously. Under other entries we have placed concepts whose definitions can be illustrated best by the way in which they differ from one another. Keywords with differing meanings are separated by a slash when they are examined under the same heading. Each keyword is followed by a definition that is further elucidated in the passage that follows, where we describe the history or origin of the concept, its general usage, and, in the event that it stems from a neighboring scientific discipline, its particular relevance for family and systems theory and therapy. This is often followed by a brief critique of the concept. To enable the reader to reconstruct the context of the keywords, we use a system of cross–references to link up similar or related concepts.

Where we associate certain concepts with names of particular researchers or "inventors," our view is naturally limited to the field of family therapy. Some authors are highlighted because they were the first to use or popularize various family therapy models. A certain amount of error could hardly be avoided here, and for this we apologize in advance.

It proved to be an exceedingly difficult task to describe the development of family therapy in a way that does justice to all those involved. This can be illustrated by the example of Gregory Bateson, whose name is linked with the shift from a lineal, cause–and–effect model, to a circular, systemic paradigm. We believe that this major epistemological shift distinguishes family therapy from most other forms of psychotherapy at present. However, the insights that Bateson introduced into psychiatric thought were not the result of his genius alone. They were the product of an exchange of ideas among many thinkers from differing scientific disciplines, including Wiener and McCulloch, to name but two. It would be futile to attempt to reconstruct exactly who put what ingredients into that fortifying, original stock. In any event, the origins and development of family therapy are a reflection of its own fundamental premise, namely, that a product emanating from a system of individuals is qualitatively different from the sum of what these individuals would produce in isolation.

Unfortunately, in the space at our disposal, much had to remain unmentioned. For this reason the list of references at the end of each article seems to us to be of particular importance. Even though we cannot say that each list is complete, we did not choose arbitrarily. Concepts related to an entire scientific field naturally contain a longer list of literature sources than those related to a single method or theory. We favored references that could serve either as introductory texts, those that in our experience are of particular value in the context of family therapy, and those of historical interest. Where the keyword has to do with a therapeutic method, we have chosen works of predominantly practical interest.

On the one hand, we intended this volume to be used as a dictionary that will enable relatively new readers to orient themselves despite the flood of publications on family therapy, and to comprehend the sometimes very abstract theories of family therapy. On the other hand, the volume is also intended as a sourcebook that will enable readers, at their own pace, to familiarize themselves systematically with much of the field of family therapy. We would like to extend our thanks to the people who helped us in the preparation and production of the German edition, above all W. D. Beiglböck, N. Bischof, I. Boszormenyi–Nagy, J. Duss–von Werdt, and P. Watzlawick, who read the manuscript in part or its entirety. Their at times severe, at times encouraging criticism was invariably helpful, even if we did not always follow their advice. Our thanks also go to Judith Landau–Stanton and M. Duncan Stanton who performed a similar function during the preparation of the English version. We are grateful for the assistance of Fr. I. von Rüdgisch–Ballas and R. Klingenberg who prepared the various versions of the German manuscript, and Mrs. A. Renner who typed the first English version.

Our special thanks go to Lyman C. Wynne who assumed the overall responsibility for editing and revision of the present English version, and to Margaret Toohey who, as editorial assistant, literary and stylistic critic, and psychological expert, gave the manuscript its final form.

Fritz B. Simon
Helm Stierlin

Jacob, F. *Le jeu des possibles: Essai sur la diversité du vivant.* Paris: Fayard, 1981.

CONTENTS

▪ A ▪

ABSTRACTION

The process of abstraction disregards idiosyncratic features and focuses instead on common elements and regularities of phenomena.

The structures of human knowledge are derived for the most part through abstraction processes. This applies to everyday thought processes as well as to the development of scientific models. To reduce complexity while retaining access to the complexity of a given subject matter is an unending task that is facilitated when abstraction processes and → **paradigms** are both subtle and flexible.

In the development of family therapy, fundamental processes of human cognition were first observed in the study of schizophrenic symptoms, and early family theories began in efforts to understand schizophrenic communication. It was noted that one characteristic of schizophrenic thought is the inability to discriminate → **logical types,** together with closely related problems in → **category formation.** Patients who show schizophrenic symptoms frequently communicate at a level of abstraction that differs from the "common–sense" level understood by others in a given verbal transaction (Kasanin, 1944). The resulting difficulty is not located in the patient, but in the relationship, in the communication process of creating shared meanings (Wynne, 1972), and in what Harry Stack Sullivan called consensual validation: "The patient feels that these are valid thoughts, suited to communicating to others—they are, of course, valid thoughts to him, but they are not *consensually* valid thoughts—and he tosses them out, to the serious detriment of clarity in the relationship with the other person" (Sullivan, 1956, p. 361). Compared to other persons, the schizophrenic may communicate on a level that either is less abstract (underinclusive, literal, and concrete), or is excessively abstract (overinclusive and global). If schizophrenic abstractions are regarded by others as → **metaphors** and → **analogic communications,** they may appear to be creatively original and sensitive to hidden meanings. When the schizophrenic is in a → **double–bind** situation, he or she will be unable to comment on the double or multiple levels of abstraction, that is, be unable to → **metacommunicate,** and subjectively will experience blocking of thought or confusion of category formation. However, such difficulties are not unique to schizophrenics; they are merely more frequently and dramatically evident.

1

The → **patterns** of abstraction that are accepted as valid in any given social situation (for example, a family) must be acquired. The investigation of the foundations, possibilities, and boundaries of these family → **rules** are in close relation to the rules of abstraction underlying the family's paradigm, model, or internal map for construing the social world (Reiss, 1981).

Two main types of abstraction processes can be distinguished: (1) generalizing abstraction and (2) isolating abstraction. Generalizing abstractions are concerned with finding invariants that are not altered by any change in the other characteristics of an observed object. An example of this would be the determination of those interactional patterns of a family that remain constant throughout changes in situations and persons involved. With isolating abstractions, certain characteristics, relations, etc., are detached from their context, thereby bestowing on them a kind of independent existence. An example of this is the reification of a certain symptom by isolating it from its → **context,** and by declaring it to be "sick." This is especially applicable to the complex of symptoms known as "schizophrenia."

Reflection on one's own rules or methods of abstraction is a necessity for anyone who wishes to make scientific statements about an object under study, for example, individual or family "pathology." Only when one understands how and where one is dismembering the continuity of chains of events by the manner of one's individual perception (→ **punctuation**), and thereby constructing a certain kind of causality (→ **lineality,** → **circularity**), can one understand the punctuations and epistemological foundations of family transactions.

Rules of abstraction are bound to particular rules of language usage (→ **syntax,** → **semantics** → **pragmatics**). As a whole, these rules affect thinking and behavior as well as affective processes (→ **affect logic**) and take the form of patterns. All human thought is bound to the use of such patterns or schemata; they are the prerequisites for survival in a given environment.

Bateson, G. Steps to an ecology of mind. New York: Ballantine Books, 1972.
Bateson, G. Mind and nature: A necessary unity. New York: E. P. Dutton, 1979.
Foerster, H. von. Thoughts and notes on cognition. In P. L. Garvin (Ed.), Cognition: A multiple view. New York: Plenum Press, 1970, 25–48.
Furth, H. Piaget and knowledge: Theoretical foundations. Englewood Cliffs, N.J.: Prentice-Hall, 1969.
Glaserfeld, E. von. An introduction to radical constructivism. In P. Watzlawick (Ed.), The invented reality. New York: W. W. Norton & Co., 1984, 17–40.
Kasanin, J. S. (Ed.). Language and thought in schizophrenia. New York: W. W. Norton & Co., 1944.
Keeney, B. P. Aesthetics of change. New York: Guilford Press, 1983.
Korzybski, A. Science and sanity. Chicago: International Non-Aristotelian Library, 1933.

Lidz, T. *The origin and treatment of schizophrenic disorders.* New York: Basic Books, 1973.

Morin, E. *La méthode. I: La nature de la nature.* Paris: Seuil, 1977.

Piaget, J. *L'équilibration des structures cognitives: Problème central du development.* Paris: Presses Universitaires de France, 1975.

Piatelli-Palmarini, M. (Ed.). *Language and learning: The debate between Jean Piaget and Noam Chomsky.* London: Routledge & Kegan Paul, 1980.

Rapaport, D. (Ed.). *Organization and pathology of thought:* New York: Columbia University Press, 1951.

Reiss, D. *The family's construction of reality.* Cambridge: Harvard University Press, 1981.

Riedel, R. *Biologie der Erkenntnis.* Hamburg: Parey, 1980.

Simon, F. B. *Der Prozess der Individuation: Über den Zusammenhang von Vernunft und Gefühlen.* Göttingen: Vandenhoeck & Ruprecht, 1984.

Sullivan, H. S. *Clinical studies in psychiatry.* New York: W. W. Norton & Co., 1956.

Watzlawick, P. *How real is real? Confusion, disinformation, communication.* New York: Random House, 1976.

Watzlawick, P. *The language of change: Elements of therapeutic communication.*

Wynne, L. C. The injection and concealment of meaning in family relationships and psychotherapy of schizophrenics. In D. Rubinstein & Y. O. Alanen (Eds.), *Psychotherapy of schizophrenia.* Amsterdam: Excerpta Medica, 1972, 180–193.

* * * * * *

ADAPTABILITY

Adaptability is the ability of a system, for example, an individual or a family, to survive and maintain its → **coherence** under changeable internal and external conditions. The term adaptation implies an outcome at a given point in time, an adjustment that is a *state* of relatedness, whereas adaptability is an ongoing process of relatedness.

Adaptability is dependent upon two regulatory mechanisms: positive and negative → **feedback loops.** In the event of negative feedback, the status quo of a certain structure is maintained (→ **morphostasis**). In the event of positive feedback, new structures are created within the system and change occurs (→ **morphogenesis**).

The adaptability of a family depends upon its ability to create a flexible balance between too much change (leading to chaotic systems) and too much stability (leading to rigid systems) (Olson, Sprenkle, & Russell, 1979). Flexibility is necessary to guarantee → **change** and development in the face of growth, aging, and variable environmental conditions (→ **coevolution,** → **mutuality**). However, some degree of system → **stability** is needed for well–defined internal family space

4

with agreed–upon → **rules** that provide each family member with a cognitive and affective frame of orientation. The manner in which families adapt to changes in internal or external conditions must be seen as decisive for their functional or dysfunctional level of adaptability (→ **healthy/functional family**). This formulation is a central principle for → **family typology** as presented in the → **Circumplex Model.**

Ashby, W. R. *Design for a brain.* London: Chapman & Hall, 1952.
Ashby, W. R. *An introduction to cybernetics.* London: Methuen, 1956.
Bales, R. F. Adaptive and integrative changes as sources of strain in social systems. In A. P. Hare, E. F. Borgatta, & R. F. Bales (Eds.), *Small groups: Studies in social interaction.* New York: Alfred A. Knopf, 1962, 127–131.
Bateson, G. *Steps to an ecology of mind.* New York: Ballentine Books, 1972.
Bertalanffy, L. von. *General systems theory.* New York: George Braziller, 1968.
Billings, A., & Moos, R. Family environments and adaptation: A clinically applicable typology. *American Journal of Family Therapy 10:* 26–38, 1982.
Buckley, W. (Ed.). *Sociology and modern systems theory: A sourcebook.* Englewood Cliffs, N.J.: Prentice-Hall, 1967.
Buckley, W. *Modern systems research for the behavioral scientist.* Chicago: Aldine Publishing Co., 1968.
Hartmann, H. *Ego psychology and the problem of adaptation.* New York: International Universities Press, 1958.
Kantor, D., & Lehr, W. *Inside the family: Toward a theory of family process.* San Francisco: Jossey-Bass, 1975.
Lidz, T. *The family and human adaptation: Three lectures.* New York: International Universities Press, 1963.
Lorenz, K. *Studies in animal and human behavior* (2 vols.). Cambridge: Harvard University Press, 1970.
Maruyama, M. The second cybernetics: Deviation-amplifying mutual causal processes. *American Scientist 5:* 164–179, 1963.
Olson, D. H., Sprenkle, D. H., & Russell, C. S. Circumplex model of marital and family systems: I. Cohesion and adaptability dimensions, family types, and clinical applications. *Family Process 18:* 3–28, 1979.
Speer, D. C. Family systems: Morphostasis and morphogenesis, or "Is homeostasis enough?". *Family Process 9:* 259–278, 1970.
Wertheim, E. S. The science and typology of family systems II. Further theoretical and practical considerations. *Family Process 14:* 285–309, 1975.

* * * * * *

Affect Logic

Affect logic (the logical structure of affect and the affective structure of logic) is a concept concerned with the development of psychological structures in a relational context. Ciompi (1982) describes the continual, close and indivisible interweaving of feelings and thinking. His description takes Piaget's (1970, 1975) fundamental statements on the differentiation of cognitive structure and combines them with concepts from psychoanalysis, → **systems theory,** and → **communication theory.**

According to Ciompi's formulation, the psyche is a hierarchically ordered complex of affective and logical relational structures. These structures are internalized schemata of thought, feeling, and behavior, with inseparable cognitive and affective components. They represent a concurrent (synchronic) manifestation of life experience that is successively gained across time (→ **diachronic**). These schemata develop with ever increasing internal complexity as information (Bateson's, 1979, "difference that makes a difference") accumulates.

In this context, thinking and feeling display two intricately bound but radically different ways of experiencing reality. (See also → **analogue/digital communication.**) Feeling apprehends unities and patterns; it is slow to evolve and to recede; its main instrument and location is the body; it is sometimes said to be centered in the right hemisphere of the brain (→ **left/right hemispheres of the brain**). Above all, thinking apprehends parts and details and is bound for the most part to the activity of the left brain. According to Ciompi, an individual's reality is optimally economical and in harmony when both modes of experience are "saying the same thing." A discrepancy of the two in either perception or communication creates a tension–laden disharmony and can lead to confusion of the internalized affect–logical relational systems and, hence, of the behavior governed by these schemata.

Ciompi's description corresponds for the most part to that which is described elsewhere as an internal map or model of the world (→ **paradigm/model/map**). These internal relational systems show, as do all cybernetic systems, the → **feedback loops** that attempt to maintain the stability of a perceived reality. In certain circumstances, which are experienced as a → **crisis,** these relational systems "snap," a situation that may lead to psychotic decompensation. Ciompi's attempt to integrate the concepts of psychoanalysis and systemic family therapy with the help of Piaget's cognitive psychology is theoretically promising. He takes into account both the synchronic and diachronic structures of human systems, hence, considering both the historicity of human experience as well as its immediate context–dependent aspects.

Simon (1984) reached quite similar conclusions. With the help of → **semiotic** concepts, he attempted to describe the principles underlying the construction of subjective models or maps of the world. In regard to the implications of this concept for therapy, Schneider (1981) has attempted to apply Piaget's theory as a paradigm for psychoanalysis. Lidz (1976) also referred to Piaget's work in his theory of disturbed → **category formation** in the etiology of schizophrenia.

6

Bateson, G. *Mind and nature: A necessary unity.* New York: E. P. Dutton, 1979.
Ciompi, L. *Affektlogik. Über die Struktur der Psyche und ihre Entwicklung. Ein Beitrag zur Schizophrenieforschung.* Stuttgart: Klett-Cotta, 1982.
Lidz, T. Skizze einer Theorie der schizophrenen Störungen. *Familiendynamik 1:* 90–112, 1976.
Lidz, T., Fleck, S., & Cornelison, A. R. *Schizophrenia and the family.* New York: International Universities Press, 1965.
Piaget, J. *Genetic epistemology* (translated by E. Duckworth). New York: Columbia University Press, 1970.
Schneider, H. *Die Theorie Piagets: Ein Paradigma für die Psychoanalyse?* Bern: Huber, 1981.
Simon, F. B. *Der Prozess der Individuation: Über den Zusammenhang von Vernunft und Gefühlen.* Göttingen: Vandenhoeck & Ruprecht, 1984.

* * * * * *

ALLIANCE/ALIGNMENT/COALITION

These synonymous terms refer to the perception or experience that two or more persons are joined together in a common endeavor, interest, attitude, or set of values; contrasting items are alienation, split, or estrangement.

The concepts of alignment/alliance and corresponding splits/alienation were introduced by Wynne (1961) to facilitate "descriptions of organizational or structural features" of family therapy systems as a supplement to communications analysis of discrete messages (p. 96). Applying the principle of systems equilibrium, Wynne hypothesized that an alignment or alliance between two or more persons automatically tends to split them off from others within the system: An emerging alignment or split "in any part of a system whose components are interdependent reverberates to produce change in other parts of the system. . . . The study of such sequences over a period of time, as the therapeutic process unfolds, will help reveal how the various levels of functioning in the family system are dramatically linked and experientially separated or dissociated" (Wynne, 1961, p. 97).

When such alignments or coalitions blur or cross over → **generational boundaries,** a disturbance of the family → **hierarchy** results (Lidz, 1963; Minuchin, 1974). These dysfunctions may take the form of → **rigid triads** (Hoffman, 1981; Minuchin, 1974), of → **perverse triangles** (Haley, 1967), and of pathological → **triangulation** (Bowen, 1976).

The intentional formation of a coalition of therapist with a family member is a therapeutic technique employed by Minuchin and Zuk as a method for restructuring the family. Zuk (1981) describes the "go–between" process in which family coalitions are broken up by the therapist's systematically taking sides with or against individual family members. By constantly switching allegiances from one individual family member to another, the therapist remains in control of family interaction and is in a position to shake up rigid family structures. Minuchin and Fishman (1981) advance similar theoretical considerations in the therapeutic technique of unbalancing, in which the therapist's goal is to change the hierarchical relationship of the members of a subsystem by temporarily aligning, affiliating, or → **joining** one individual or one subsystem at the expense of the others. New perspectives, roles, and solutions may thereby be opened up.

Bowen, M. The use of family theory in clinical practice. *Comprehensive Psychiatry 7:* 345–374, 1966.

Bowen, M. Theory in the practice of psychotherapy. In P. J. Guerin (Ed.), *Family therapy: Theory and practice.* New York: Gardner Press, 1976, 42–90.

Caplow, T. *Two against one: Coalitions in triads.* Englewood Cliffs, N.J.: Prentice-Hall, 1968.

Haley, J. Toward a theory of pathological systems. In G. H. Zuk & I. Boszormenyi-Nagy (Eds.), *Family therapy and disturbed families.* Palo Alto: Science and Behavior Books, 1967, 11–27.

Hoffman, L. *Foundations of family therapy: A conceptual framework for systems change.* New York: Basic Books, 1981.

Lidz, T. *The family and human adaptation: Three lectures.* New York: International Universities Press, 1963.

Minuchin, S. *Families and family therapy.* Cambridge: Harvard University Press, 1974.

Minuchin, S., & Fishman, H. C. *Family therapy techniques.* Cambridge: Harvard University Press, 1981.

Minuchin, S., Montalvo, B. G., Guerney, B., Rosman, B. L., & Schumer, F. *Families of the slums: An exploration of their structure and treatment.* New York: Basic Books, 1967.

Minuchin, S., Rosman, B. L., & Baker, L. *Psychosomatic families: Anorexia nervosa in context.* Cambridge: Harvard University Press, 1978.

Penn, P. Coalitions and binding interactions in families with chronic illness. *Family Systems Medicine 1* (2): 16–25, 1983.

Wynne, L. C. The study of intrafamilial alignments and splits in exploratory family therapy. In N. Ackerman, F. L. Beatman, & S. N. Sherman (Eds.), *Exploring the base for family therapy.* New York: Family Service Association of America, 1961, 95–115.

Zuk, G. H. The side-taking function in family therapy. In C. J. Sager & H. S. Kaplan (Eds.), *Progress in group and family therapy.* New York: Brunner/Mazel, 1972, 376–384.

Zuk, G. H. *Family therapy: A triadic-based approach* (revised ed.). New York: Human Sciences Press, 1981.

* * * * * *

ANALOGUE/DIGITAL COMMUNICATION

Human communication processes can be separated into two types, analogue and digital, associated with two different media that use different signs and signals.

In digital communication processes there exists no similarity between the expressed sign and its meaning, that is, betwen an object and its name. Signs are generally used as the result of tacit agreement (→ semiotics). A good example of digital communication are words themselves. Words and their meanings have for the most part little to do with one another. The word "table" has little or nothing essentially "table-like" about it.

In analogue communication there exists a fundamental similarity between what is expressed and the manner in which it is expressed. Analogue communication is exhibited in human interaction by nonverbal behavior, including speech variations such as tone, tempo, and so forth. Whereas digital communication has a highly complicated → syntax but is only able to describe limited aspects of human relational processes, the expressive value of analogue communication in relational processes is high but the syntax is limited.

The division and classification of human interactional and communication phenomena into analogue and digital processes is artificial but useful. This distinction has been commonly used in → cybernetics. In data processing a general distinction can be made between digital and analogue computers. Digital computers function on the "all or nothing" principle, using digits [Latin digitus, finger]. Analogue [Greek ana logon, correct relation] computers perform arithmetical operations by using variable physical qualities to represent numbers. Perhaps the simplest example of this type of analogue machine is the abacus where spatial changes "imitate" abstract processes. The most important difference between analogue and digital signs is that the transition between the digital signs is discontinuous, whereas it is continuous in the analogue sign system. The difference between two digital signs is understood as either a "yes" or a "no." Analogue signs express continuously changeable quantities and qualities.

The difference between analogue and digital communication has been systematically described by Watzlawick, Beavin, and Jackson (1967) and is the foundation of their → communication theory. The differentiation between the various levels of communication came to the full attention of family therapy research after the publication of the → double-bind hypothesis. This hypothesis is sometimes erroneously understood to begin with the distinction between verbal and nonverbal channels, but this dichotomy is not equivalent to that between analogue and digital communication or to the concept of logical types that is used in the double–bind theory.

In general, it can be said that digital communication allows for the expression of considerably more detailed material than does analogue communication. Digital communication has an articulate → **semantic** system at its disposal, i.e., the meaning of each digital sign is prototypically unequivocal. Analogue signs by contrast are polysemous, that is, open to many interpretations: Tears can be the expression of joy or sorrow, relief, or other emotions. Digital communication allows for the possibility of negation whereas analogue communication can only represent messages positively. Hierarchically linked abstractions need to be expressed almost exclusively in a digital fashion. Yet, when one studies how two people form and understand their emotional relationship to each other, one discovers that analogue communication lends itself to greater depth of expression. Emotions that are felt for another person manifest themselves in bodily reactions, which in turn become signs for emotions. There exists a close relationship between these types of signs and their meanings. The verbal statement "I love you" says a great deal less than the accompanying bodily reactions.

One of the problems in communication theory with the use of the analogue/digital distinction is that the potential of "word–speech" for digital communication is limited. Word–speech is only *relatively* digital. Words themselves also tend to be polyvalent. They can be used poetically as → **metaphors,** as pictures whose exact, stable meaning cannot always be identified or confirmed. In cybernetic engineering, "digital" is used to refer to a code admitting only "yes" or "no" differentiations, for example, binary figures made up of one and zero.

In the course of the acquisition of human speech, words become increasingly "digitalized." A young child at first uses the word "mama" as an analogue communication tool to emit an appeal for nurturance, to express sensations, and to describe situations that are closely related to this term. In later development the concept "mama" is more narrowly defined, becoming finally crystalized into the name of the person "Mother." Therefore, when we speak in terms of analogue and digital communication in human interactional processes, it should be understood that there exists no absolute and clear division between the two types of communication modes.

Bateson, G., & Jackson, D. D. Some varieties of pathogenic organization. In D. McK. Rioch & E. A. Weinstein (Eds.), *Disorders of communication. Proceedings of the Association for Research in Nervous and Mental Disease, Research Publications, Vol. 42.* Baltimore: Williams & Wilkins Co., 1964, 279–290.

Bateson, G., Jackson, D. D., Haley, J., & Weakland, J. H. Toward a theory of schizophrenia. *Behavioral Science 1:* 251–264, 1956.

Madanes, C. *Strategic family therapy.* San Francisco: Jossey-Bass, 1981.

Watzlawick, P., Beavin, J. H., & Jackson, D. D. *Pragmatics of human communication: A study of interactional patterns, pathologies and paradoxes.* New York: W. W. Norton & Co., 1967.

* * * * * *

ATTRIBUTION/LABELING/DELINEATION

The overt or covert attribution of characteristics, intentions, and roles to the members of a social system.

Attribution is an element of all social interaction and organization. The behavior, status, and functioning of individual persons are seen as elements of a representational system comparable to the system of language or speech (→ **semiotics**). Each of these elements is assigned a meaning. This meaning is not objectively given, but is dependent upon the relational system (→ **context**) in which it occurs. Context and attribution are elements of a circular process (→ **circularity**); a person whose behavior is labeled as belonging to a certain role is often coerced to behave in a manner that accords with the role attributed to him or her, which confirms the "validity" of the original attribution.

In the mid-1960s, labeling theory, linked to attributions, gained considerable attention in medical sociology and psychiatry. It concerns itself, *inter alia,* with the conditions under which diagnoses are made and the effects that these diagnoses have on the persons to whom they assigned (*cf.* Scheff, 1966).

In the field of family therapy, Ivan Boszormenyi–Nagy, Ronald Laing, and Helm Stierlin have described this problem and the impact of labeling phenomena. As mentioned above, attribution is an element of all socialization processes. It becomes problematic in three sets of circumstances. More generally, it is difficult for an individual to find a meaningful social role, a meaning in life, and a feeling of personal importance; this hinders the development of → **self–esteem.** More specifically, when attribution (diagnosis) is unclear, inappropriate, or lacking entirely in treatment settings, a framework for initiating therapy may be difficult to construct. Even a pathological label may be a starting point that can be reframed (→ **reframing**) (Grunebaum & Chasin, 1978). In the third situation, attribution proves to be too rigid; labeling, in these instances, is a forcible invasion of an individual's self. An example of this is the attribution to a child of characteristics, roles, or intentions that have a negative effect on the child's age–appropriate → **individuation** and the processes of the adolescent's detachment from his or her family (→ **separating parents and adolescents**).

Three areas of attribution have proven to be of particular clinical interest: (1) the attribution of illness, weakness, and general ineptitude in daily affairs; (2) the attribution of badness, meanness, or criminality; and (3) the attribution of insanity, abnormality, or craziness. Attribution is an important element of → **delegation** and → **projective identification;** it also manifests itself in certain → **binding** mechanisms. Boszormenyi–Nagy (1965) views attribution as a mechanism through which multigenerational → **loyalties,** which can have both negative and positive effects on the familiy system, are established and maintained.

Acock, A. C., & Bengston, V. L. Socialization and attribution processes: Actual versus perceived similarity among parents and youth. In D. Olson & B. Miller (Eds.), *Family studies review yearbook, Vol. 2.* Beverly Hills: Sage Publications, 1984, 305–319.

Boszormenyi-Nagy, I. Intensive family therapy as process. In I. Boszormenyi-Nagy & J. L. Framo (Eds.), *Intensive family therapy: Theoretical and practical aspects.* New York: Harper & Row, 1965, 87–142.

Grunebaum, H., & Chasin, R. Relabeling and reframing reconsidered: The beneficial effects of a pathological label. *Family Process 17:* 449–455, 1978.

Herkner, W. (Ed.). *Attribution: Psychologie der Kausalität.* Bern: Huber, 1980.

Jones, R. A. *Self-fulfilling prophecies: Social, psychological and physiological effects of expectancies.* Hillsdale, Cal.: Erlbaum, 1977.

Kaslow, F. W. A dialectic approach to family therapy and practice: Selectivity and synthesis. *Journal of Marital and Family Therapy 7:* 345–351, 1981.

Laing, R. D., & Esterson, A. *Sanity, madness, and the family. Vol. I, Families of schizophrenics.* London: Tavistock Publications, 1964.

Scheff, T. J. *Being mentally ill: A sociological theory.* Chicago: Aldine Publishing Co., 1966.

Stierlin, H. *Das Tun des Einen ist das Tun des Anderen.* Frankfurt: Suhrkamp, 1971.

Stierlin, H. *Delegation und Familie.* Frankfurt: Suhrkamp, 1978.

Szasz, T. *The myth of mental illness: Foundations of a theory of personal conduct.* New York: Harper & Row, 1961.

AUTONOMY/EMANCIPATION

Living systems are able to develop a certain independence from their environment. The behavior of living systems is to a variable degree internally or externally controlled. The concept of autonomy or emancipation (be it of an individual or of a family) must encompass this aspect of constant interaction with the environment. From a systems point of view, autonomy or emancipation can be seen as an aspect of → **self-organization.**

Goodwin (1970) describes autonomous systems as follows: " 'Living systems' are engaged in a perpetual process of self–maintenance and self–realisation directed by internally–defined criteria of stability and organisation. Phenomenologically it is this attribute of living beings which allows us to identify them as discrete, autonomous systems: autonomous not in the sense that they are independent of their environment, but in the sense that their 'goals' are different from those of the physical environment, and these goals are internally defined" (p. 1). The ontogenesis of the individual as well as the structuring of the family can be understood as a process of self–organization. In constant interaction with the environment, structures are formed whose function it is to insure the survival of the system. There are two possibilities of influencing these processes: (1) internal control and (2) external control (Riesman, Glazer, & Denney, 1950). In the development of the individual, it is possible to determine differing phases and degrees of dependence from external influence. Babies and small children are dependent to a large degree upon external control. In the process of development this dependence lessens, and to an increasing degree the individual takes over self–preserving and self–directive functions. This process of emancipation can be understood as an increasing structural refinement of an individual's internal system. The development of psychic structures can be understood as the evolution of internal structures, with both individual and family representing a coevolving, individuating ecological structure (→ **individuation**).

In more abstract terms. Foerster (1984) has defined autonomy as self–regulation, or the regulation of regulation. In a similar vein, Keeney (1983) has stated: "A system's *highest* order of recursion or feedback process defines, generates, and maintains the autonomy of a system. The range of deviation this feedback seeks to control concerns the organization of the whole system itself. If the system should move beyond the limits of its own range of organization, it would cease to be a system. Thus, autonomy refers to the maintenance of a system's wholeness. In biology it becomes a definition of what maintains the variable called 'living' " (p. 84).

The autonomy, or organizational closure of a system, in the case of an individual or a family, is bound up with the ability to maintain certain → **boundaries,** i.e., the ability to discriminate between internal and external events. A system that is capable of reaching an internally defined goal irrespective of environmental conditions can be said to have a certain autonomy. Autonomy implies responsibility (Foerster, 1984). This independence, however, is *never* total; it functions only within a certain range. Autonomy is always relative to a particular environment. This environment itself is never static because it in turn is changed (within limits) by the behavior of the system of which it is a part. The achievement and maintenance of autonomy is thus always bound to take into account such processes of change. Keeney (1983) argues that what we do in interaction with an autonomous system never gets "inside" the system, but takes place with the wholeness of the system that is maintained in the process of → **autopoiesis.** Reasoning along these lines, Maturana and Varela (1980) propose that interactions with an autonomous system should be called "perturbations," rather than "inputs."

Emancipation or, expressed psychologically, individuation, in the sense of the acquisition of autonomy, thus has two prerequisites: (1) the establishment of internal stability and (2) the establishment of a relation to a → **context** or to the entire ecosystem (→ **ecology**). During the early mother–child relationship the child will hardly be able to emancipate itself, as the child's survival is dependent to a great extent on external control. In the course of time, the child achieves maintenance of its own → **stability.** Whether this developmental process is successful or not depends upon both partners (or the entire family) because the definition of relationship cannot be one–sided.

Ideally, the child's relationship to its parents changes in accord with its epigenetic development, so that it is able to attain → **self/object differentiation** and the formation of an → **identity** conforming to the norms of its sociocultural environment. This process is a constant oscillation between conformity and nonconformity in which involved individuals change the conditions of interaction for themselves and for others. This is true of all coevolving systems. Each member determines to a certain extent the environment of the interactional partners. The type, the extent, and the impulse of these determinations change with the stages of the individual's and the → **family's life cycle,** both of which are closely interconnected. In childhood it is the parents who constitute a significant part of the environment of the child. For married adults, to a lesser degree, the spouse and/or children usually serve this function. Finally, in old age, given one's reduced autonomy, one's own children, relatives, or institutions take over and become an external source of control.

In the life–cycle of the individual as well as in the life–cycle of the family, change is occurring constantly; therefore, it is of the utmost importance that the balance between stability and flexibility be guaranteed (→ **relational balance**).

In family therapy, in contrast to individual therapy, the reciprocal relationship between emancipation of the individual and of the family or, analogously, between the species and its ecological niche, is always taken into consideration. It is not the goal of family therapy to preserve the family at any cost, even though some critics of family therapy believe that this is so. The goal of family therapy is to render development possible for the individual as well as for the family as a whole.

Foerster, H. von. On constructing a reality. In P. Watzlawick (Ed.), *The invented reality*. New York: W. W. Norton & Co., 1984, 41–61.

Goodwin, B. C. Biological stability. In C. H. Waddington (Ed.), *Towards a theoretical biology, Vol. 3: Drafts*. Edinburgh: Edinburgh University Press, 1970, 1–17.

Hartmann, H. *Essays on ego psychology*. New York: International Universities Press, 1964.

Jantsch, E. *Design for evolution*. New York: George Braziller, 1975.

Jantsch, E. *The self-organizing universe*. Elmsford, N.Y.: Pergamon Press, 1980.

Jantsch, E., & Waddington, C. H. (Eds.). *Evolution and consciousness: Human systems in transition*. Reading, Mass.: Addison-Wesley, 1976.

Keeney, B. P. *Aesthetics of change*. New York: Guilford Press, 1983.

Maturana, H. R., & Varela, F. J. *Autopoiesis and cognition: The realization of living*. Boston: Reidel, 1980.

Riesman, D., Glazer, N., & Denney, R. *The lonely crowd: A study of the changing American character*. New York: Yale University Press, 1950.

Varela, F. J. A calculus for self-reference. *International Journal of General Systems* 2: 5–24, 1975.

Varela, F. J. *Principles of biological autonomy*. New York: Elsevier North Holland, 1979.

* * * * * *

■ B ■

BEAVERS SYSTEMS MODEL

The Beavers Systems Model is a dimensionalized approach to the classification of family functioning. It provides for ratings of (1) competence (→ **adaptability**) in whole families who are engaged in current task performance and (2) the style of family interaction (→ **centripetal/ centrifugal patterns**). From a grid of ratings on these two dimensions, a → **family typology** is constructed that is clinically useful and empirically supported.

The Beavers Systems Model was designed to represent data from direct observations of family interaction rather than from self–reports, as in Olson's → **Circumplex Model.** Family members are asked to discuss for about ten minutes a topic such as, "What would you like to see changed in your family?". Prior research by Lewis, Beavers, Gossett, and Phillips (1976) showed that competence in small tasks of

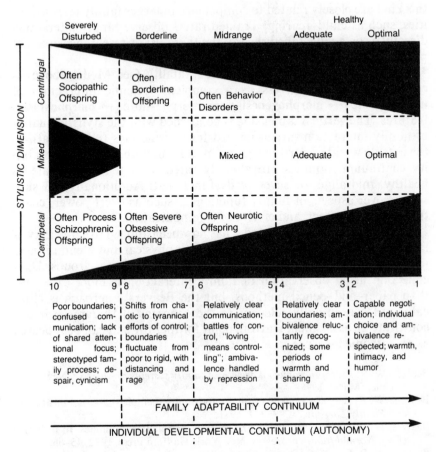

(adapted from Beavers and Voeller, 1983, p. 90)

DEFINITIONS

Autonomy: A continuous or infinite dimension, related to the family system's capacity to allow and encourage members to function competently in making choices, assuming responsibility for self, and negotiating with others.

Adaptability: A continuous or infinite dimension, related to the capacity of a family to function competently in effecting change and tolerating differentiation of members.

Centripetal / Centrifugal: A curvilinear, stylistic dimension with extreme styles associated with severely disturbed families and the most competent families avoiding either extreme.

Inflexibility: The inability to change. The most chaotic families are the most inflexible owing to their lack of a shared focus of attention.

Severely Disturbed: The lowest level of functioning along the adaptiveness continuum manifested by poorly defined subsystem boundaries and confusion owing to nonautonomous members having little tolerance for clear, responsible communication.

Borderline: A level of functioning between severely disturbed and midrange, manifested by persistent and ineffective efforts to rid the system of confusion by simplistic and often harsh efforts at control.

Midrange: Families that typically turn out sane but limited offspring, with relatively clear boundaries but continued expectations of controlling and being controlled.

this kind are closely related to competence in larger family responsibilities, such as child–rearing. Trained raters observe family interaction directly or on a videotaped record; the therapist or researcher does not participate in the family interaction.

The horizontal dimension of adaptability (see Model above) is conceptualized by Beavers as a complex, systemic interaction of morphogenic (→ **morphogenesis**) and morphostatic (→ **morphostasis**) features. The vertical dimension is concerned with the stylistic quality of family interaction turned inward for satisfactions (centripetal), to the outside world (centrifugal), or a mixture of both. On the adaptability continuum, families are globally rated on a ten–point scale as healthy, midrange, or severely dysfunctional. Additionally, 13 subscales cover aspects of family functioning such as overt power, coalitions, range of affect, and clarity of communication.

The Beavers Systems Model has now been applied to a diversity of families, without identified disorders, with physical and mental illness in one or more family members, and in various cultural groups. Data collection using observation of family interaction is more expensive than paper–and–pencil methods, but the Beavers' approach is clinically and conceptually relevant to the concerns of therapists; it can constitute an assessment starting point for therapy and can be repeated as an outcome measure.

Beavers, W. R. *Psychotherapy and growth: A family systems perspective.* New York: Brunner/Mazel, 1977.

Beavers, W. R. A systems model of family for family therapists. *Journal of Marital and Family Therapy 7:* 299–307, 1981.

Beavers, W. R. Healthy, midrange, and severely dysfunctional families. In F. Walsh (Ed.), *Normal family processes.* New York: Guilford Press, 1982, 45–66.

Beavers, W. R. *Successful marriage: A family systems approach to couples therapy.* New York: W. W. Norton & Co., 1985.

Beavers, W. R., & Voeller, M. N. Family models: Comparing and contrasting the Olson Circumplex Model with the Beavers Systems Model. *Family Process 22:* 85–98, 1983.

Lewis, J. M., Beavers, W. R., Gossett, J. T., & Phillips, V. A. *No single thread: Psychological health in family systems.* New York: Brunner/Mazel, 1976.

Stierlin, H., Levi, L. D., & Savard, R. J. Centrifugal versus centripetal separation in adolescence: Two patterns and some of their implications. In S. C. Feinstein & P. Giovacchini (Eds.), *Adolescent psychiatry, Vol. II: Developmental and clinical studies.* New York: Basic Books, 1973, 211–239.

* * * * * *

BEHAVIORAL FAMILY THERAPY

This form of therapy is based on a blend of operant learning principles, social exchange theory, and cognitive psychology (Bandura, 1974; Jacobson & Margolin, 1979; Mahoney, 1974; Rappaport & Harrell, 1972; Thibaut & Kelly, 1959). Interventions are derived from empirical research and are oriented to learning and to the development of mutually acceptable problem–solving skills, often combined with communication skill training.

Behavioral therapists were relatively late in applying their methods to the field of relationship problems, doing so at first primarily with marital problems and, more recently, with whole families. Interest in this approach began in the late 1960s (Liberman, 1970; Stuart, 1969). Behavior therapists began by treating each family member, using the traditionally established methods of learning theory such as positive and negative reinforcement, etc. Families were engaged, for example, by training the parents of children who exhibited deviant behavior to reinforce positively or negatively (reward or punish) certain child behaviors in order to establish a therapeutic "field of learning" (Patterson & Hops, 1972; Patterson & Reid, 1970). Individual operant conditioning was found to be of limited value if dysfunctional patterns of interaction and relatedness were neglected. For example, it was discovered that both spouses exhibited behaviors that reinforced the pathological behavior of the partner.

When the theories of social learning and exchange were taken into consideration, it became possible to grasp the complexity of such interactional problems more readily. A fundamental proposition of these theories is that in interactional situations behaviors are exchanged between partners. Each interactional partner attempts to achieve maximal "profit" with minimal "loss." The degree of profit that one receives from one's own behavior or that of the interactional partner will have a more or less reinforcing effect. The choice of manifest behaviors is thus determined by the "rate of exchange" currently valid in the couple's relationship. This then determines the →
rules of a partnership. These rules develop in the course of the couple's mutual "learning history" (or interactional experience with one another). If punishment or negative reinforcement between spouses predominates in the marital relationship, then the relationship will be (according to the tenets of behavioral therapy) problematic. The predominance of positive reinforcement or reward, however, fosters a functional relationship between the partners (Jacobson, 1981).

Hence, according to behavioral therapy, the emotional state of one partner is a consequence of the behavior of the other partner.

Inability to articulate one's needs and to communicate clearly about them to the other partner leads to reciprocal, pathological cycles of reinforcement. The inability to differentiate between affective and factual levels makes the solution of conflicts difficult. Behavioral therapy concerns itself first with determining the rules of interaction, the chains of reciprocal stimuli and reaction, and the matrix of negative and positive reinforcement. In a given context, desired and undesired behavior and corresponding forms of relationship are established, and rewards and punishments are negotiated. Communication training is taught so that the partners learn to express their needs and to resist demands that they find undesirable. In general, the therapist attempts to potentiate the couple's ability to solve problems and conflicts. A good example of this approach is → **sex therapy.**

An important aspect of interpersonally oriented behavioral therapy is "contingency contracting." Here, contracts are devised with the couple or family, which include specific expectations that certain behaviors will occur or diminish, with explicit consequences (positive or negative) to follow designated behavior. For example, a therapist might negotiate with a couple that the husband compliment the wife at least three times during the upcoming week and, if she had prepared his favorite dish, to criticize her only once afterward. The wife's part of the contract could be to agree not to wake up the husband with complaints during the night after he had complimented her, and to prepare his favorite dish once during the week.

If one takes into consideration the reciprocal relationship between the identity development and the behavior of oneself and others, it becomes entirely possible to integrate psychoanalytic and behavioral concepts, as well as the concepts of learning theory. From a systems viewpoint, one should, however, be skeptical of intervention methods that attempt to change behavior while disregarding the overarching → **context** in which the behavior takes place. Current behavioral family and marital therapy does not fall into this trap. For example, Barton and Alexander (1981) have broadened an earlier behavioral approach into what they call functional family therapy. In this approach, the meaning of behavior is "derived from an examination of the relational processes in which it is embedded, as well as the relational outcomes that the behavior functionally elicits from others" (p. 406). Stuart (1980) also incorporates systems theory into his thinking in a highly structured, six–stage approach to marital therapy. Liberman and associates (1980), and Falloon, Boyd, and McGill (1984) teach problem–solving and communication skills within a marital and family framework. The work of Falloon's team is especially outstanding because of their success in treating chronic schizophrenics within a family context. With this approach, they have obtained significantly better results than with a comparison group that received individual therapy. Margolin (1983) states that there has been "a misleading tendency to equate behavioral marital therapy with specific procedures. What distinguishes the behavioral model from other marriage therapies is not its procedures *per se* but its commitment to an integration between clinical and research endeavors . . . Behavior marital therapy is best described as a method of inquiry, both for analyzing clinical problems and for designing intervention techniques. Clinical observations, whether systematic or serendipitous, prompt theoretical refinements and additional empirical study. Through continued empirical investigation, clinical procedures undergo considerable change over time. A self–corrective process thus ensues from this constant interplay between clinical and research endeavors" (p. 247).

Bandura, A. *Social learning theory*. Englewood Cliffs, N.J.: Prentice-Hall, 1974.
Barton, C., & Alexander, J. F. Functional family therapy. In A. S. Gurman & D. P. Kniskern (Eds.), *Handbook of family therapy*. New York: Brunner/Mazel, 1981, 403–443.
Birchler, G., & Spinks, S. Behavioral-systems marital and family therapy: Integration and clinical application. *American Journal of Family Therapy 8:* 6–28, 1980.
Falloon, I. R. H., Boyd, J. L., & McGill, C. W. *Family care of schizophrenia: A problem-solving approach to the treatment of mental illness*. New York: Guilford Press, 1984.
Gurman, A. S. Behavioral marriage therapy in the 1980's: The challenge of integration. *American Journal of Family Therapy 8:* 86–96, 1980.
Gurman, A. S., & Kniskern, D. P. Behavioral marriage therapy: II. Empirical perspective. *Family Process 17:* 139–148, 1978.
Gurman, A. S., & Knudson, R. M. Behavioral marriage therapy: I. A psychodynamic-systems analysis and critique. *Family Process 17:* 121–138, 1978.
Gurman, A. S., Knudson, R. M., & Kniskern, D. P. Behavioral marriage therapy: IV. Take two aspirin and call us in the morning. *Family Process 17:* 165–180, 1978.
Hahlweg, K., & Jacobson, N. S. (Eds.). *Marital interaction: Analysis and modification*. New York: Guilford Press, 1984.
Jacobson, N. S. Behavioral marital therapy: Current trends in research, assessment and practice. *American Journal of Family Therapy 8:* 3–5, 1980.
Jacobson, N. S. Behavioral marital therapy. In A. S. Gurman & D. P. Kniskern (Eds.), *Handbook of family therapy*. New York: Brunner/Mazel, 1981, 556–591.
Jacobson, N. S., & Margolin, G. *Marital therapy: Strategies based on social learning and behavior exchange principles*. New York: Brunner/Mazel, 1979.
Liberman, R. P. Behavioral approaches to family and couple therapy. *American Journal of Orthopsychiatry 40:* 106–118, 1970.
Liberman, R. P., Wheeler, E. G., deVisser, L. A. J. M., Kuehnel, J., & Kuehnel, T. *Handbook of marital therapy: A positive approach to helping troubled relationships*. New York: Plenum Press, 1980.
Mahoney, M. J. *Cognition and behavior modification*. Cambridge, Mass.: Ballinger, 1974.

20

Margolin, G. Behavioral marital therapy. In B. B. Wolman & G. Stricker (Eds.), *Handbook of marital and family therapy.* New York: Plenum Press, 1983, 247–276.

Patterson, G. R., & Hops, H. H. Coercion, a game for two: Intervention techniques for marital conflict. In R. E. Ulrich & P. Mountjoy (Eds.), *The experimental analysis of social behavior.* New York: Appleton-Century-Crofts, 1972, 424–440.

Patterson, G. R., & Reid, J. B. Reciprocity and coercion: Two facets of social systems. In C. Neuringer & J. L. Michael (Eds.), *Behavior modification in clinical psychology.* New York: Appleton-Century-Crofts, 1970, 133–177.

Rappaport, A. F., & Harrell, J. A behavioral-exchange model for marital counseling. *Family Coordinator 21:* 203–213, 1972.

Stuart, R. B. Operant-interpersonal treatment for marital discord. *Journal of Consulting and Clinical Psychology 33:* 675–682, 1969.

Stuart, R. B. *Helping couples change: A social learning approach to marital therapy.* New York: Guilford Press, 1980.

Thibaut, J. W., & Kelly, H. H. *The social psychology of groups.* New York: John Wiley & Sons, 1959.

* * * * * *

BIFOCAL FAMILY THERAPY

Bifocal family therapy, derived from psychoanalytic and group therapy methods, combines nondirective, directive, and manipulative techniques. The goal is to change deadlocked family systems. This therapy especially focuses on removing schizophrenic patients from the role of the family outsider. It is one of the few therapeutic methods developed within an institutional setting and is designed to take into consideration the conditions prevailing in a psychiatric hospital.

In the late 1940s, Schindler developed this method to treat institutionalized schizophrenic patients. He assumed that the institutionalization was the result of a tension–laden situation or crisis within the family. He noticed that families did not necessarily hospitalize the person who was most central in the family or the one who had the most symptoms, but, rather, the family member who occupied an outsider, or omega–position in the family system. Schindler considered the family to be a "forced group," and he derived certain → strategies for change from its group dynamics.

The principles of bifocal family therapy can be described as follows. A certain number of patients, usually about six, form a small therapy group. Concurrently, the family members of these six patients form an outpatient group. Both groups receive therapy from the same therapist and/or cotherapist. During the initial phase of therapy the group members assume that the therapist will take a leading (dominant and didactic) position. Apparently, the concept of the "omnipotent doctor" tends to have a stabilizing effect because the inpatient group in particular tends to become unsettled and to respond with varying degrees of uncertainty when this expectation is not met. The degree of fear, impatience, and aggressive behavior directed toward the therapist varies according to the amount of insecurity the patients feel. Through a specific gambit (the omega opening), the therapist places the patient with the most conspicuous illness at the center of attention. This introduces the group to the phenomenon of illness literally in their midst, and leads to a recognition of their denial of this process. In the parallel therapy with family members, the therapist creates even greater confusion by avoiding the dominant role. Attempts are made to force the therapist into the role of the expert, and endless questions are directed at him or her in order to achieve this end.

This first phase is gradually replaced by the second, in which the group members themselves take the lead. Central topics in the second phase of therapy are communication problems with the inpatients, their unrealistic expectations, their fears and uncertainties in their relationships with their families. Through manipulative maneuvers by the therapist, a "voluntary restriction" of visiting rights is effected. This increases the ambivalence of the patient–family relationship; the wish to reject the patient as well as the wish to bind him or her are intensified. Guilt feelings increase. The conflict created by typical bifocal therapy puts the therapist in a "transference crossover" between patients and family members (Schindler, 1976). In the patient group, the therapist becomes the object of parental transference; each patient in turn projects his or her particular view of his or her parents onto the therapist. In the group of family members, the characteristics, impulses, and potentialities of the patient in question are attributed to the therapist. Hence, the therapist is in the midst of each → **transference** process. Through various interventions, the therapist is able, in a dialectical manner, to bring into play the respective counterpart to the parents' and the patients' transference patterns. During the stage of "realizing coping" (*realisierende Bewältigung*), the patients begin their first steps toward separation from the family of origin (→ **separating parents and adolescents**). During this stage the family members and/or parents show signs of being deeply perturbed. The therapist reinforces the patient's position at this point with the help of the therapeutic strategy Schindler calls the "omega rochade"; the therapist displays understanding for the patient's "crazy ideas" and does not enforce any normative demands. The binding, emotional forces of the parents are now directed toward the therapist, which lessens the burden on the patient.

The goal of bifocal family therapy, oriented as it is toward inpatient care systems, is to advance the process of separation and → **individuation** within the family. At the same time, it attempts to free the psychiatrist and the hospital from any tendency toward homeostatic functioning (maintenance of status quo). Generally speaking, bifocal family therapy takes about a year.

In summary, with the help of diagnostic transference strategies and countertransference reactions, bifocal family therapy attempts to change rigid family structures. In this attempt, the → **paradoxical intervention** strategy, whereby the therapist does not meet the expectations of the group therapy members about a therapist's role, very likely is crucial to the success of the therapy.

Schindler, R. Bifocal group therapy. In J. H. Masserman & J. L. Moreno (Eds.), *Progress in psychotherapy, Vol. III: Techniques of psychotherapy.* New York: Grune & Stratton, 1958, 176–186.

Schindler, R. Bifokale Gruppentherapie und Familientherapie. In E. Pakesch (Ed.), *Die Familie als Patient.* Graz: Akademie Druck– und Verlagsanstalt, 1974, 143–151.

Schindler, R. Bifokale Familientherapie. In H. E. Richter, H. Strotzka, & J. Willi (Eds.), *Familie und seelische Krankheit: Eine neue Perspektive der psychologischen Medizin und der Sozialtherapie.* Reinbek: Rowohlt, 1976, 216–235.

* * * * * *

BINDING

Binding is a relational mode that comes into effect (mostly covertly) in all types of relationships. In the context of the Heidelberg model, it contrasts with the → **expelling** mode and stands at the same time in dialectical relationship to it. The binding mode is of particular importance within the context of → **separating parents and adolescents.** Binding reflects the dominance of → **centripetal patterns.**

If the binding mode predominates, the relationship partners—particularly parents and children—act in accord with the tacit assumption that "real" satisfaction of emotional needs and security can only be found within their relationship. The world outside the family is seen as a hostile and frightening place. This assumption is reflected in the attitude of the parents who see no other alternative, when confronted with their own developmental crisis, than to bind their children even more closely in the family ghetto, to impede and even prevent the development of their children's autonomy. This attitude is then internalized by the children who, in turn, contribute to binding interactions. Detachment from the family and autonomy are equated with extreme (existential) loneliness, abandonment, and defenselessness against the hostile outside forces.

Using psychoanalytic terms, three levels of binding can be discriminated. On the first, more affective level, the predominantly elementary need for satisfaction of urges is addressed and/or abused. This may be termed "id–binding." The second level of binding occurs primarily on the level of cognitive processes, referred to as "ego–binding." On the third level, "superego–binding," the loyalty of the bound–up individual is exploited. On all three levels the interactional partners offer each other relationship modes that strengthen the centripetal patterns in the family.

Binding on the id–level can be defined as reciprocal, regressive gratification that stimulates and satisfies desires and needs. This often takes the form of partially satisfying oral drives, but sexual stimulation (which at times can go as far as incest) also occurs. The atmosphere in id–binding families tends to be heavy, stuffy, and charged with emotion.

Binding on the cognitive level is primarily concerned with the exchange of perceptions, thoughts, and feelings. In extreme cases, family members may think that they share the same beliefs, that their view of the world is the same, and that their feelings are similar. This is of course not possible, and it results in a great many perceptual distortions, disqualifications (devaluations), → mystifications, and projective → attributions. Family members believe that they can read each other's thoughts and speak the other's mind. The parents know "instinctively" how strong or weak, sick or healthy, sane or crazy their children are. Children bound up in this manner tend to be restricted in related → individuation; they do tend, however, to reflect strong → consensus sensitivity. Any form of independence is prohibited, and there exists a strong orientation toward each other.

Binding on the superego level has to do with ethical aspects of relationships, above all, betrayal of overt or covert → loyalty can cause massive, break–away guilt, which in turn can lead to self–destructive life styles. Many self–destructive careers, characterized, for example, by alcoholism, drug abuse, continual occupational failures, or the tendency toward suicidal preoccupations, can be understood as the result and expression of a massive binding on the superego level, with concomitant break–away guilt.

Although family therapists are confronted primarily with pathological forms of binding, binding in itself is a highly functional mechanism for the survival of the individual as well as for the species. Bowlby (1969) thoroughly researched human binding ("attachment")

24

behavior during early childhood. It appears that mother and child innately have the potentiality for certain behavioral patterns that establish an emotional bond between them. The cries and smiles of the child guide the mother to it. The child's clinging and following instincts lead the child to the mother and keep her in the vicinity. The interactional circle, present in early infancy, is thus dependent upon both partners. Similar mechanisms have been described by other behavior researchers (see Wickler & Seibt, 1977). Binding mechanisms link innate behavior patterns and learning. Binding becomes pathological only when the possibility of change is thwarted for the individual, or within the → **family life cycle,** and → **adaptability** to the changed demands of the surrounding social system is impeded.

More recently, Wynne (1984) has placed the relational dynamics of binding/attachment in an epigenetic perspective. He hypothesizes a sequence of four major relational processes or patterns, identified as (1) attachment/caregiving, (2) communicating, (3) joint problem solving, and (4) mutuality. These can be viewed as elucidating age–appropriate dynamics, of binding and un–binding, as well as related individuation and family–wide → **coevolution** within the individual and family life cycle.

Boszormenyi-Nagy, I., & Spark, G. M. *Invisible loyalties: Reciprocity in intergenerational family therapy.* New York: Harper & Row, 1973.
Bowlby, J. *Attachment and loss. Vol. I, Attachment.* New York: Basic Books, 1969.
Schaffer, H. R., & Emerson, P. E. The development of social attachments in infancy. *Monograph, Society for Research in Child Development 29:* 1–77, 1964.
Spitz, R. A. Hospitalism: A follow-up report. *Psychoanalytic Study of the Child 2:* 113–117, 1946.
Stierlin, H. *Separating parents and adolescents: A perspective on running away, schizophrenia, and waywardness.* New York: Quadrangle, 1974.
Stierlin, H. *Delegation und Familie.* Frankfurt: Suhrkamp, 1978.
Stierlin, H., Levi, L. D., & Savard, R. J. Centrifugal versus centripetal separation in adolescence: Two patterns and some of their implications. In S. C. Feinstein & P. Giovacchini (Eds.), *Adolescent psychiatry, Vol. II. Developmental and clinical studies.* New York: Basic Books, 1973, 211–239.
Wickler, W., & Seibt, U. *Das Prinzip Eigennutz: Ursachen und Konsequenzen sozialen Verhaltens.* München: Piper, 1977.
Wynne, L. C. The epigenesis of relational systems: A model for understanding family development. *Family Process 23:* 297–318, 1984.

* * * * * *

BINOCULAR THEORY OF CHANGE

Binocular theory of change is a short–term therapy concept based on the epistemological insights of Gregory Bateson.

According to this concept, a therapist is never able through interventions to completely change the interactional pattern based upon a family's epistemology. It is possible, however, to introduce another point of view that is slightly different from the family's. From these two points of view a third one can be formed that is novel for the family. According to de Shazer's (1982) concept of short–term therapy, the interventions of a therapy team must be compatible with the family's beliefs about itself and yet be different enough to make possible the creation of a third, new perspective. The idea for this concept stems from "plastic seeing" and gives rise to the requirements of a "double description." Two pictures, taken from slightly different perspectives, are combined to create a three–dimensional effect (Bateson, 1979; Keeney, 1979).

On the formal level, the intervention procedure should be isomorphic (→ **isomorphism**) with the structure of the family's model of the world (→ **paradigm/ model/ map**). Only then, in de Shazer's opinion, is the family willing to integrate a new perspective into their own epistemology. Hence, a therapeutic team can employ the tactic of dividing itself so as to portray two different, opposing interpretations of a family problem when such a division of views is already present within the family therapeutic system. If clumsily applied, this tactic may reinforce a family's conviction that consensus is dangerous, but, ordinarily, useful new → **information** can be introduced into the family with this approach.

Bateson, G. *Mind and nature: A necessary unity.* New York: E. P. Dutton, 1979.
de Shazer, S. *Patterns of brief family therapy: An ecosystemic approach.* New York: Guilford Press, 1982.
Keeney, B. P. Ecosystemic epistemology: An alternative paradigm for diagnosis. *Family Process 18:* 117–129, 1979.
Keeney, B. P. *Aesthetics of change.* New York: Guilford Press, 1983.

BOUNDARIES

Most family therapists consider the processes of boundary demarcation between individuals, family subsystems, and the family and the external environment to be of central importance.

Dysfunctional families show disturbances of boundary differentiation (→ **healthy/ functional familes**). Boundaries allow for the differentiation and development of → **structures**. A disturbance in boundary formation is thus synonymous with pathological structure. The boundaries of a system or subsystem are determined by "the rules defining who participates [in the family or subsystem], and how" (Minuchin, 1974, p.53).

Internal family boundaries are recognizable by the different rules for behavior that are applicable for different family subsystems. The rules that apply to parental behavior (parental subsystems) are usually different from those that apply to child behavior (child subsystem). The boundaries between the family and the external environment are determined by the difference in the interactional behavior that family members exhibit toward other family members and toward nonfamily members.

These interactional rules on the behavioral level are reflected in the rules underlying the family's → **epistemology** of itself. Most constructs about family pathology or dysfunctionality include the concept of disturbances in the formation of boundaries. Disorders of boundary formation are also linked to disturbances in cognitive and affective styles and the ensuing problems in interactional styles. The formation of boundaries is a prerequisite for any type of → **system,** be it interactional or epistemological. Rules must be developed within complex living systems, which include families. Such rules delineate how behavior or a class of behaviors is to be understood. There must be rules or boundaries that define where, when, and under what conditions a given member may behave in such and such a manner. From a cybernetic perspective, Ashby (1956) defined the concept of boundaries as "a relation between two sets" that "occurs when the variety that exists under one condition is less than the variety that exists under another" (p. 127). The delineation of boundaries, in effect, selectively reduces complexity. This process of complexity–reduction through boundary–definition is similar to what is called "demarcation" of behavior patterns and → **punctuation** of sequences of communication. Where and when demarcation/punctuation occurs, and what kind of selections result are culture–dependent, and, hence, variable. Without doubt, language plays a major role in determining the processes of demarcation and punctuation (Shands, 1971; Whorf, 1942).

The concept of the *Individual* in Indo–European languages postulates an "I," a boundary and independence from the surrounding environment (→ **autonomy**). This concept is in accord with the agreed–upon cultural definition that the norm of individual development is successful → **individuation** (self/other differentiation) and stable → **identity.** The development of a child's affective and cognitive styles is an expression of the child's → **adaptability** to the → **rules** of family communication and interaction, which are translated into epistemological rules (→ **paradigm/ model/ map**). This internalized model of the world is a set of relationship → **roles,** i.e., the demarcation of boundaries.

Two types of boundary formation disturbances are of particular importance in family therapy: boundaries that are too weak, and those that are overly strong. The latter disturbance, expressed in the concept of → **disengagement,** is an overlooking or denying of the fact that people are engaged in some kind of relationship to one another. Overly strong boundary demarcation leads to autism and isolation. Overly weak boundaries are conceptualized as → **enmeshment,** → **fusion,** → **undifferentiated family ego mass,** or, in psychoanalytic terminology, as disturbances in self/other differentiation (particularly implicated in the formation of schizophrenic symptoms). Disturbances of this sort are found in families that strive toward, or at least hope to attain, a unity of thinking and feeling among all family members about their need for physical and mental privacy and independence. Families who believe that family members are incapable of survival on their own, and that total family unity (real or ideal) is the only mode in which they can function, may be said to be extremely bound up (→ **binding,** → **rubber fence**).

Experience has shown that only related individuation is functional, that is, when the balance between separation and unity remains in a constant state of negotiation. This system principle applies to family subsystems as well as to the relationship between the family and its external social environment. In these circumstances, communication about the rules (metarules) must take place in order to determine when the boundaries are functional, and when they are not. Parents and children, for example, may exchange roles in play, but only if it is clear to them that this is being done in play (→ **context marking,** → **generational boundaries**). If the roles were exchanged without first delineating the context, confusion about the validity of boundaries would result and lead to misunderstanding, or in more extreme forms, to → **collective cognitive chaos** and → **mystification.**

Finally, boundaries are an indication of the extent to which systems are or can become open. The crossing of boundaries changes closed systems into open ones; in other words, it transforms stable structures (→ **morphostasis**) into flexible structures (→ **morphogenesis**). The boundaries of a system thus determine to a major degree the processes of its → **self-organization.**

Ashby, W. R. *An introduction to cybernetics.* London: Methuen, 1956.

Boss, P., & Greenberg, J. Family boundary ambiguity: A new variable in family stress theory. *Family Process 23:* 535–546, 1984.

28

Elkaïm, M., Prigogine, I., Guattari, F., Stengers, I., & Denenbourg, J.–L. Openness: A round-table discussion. *Family Process 21:* 57–70, 1982.

Haley, J. Toward a theory of pathological systems. In G. H. Zuk & I. Boszormenyi-Nagy (Eds.), *Family therapy and disturbed families.* Palo Alto: Science and Behavior Books, 1967, 11–27.

Hoffman, L. "Enmeshment" and the too richly cross-joined system. *Family Process 14:* 457–468, 1975.

Koehler, W. Closed and open systems. In F. E. Emery (Ed.), *Systems thinking.* Harmondsworth, England: Penguin Books, 1974, 59–69.

Miller, J. G. *Living systems.* New York: McGraw-Hill, 1978.

Minuchin, S. *Families and family therapy.* Cambridge: Harvard University Press, 1974.

Shands, H. G. *The war with words.* The Hague-Paris: Mouton, 1971.

Shapiro, E. On curiosity: Intrapsychic and interpersonal boundary formation in family life. *International Journal of Family Psychiatry 3:* 69–90, 1982.

Simon, F. B. Die Evolution unbewusster Strukturen. *Psyche 37:* 520–544, 1983.

Simon, F. B. *Der Prozess der Individuation: Über den Zusammenhang von Vernunft und Gefühlen.* Göttingen: Vandenhoeck & Ruprecht, 1984.

Simon, F. B., & Pritz, A. Aussenseiterstrategien: Die Paradoxe Logik sozialer Innovationen. *Gruppenpsychotherapie Gruppendynamik 19:* 77–87, 1983.

Spencer-Brown, G. *Laws of form.* New York: Dutton, 1979.

Whorf, B. L. *Language, thought, and reality.* Cambridge: Massachusetts Institute of Technology Press, 1942.

Wynne, L. C., Ryckoff, I. M., Day, J., & Hirsch, S. I. Pseudo-mutuality in the family relations of schizophrenics. *Psychiatry 21:* 205–220, 1958.

* * * * * *

BRIEF THERAPY

This therapeutic procedure developed from the implications of systems theory concepts. An understanding of second–order → **change** has shown that the structure of a system is capable of discontinuous and erratic change. Brief therapy aims at removing the barriers to the development and → **adaptability** of family systems (→ **coevolution**) and reinstating the family's potential for → **self–organization.**

In contrast to psychoanalytically based, brief therapy approaches, which of necessity limit themselves to focusing on one problem, systematically oriented, brief therapy methods are not merely "second best." Both → **cybernetics** and → **systems theory** have proven that the self–organizational processes of systems can change in either a continuous or discontinuous manner. In psychoanalytic treatment, change is expected to take place through continuous, not discontinuous, working–through. The success of such change is related to a great extent to the length of treatment, the number of therapy hours, and so on.

Systemically oriented procedures, on the other hand, attempt to effect, by means of a few interventions, a second–order or discontinuous change in system patterns in the entire family as well as in each individual family member. The intervention strategies of systemic therapy are as a rule directive. Brief therapy consists of a limited number of sessions (usually six to fifteen) spaced at intervals of one to six weeks. These sessions are problem oriented, sometimes with a supportive and psychoeducational approach when the brief therapy takes place around crisis intervention and prevention (→ **crisis family therapy**). In brief therapy that is also → **systemic therapy,** the therapist endeavors to change the epistemological (→ **epistemology**) foundations of the problem. The decisive change process often does not take place in the therapy sessions themselves but, rather, in the intervals between sessions.

Brief therapy forms belong to the larger context of therapeutic communication (→ **communication therapy**). One speaks of → **strategic therapy** when the solution of a specific, delimited problem is the focus of therapeutic interest; if, however, the focus is a relational problem, one tends to speak of systemic therapy. Other forms of therapy, such as → **hypnotherapy** and → **neurolinguistic programming,** tend to be used mostly with individual patients, although in recent years both have found increasing admittance into the realm of family therapy.

Bandler, R., & Grinder, J. *Frogs into princes.* Moab, Utah: Real People Press, 1979.

Bergman, J. E. *Fishing for barracuda: Pragmatics of brief systemic therapy.* New York: W. W. Norton & Co., 1985.

de Shazer, S. Brief family therapy: A metaphorical task. *Journal of Marital and Family Therapy 6:* 471–476, 1980.

de Shazer, S. *Patterns of brief family therapy: An ecosystemic approach.* New York: Guilford Press, 1982.

de Shazer, C. *Keys to solution in brief therapy.* New York: W. W. Norton & Co., 1985.

Duss-von Werdt, J., & Welter-Enderlin, R. Kurztherapie mit einer Paargruppe. *Familiendynamik 3:* 86–90, 1978.

Fisch, R., Weakland, J. H., & Segal, L. *The tactics of change: Doing therapy briefly.* San Francisco: Jossey-Bass, 1982.

Goldstein, M. J., & Kopeikin, H. S. Short– and long–term effects of combining drug and family therapy. In M. J. Goldstein (Ed.), *New developments in interventions with families of schizophrenics.* San Francisco: Jossey-Bass, 1981, 5–26.

Papp, P. *The process of change.* New York: Guilford Press, 1983.

Saposnek, D. T. Aikido: A model for brief strategic therapy. *Family Process 19:* 227–238, 1980.

Watzlawick, P., Weakland, J. H., & Fisch, R. *Change: Principles of problem formation and problem resolution.* New York: W. W. Norton & Co., 1974.

Weakland, J. H., Fisch, R., Watzlawick, P., & Bodin, A. M. Brief therapy: Focused problem resolution. *Family Process 13:* 141–168, 1974.

* * * * * *

■ C ■

CATASTROPHE THEORY

This mathematical theory describes how systems may flip from one postulated state of equilibrium to another state of equilibrium ("catastrophe") (→ **crisis**).

Continuous causes may have discontinuous effects, that is, a system may show either → **stability** (→ **equilibrium**) or → **change.** One can represent the relation between environment and system as follows: A ball rolling in a hilly terrain will usually come to rest in its deepest depression; however, it may come to a stop in a trough at a higher elevation where it also may stabilize and be in a state of equilibrium. If we think of living systems, we can imagine such troughs as ecological niches to which a given system, for example, an individual or a family, has adapted (→ **adaptability**).

Although catastrophe theory, as developed by Thom (1975), had become popularized, it recently has been widely criticized because it offers a relatively static concept that does not do justice to the phenomenon of → **self–organization.** Catastrophe theory is unable to demonstrate how, in our example, the ball gets from one trough to another, and how the necessary energy to overcome the inertia is supplied. Thus, this theory postulates a passive system that lacks creativity and is unable to test out other possible behaviors or to influence its environment (→ **fluctuation/dissipative structures,** → **chaos theory,** → **synergetics,** → **coevolution**).

Poston, T., & Stewart, J. *Catastrophe theory and its applications:* London: Pitman, 1978.
Thom, R. *Structural stability and morphogenesis.* Reading, Mass.: Benjamin, 1975.
Zeman, E. C. *Catastrophe theory: Selected papers.* Reading, Mass.: Addison-Wesley, 1977.

* * * * * *

CATEGORY FORMATION

The formation of categories aids in the → **punctuation** of communication and the structuring of thought and emotion.

Since 1911, when Eugen Bleuler (1950) formulated the concept of schizophrenia, "loosening of associations" has been considered an essential aspect of schizophrenic thought disorder. A number of researchers have conceptualized this phenomenon as faulty category formation. This view has been advanced explicitly by Lidz (1968), who posited that an essential characteristic of thought disorder is the inability to form categories:"A category serves as a filter that permits attention to essentials and eliminates the intrusion of non–essentials into the train of thought" (p. 178). Overinclusiveness, regarded as a form of schizophrenic thought disorder by Cameron (1938), is egocentric. Typically, a person believes that what others say and do involves him or her even when this is not the case. This leads to feelings of reference, ideas of persecution, and so forth.

Individuals with schizophrenic thought disturbances may also believe that their actions, thoughts, feelings, and wishes influence others, or that they can magically influence the inanimate universe. Lidz refers to Piaget's (1952) work, which states that thought processes of this type are part of a normal developmental stage in the cognitive maturation of the child. It is only after the child has achieved "object constancy" in the "separation and individuation" phase (as described by Mahler, 1968) that the child eventually overcomes cognitive egocentricity. At this developmental point, the child is able to discriminate between those experiences that involve self and those experiences that involve object, and can conceptualize two types of categories for the two types of experiences.

Attainment of → **self/object differentiation** is therefore the prerequisite for any kind of genuine category formation. The thought processes of those individuals who do not advance to this level remain pre–categorical and overinclusive. If an individual remains in the pre–categorical stage of thinking, the developmental stage of → **separating parents and adolescents** may culminate in decompensation. An overinclusive → **identity,** i.e., an identity that has an inclusive attitude toward the family, makes separation seem impossible. Likewise, every situation that is intimate threatens the individual with the loss of individual → **boundaries**.

As an aspect of communication processes, category formation, in Lidz's conceptualization, shows similarities to what other authors prefer to call punctuation and → **logical types.** Like Lidz, Ciompi (1982) draws upon Piaget's discoveries in his conceptualization of the structure of psychic systems (→ **affect logic**).

Bleuler, E. *Dementia praecox or the group of schizophrenias* (translated by J. Zinkin). New York: International Universities Press, 1950.

Cameron, N. Reasoning, regression and communication in schizophrenics. *Psychological Monographs 50* (whole no. 221), 1938.

Ciompi, L. *Affektlogik: Über die Struktur der Psyche und ihre Entwicklung. Ein Beitrag zur Schizophrenieforschung.* Stuttgart: Klett-Cotta, 1982.

Lidz, T. The family, language, and the transmission of schizophrenia. In D. Rosenthal & S. S. Kety (Eds.), *The transmission of schizophrenia.* Oxford: Pergamon Press, 1968, 175–184.

Lidz, T. *The origin and treatment of schizophrenic disorders.* New York: Basic Books, 1973.

Lidz, T. Skizze einer Theorie der schizophrenen Störungen. *Familiendynamik 1:* 90–112, 1976.

Mahler, M. *On human symbiosis and the vicissitudes of individuation. Vol. I, Infantile psychosis.* New York: International Universities Press, 1968.

Piaget, J. *The language and thought of the child.* London: Routledge & Kegan Paul, 1952.

* * * * * *

CENTRIPETAL/CENTRIFUGAL PATTERNS

These concepts were introduced into family therapy theory by Helm Stierlin to depict two differing family constellations during the period of → separating parents and adolescents.

Stierlin et al. (1973) describe two patterns of adolescent separation from the family as centrifugal and centripetal:

These patterns reflect forces in the family that are either outward (centrifugal) or inward (centripetal) directed. We consider these patterns extreme variants of the separation course of adolescence. These separation patterns, we try to show, can illuminate those sequences and configurations which in adolescents give rise to various forms of psychopathology, particularly certain forms of schizophrenia and sociopathy. . . .

With this model in mind, we can distinguish between two extreme vicissitudes of separation. In one of these, the orbit of the family and parents exerts an unusual attraction for the adolescent: Centripetal forces are here predominant. These forces tend to delay or abort the adolescent's endeavors at separation. They may nonetheless facilitate certain enriching experiences, conflictive and painful though these may be.

In the other extreme configuration suggested by this model, the adolescent evades or attenuates the attraction of the parental orbit. At the same time he maximizes the importance of peers or alternate adults. Here we find centrifugal forces strongly at work: Instead of delaying his separation, the adolescent is rushing it. In so doing, he subjects himself to experiences and problems different from those found in the first–mentioned configuration.

These two different separation patterns imply thus different vicissitudes in relationships and different potentials for growth. (pp. 211–212)

As Stierlin further developed his model of adolescent separation processes, he tended to speak more of the forces of → **binding** and → **expelling,** which essentially determine whether the process of related individuation will be attained. Extreme forces of binding can be found in families with schizophrenic members (so–called "schizo–present" families); extreme forms of binding *and* explusion tend to be observed in families exhibiting serious and chronic psychosomatic symptoms. The → **Beavers Systems Model,** in particular, uses such distinctions as a central dimension in its description of various family systems.

Beavers, W. R. *Psychotherapy and growth: A family systems perspective.* New York: Brunner/Mazel. 1977.

Kelsey-Smith, M., & Beavers, W. R. Family assessment: Centripetal and centrifugal family systems. *American Journal of Family Therapy 9:* 3–12. 1981.

Stierlin, H. *Separating parents and adolescents: A perspective on running away, schizophrenia, and waywardness.* New York: Quadrangle, 1974.

Stierlin, H., Levi, L. D., & Savard, R. J. Centrifugal versus centripetal separation in adolescence: Two patterns and some of their implications. In S. C. Feinstein & P. Giovacchini (Eds.), *Adolescent psychiatry, Vol. II: Developmental and clinical studies.* New York: Basic Books, 1973, 211–239.

* * * * * *

CHANGE, FIRST AND SECOND ORDER

A system is able to change in two ways: (1) Individual parameters change in a continuous manner but the structure of the system does not alter; this is known as "first–order change." (2) The system changes qualitatively and in a discontinuous manner; this is known as "second–order change." This second type of change in systems occurs with "changes in the body of rules governing their structure or internal order" (Watzlawick, Weakland, & Fisch, 1974). Second–order change is change of change.

In a relatively stable environment, the required values of a system can be held constant through quantitative changes in the system's behavior; an example of this is the maintenance of constant body temperature by means of perspiration. Ashby (1952) referred to these continuous, purely corrective changes in a system as first–order change, occurring within a system that itself remains unchanged. In contrast to these mechanisms, Ashby described second–order changes, whose occurrence changes the system itself. Those systems that possess the ability to change in a qualitative manner are far better able to adapt to changes in their environment than those systems that are merely capable of first–order change. The ability to learn (→ **learning**) is linked to second–order change. The above description applies to all developmental processes that are capable of changing structures (→ **coevolution,** → **morphogenesis**).

A system that is merely capable of first–order change is able to maintain its → **stability** in a relatively constant environment through the mechanisms of → **morphostasis** and → **homeostasis.** If, however, the environment changes, then the system's ability to adapt is limited. In order to survive, second–order change is necessary so that the system can either remove itself from the changed environment or change its own internal structures in such a way that its → **coherence** is maintained.

The concept of second–order change was introduced into psychotherapy in general and into family therapy in particular by Watzlawick, Weakland, and Fisch (1974). The concept has proven to be of immense importance because, in contrast to traditional ideas regarding change, the concept of second–order change provided a plausible explanation of how well–aimed therapeutic interventions could produce disproportionately large changes in family systems (→ **brief therapy**). Whereas in first–order change the linkage between cause and effect is in general proportional (linear) (→ **lineality/linearity**), causality is nonlinear (→ **nonlinearity**) in second–order change. These differing types of change and adaptation are based on differing types of → **feedback.**

First–order change is largely based on negative feedback, which balances out deviations and keeps the system at a constant level. Second–order change, on the other hand, is based on positive feedback, which augments deviations (→ **fluctuation**) and thus initiates the development of new structures (→ **self–organization**). The goals of therapy determine largely in advance which type of change is being consciously or unconsciously sought. The attempt to establish a *status quo ante* (the condition that existed in the family before the appearance of the symptoms) implies a mere first–order change; this approach accords with the traditional medical view of therapy. If, however, one aims for new patterns of behavior, new family structures, and the development of improved problem–solving abilities, then one is aiming for second–order change.

Ashby, W. R. *Design for a brain.* London: Chapman & Hall, 1952.
Ashby, W. R. *An introduction to cybernetics.* London: Methuen, 1956.
Bateson, G. *Steps to an ecology of mind.* New York: Ballantine Books, 1972.
Speer, D. C. Family systems: Morphostasis and morphogenesis, or "Is homeostasis enough?". *Family Process 9:* 259–278, 1970.
Watzlawick, P., Weakland, J. H., & Fisch, R. *Change: Principles of problem formation and problem resolution.* New York: W. W. Norton & Co., 1974.

* * * * * *

CHAOS THEORY

This mathematical theory takes into account the disorderly, chaotic behaviors of systems.

Our everyday world view as well as most traditional sciences are based on the assumption that causality (→ **lineality**) operates unidirectionally over time. Accordingly, the past shapes the present, the present shapes the future, and a physical system that originates under exactly the same conditions will each time show exactly the same subsequent behaviors. Hence the conclusion: Same causes have same effects. This conclusion, however, is reductionistic. Neither in nature nor in an experimenter's laboratory can causes be exactly reproduced and their effects be exactly determined. Yet, as our daily experience shows, we can compute a reliable reality only when we assume that similar causes have similar effects (→ **constructivism**, → **paradigm/model/ map**). Only in this way can a basic requirement of natural science research—the reproducibility of experiments—be fulfilled. This means that minor deviations can be tolerated because it can be assumed that minor deviations in the starting conditions of an experiment will similarly result in minor deviations in the end–state.

Recently, however, the basic assumption of scientific and everyday thinking has been shaken. For example, in classical mechanics it can be demonstrated that under certain conditions even minimal alterations in a system's starting conditions may radically change its subsequent behavior. Accordingly, similar "causes" may have very dissimilar effects because any behavior reveals a sensitive dependence on its starting conditions. These phenomena constitute the research domain of chaos theory.

Around the turn of the century, the mathematician Poincaré supplied an example of possible chaotic movement. He had devised a model of a solar system consisting of two suns but only one planet. He showed that this planet is bound to carry out incredibly complicated movements comparable to those of a ball in a soccer game. (What world view, or epistemology, might the inhabitants of such a planet develop?) This example shows that the long–term computation of behaviors in physical systems may be impossible even when the rules and laws of natural science are applied. The planet influenced by two suns obeys ordinary gravitational laws and yet displays unpredictable behaviors that result from minimal alterations in its starting conditions (including the starting conditions of observation, of computation, etc.), which can never be exactly determined. This is the reason why meteorological predictions turn out to be so unreliable and prognoses regarding evolution processes remain, in the last analysis, merely speculative (→ **coevolution**).

Chaos theory has special relevance for family theory as it makes understandable how minimal differences may make a huge difference (→ **information**). There are no two families that live under exactly the same conditions; small changes in developmental conditions may have massive effects (→ **reframing**, → **brief therapy**). Thus, we glimpse new domains of research in which, for example, the seemingly unruly and chaotic character of schizophrenic thinking may be found to obey certain general rules (→ **synergetics**). Chaos theory postulates a fluid transition between order and chaos whereby structures (→ **structure/ function/process**) may disintegrate into chaos while new structures may evolve out of disorder (→ **entropy/negentropy**).

Collet, P., & Eckmann, J. P. *Iterated maps of the interval as dynamical systems.* Basel: Birkhäuser, 1980.

Feigenbaum, M. J. Universal behavior in nonlinear systems. *Los Alamos Science* (Summer): 4–27, 1980.

May, R. M. *Stability and complexity in model ecosystems.* Princeton, N.J.: Princeton University Press, 1973.

Poincaré, H. *Les méthodes nouvelles de la méchanique celeste.* New York: Dover, 1957.

CIRCULAR QUESTIONING

This technique, used in → **systemic therapy,** aims at gathering and, at the same time, introducing information into the family system. The gathering of information aids in the formulation and validation of hypotheses regarding the family's dynamic structure (→ **hypothesis formation**). The transmission of information aims at changing the individual's and the family's → **epistemology** of themselves. According to Bateson (1979), "information is the difference which makes a difference." For example, each participant in a family therapy session is asked in turn to express his or her views on the relationships and the differences between other family members. Thus, each family member contributes on a metalevel (→ **metacommunication**) to the development of an image of the family structure, and to an understanding of the circular (→ **circularity**) nature of the relationships in the family.

The technique of circular questioning was developed by the Milan School of Selvini–Palazzoli and associates; the technique enables the therapist to gain extensive information about the family in a short period of time. Throughout the questioning sequence, → **neutrality** and → **positive connotation** are maintained. Communication largely takes the form of metacommunication about the behavior of others. Hence, the dangers of → **self-reference** in responses to questioning are avoided. If, for example, in other therapy forms, a child is questioned about his or her relationship to one of the parents, the answer given in the presence of the parents becomes itself an element of the parent-child relationship, and may consolidate and intensify an already existing → **loyalty** conflict. Taboos and → **family secrets** that remain in effect during a therapy session can be indirectly touched upon through the technique of circular questioning. For example, one can respect the content of a secret and still ask hypothetical questions about the effects of disclosure on the various family members. Along the same lines, covert coalitions between individual family members can be detected in a fairly unproblematic manner, e.g., "Who can comfort mother better when she is sad, father or daughter?" "What does father do when daughter is able to comfort mother?"

The technique of circular questioning both achieves quick access to a rich source of information and serves as an effective therapy instrument. The constant change of perspectives and the introduction of new systems of evaluation are sufficient to place the pathogenic aspects of the family's epistemology of itself in question. Further, the indirect transmission of information blocks the formation of possible family → **resistance** and the establishment of a united front against the therapist. Each family member is free to make use of the information in his or her own way, and free to express his or her opinion about that information. Changes that are promoted through this questioning technique are further reinforced by the specific intervention strategies of systemic therapy (→ **paradoxical intervention**).

Bateson, G. *Mind and nature: A necessary unity.* New York: E. P. Dutton, 1979.
Penn, P. Circular questioning. *Family Process 21:* 267–280, 1982.
Selvini-Palazzoli, M., Boscolo, L., Cecchin, G., & Prata, G. *Paradox and counter-paradox: A new model in the therapy of the family in schizophrenic transaction* (Translated by E. V. Burt). New York: Jason Aronson, 1978.
Selvini-Palazzoli, M., Boscolo, L., Cecchin, G., & Prata, G. Hypothesizing-circularity-neutrality: Three guidelines for the conductor of the session. *Family Process 19:* 3–12, 1980.

✳   ✳   ✳   ✳   ✳   ✳

CIRCULARITY/RECURSIVENESS/ CIRCULAR CAUSALITY

These terms refer to a sequence of cause and effect that leads back to a first cause and either confirms or changes that first cause. This principle also applies to the processes of logical conclusions and argument. The most elementary model of circularity is the so-called → **feedback loop;** its conceptual opposite is → **lineality.**

Circular processes are the central concern of → **cybernetics,** in which innumerable elements of a system are reciprocally contingent and influence each other's behavior in a complex manner. Many phenomena can only be explained by reference to the reciprocal contingency of different variables. This applies in particular to evolutionary processes (→ **coevolution**), processes in the maintenance and establishment of → **stability** and → **homeostasis,** and the development and alteration of the structures of systems (→ **morphogenesis,** → **morphostasis**). Cybernetics attempts to answer questions that arise in connection with these complex processes of systems in general, regardless of their material composition. These questions are of special interest to family therapy.

The fundamental instrument of cybernetic analysis is the discounting of the dimension of time, that is, only synchronic or, at least, very rapidly occurring interactional relations are taken into consideration. Circularity is not comprehensible within the dimension of time as humans experience it, because time is not reversible; the past cannot be changed retroactively. Yet, wherever the past does leave its mark on personal or family structures (in memory, in family rules, family structures, etc.) circularity plays a role. As Shakespeare has said, "past is prologue." A family rule that has been established in the past is applied to the present and can be confirmed or changed in the future. The prerequisite of this occurrence is a process of abstraction whereby situations are classified as being similar to one another and as having identical → **contexts.** It is only when an internal model of the world has been established, and concrete events, behaviors, and experiences have been translated in some manner into signs that circularity can be applied to the regulation of human behavior (→ **paradigm/model/ map**).

Recursiveness [Latin *recurrere,* to flow back], like circularity, characterizes the reversibility of causes and effects back to their initial starting point. In individual human development, as in the development of relational systems, we may assume that recursiveness occurs through individual as well as collective storage of experience (memory). Recursiveness allows the endless stream of perceptions and experiences that occur in the passage of time to be punctuated (→ **punctuation**) in such a way as to reduce the complexity of experience. The experiences of yesterday are equated with those of today, and rules of behavior are established. This process is both functional and economical, but it can become dysfunctional when rules are so rigid that they resist all change.

In family systems in particular, the thoughts and feelings of each individual are embedded in the family context and sustained by the family rules. The reverse is also true: The patterns of each family member's thoughts and feelings maintain the status quo of the family rules. This represents a process of reciprocal stabilization. Thus, a situation is created in which circularity conditions a type of stability that is inadequate in the face of the demands of changing internal and external circumstances (→ **family life cycle**). The result is dysfunction or pathology of the family system (→ **adaptability**).

Ashby, W. R. *An introduction to cybernetics*. London: Methuen, 1956.
Bateson, G. *Steps to an ecology of mind*. New York: Ballantine Books, 1972.
Bateson, G. *Mind and nature: A necessary unity*. New York: E. P. Dutton, 1979.
Deissler, K. Die rekursive Kontextualisierung natürlicher Prozesse. *Familiendynamik* 8: 139–165, 1983.
Hoffman, L. *Foundations of family therapy: A conceptual framework for systems change*. New York: Basic Books, 1981.
Morin, E. *La méthode. I: La nature de la nature*. Paris: Seuil, 1977.
Selvini-Palazzoli, M., Boscolo, L., Cecchin, G., & Prata, G. *Paradox and counterparadox: A new model in the therapy of the family in schizophrenic transaction* (translated by E. V. Burt). New York: Jason Aronson, 1978.
Selvini-Palazzoli, M., Boscolo, L., Cecchin, G., & Prata, G. Hypothesizing-circularity-neutrality: Three guidelines for the conductor of the session. *Family Process* 19: 3–12, 1980.

* * * * * *

CIRCUMPLEX MODEL

In this model, families are assessed on the dimensions of → **cohesion,** → **adaptability** (change), and communication.

In the Circumplex Model of marital and family systems, "[f]amily cohesion, adaptability, and communication are three dimensions of family behavior that emerged from a conceptual clustering of over fifty concepts developed to describe marital and family dynamics" (Olson, Russell, & Sprenkle, 1983, pp. 69–70). On the dimension of cohesion, too much closeness leads to → **enmeshment,** and too little closeness results in → **disengagement:** "Some specific variables that can be used to assess the degree of family cohesion are: *emotional bonding, independence, boundaries, coalitions, time, space, friends, decision-making,* and *interests* and *recreation*" (Olson, Sprenkle, & Russell, 1979, p. 6). On the dimension of adaptability, the extent to which the family system is flexible and able to change, a balance must be found between too little flexibility for change, and too much flexibility. The model developed by Olson and his coworkers serves as an aid in diagnosis and in the determination of specific therapy goals:

40

The definition of adaptability used . . . is: *the ability of a marital/family system to change its power structure, role relationships, and relationship rules in response to situational and developmental stress.* The assumption is that an adaptive system requires balancing both morphogenesis (change) and morphostasis (stability).

The specific variables that are of interest in terms of this dimension are: *family power structure* (assertiveness and control), *negotiation styles, role relationships* and *relationship* rules, and *feedback* (positive and negative). (Olson, Sprenkle, & Russell, 1979, p. 12)

The Circumplex Model:
Sixteen Possible Types of Marital and Family Systems

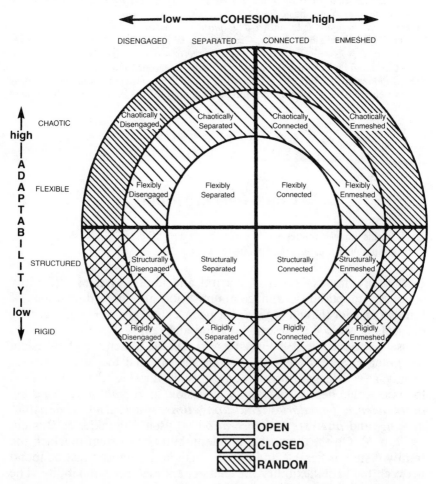

(from C.S. Russell, 1979)

The diagram depicts the various combinations of cohesive forces that determine distance and closeness within a family system, as well as the family's willingness and ability to adapt. Thus, it illustrates the family system's propensity for → **stability** and → **change.** The extreme poles of adaptability are accordingly either rigid or chaotic family structures, whereas the extreme poles of cohesion are enmeshment or a general diffusion of organization in the family system. The third dimension in the Circumplex Model is family communication. It is considered to be a facilitating dimension, "critical to movement on the other two dimensions" (Olson, McCubbin, Barnes, Larsen, Muxen, & Wilson, 1983, p. 49), that enables couples and families to share their needs and preferences as they relate to cohesion and adaptability.

Olson, D. H., McCubbin, H. C., Barnes, H., Larsen, A., Muxen, M., & Wilson, M. *Families: What makes them work?* Beverly Hills: Sage Publications, 1983.
Olson, D. H., Russell, C. S., & Sprenkle, D. H. Circumplex Model of marital and family systems: VI. Theoretical update. *Family Process 22:* 69–83, 1983.
Olson, D. H., Sprenkle, D. H., & Russell, C. S. Circumplex Model of marital and family systems: I. Cohesion and adaptability dimensions, family types, and clinical applications. *Family Process 18:* 3–28, 1979.
Russell, C. S. Circumplex Model of marital and family systems: III. Empirical evaluation with families. *Family Process 18:* 29–45, 1979.
Sprenkle, D. H., & Olson, D. H. Circumplex Model of marital systems: An empirical study of clinic and non-clinic couples. *Journal of Marriage and Family Counseling 4* (2): 59–74, 1978.

* * * * * *

CLOSENESS/DISTANCE

In every relationship the psychic distance between partners must be regulated both in fantasy and in reality. A balance must be found between the extremes of being too close (fantasies of fusion) and being too distant (autism) (→ **relational balance,** → **cohesion**). The fear of loss of individual autonomy and the fear of isolation characterize the ambivalence that is bound up with the negotiation of closeness and distance.

Interpersonal relationships are unavoidably marked by ambivalence between wishes for and fears of closeness, and wishes for and fears of distance. During the process of → **individuation,** new ways of balancing closeness and distance must constantly be sought. For the helpless neonate, the closeness of the person taking care of it is of vital importance. The loss of this caretaker would be a catastrophe. The experience that a mother's absence is followed by her return, enables the child to develop a feeling of security; the initial, concrete–spatial feeling of trust is replaced by trust in the mother's emotional closeness. The increasing development of autonomy changes a person's evaluation of this closeness; it also begins to be experienced as a limitation of one's personal activity radius and an invasion of one's personality. How much distance and closeness a person needs or can tolerate depends on the extent to which personal → **boundaries** are developed and how → **self/object differentiation** is regulated in families.

What an individual experiences as the wish for or the fear of closeness and distance is determined to a great extent by the family's interactional patterns. Nearly all family therapy theoreticians supply descriptions of families in which too much closeness leads to the creation of symptoms (→ **enmeshment,** → **fusion,** → **undifferentiated family ego mass**) and emotional overinvolvement (→ **expressed emotion**). Too much distance leads to dysfunctionality (→ **disengagement,** → **emotional cutoff**). In the development of every family system → **centripetal/centrifugal patterns** must constantly be balanced. If an established form of balance is maintained despite the changing circumstances of the family's environment, then the structures within the family become rigid. When this happens, one aspect of a family's ambivalence—distance or closeness—may be openly communicated, while the other aspect may only be communicated in a covert manner (→ **pseudomutuality/pseudohostility**).

The fact that wishes for closeness and distance are generally quite ambivalent often leads to the distribution of these two aspects between the two partners (→ **collusion**). Superficially, it appears as if one partner is hanging onto the other, while the other partner appears to have massive escapist tendencies. In such instances, the possibility of → **triangulation** presents itself, and a child takes over the regulation of distance by developing symptoms (see Byng–Hall, 1980). In caring for the sick child, a situation is created in which the couple can feel close to each other, joined as they are in their efforts to master the difficult situation; however, the possibility of employing distancing tactics and mutual devaluation is also present, that is, one's partner can be reproached for not being concerned enough or not doing enough for the "poor sick child."

Specific problems arise in families with adolescent children. The vicissitudes of → **separating parents and adolescents** make it necessary for parents and children to learn to tolerate more distance from one another. This, however, affects all the relationships in the family. A new form of closeness with new partners is sought by the adolescent or, when this is too much of a threat, is feared and avoided. The parents, again left alone together, must develop new ways of regulating their needs for closeness and distance.

Singer and Wynne (1965a) have formulated similar problems in terms of the concept of "proper distancing," referring to "the observation that most persons while growing up learn to gauge the proper distance, or focal length, for dealing with objects, ideas, people, and events under various circumstances, and also learn how to change distance flexibly, smoothly, and unobtrusively as transactions unfold." Inappropriate "distance and closeness in making contact with the environment, both human and nonhuman" was found to be commonly associated with → **communication deviance** (p. 196; see also Singer & Wynne, 1965b).

More recently, Wynne (1984) has reconceptualized closeness/distance in terms of attachment/caregiving, epigenetically followed in the development of relational systems by focal emphases on communication, joint problem solving, and → **mutuality.**

In summary, one can say that the attempt to eliminate or deny ambivalence in a relationship is almost certainly a significant factor in psychopathological development. Every attempt at distancing by one of the partners is seen as a threat to the relationship altogether, and every move toward greater closeness awakens fears of being devoured by the other.

Byng-Hall, J. Symptom bearer as marital distance regulator: Clinic implications. *Family Process 19:* 355–365, 1980.

Byng-Hall, J., & Campbell, D. Resolving conflicts in family distance regulation: An integrative approach. *Journal of Marital and Family Therapy 7:* 321–330, 1981.

Cheek, F. E., & Anthony, R. Personal pronoun usage in families of schizophrenics and social space utilization. *Family Process 9:* 431–447, 1970.

Olson, D. H., Sprenkle, D. H., & Russell, C. S. Circumplex Model of marital and family systems: I. Cohesion and adaptability dimensions, family types, and clinical applications. *Family Process 18:* 3–28, 1979.

Scheflen, A. *Human territories: How we behave in space-time.* Englewood Cliffs, N.J.: Prentice-Hall, 1976.

Singer, M. T., & Wynne, L. C. Thought disorder and family relations of schizophrenics: III. Methodology using projective techniques. *Archives of General Psychiatry 12:* 187–200, 1965. (a)

Singer, M. T., & Wynne, L. C. Thought disorder and family relations of schizophrenics: IV. Results and implications. *Archives of General Psychiatry 12:* 201–212, 1965. (b)

Stierlin, H. *Das Tun des Einen ist das Tun des Anderen.* Frankfurt: Suhrkamp, 1971.

Stierlin, H., Levi, L. D., & Savard, R. J. Centrifugal versus centripetal separation in adolescence: Two patterns and some of their implications. In S. C. Feinstein & P. Giovacchini (Eds.), *Adolescent psychiatry, Vol. II. Developmental and clinical studies.* New York: Basic Books, 1973, 211–239.

Warner, S. M. Soft meaning and sincerity in the family system. *Family Process 22:* 523–535, 1983.

Wynne, L. C. The epigenesis of relational systems: A model for understanding family development. *Family Process 23:* 297–318, 1984.

* * * * * *

CODE/CODING

Code or coding is the key for transferring information from one language to another. It is to a certain extent a translation specification.

This type of translation (coding) is at the basis of all psychic processes. Events and conditions that take place outside the sphere of the body of an individual are perceived as alterations of one's own condition. These events and processes are represented, stored, and interpreted in some way. On the basis of this, decisions are then made that determine behavior.

Communication processes require agreement between the communication partners about how something is to be understood, in other words, which code is being applied. Questions regarding coding fall into the domain of → semiotics (→ semantics, → syntax, → pragmatics), and → communication theory, → ethnomethodology, and → sociolinguistics are concerned with the social circumstances governing the formation of code systems; → psycholinguistics examines the reciprocal relationship between linguistic codes and psychological processes.

Bateson, G. *Steps to an ecology of mind.* New York: Ballantine Books, 1972.
Melson, A., & Martin, E. (Eds.). *Coding processes in human memory.* New York: Winston, 1972.
Newell, A. A theoretical exploration of mechanisms for coding the stimulus. In A. Melson & E. Martin (Eds.), *Coding processes in human memory.* New York: Winston, 1972.

* * * * * *

COEVOLUTION

Systems never develop in a static environment; systems influence the environment and are contributory determinants in its development. An example of this is the reciprocal dependence of two biological species, prey and predator. This reciprocal dependence determines the conditions of evolution for both species.

The importance of the concept of coevolution was first recognized in the field of biology, but it applies to every process of → self–organization in the known universe. Two types of processes can be distinguished: (1) those that are nonreversible (in the time dimension) and (2) those that are concurrent. These processes have been described by Bateson (1979) and Jantsch (1980). The momentum that initiates a process of coevolution is derived from a state of disequilibrium that will force a system toward → **adaptation;** however, it is unpredictable *which* activity will lead to the reestablishment of balance within the system (→ **fluctuation,** → **trial–and–error method,** →**crisis,** → **stability**).

Bateson (1979) described coevolution as a "stochastic" system of evolutionary change, stochastic meaning that events occur in a *partially* random manner, that is, "a sequence of events combines a random component with a selective process so that only certain outcomes of the random are allowed to endure" (p. 230). In coevolution, interaction takes place in such a way that species A sets the stage for the natural selection of changes in species B, and conversely.

For a developing individual the family represents the coevolutionary → **ecosystem.** Within the family system, each family member determines the conditions for the development of all the other family members. For the family as a unit, the surrounding sociocultural system forms the coevolutionary ecosystem. Individual, family, and social environment represent a complex, close–knit, three–tier feedback system with each of its units belonging to a different → **logical type,** i.e., a unit of a lower order is an element of a unit of a higher order.

Normally, a family is not a closed system with impermeable → **boundaries** that keep out all outside information. To a large extent, the rules that parents and children are expected to abide by are determined by social norms. However, there are families that act almost as if they were closed systems. Such families have been described by Wynne et al. (1958), using the concept of the → **rubber fence.** In these families, the process of coevolution is disturbed. Neither the norms of the family nor of society (such as how children are to be treated) may be queried or revised in these families. A child growing up in a closed family system must unswervingly adhere to the family rules. This means that both the child and the family are hindered in their potential development. Jantsch (1980) has noted that any system isolated from its environment can only move in the direction of a state of equilibrium; after achieving this state of equilibrium, its dynamic potential comes to a standstill.

Families with a schizophrenic member present themselves from the beginning as blocked in their development and as almost completely closed systems. Jackson (1957) used the term → **homeostasis** to describe this phenomenon. In closed family systems the child finds itself in a paradoxical situation. On the one hand, sheer biological necessity demands the child's maturation; on the other hand, the child is caught in a homeostatic system that rigidly maintains its state of equilibrium. To change oneself without changing the environment (the family) is an all but impossible task (→ double bind).

The development of a family is reciprocally determined by the development of each individual family member; hence, family coevolution also involves family–wide coindividuation (→ individuation/related individuation/coindividuation). Where the goal of therapy is to remove barriers that impede family coevolution and coindividuation, it must aim at the opening of family boundaries and the introduction of new → information. This requires a circular process between therapist and family that demands revision of the therapist's concepts and hypotheses in line with the success or failure of the information collection and transmission strategies he or she has employed. Hence, the evolution of effective therapeutic concepts is a supplementary aspect of family–wide coevolution and coindividuation.

Insight into the principle of coevolution will entail relinquishing hitherto accepted assumptions about lineal subject–object split of subject–object epistemology. Jantsch (1980) uses an extended metaphor to illustrate how differing epistemologies determine views of the self and its relationship to the world: A man standing on a river bank describing the river as it flows by can be seen as analogous to an observer applying a lineal (→ lineality) concept of cause and effect. In the circular (→ circularity) model, which conceives of system and environment as joined in a reciprocal relationship, the observer is similar to a ship's captain who must be constantly on guard so as to adapt his steering to the flow of the river. A wholistic perspective, for example, an Oriental, Taoist view, might perceive the relationship between observer and world in such a way that the observer would be the river (→ holism).

Bateson, G. Mind and nature: A necessary unity. New York: E. P. Dutton, 1979.

Dell, P. F. Beyond homeostasis: Toward a concept of coherence. Family Process 21: 21–41, 1982.

Dell, P. F., & Goolishian, H. A. Order through fluctuation: An evolutionary epistemology for human systems. Australian Journal of Family Therapy 2: 175–184, 1981.

Eigen, M., & Winkler, R. Laws of the game. New York: Alfred A. Knopf, 1975.

Fivaz, E., Fivaz, R., & Kaufmann, L. Agreement, conflict, symptom: An evolutionary paradigm. In R. Welter-Enderlin & J. Duss-von Werdt (Eds.), Menschliche Systeme: Ein Rahmen für das Denken, die Forschung und das Handeln. Zürich: Institut für Ehe und Familie, 1982, 140–178.

Hill, R., & Rodgers, R. H. The developmental approach. In H. T. Christensen (Ed.), Handbook of marriage and the family. Chicago: Rand McNally, 1964, 171–211.

Hoffman, L. A co-evolutionary framework for systemic family therapy. Australian Journal of Family Therapy 4: 9–21, 1982.

Jackson, D. D. The question of family homeostasis. Psychiatric Quarterly, Suppl. 31: 79–90, 1957.

Jantsch, E. *Design for evolution.* New York: George Braziller, 1975.
Jantsch, E. *The self-organizing universe.* Elmsford, N.Y.: Pergamon Press, 1980.
Jantsch, E., & Waddington, C. H. (Eds.). *Evolution and consciousness: Human systems in transition.* Reading, Mass.: Addison-Wesley, 1976.
Kegan, R. *The evolving self: Problem and process in human development.* Cambridge: Harvard University Press, 1979.
Lorenz, K. *Evolution and modification of behavior.* Chicago: University of Chicago Press, 1965.
Simon, F. B. Die Evolution unbewusster Strukturen. *Psyche 37:* 520–554, 1983.
Werner, H. *Comparative psychology of mental development* (revised ed.). New York: International Universities Press, 1957. (a)
Werner, H. The concept of development from a comparative and organismic point of view. In D. B. Harris (Ed.), *The concept of development.* Minneapolis: University of Minnesota Press, 1957, 125–148. (b)
Wertheim, E. S. The science and typology of family systems II. Further theoretical and practical considerations. *Family Process 14:* 285–309, 1975.
Wynne, L. C. The epigenesis of relational systems: A model for understanding family development. *Family Process 23:* 297–318, 1984.
Wynne, L. C., Ryckoff, I. M., Day, J., & Hirsch, S. I. Pseudo-mutuality in the family relations of schizophrenics. *Psychiatry 21:* 205–220, 1958.

* * * * * *

COHERENCE

Coherence [Latin *cohaerere,* to hang together] refers to the unity of single elements in a superordinate whole. In reference to a system, the concept describes "the behavior of a system–being–self" (Dell, 1982, p. 31). Dell argues that the term coherence should replace → **homeostasis.**

Paul Dell has defined coherence as "congruent interdependence in functioning whereby all the aspects of a system fit together" (Dell, 1982, p. 31). From a dynamic perspective, which considers neither the environment nor any system to be static but, rather, as being in a state of mutual interdependence and → **coevolution,** coherence is the decisive criterion of → **stability.** The → **adaptability** of a → **system** manifests itself in its ability to survive.

The coevolution of an individual's coherence and a family system's coherence is the fit, or → **"complementarity** that can neither be separated into its components nor reduced to one or the other" (Dell, 1982, p. 32). In family therapy, the therapist and the family may undergo a "coevolution of coherences" if a family stays in therapy, whereby the therapist becomes part of the family system and is ineffective as a therapist.

48

Dell, P. F. Beyond homeostasis: Toward a concept of coherence. *Family Process 21:* 21–41, 1982.

Dell, P. F. Understanding Bateson and Maturana: Toward a biological foundation for the social sciences. *Journal of Marital and Family Therapy 11:* 1–20, 1985.

Maturana, H. R. The organization of the living: A theory of the living organization. *International Journal of Man-Machine Studies 7:* 313–332, 1975.

Maturana, H. R. Biology of language: The epistemology of reality. In G. A. Miller & E. Lenneberg (Eds.), *Psychology and biology of language and thought.* New York: Academic Press, 1978.

* * * * * *

COHESION

In family assessment, the dimension of cohesion reflects the manner in which → **closeness/distance,** as well as → **centripetal/centrifugal patterns,** are balanced during the → **family life cycle.**

Olson, Russell, and Sprenkle (1983) have defined family cohesion as *"the emotional bonding that family members have toward one another. . . .* There are four levels of cohesion, ranging from *disengaged* (very low) to *separated* (low to moderate) to *connected* (moderate to high) to *enmeshed* (very high)" (p. 70). If cohesion is strong, centripetal forces predominate, together with the transactional mode of → **binding,** and → **enmeshment** occurs. Under such conditions, it is difficult for individual family members to achieve a level of related → **individuation,** → **self/object differentiation,** and → **autonomy** that would be considered adequate by the norms of the family system social environment. When binding does not exist and centrifugal forces predominate, the transactional mode leads to the → **expelling** of individual family members and to → **disengagement.**

It is a paradox of family cohesion that the more the family strives to maintain it at all costs, the more likely it is that these efforts will have the opposite effect; in its attempt to maintain it, the family develops rigid interactional structures that prevent the family from meeting the demands of a constantly changing internal and external world. The → **Circumplex Model** attempts to chart the relationship between the dimensions of adaptability (rigidity versus flexibility) and cohesion for diagnostic and prognostic purposes.

Moos and Moos (1976) also have used the term "cohesion," which is one of ten dimensions in their Family Environment Scale (FES). They define cohesion as "the extent to which family members are concerned and committed to the family and the degree to which they are helpful and supportive to each other" (p. 360).

Beavers, W. R. *Psychotherapy and growth: A family systems perspective.* New York: Brunner/Mazel, 1977.

Beavers, W. R., & Voeller, M. N. Family models: Comparing and contrasting the Olson Circumplex Model with the Beavers Systems Model. *Family Process 22:* 85–98, 1983.

Moos, R. H., & Moos, B. S. A typology of family social environments. *Family Process 15:* 357–371, 1976.

Olson, D. H., Russell, C. S., & Sprenkle, D. H. Circumplex Model of marital and family systems: VI. Theoretical update. *Family Process 22:* 69–83, 1983.

Olson, D. H., Sprenkle, D. H., & Russell, C. S. Circumplex Model of marital and family systems: I. Cohesion and adaptability dimensions, family types, and clinical applications. *Family Process 18:* 3–28, 1979.

Stierlin, H., Levi, L. D., & Savard, R. J. Centrifugal versus centripetal separation in adolescence: Two patterns and some of their implications. In S. C. Feinstein & P. Giovacchini (Eds.), *Adolescent psychiatry, Vol. II: Developmental and clinical studies.* New York: Basic Books, 1973, 211–239.

* * * * * *

COLLECTIVE COGNITIVE CHAOS

This term was used by Wynne (1965, 1971) to describe the ways in which certain families with a schizophrenic member manifest overall transactional sequences that are disjointed, fragmented, and sometimes bizarre, even though individual, isolated statements, considered out of context, may appear quite ordinary.

Family interaction with a high level of → **communication deviance** also is characterized by erratic failures in establishing a "proper distance" between family members (Singer & Wynne, 1965), that is, in achieving a → **relational balance** of → **closeness/distance.**

Schaffer et al. (1962) describe the subculture of these disturbed families as having an "institutionalization of fragmentation" of deep significance for each family member and for the family as a social subsystem. Another closely related concept is "transactional thought disorder" (Wynne & Singer, 1963), in which the degree of disturbance in family transactions is greater and qualitatively different from that found in the contributions of any individual family member. The common theme in these observations is that the fragmentation, disruptive quality, and blurring of attention and meaning found in *sequences* of family interactions cannot be adequately described by mechanically adding up the degree of cognitive disturbance of the individuals taken out of their family context. Hence, the systemic collectivity of the family must be seen or imagined in order to grasp the functioning of the family as a whole.

As is the case with the analogous concepts of → **fusion** and → **undifferentiated family ego mass,** a disturbance in → **self/object differentiation** can be hypothesized as at the root of the disorder. Disturbances of this type manifest themselves as an erratic zig-zagging between the extremes of fusion and exaggerated attempts at distancing (→ **emotional cutoff**).

Schaffer, L., Wynne, L. C., Day, J., Ryckoff, I. M., & Halperin, A. On the nature and sources of the psychiatrist's experience with the family the schizophrenic. *Psychiatry 25:* 32–45, 1962.

Singer, M. T., & Wynne, L. C. Thought disorder and family relations of schizophrenics: III. Methodology using projective techniques. *Archives of General Psychiatry 12:* 187–200, 1965.

Wynne, L. C. Some indications and contra-indications for exploratory family therapy. In I. Boszormenyi-Nagy & J. L. Framo (Eds.), *Intensive family therapy: Theoretical and practical aspects, with special reference to schizophrenia.* New York: Harper & Row, 1965, 289–322.

Wynne, L. C. Some guidelines for exploratory conjoint family therapy. In J. Haley (Ed.), *Changing families: A family therapy reader.* New York: Grune & Stratton, 1971, 96–115. (Updated revision in *Psychotherapeutica Schizophrenia, Third International Symposium, Lausanne.* Basel: Karger, 1965, 24–31.)

Wynne, L. C., & Singer, M. T. Thought disorder and family relations of schizophrenics: I. A research strategy. *Archives of General Psychiatry 9:* 191–198, 1963.

* * * * * *

COLLUSION

Collusion [Latin *com-*, together + *ludere*, to play] is an unconscious and unavowed acting or playing together by two partners in an attempt to master their fears and conflicts. In order to deal with conflicts that stem from personal biography, partners delegate each other to embody one aspect of an ambivalence that otherwise would be unbearable for the individual concerned. Hence, the concept of collusion is an attempt to understand the dynamics of couple and marital conflicts both in the light of psychoanalysis and its concentration on individual biographies, and of systems theory and its preoccupation with functional → **mutuality.**

The term "collusion" is frequently found in the literature on couples therapy. Laing (1969) pointed out that the Latin word *ludere* has two meanings: (1) to play and (2) to deceive. Both of these aspects—the ordered structure of game rules and mutual deception—are characteristics of collusion, defined in English as "a secret agreement between two or more persons for a deceitful or fraudulent purpose" (*American Heritage Dictionary, 2nd College Edition,* 1982). In Germany, "Kollusion" is understood in more neutral terms and, as discussed by Willi (1982, 1984a, b), is more akin to → **complementarity.**

Dicks (1967) outlined the principal features of the collusion concept, which were then further developed by Willi. In forming a relationship, each partner discovers in the other lost and/or repressed aspects of himself or herself. Psychodynamically, these aspects may be regarded as manifestations of needs and wishes that have been repressed and are kept repressed by various defense mechanisms. A partner's attraction is based to a large extent on his or her being seen as embodying those parts of the self that have been repressed. In other words, it derives largely from the mechanism of → **projective identifi-cation.** In the course of the relationship, however, that which was originally attractive becomes again ambivalently cathected, i.e., is experienced as an element of conflict. Interpersonal (marital) strife then ensues. The choice of a partner thus both creates the possibility of supplementing (completing) one's self and sets the stage for a resurrec-tion of conflicting instinctual wishes and needs. The burdens involved in such concerted acting (within relationships or through a change in social environment) mean that the partners become more and more polarized within the context of jointly repressed, basic conflicts. The wishes and needs that each partner has delegated (→ **delegation**) onto the other become increasingly threatening, and the partner, as their embodiment, needs to be vigorously fought against.

Willi (1982) described the two possible roles in a couple's relationship as being either regressive or progressive. The regressive role is characterized by decompensation and hypofunctionality, the progressive role by overcompensation and hyperfunctionality. Willi (1984a) emphasizes the developing process in the relationship: "The terms progressive and regressive correspond to the relationship as a process of coevolution" (p. 179) (→ **coevolution**). "In terms of the dyadic wholeness, increased complementarity reduces fears of part-ner–loss and reinforces interdependency and cohesion of the marital system" (p. 180).

Willi based his definition of collusion on his belief that there exists "a similarly neurotic propensity to enter into a relationship on the part of both partners," which then develops into a "sympathetic vibration" (1982, p. 190). It can hardly be doubted that the vicissitudes of one's individual history influence an individual in the choice of a partner; however, it remains doubtful whether the collusion concept can be restricted to specifically neurotic tendencies. Partners daily face the need for decisions, and some "casting" into progressive and regressive roles is inevitable. What this means is that the interactional partner who always plays the same role only lives out one aspect of his or her ambivalence with regard to activity and passivity. When one partner in a cooperative couple relationship always plays the more progressive role, and the other always behaves in a somewhat more regressive manner, it does not necessarily mean that this behavior is a product of each partner's past developmental history. Jackson (1965) made a similar point in describing the inevitability of the marital quid pro quo.

In couples therapy, the type of intervention will vary according to whether the presence of collusion and its adjunct conflicts seems to be mostly based in the developmental history of the individuals or to be an expression of current interaction. In the first instance, one would attempt to disclose and deal with the underlying neurotic conflicts via, say, psychoanalytic therapy. In the second instance, one would attempt to change the interactional rules via → **systemic therapy,** or → **strategic therapy.**

Phenomena similar to those labeled as collusion by Dicks and Willi have been described by Ackerman (1958) as "negative complementarity," by Boszormenyi–Nagy (1967) as "merger," by Bowen (1965) as "family projection process," by Jackson (1965) as the "marital quid pro quo," by Lidz et al. (1957) as → **marital skew,** and by Wynne (1965) as "trading of dissociations."

Ackerman, N. W. *The psychodynamics of family life: Diagnosis and treatment of family relationships.* New York: Basic Books, 1958.

American heritage dictionary, second college edition. Boston: Houghton Mifflin Co., 1982.

Boszormenyi-Nagy, I. Relational modes and meaning. In G. H. Zuk & I. Boszormenyi-Nagy (Eds.), *Family therapy and disturbed families.* Palo Alto: Science and Behavior Books, 1967, 58–73.

Bowen, M. Family psychotherapy with schizophrenia in the hospital and in private practice. In I. Boszormenyi-Nagy & J. L. Framo (Eds.), *Intensive family therapy: Theoretical and practical aspects.* New York: Harper & Row, 1965, 213–242.

Dicks, H. V. *Marital tensions: Clinical studies toward a psychological theory of interaction.* New York: Basic Books, 1967.

Jackson, D. D. Family rules: The marital quid pro quo. *Archives of General Psychiatry 12:* 589–594, 1965.

Laing, R. D. *The politics of the family.* Toronto: Canadian Broadcast Corporation Publications, 1969.

Lidz, T., Cornelison, A. R., Fleck, S., & Terry, D. The intrafamilial environment of schizophrenic patients: II. Marital schism and marital skew. *American Journal of Psychiatry 114:* 241–248, 1957.

Willi, J. *Couples in collusion.* New York: Jason Aronson, 1982. (German edition: *Die Zweierbeziehung.* Reinbek bei Hamburg: Rowohlt Verlag, 1975.)

Willi, J. The concept of collusion: A combined systemic-psychodynamic approach to marital therapy. *Family Process 23:* 177–185, 1984. (a)

Willi, J. Dynamics of couple therapy. New York: Jason Aronson, 1984. (b) (German edition: *Therapie der Zweierbeziehung.* Reinbek bei Hamburg: Rowohlt Verlag, 1978.)

Wynne, L. C. Some indications and contra-indications for exploratory family therapy. In I. Boszormenyi-Nagy & J. L. Framo (Eds.), *Intensive family therapy: Theoretical and practical aspects, with special reference to schizophrenia.* New York: Harper & Row, 1965, 289–322.

* * * * * *

COMMUNICATION, CONTENT AND RELATIONSHIP ASPECTS

An axiom in the → **communication theory** developed by Paul Watzlawick, Beavin, and Jackson (1967) posits that every interpersonal communication is not only an exchange of information about some subject matter, but also concurrently contains a message regarding the relationship between the interactional partners. This second aspect of communication belongs to a higher → **logical type** and represents a form of → **metacommunication.**

The difference between content and relational aspects of communication can best be described by an example. When two scientists discuss a particular scientific problem at a scientific congress, the discussion serves not only to clarify that problem but also to define the type of → **relationship** between the two scientists. This relationship can be either complementary or symmetrical (→ **complementarity,** → **symmetry**). Is one of the scientists superior; is he right? Or do both scientists stand on equal ground? Merton (1965) noted that these modes of scientific interaction were mentioned as early as the era of Sir Isaac Newton. Once it is apparent to both discussants as to what type of relationship they have—a complementary one such as a teacher–pupil, or a symmetrical one as in a discourse between equals who respect and recognize each other—only then can a discussion of the problem at hand ensue. If, however, the definition of relationship is unresolved, then a discussion of the problem may serve to clarify the relationship, but also may degenerate into a contest over who will "have the last word." Hence, in each instance it must be determined whether the definition of relationship between interactional partners has been clarified within the communication processes and, if it has, which definition of relationship the interactional partners have agreed upon.

If family members are rivals for a → **dominant** position, a symmetrical escalation ensues that can lead to a → **malign clinch;** none of those involved are willing to place themselves in the inferior position. This leads to "a game without end" in which everyone will try against all odds to "win." In such a situation, the relationship that is offered by one partner ("I am superior; you are inferior") is unacceptable to the other, as is any attempt by either partner to agree upon a symmetrical relationship. Leaving a relationship undefined also leaves unclear what is "real" or "not real" in the relational sphere. Acknowledging an unequivocal "family reality" (→ **relational reality**) is also an aspect of → **power** and individual → **autonomy** within the family.

Haley, J. An interactional description of schizophrenia. *Psychiatry 22:* 321–332, 1959.

Haley, J. Family experiments: A new type of experimentation. *Family Process 1:* 265–293, 1962.

Haley, J. Toward a theory of pathological systems. In G. H. Zuk & I. Boszormenyi-Nagy (Eds.), *Family therapy and disturbed families.* Palo Alto: Science and Behavior Books, 1967, 11–27.

Merton, R. K. *On the shoulders of giants: A Shandean postscript.* New York: Macmillan & Co., 1965.

Watzlawick, P. *An anthology of human communication; text and tape.* Palo Alto: Science and Behavior Books, 1964.

Watzlawick, P., Beavin, J. H., & Jackson, D. D. *Pragmatics of human communication: A study of interactional patterns, pathologies and paradoxes.* New York: W. W. Norton & Co., 1967.

Watzlawick, P., & Weakland, J. H. (Eds.). *The interactional view.* New York: W. W. Norton & Co., 1977.

Watzlawick, P., Weakland, J. H., & Fisch, R. *Change: Principles of problem formation and problem resolution.* New York: W. W. Norton & Co., 1974.

* * * * * *

COMMUNICATION DEVIANCE

This term was introduced by Wynne and Singer to refer to those varieties of communication patterns that distract and befuddle a listener who is attempting to share meaning and a focus of attention with a speaker. These features were first found with high frequency in Rorschach and TAT records of the parents of schizophrenic and borderline patients, but they represent a broader communicational process that is not restricted to such protocols or persons.

In an effort to test systematically earlier clinical hypotheses about the families of schizophrenics (see Bateson et al., 1956; Lidz et al., 1957, 1958; and Wynne et al., 1958), Wynne and Singer (1963a) devised a research strategy for studying communication disorders. Initially, they used verbatim Rorschach and TAT protocols, not as projective techniques but as a means of sampling communication of family members while in a standardized task and context. Their procedure assessed the transactions between subject and tester and provided information about the subject's focus of attention, modes of thought, communication, and relating. The task of perceiving and describing standardized test stimuli (Rorschach cards) in a semi–structured procedure is analogous to the task that parents face when they attempt to convey a consistent and adequate picture of reality that for their children is as yet relatively unstructured. Wynne and Singer postulated that individual schizophrenic thought disorders may be seen as the expression and consequence of interpersonal family communication disturbances.

First, they classified disordered communication as amorphous, fragmented, or constricted (Wynne & Singer, 1963b), and then found links, specific within each family system, between the communication features of parents and their offspring. Protocols of family members were identified blindly as fitting together, not only between schizophrenics and their parents, but also between borderline, neurotic, and normal index offspring, their well siblings, and their parents. Thus, the systemic qualities of family communication were found to extend far beyond the research focus on schizophrenia (Singer & Wynne, 1965a, b).

Later, Singer and Wynne (1966) developed manuals for scoring what they began calling "communication deviances" (CD), assessed by their transactional impact on the listener. They concluded that in the families of schizophrenics, communication processes begin to be disturbed at a basic phase of sharing foci of attention. These difficulties lead to failures in sharing meaning, in establishing appropriate → **closeness/distance,** and in acquiring a sense of trust in the family's → **relational reality.** CD categories include features of amorphous and fragmented communication such as inconsistent and ambiguous references, disqualifications, and nihilistic and distracting remarks. The frequency of parental CD/number of words used was found to be very highly significantly related to severity of illness in an index offspring, both in biologic and adoptive families (Doane, 1978; Singer, Wynne, & Toohey, 1978; Wynne, Singer, Bartko, & Toohey, 1977; Wynne, Singer, & Toohey, 1976). However, recent data by Sass, Gunderson, Singer, and Wynne (1984) suggest that parents of stably delusional, paranoid schizophrenics do not show high CD but, rather, have a constricted form of communication. This finding confirms earlier work of Singer and Wynne (1965b) that identified qualitatively different forms of communication problems.

The principles developed for communication deviance scoring in the individual Rorschach have also been applied to protocols of Family and Spouse Consensus Rorschachs (Doane, Jones, Fisher, Ritzler, Singer, & Wynne, 1982; Loveland, Wynne, & Singer, 1963); the TAT

(Doane, West, Goldstein, Rodnick, & Jones, 1981; Jones, 1977); family therapy excerpts (Morris & Wynne, 1965); the Object Sorting Test (Wild, Singer, Rosman, Ricci, & Lidz, 1965); and the Twenty Questions Test (Wild, Shapiro, & Goldenberg, 1975).

The positive counterpart of communication deviance is "healthy communication" (Wynne & Cole, 1983; Wynne, Jones, & Al-Khayyal, 1982), scored on protocols of the Consensus Family Rorschach.

The results of Wynne's and Singer's investigations of families studied at a given point in time now have been further corroborated by longitudinal studies in which evidence of the presence of parental communication deviance in the early rearing environment enables one to make significantly correct predictions as to the later appearance of schizophrenia spectrum disorders in the index offspring (Goldstein, 1983; Goldstein, Rodnick, Jones, McPherson, & West, 1978). Other research has shown that family CD can be used as a predictor of children who show impaired functioning in the school setting (Wynne & Cole, 1983).

Conceptually, communication deviance has much in common with communication in the → **double bind** (Bateson, Jackson, Haley, & Weakland, 1956) and in transactional disqualifications (Sluzki, Beavin, Tarnopolsky, & Verón, 1967). Recently, Wynne (1984) has placed normative communication processes and CD within an epigenetic framework; the relational process of communication comes into ascendancy after the attachment/caregiving phase of development.

Bateson, G., Jackson, D. D., Haley, J., & Weakland, J. H. Toward a theory of schizophrenia. *Behavioral Science 1:* 251–264, 1956.

Doane, J. A. Family interaction and communication deviance in disturbed and normal families: A review of research. *Family Process 17:* 357–376, 1978.

Doane, J. A., Jones, J. E., Fisher, L., Ritzler, B., Singer, M. T., & Wynne, L. C. Parental communication deviance as a predictor of competence in children at risk for adult psychiatric disorder. *Family Process 21:* 211–223, 1982.

Doane, J. A., West, K. L., Goldstein, M. J., Rodnick, E. H., & Jones, J. E. Parental communication deviance and affective style: Predictors of subsequent schizophrenia spectrum disorders in vulnerable adolescents. *Archives of General Psychiatry 38:* 679–685, 1981.

Goldstein, M. J. Family interaction: Patterns predictive of the onset and course of schizophrenia. In H. Stierlin, L. C. Wynne, & M. Wirsching (Eds.), *Psychosocial interventions in schizophrenia: An international view.* Berlin: Springer-Verlag, 1983, 5–19.

Goldstein, M. J., Rodnick, E. H., Jones, J. E., McPherson, S. R., & West, K. L. Familial precursors of schizophrenia spectrum disorders. In L. C. Wynne, R. L. Cromwell, & S. Matthysse (Eds.), *The nature of schizophrenia: New approaches to research and treatment.* New York: John Wiley & Sons, 1978, 487–498.

Helmersen, P. *Family interaction and communication in psychopathology: An evaluation in recent perspectives.* New York: Academic Press, 1983.

Jones, J. E. Patterns of transactional style deviance in the TAT's of parents of schizophrenics. *Family Process 16:* 327–337, 1977.

Lidz, T., Cornelison, A. R., Fleck, S., & Terry, D. The intrafamilial environment of schizophrenic patients: II. Marital schism and marital skew. *American Journal of Psychiatry 114:* 241–248, 1957.

Lidz, T., Cornelison, A. R., Terry, D., & Fleck S. The intrafamilial environment of the schizophrenic patient: VI. The transmission of irrationality. *Archives of Neurology and Psychiatry 79:* 305–316, 1958.

Loveland, N. T. The relation Rorschach: A technique for studying interaction. *Journal of Nervous and Mental Disease 142:* 93–105, 1967.

Loveland, N. T., Wynne, L. C., & Singer, M. T. The Family Rorschach: A method for studying family interaction. *Family Process 2:* 187–215, 1963.

Morris, G. O., & Wynne, L. C. Schizophrenic offspring and styles of parental communication: A predictive study using family therapy excerpts. *Psychiatry 28:* 19–44, 1965.

Sass, L. A., Gunderson, J. G., Singer, M. T., & Wynne, L. C. Parental communication deviance and forms of thinking in male schizophrenic offspring. *Journal of Nervous and Mental Disease 172:* 513–520, 1984.

Singer, M. T., & Wynne, L. C. Thought disorder and family relations of schizophrenics: III. Methodology using projective techniques. *Archives of General Psychiatry 12:* 187–200, 1965. (a)

Singer, M. T., & Wynne, L. C. Thought disorder and family relations of schizophrenics: IV. Results and implications. *Archives of General Psychiatry 12:* 201–212, 1965. (b)

Singer, M. T., & Wynne, L. C. Principles for scoring communication defects and deviances in parents of schizophrenics: Rorschach and TAT scoring manuals. *Psychiatry 29:* 260–288, 1966.

Singer, M. T., Wynne, L. C., & Toohey, M. L. Communication disorders and the families of schizophrenics. In L. C. Wynne, R. L. Cromwell, & S. Matthysse (Eds.), *The nature of schizophrenia: New approaches to research and treatment.* New York: John Wiley & Sons, 1978, 499–511.

Sluzki, C. E., Beavin, J., Tarnopolsky, A., & Verón, E. Transactional disqualification: Research on the double bind. *Archives of General Psychiatry 16:* 494–504, 1967.

Wild, C. M., Shapiro, L. N., & Goldenberg, L. Transactional communication disturbances in families of male schizophrenics. *Family Process 14:* 131–160, 1975.

Wild, C. M., Singer, M. T., Rosman, B., Ricci, J., & Lidz, T. Measuring disordered styles of thinking. *Archives of General Psychiatry 13:* 471–476, 1965.

Wynne, L. C. Knotted relationships and communication deviance. In M. Berger (Ed.), *Beyond the double bind.* New York: Brunner/Mazel, 1978, 177–187.

Wynne, L. C. The epigenesis of relational systems: A model for understanding family development. *Family Process 23:* 297–318, 1984.

Wynne, L. C., & Cole, R. E. The Rochester risk research program: A new look at parental diagnoses and family relationships. In H. Stierlin, L. C. Wynne, & M. Wirsching (Eds.), *Psychosocial intervention in schizophrenia: An international view.* Berlin: Springer-Verlag, 1983, 35–48.

Wynne, L. C., Jones, J. E., & Al-Khayyal, M. Healthy family communication patterns: Observations in families "at risk" for psychopathology. In F. Walsh (Ed.), *Normal family processes: Implications for clinical practice.* New York: Guilford Press, 1982, 142–164.

Wynne, L. C., Ryckoff, I. M., Day, J., & Hirsch, S. I. Pseudo-mutuality in the family relations of schizophrenics. *Psychiatry 21:* 205–220, 1958.

58

Wynne, L. C., & Singer, M. T. Thought disorder and family relations of schizophrenics: I. A research strategy. *Archives of General Psychiatry 9:* 191–198, 1963. (a)

Wynne, L. C., & Singer, M. T. Thought disorder and family relations of schizophrenics: II. A classification of forms of thinking. *Archives of General Psychiatry 9:* 199–206, 1963. (b)

Wynne, L. C., Singer, M. T., Bartko, J. L., & Toohey, M. L. Schizophrenics and their families: Recent research on parental communication. In J. M. Tanner (Ed.), *Developments in psychiatric research.* London: Hodder & Stoughton, 1977, 254–286.

Wynne, L. C., Singer, M. T., & Toohey, M. L. Communication of the adoptive parents of schizophrenics. In J. Jørstad & E. Ugelstad (Eds.), *Schizophrenia 75: Psychotherapy, family studies, research.* Oslo: Universitetsforlaget, 1976, 413–452.

Wynne, L. C., Toohey, M. L., & Doane, J. A. Family studies. In L. Bellak (Ed.), *Disorders of the schizophrenic syndrome.* New York: Basic Books, 1979, 264–288.

* * * * * *

COMMUNICATION THEORY

In a field of the humanities that is closely related to psychology and sociology, communication theory concerns itself mainly with the conditions and variations of information exchange between humans.

Contemporary information theory relevant to family therapy has its foundations in → **information theory** and → **semiotics**. In particular, pragmatic communication theory, first systematically outlined by Watzlawick, Beavin, and Jackson in 1967 (*Pragmatics of Human Communication*) and in the two–volume edition of *Human Communication* (Jackson, 1968), has proven to be of central importance for family theory and therapy. These authors integrated clinical data with the ideas, observations, and investigations of the → **double–bind** hypothesis of Bateson et al. (1956). They posited principles, or five "pragmatic axioms," which they believed could elucidate all forms of functional, interpersonal communication. (The following excerpt is taken from Watzlawick et al., 1967; the italics in various quotations have been omitted.)

Axiom 1: In an interpersonal context "one cannot not communicate" (p. 51). Every behavior thus contains a message. Hence the paradoxical situation that a person who is not attempting to communicate will still communicate; noncommunication itself is a form of communication.

Axiom 2: "Every communication has a content and relationship aspect such that the latter classifies the former and is therefore a metacommunication" (p. 54) (→ **communication, content and relational aspects**).

Axiom 3: This relates to → **punctuation** phenomena and states that the nature of a relationship between two partners is determined by the manner in which they punctuate the communication between them.

Axiom 4: "Human beings communicate both digitally and analogically. Digital language has a highly complex and powerful logical syntax but lacks adequate semantics in the field of relationship, while analogic language possesses the semantics but has no adequate syntax for the unambiguous definition of the nature of relationships" (pp. 66–67) (→ **analogue/digital communication**, → **syntax**, → **semantics**).

Axiom 5: "All communicational interchanges are either symmetrical or complementary, depending on whether they are based on equality or difference" (p. 70) (→ **complementarity**, → **symmetry**).

With the help of this conceptual framework it became possible to understand highly complicated communication processes, in particular the rules governing family interaction. The impossibility of not communicating means that all interpersonal situations are communication situations. Their relational features are in the forefront of interest here. The differentiation between digital and analogue modes of communication has proven to be important because analogue messages and definition of relationship exhibit a high degree of → **isomorphism**. The ambiguity involved in the simultaneous exchange of messages concerning both the relationship itself and things outside the relationship leads to problems of interpretation and translation, which, if left unclarified, lead to pathological interaction patterns.

The concept of punctuation allows the possibility of talking about the reciprocity of human relationships in a manner that is at once different from and more complex than that of the traditional stimulus–response model of behavior. Finally, the concepts of symmetrical and complementary relationships introduce the important aspects of mutual evaluation and their relativity in interpersonal relationships. While it is moot whether these communication concepts and axioms encompass the multifaceted range of human communication processes, their importance for the field of family therapy remains undisputed.

Bateson, G. *Steps to an ecology of mind.* New York: Ballantine Books, 1972.
Bateson, G., Jackson, D. D., Haley, J., & Weakland, J. H. Toward a theory of schizophrenia. *Behavioral Science 1:* 251–264, 1956.
Blakar, R. M. *Studies of familial communication and psychopathology: A social-developmental approach to deviant behavior.* Oslo: Universitetsforlaget, 1980.

60

Blakar, R. M. *Communication: A social perspective on clinical issues.* Oslo: Universitetsforlaget, 1984.
Jackson, D. D. (Ed). *Human communication, Vol. 1: Communication, family, and marriage; Vol. 2: Therapy, communication, and change.* Palo Alto: Science and Behavior Books, 1968.
Laing, R. D., Phillipson, H., & Lee, A. R. *Interpersonal perception: A theory and a method of research.* New York: Tavistock Publications, 1966.
Ricci, C., & Selvini-Palazzoli, M. Interaction complexity and communication. *Family Process 23:* 169–176, 1984.
Ruesch, J., & Bateson, G. *Communication: The social matrix of psychiatry.* New York: W. W. Norton & Co., 1951.
Sluzki, C. E., & Ransom, D. C. (Eds.). *Double bind: The foundation of the communicational approach to the family.* New York: Grune & Stratton, 1976.
Watzlawick, P. *An anthology of human communication; text and tape.* Palo Alto: Science and Behavior Books, 1964.
Watzlawick, P., Beavin, J. H., & Jackson, D. D. *Pragmatics of human communication: A study of interactional patterns, pathologies and paradoxes.* New York: W. W. Norton & Co., 1967.

COMMUNICATION THERAPY

Communication therapy is an umbrella term for various forms of therapy based on cybernetic concepts. The theoretical framework, formulation of hypotheses, and intervention strategies are based on the findings of → **communication theory,** → **systems theory,** and → **game theory.** Within the field of communication therapy one can differentiate between → **strategic therapy** and → **systemic therapy.**

The intellectual forefathers of these therapy forms were Gregory Bateson and Milton Erickson. After years of experience in cultural–anthropological field research that led, among other innovations, to the concept of → **schismogenesis,** Bateson became interested in cybernetics. The application of cybernetic concepts in the field of psychiatry and, more specifically, the communication structures of schizophrenics, led to the development of the → **double–bind** hypothesis. Among those credited with the development of this hypothesis, besides Bateson, are Jay Haley, John Weakland, William Fry, and Don D. Jackson, the latter also introducing the concept of family → **homeostasis.** The symptomatology or "craziness" of the patient was not reduced merely to the personality characteristics of the patient, but was traced back to the communication patterns within the patient's family and in other social contexts.

Since its initial formulation, this uncommonly fertile idea has been investigated and expanded at the Mental Research Institute in Palo Alto, California. Members of this Institute have included: John E Bell, Arthur Bodin, Richard Fisch, Jay Haley, Jules Riskin, Virginia Satir, Carlos Sluzki, Paul Watzlawick, and John Weakland. In their own publications, theoretical and therapeutic approaches, these people are largely oriented to the intervention strategies of Milton Erickson. In particular, Haley and Weakland analyzed Erickson's hypnotic techniques, paradoxical interventions, and manipulative procedures (Haley, 1963, 1967, 1973, 1976). The short–term therapy methods originally developed in Palo Alto, and now applied in many other places, could not have been developed without the groundwork laid by Bateson and Erickson.

In 1967, Watzlawick, Beavin, and Jackson published *Pragmatics of Human Communication,* a survey of the basic theoretical premises and pragmatic aspects of human interaction. This book has greatly influenced thought in Europe and America. The publication by Watzlawick, Weakland and Fisch (1974) of their formulations about the principles of change in human beings may be understood as an attempt to integrate Bateson's theoretical work with Erickson's practical principles. Methodological application of the strategies developed by Erickson led to the development of → **hypnotherapy** and → **neurolinguistic programming.**

In comparison, → **systemic therapy** was developed at the Institute for Family Studies in Milan, Italy, founded in 1967 under the directorship of Mara Selvini–Palazzoli. Whereas → **strategic therapy** places its main emphasis on understanding of and intervening in the presenting problems, systemic therapy concentrates on the comprehension and modification of self–maintaining feedback mechanisms within the family. Thus, Erickson has influenced the Milan group far less than has Bateson. Correspondingly, the Milan group is more concerned with the questions that Bateson raised, such as the processes of evolution and → **coevolution,** → **entropy,** and → **negentropy,** as well as the → **epistemology** of individuals and systems (compare → **cybernetics,** → **communication theory,** → **systems theory,** and → **game theory**).

Andolfi, M. *Family therapy: An interactional approach* (translated by M. R. Cassin). New York: Plenum Press, 1979.

Bateson, G., Jackson, D. D., Haley, J., & Weakland, J. H. Toward a theory of schizophrenia. *Behavioral Science 1:* 251–264, 1956.

Bodin, A. M. The interactional view: Family therapy approaches of the Mental Research Institute. In A. S. Gurman & D. P. Kniskern (Eds.), *Handbook of family therapy.* New York: Brunner/Mazel, 1981, 267–309.

Greenberg, G. S. The family interactional perspective: A study and examination of the work of Don D. Jackson. *Family Process 16:* 385–412, 1977.

62

Haley, J. *Strategies of psychotherapy.* New York: Grune & Stratton, 1963.
Haley, J. Toward a theory of pathological systems. In G. H. Zuk & I. Boszormenyi-Nagy (Eds.), *Family therapy and disturbed families.* Palo Alto: Science and Behavior Books, 1967, 11–27.
Haley, J. *Uncommon therapy: The psychiatric techniques of Milton H. Erickson, M.D.: A casebook of an innovative psychiatrist's work in short-term therapy.* New York: W. W. Norton & Co., 1973.
Haley, J. *Problem-solving therapy.* San Francisco: Jossey-Bass, 1976.
Lederer, W., & Jackson, D. D. *Mirages of marriage.* New York: W. W. Norton & Co., 1968.
Selvini-Palazzoli, M., Boscolo, L., Cecchin, G., & Prata, G. *Paradox and counter-paradox: A new model in the therapy of the family in schizophrenic transaction* (translated by E. V. Burt). New York: Jason Aronson, 1978.
Simon, F. B., Albert, B., & Klein, C. Organisationsstruktur und therapeutische Strategie: Kommunikationstherapie in der Institution. *Gruppenpsychotherapie Gruppendynamik 17:* 19–36, 1981.
Simon, F. B., Albert, B., & Rech, C. Communication therapy in an institutional setting. *International Journal of Family Psychiatry 3:* 91–104, 1982.
Watzlawick, P., Beavin, J. H., & Jackson, D. D. *Pragmatics of human communication: A study of interactional patterns, pathologies and paradoxes.* New York: W. W. Norton & Co., 1967.
Watzlawick, P., & Weakland, J. H. (Eds.). *The interactional view.* New York: W. W. Norton & Co., 1977.
Watzlawick, P., Weakland, J. H., & Fisch, R. *Change: Principles of problem formation and problem resolution.* New York: W. W. Norton & Co., 1974.
Weakland, J. H., Fisch, R. Watzlawick, P., & Bodin, A. M. Brief therapy: Focused problem resolution. *Family Process 13:* 141–168, 1974.

* * * * * *

COMPLEMENTARITY

Complementarity [Latin *complementum,* complement] describes a pattern of relationship wherein the behavior and aspirations of individuals or groups differ but fit together in dynamic equilibrium.

Bateson (1935, 1936, 1972) introduced the terms "complementary" and "symmetrical" into social science research as a result of his research on the Iatmul natives of New Guinea. He hypothesized that persisting differentiation of groups in dynamic equilibrium falls into two patterns of → **schismogenesis,** in which the relationships are either complementary (differ but fit together) or are symmetrical (are similar but differently oriented).

Examples of complementary relationships include that between a doctor and patient, between mother and infant, between a dominant person or group and a submissive person or group. The concepts of →

dominant/inferior denote hierarchical positions within complementary relationships. In contrast, the relationship between two competing athletes or between two boasters is symmetrical. Jackson (1959), Haley (1963), Watzlawick, Beavin, and Jackson (1967), and Lederer and Jackson (1968) elaborated on the application of Bateson's concept for marital and family therapy. Haley (1963) distinguished two "positions" of complementary behavior: "one–up" (who is in control or in charge) and "one–down" (who is accepting or being taken care of).

Bateson (1935, 1972) used the term "reciprocal" and Jackson the term "parallel" to refer to alterations between complementary and symmetrical patterns that are balanced and do not tend toward schismogenesis. Jackson also described marital complementarity in terms of a "quid pro quo" rule that can be viewed as the benign, nondeceitful → **collusion** that develops inevitably in an ongoing, goal–oriented marital relationship. Bowen's version of complementarity emphasized "overadequate–inadequate reciprocal functioning" (1960, p. 369). Wynne et al. (1958) contrasted nonmutual complementarity (as in the interchange of customer and sales clerk) and the more enduring, affectively charged complementarity of → **mutuality** and → **pseudomutuality/pseudohostility.** The concept of complementarity is closely linked to the concepts of fit (de Shazer, 1985; Glaserfeld, 1984; Wynne, 1968) and → **coherence** (Dell, 1982). Starting from a non–Batesonian perspective, family sociologists have described the concept of complementarity of needs as a major factor in mate selection (Winch, 1958).

Bateson, G. Culture contact and schismogenesis. *Man 35:* 178–183 (article 199), 1935. (Reprinted in G. Bateson, *Steps to an ecology of mind.* New York: Ballantine Books, 1972, 61–72.)

Bateson, G. *Naven: A survey of the problems suggested by a composite picture of the culture of a New Guinea tribe drawn from three points of view* (1st ed.). Cambridge: Cambridge University Press, 1936. (second edition, Stanford: Stanford University Press, 1958.)

Bateson, G. *Steps to an ecology of mind.* New York: Ballantine Books, 1972.

Beavers, W. R. *Successful marriage: A family systems approach to couples therapy.* New York: W. W. Norton & Co., 1985.

Bowen, M. A family concept of schizophrenia. In D. D. Jackson (Ed.), *The etiology of schizophrenia.* New York: Basic Books, 1960, 346–372.

Dell, P. F. Beyond homeostasis: Toward a concept of coherence. *Family Process 21:* 21–42, 1982.

de Shazer, S. *Keys to solution in brief therapy.* New York: W. W. Norton & Co., 1985.

Dicks, H. V. *Marital tensions: Clinical studies toward a psychological theory of interaction.* New York: Basic Books, 1967.

Glaserfeld, E. von. An introduction to radical constructivisn.. In P. Watzlawick (Ed.), *The invented reality.* New York: W. W. Norton & Co., 1984, 17–40.

Haley, J. *Strategies of psychotherapy.* New York: Grune & Stratton, 1963.

64

Jackson, D. D. Family interaction, family homeostasis and some implications for conjoint family psychotherapy. In J. H. Masserman (Ed.), *Individual and familial dynamics*. New York: Grune & Stratton, 1959, 122–141.

Jackson, D. D. Family rules: The marital quid pro quo. *Archives of General Psychiatry 12:* 589–594, 1965.

Lederer, W., & Jackson, D. D. *Mirages of marriage*. New York: W. W. Norton & Co., 1958.

Sluzki, C. E., & Beavin, J. Symmetry and complementarity: An operational definition and a typology of dyads. In P. Watzlawick & J. H. Weakland (Eds.), *The interactional view*. New York: W. W. Norton & Co., 1977.

Watzlawick, P., Beavin, J. H., & Jackson, D. D. *Pragmatics of human communication: A study of interactional patterns, pathologies and paradoxes*. New York: W. W. Norton & Co., 1967.

Winch, R. F. *Mate-selection: A study of complementary needs*. New York: Harper, 1958.

Wynne, L. C. Methodological and conceptual issues in the study of schizophrenics and their families. *Journal of Psychiatric Research 6 (Suppl. 1):* 185–199, 1968.

Wynne, L. C., Ryckoff, I. M., Day, J., & Hirsch, S. I. Pseudo-mutuality in the family relations of schizophrenics. *Psychiatry 21:* 205–220, 1958.

* * * * * *

CONSENSUS SENSITIVITY/DISTANCE SENSITIVITY/ENVIRONMENT SENSITIVITY

Reiss used these terms in a typology of problem–solving behavior in families, as observed in a → **family test**, the Card Sort Procedure (CSP). A family exhibits "consensus sensitivity" [Latin *consensus,* being of one mind] when mutual agreement and the avoidance of conflict are valued more highly than the optimal solution to a given problem. Families that employ this strategy tend toward a blurring of boundaries between family members; however, as a family unit, they tend to be hermetically sealed off from the external environment. Reiss applied the term "interpersonal distance sensitivity" when each family member strives to maintain his or her independence at the cost of family–wide cooperation. "Environment sensitivity" describes a family whose members possess the ability to cooperate with one another as well as the ability to admit information from the surrounding environment. This is characteristic of a → **healthy/ functional family.**

Reiss (1981) has explored the hypothesis that a family's approach to constructing reality, to construing its social world, will be manifest in its style of processing information and problem solving, as measured in an ambiguous laboratory setting. Reiss (1971a, b, c) investigated three kinds of families: those with a schizophrenic member, those with a delinquent member, and those exhibiting no serious dysfunction. Each of these families was given a task that required the optimal solution of communication within the family and communication between the family and the external environment, and, finally, reaching a group decision. In their endeavors to complete the task, the families form a shared construct that reflects "how the family may react to a variety of novel, challenging problems in its everyday life" (Reiss, 1981, p. 68).

Reiss found that families developed three types of shared constructs that became, in a sense, a → **family typology**: (1) *consensus–sensitive* families, usually with a schizophrenic member, took extraordinary pains to maintain a close and uninterrupted agreement at all times (→ **pseudomutuality**). In doing so, they were willing to forfeit an optimal solution to the problem. Family members quickly surrendered their individual ideas and hastily forced a consensus with little reference to external cues that could facilitate problem solution. Internally, they showed a tendency toward blurring of → **boundaries** and a concomitant tendency toward → **enmeshment.**

(2) *Interpersonal distance–sensitive* families, who in this sample most often had a delinquent member, also had difficulty in finding an optimal solution to the task. Each family member failed to accept suggestions, observations, or ideas of the others. Each appeared to maintain distance from one another in order to insure that his or her independence would not be threatened. When family members were asked individually to solve the problem, better results were achieved than when the family was requested to cooperate as a unit. Distance–sensitive families of this type show features of what have been described as → **disengagement** and → **pseudohostility.**

(3) *Environment–sensitive families,* in which no member exhibited serious dysfunction, jointly experienced a need to observe as many cues as possible, both from one another and directly from the external environment. These families were capable, as individuals and as a unit, of developing hypotheses regarding the optimal solution to the problem. They were able to defer a decision until they had gathered and assessed all obtainable information. There was a good balance between demarcation of personal boundaries and closeness in the family as well as delimitation from and openness toward the external environment.

In the next phase of the studies by Reiss (1981), he shifted from a typological approach to the articulation of three underlying *dimensions* of family functioning. Each family can be characterized on each systemic dimension: (1) *Configuration:* the contribution that the family, working as a group, makes to problem solving beyond whatever individual family members could achieve by acting separately; (2) *Coordination:* the ability and willingness of family members to develop similar problem solutions; (3) *Closure:* the family's tendency to remain

66

open to new information and experience (delay of closure) or to reach closure very early.

Moving to a higher level of → **abstraction,** Reiss introduced the notion of a family → **paradigm** to describe how families frame assumptions about the properties of the world. These paradigms manifest themselves as "the family's organizing patterns of daily living" (Reiss, 1981, p. 174). (Also see Reiss and Oliveri, 1980.)

Reiss also has studied how the dimensions of family functioning measured in the laboratory are evident in other circumstances: in the family's perception of psychiatric wards (Costell et al., 1981; Reiss, et al, 1980); the perception of other families in multiple family therapy groups; and the effects on family functioning of a small dose of a psychoactive drug (Reiss & Salzman, 1973).

Costell, R., Reiss, D., Berkman, H., & Jones, C. The family meets the hospital: Predicting the family's perception of the treatment program from its problem solving style. *Archives of General Psychiatry 38:* 569–577, 1981.

Reiss, D. Individual thinking and family interaction: I. Introduction to an experimental study of problem solving in families of normals, character disorders, and schizophrenics. *Archives of General Psychiatry 16:* 80–93, 1967. (a)

Reiss, D. Individual thinking and family interaction: II. A study of pattern recognition and hypothesis testing in families of normals, character disorders, and schizophrenics. *Journal of Psychiatric Research 5:* 193–211, 1967. (b)

Reiss, D. Varieties of consensual experience: I. A theory for relating family interaction to individual thinking. *Family Process 10:* 1–28, 1971. (a)

Reiss, D. Varieties of consensual experience: II. Dimensions of a family's experience of its environment. *Family Process 10:* 28–35, 1971. (b)

Reiss, D. Varieties of consensual experience: III. Contrasts between families of normals, delinquents, and schizophrenics. *Journal of Nervous and Mental Disease 152:* 73–95, 1971. (c)

Reiss, D. *The family's construction of reality.* Cambridge: Harvard University Press, 1981.

Reiss, D. The working family: A researcher's view of health in the household. *American Journal of Psychiatry 139:* 1412–1420, 1982.

Reiss, D., Costell, R., Jones, C., & Berkman, H. The family meets the hospital: A laboratory forecast of the encounter. *Archives of General Psychiatry 37:* 141–154, 1980.

Reiss, D., & Elstein, A. S. Perceptual and cognitive resources of family members: Contrasts between families of paranoid and nonparanoid schizophrenic psychiatric patients. *Archives of General Psychiatry 24:* 121–134, 1971.

Reiss, D., & Oliveri, M. E. Family paradigm and family coping: A proposal for linking the family's intrinsic adaptive capacities to its responses to stress. *Family Relations 29:* 431–444, 1980.

Reiss, D., & Salzman, C. Resilience of family process: Effect of secobarbital. *Archives of General Psychiatry 28:* 425–433, 1973.

* * * * * *

CONSTRUCTIVISM

This school of thought, which considers the relation between knowledge and reality (→ **epistemology**) within an evolutionary perspective, posits that an organism is never able to recognize, depict, or mirror reality, and that it can only construct a "model that fits" (Glaserfeld, 1984). This model (→ **paradigm/model/map**) evolves in the organism's interactions with its environment and obeys evolutionary principles of selection.

Traditional epistemologies view cognition as mirroring a reality that exists independently of the observer. Radical constructivism, in contrast, posits that any statement about reality is primarily a statement about the observer. This follows from the recursive nature of all knowledge (→ **self–reference**). One needs to ask how and at what point can knowledge be related to reality if one realizes that such knowledge is in itself an element of this reality. This question, however, defies common logic because it inevitably leads to paradoxes. Constructivism, therefore, does not aim at knowing reality but only seeks to understand how models that serve differing pragmatic purposes are constructed. Because species, organisms, and humans differ with respect to their pragmatic (or survival) goals, there exist nearly unlimited possibilities for the construction of diverse realities.

It is a tenet of constructivism that organic and cognitive structures evolve in similar fashion; in each case selection processes operate through → **trial and error**. Experiences gained through action become hypotheses (→ **hypothesis formation**), which in turn serve to guide further action. To the extent that these hypotheses fail the test of experience, they require modification. However, such "test of experience" will not validate only one hypothesis but, rather, any number that will satisfy the experiential requirements. Glaserfeld (1984) illustrated this with the following metaphor: A key "fits" if it opens a lock. The "fit" describes the capacity of the key but not of the lock. Professional criminals know only too well that there exist many keys that are different from that possessed by the owner of the lock, yet which will open the lock.

Such a perspective is no longer concerned with the subject–object split that preoccupied traditional epistemologies. Rather, it views cognition as an aspect of interaction; life processes can be comprehended as processes of cognition (→ **learning**). Cognitive systems organize themselves in ways that allow them to define an interactional domain in which they can successfully pursue their quest for survival. Thus, cognition constitutes factual, inductive action or behavior in this domain. Accordingly, we can view living systems as cognitive systems and life as a process of cognition (see Maturana, 1978).

Within such a perspective, biological structures also can be viewed as cognitive structure. When compared with cognitive structures in the narrower meaning of the term, they reveal only lesser flexibility, i.e., a relative inertia or slowness to change. We may speak of two levels of cognitive structures—the biological and the cognitive—in which the former determines the premises of the latter. Accordingly, cognitive processes do not start at some zero point but, instead, follow the guidelines of a biologically coded basis for hypothesis formation. Riedel (1980) details four hypotheses about the processes by which knowledge is acquired.

1. "The hypothesis of the apparent true" designates a functional principle that contains the "expectation that certain experiences can probably be predicted to recur under like conditions, i.e., can be confirmed through their recurrence" (p. 53).

2. The "hypothesis of the comparable" implies that things may be compared even when they are not totally alike. There is the "expectation" that some things, even though they are not the same in all respects, will be found comparable with respect to certain as yet not perceived characteristics (p. 93). All expectation and comparison take place in similarly constituted domains, e.g., domains with similar structures or functions. Anticipation builds on confirmed expectation.

3. The third hypothesis built into man's phylogenetic heritage is that of the "basic cause" (*Ursache*). It acknowledges the fact that all human experience is irreversible with regard to the dimension of time (→ **diachronic/synchronic**); and it contains the "expectation" that "similar events or conditions may allow one to predict similar sequences of events or conditions and that . . . a certain domain of similarities, i.e., one and the same amount of events or conditions will allow one to anticipate one and the same sequence of events or conditions" (p. 130).

4. The "hypothesis of purposefulness" contains the "expectation" that functions of similar systems can be comprehended as functions of the same superordinate system. One could also say that "same structures will meet or satisfy the same purpose" (p. 159).

These hypotheses guide action and are in turn confirmed through action. They constitute an orienting frame whereby subjective meanings may be ordered and a reliable world (*Lebenswelt*) be constructed. Within such a world, an individual can exert a certain amount of → **autonomy.** Foerster's "postulate of an epistemic homeostasis" (1970, 1974, 1984) implies that the central nervous system as a whole is so organized that it can compute a stable reality. He would like to replace the term "knowing" with the phrase "computing a reality," which would comprise all operations (numerical, syntactic, semantic, etc.) carried out with any kind of symbols. This subjectively constructed (computed) reality serves to reduce the incredible complexity of the world. Order is created out of disorder, form out formlessness (→ **entropy**).

Philosophical positions akin to those of present–day constructivism were held by Giambattista Vico (1710) and Immanuel Kant (1781), among others. Kant, for example, posited in his *Critique of Pure Reason* that we can infer the mental operations whereby we construct our experiential world. More recently, Jean Piaget made substantial contributions to constructivism. In his genetic epistemology, he differentiated between two tendencies of an organism when dealing with events in its environment—the tendency to draw such events onto itself, and the tendency to adapt to them. In the first case, Piaget speaks of "assimilation," in the second of "accommodation" (Piaget, 1970, 1971). The rules of "operant thinking" develop thus in the organism's interaction with its environment a long time before they can be confirmed or disconfirmed by abstract thinking processes. Due to the capacity to symbolize, mankind has at its disposal a most economical method of "trial and error," i.e., one exercised on a symbolic, even playful, level. The structure of this "inner map" both reflects the precipitate of experienced interactions and serves to direct one toward forthcoming interaction.

In family therapy, the theories of constructivism became highly significant. This is true of the picture a therapist forms of a particular family as well as of the world views (or realities) that various families construct. Family adaptive as well as nonadaptive interactional patterns are closely linked to its specific constructions of reality and, therefore, are changeable through interventions aimed at the reconstruction of such realities (→ **reframing**).

Bannister, D., & Fransella, F. *Inquiring man: The theory of personal constructs.* Harmondsworth, England: Penguin Books, 1977.

Foerster, H. von. Thoughts and notes on cognition. In P. L. Garvin (Ed.), *Cognition: A multiple view.* New York: Plenum Press, 1970, 25–48.

Foerster, H. von. Kybernetik einer Erkenntnistheorie. In W. D. Keidel, W. Handler, & M. Spring (Eds.), *Kybernetik und Bionik.* München-Wien: Oldenburg, 1974, 27–46.

Foerster, H. von. On constructing a reality. In P. Watzlawick (Ed.), *The invented reality.* New York: W. W. Norton & Co., 1984, 41–61.

Glaserfeld, E. von. An introduction to radical constructivism. In P. Watzlawick (Ed.), *The invented reality.* New York: W. W. Norton & Co., 1984, 17–40.

Kant, I. [1781] *Critique of pure reason.* Garden City, L. I.: Doubleday, 1961.

Kelly, G. A. *The psychology of personal constructs* (2 vols.). New York: W. W. Norton & Co., 1955.

Maturana, H. R. Biology of language: The epistemology of reality. In G. A. Miller &

70

E. Lenneberg (Eds.), *Psychology and biology of language and thought.* New York: Academic Press, 1978.

Piaget, J. *Genetic epistemology* (translated by E. Duckworth). New York: Columbia University Press, 1970.

Piaget, J. *Biology and knowledge.* Chicago: University of Chicago Press, 1971.

Riedel, R. *Biologie der Erkenntnis.* Hamburg: Parey, 1980.

Vico, G. [1710] *De antiquissima Italorum sapientia.* Naples: Stamperia de Classici Latini, 1958.

Watzlawick, P. *How real is Real? Confusion, disinformation, communication.* New York: Random House, 1976.

Watzlawick, P. (Ed.). *The invented reality: How do we know what we believe we know? Contributions to constructivism.* New York: W. W. Norton & Co., 1984.

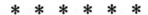

CONTEXT

Context [Latin *contextus,* a weaving together] is the frame in which behavior, verbal and nonverbal messages become meaningful.

Just as the meaning of a sentence needs to be considered within its text, so must behavior be understood within its context. Different interpersonal contexts are governed by different rules of behavior. For example, the context of a parent–child relationship is governed by a different set of rules from that of the relationship between a doctor and a patient; the rules that govern a sibling relationship differ from relational rules between chance acquaintances. If interaction is to flow smoothly, agreement must be reached regarding which context is currently valid (→ **context marking**). If it were not possible to reach an agreement regarding the validity of context, human communication would be a complicated affair indeed. No one would know which rules of behavior to follow. A situation, for example, in which one interactional partner is "just kidding" and the other is serious will lead inevitably to confusion.

The development of family therapy is based on an expansion of the traditional therapeutic context. The symptomatology of the individual is seen not only in the context of some kind of organic change, but also in the context of its meaning within the family and the wider social environment. Instead of focusing solely upon the individual, the perspective is extended to include the system in which the individual is embedded. However, it is part of every form of therapy, not just family therapy, to assess clearly what the relevant context is. The context and, hence, the rules that govern behvaior, the definition of → **roles**, and the expectations of patients and therapists, vary according to whether the setting is clinical–institutional or private.

The assessment of the relevant context from a diagnostic perspective is synonymous with the assessment of the relevant → **system.** As both behavior and interaction can be punctuated (→ **punctuation**) differently, it must be assumed that each individual has his or her own frame of reference that accordingly structures perception. In other words, one's perception is geared to one's specific context and determined by one's personal view of the world. Individual behavior is oriented to such a framework, and this framework, in turn, is embedded within the framework of the family system. Therefore, in families with a symptomatic member, therapy always means a change in the individual, subjective context, as well as in the collective context (→ **epistemology,** → **paradigm/model/map,** → **reframing,** → **ecology,** → **network**).

There exists a reciprocal relationship between a given context and the → **learning** and the internalized programs that determine individual behavior. The individual is not the "smallest survival unit" (Bateson, 1972) but an element of a superordinate ecosystem. One is embedded in a "transactional field" (Guntern, 1979, 1980) whose rules codetermine the meaning one's behavior will have.

From the vantage of therapy in institutional settings, institutional rules and interactional patterns have special significance and constitute a contextual framework that gives varying meanings to individual symptoms. At the same time, these meanings are shaped by social role definitions and expectations. Thus, the meanings and expectations that come into play will depend on whether a family consults a general practitioner, a psychiatrist, a minister, a hospital, or a counseling service. For these reasons, it is important to clarify how a patient or a family has found its way to a therapist or institution, i.e., how, by whom, and why the referral was made. The answers to these questions will have great significance for the role that the patient or family assigns to the therapist. Such contextual conditions always imply that a certain type of relationship is offered and/or expected. Therefore, any therapist must be aware that relationship to a client will never start at point zero but has already been pre–formed by such social definitions and expectations. (Note: The definition of context presented here differs in part from the definition that applies to → **contextual therapy.**)

Bateson, G. *Steps to an ecology of mind.* New York: Ballantine Books, 1972.
Guntern, G. *Tourism, social change, stress and mental health in the pearl of the Alps.* Berlin: Springer-Verlag, 1979.

72

Guntern, G. Das syngenetische Programm und seine Rolle in der Verhaltenssteuerung. In J. Duss-von Werdt, & R. Welter-Enderlin (Eds.), *Der Familienmensch.* Stuttgart: Klett-Cotta, 1980, 97–115.

Mosher, L. R., Wild, C., Valcov, A., & Feinstein, A. E. Cognitive style, schizophrenia and the family: Methodological implications of contextual effects. *Family Process 11:* 125–146, 1972.

Scheflen, A. E. Susan smiled: On explanation in family therapy. In J. G. Howells (Ed.), *Advances in family psychiatry, Vol. II.* New York: International Universities Press, 1980, 385–400.

Selvini-Palazzoli, M. Why a long interval between sessions? The therapeutic control of the family-therapist suprasystem. In M. Andolfi & I. Zwerling (Eds.), *Dimensions of family therapy.* New York: Guilford Press, 1980, 161–169.

Selvini-Palazzoli, M., Boscolo, L., Cecchin, G., & Prata, G. Hypothesizing-circularity-neutrality: Three guidelines for the conductor of the session. *Family Process 19:* 3–12, 1980.

Simon, F. B. Familientherapie: Grundlage einer "sozialen Psychiatrie." *Psychiatrische Praxis 7:* 195–198, 1980.

Simon, F. B. Das verlorene Vertrauen und der Ruf nach Kontrolle: Systemtheoretische Aspekte der "Ausgrenzung." *Psychiatrische Praxis 9:* 59–63, 1982.

Simon, F. B., Albert, B., & Klein, C. Gefahren paradoxer Kommunikation im Rahmen der "Therapeutischen Gemeinschaft." *Psychiatrische Praxis 4:* 38–43, 1977.

* * * * * *

CONTEXT MARKING

Context marking provides → **information** and → **punctuation** about the valid frame of reference (→ **context**) for interactional behavior, including communication (→ **metacommunication**).

In interpersonal communication countless signals are exchanged, most of them preconscious, that determine the interactional → **rules.** A patient visiting a doctor usually behaves like a patient; the doctor behaves in a way appropriate to the role of a doctor. The context for both is marked by signals that imply acceptance of the rules valid for institutions, consulting rooms, or clinics. But context marking also plays a central role in less formalized relationships. For example, if a man tells his wife to speak quietly, and she complies, he has marked the context in such a way that it inevitably influences all further interaction. This particular marking of context illustrates a complementary relationship (→ **complementarity**).

Without a continual marking of contexts, it is probable that social systems could not function; there would be constant conflict with regard to what rules of behavior were currently valid. The allocation of certain rules to specific contexts is an aspect of → **learning,** i.e., it is determined by experience and takes place via → **trial and error.**

If human beings find themselves in a context of vital importance in which the usual rules of communication are found to be unsuitable, a condition of confusion, pain, and maladjustment results (→ **double bind**). If, however, a person is able to survive and cope with such a situation, his or her creativity may be enhanced (Wynne, 1976). In the framework of these theoretical considerations, it cannot be determined whether this individual will become a clown, a poet, a schizophrenic, or any combination of the three. Bateson (1972, pp. 271–278) pointed out that this is not an isolated individual syndrome, but a species of "transcontextual" syndromes that are not necessarily "pathological." Each situation will involve a *re*-marking of the context, i.e., differentiating between rules that are valid or invalid in any given context.

Bateson, G. *Steps to an ecology of mind*. New York: Ballantine Books, 1972.
Bateson, G. *Mind and nature: A necessary unity*. New York: E. P. Dutton, 1979.
Wynne, L. C. On the anguish and creative passions of not escaping double binds: A reformulation. In C. E. Sluzki & D. C. Ransom (Eds.), *Double bind: The foundations of the communicational approach to the family*. New York: Grune & Stratton, 1976. 243–250.

* * * * * *

CONTEXTUAL THERAPY

Contextual therapy is a nondirective form of therapy that, through promotion of mutual understanding and trust, fosters a dialogue between family members and, hence, makes change possible. This school of therapy was founded by Ivan Boszormenyi–Nagy in an attempt to integrate the findings of psychoanalysis, existential philosophy, systems theory, and ethics. His central thesis is that disturbances in individuals and families are an expression and consequence of an imbalance in giving and taking, entitlement and fulfillment, particularly in the realm of caring. Contextual therapy tries to balance the given → **ledger of merits** and demerits by establishing a sense of mutual responsibility. The therapeutic dimension attempts to do justice not only to the external facts, but also to the psychology of the individual, the patterns of transaction, and, above all, the integrity of the interpersonal relationships.

The terminology of contextual therapy—legacy, merit, ledger of merits, entitlement, accountability—underlines its concern about interpersonal → **relational ethics.** Boszormenyi–Nagy attributes to merit, or the consciousness of achieving merit, the same motivational force that individual–centered psychodynamic theories accord to instinctual drives. The fulfillment or nonfulfillment of legacies affects the ledger of merits of each family member; it determines whether one feels he or she has been fairly treated, possesses integrity, and has a meaning in life.

Therapists are guided by the fundamental principle of → **multidirectional partiality,** which means that they empathize with each family member and make each family member's (ethical) standpoint their own. Above all, therapists attempt to make visible the previously invisible ties of → **loyalty,** which underlie the attachments between family members. The → **context** that therapists must consider spans a number of generations (→ **multigenerational perspective**).

It often happens that vertical ties, for example, between parents and their parents, are more vital than horizontal ties, such as those between spouses. In such instances, the therapist elucidates the behavior of the spouses in the light of what each has experienced in his or her family of origin; and what seems to be pathological or self–destructive behavior often is an expression of a deep, invisible bond of loyalty. Loyalty, however, can be misused, for example, when a child is recruited to balance out or to make good that which the parents themselves did not receive from, or were subjected to by their own parents (→ **parentification**). With an understanding of these dynamics, it becomes possible for the family to balance the ledger of merits, recognize and "reimburse" individual family members, and, thereby, change the structure of family relationships. This, above all, has the important effect of unburdening later generations.

Boszormenyi-Nagy, I. A theory of relationships: Experience and transaction. In I. Boszormenyi-Nagy & J. L. Framo (Eds.), *Intensive family therapy: Theoretical and practical aspects.* New York: Harper & Row, 1965, 33–86.
Boszormenyi-Nagy, I., & Krasner, B. R. Trust-based therapy: A contextual approach. *American Journal of Psychiatry 137:* 767–775, 1980.
Boszormenyi-Nagy, I., & Spark, G. M. *Invisible loyalties: Reciprocity in intergenerational family therapy.* New York: Harper & Row, 1973.
Boszormenyi-Nagy, I., & Ulrich, D. N. Contextual family therapy. In A. S. Gurman & D. P. Kniskern (Eds.), *Handbook of family therapy.* New York: Brunner/Mazel, 1981, 159–186.

* * * * * *

CONTROL THEORY

This theory (located within the field of → **cybernetics**) concerns itself with the structures and functions that determine the → **stability** and development of dynamic systems. In a control system, the values of a variable quantity are controlled, either held constant or varied to conform to a prescribed norm. In this broad sense, living organisms contain numerous natural control systems, such as body temperature and acidity. The application of control theory in modern technology is far advanced, as in the development of computers, but it is still relatively primitive and speculative for biological systems, and especially for social systems. On a theoretical level, the function and structure of control systems is concerned with the transmission and processing of signals and/or information (→ **information theory**). The two fundamental types of control systems are feedback (closed loop) and feedforward (open loop) (→ **feedback loop**).

Whereas in the early stages of its development control theory concerned itself with the stability of relatively simple systems, it later broadened its focus to include the study of adaptive processes in living systems. It has become apparent that there are also more highly developed forms of control (regulation), such as those that, in the course of evolution (→ **coevolution**), have made possible the development of increasingly complex systems. Such systems show a large degree of independence from environmental influence and, under certain conditions, are in a position to change their internal structures. Such forms of stability manifest not only deviation–reducing, "negative" feedback (those processes that restabilize a structure after or during disturbance from outside) but also "cumulative," "positive" feedback (those processes that amplify deviations) that can lead to the creation of a new form of stability or to the destruction of the system (→ **change, first and second order**).

The ideas of control theory, like those of practically all other areas of cybernetics, now form a conceptual basis for most modern sciences. In physiology, control formulations especially derived from the research of Cannon (1932) on → **homeostasis,** and from Ashby (1952). In the family therapy field, Haley has given special attention to the concept of control, in part from the broad, theoretical viewpoint described above and in part as a way of describing specific processes in families (1959b), in hypnosis (1958), and in psychotherapy (1959a; 1961a, b). As early as 1956, Haley argued that a central struggle in families and in therapy is control over *who* is to determine the type of relationship they will have (Haley, 1976).

Family theorists have been preoccupied with closed–loop feedback control systems and have largely overlooked the concept of open–loop feedforward systems in control theory. In feedforward control systems, information is programmed to produce a desired result, but information from the process is not used to correct the pattern. Such control systems are common in industrial automation, for example, in cutting tools that follow the shape of a model. Analogously, directive techniques in family therapy might be construed to be feedforward control processes. The → **lineality** of the feedforward concept is anathema to systems–oriented family therapists, but actual therapy techniques, especially those in → **behavioral family therapy** and → **structural family therapy,** incorporate, with great efficacy, lineal principles of feedforward control processes (Wynne, 1985). To be sure, sophisticated family therapists conceptualize these treatment techniques (hopefully) within a broader systemic or ecosystemic context.

Ashby, W. R. *Design for a brain.* London: Chapman & Hall, 1952.

Cannon, W. B. *Wisdom of the body.* New York: W. W. Norton & Co., 1932.

Haley, J. An interactional explanation of hypnosis. *American Journal of Hypnosis 1:* 41–57, 1958.

Haley, J. Control in psychoanalytic psychotherapy. In J. Masserman & J. L. Moreno (Eds.), *Progress in psychotherapy, Vol. IV.* New York: Grune & Stratton, 1959, 48–65. (a)

Haley, J. An interactional description of schizophrenia. *Psychiatry 22:* 321–332, 1959. (b)

Haley, J. Control in brief psychotherapy. *Archives of General Psychiatry 4:* 139–153, 1961. (a)

Haley, J. Control in psychotherapy with schizophrenics. *Archives of General Psychiatry 5:* 340–353, 1961. (b)

Haley, J. Development of a theory: A history of a research project. In C. E. Sluzki & D. C. Ransom (Eds.), *Double bind: The foundation of the communicational approach to the family.* New York: Grune & Stratton, 1976, 59–104.

Klaus, G., & Liebscher, H. *Wörterbuch der Kybernetik* (4th revised ed.). Frankfurt: Fischer, 1979.

Wynne, L. C. Structure and lineality. In C. Fishman & B. Rosman (Eds.), *Evolving models for family change: A volume in honor of Salvador Minuchin.* New York: Guilford Press, in press.

✳ ✳ ✳ ✳ ✳ ✳

COUPLES THERAPY

Couples therapy has developed in conjunction with as well as independently of family therapy. From the perspective of family therapy, a couple is a system; from the perspective of an individually oriented therapy, a couple is seen as an interactional network of two individuals whose needs harmonize and/or collide.

The central theories about the psychology of couple relationships reflect fundamentally different opinions about the essence of a couple's relationship. Willi (1982) postulated that the individual's choice of a partner and the resultant dynamics of a couple's relationship have their roots in the life history of each individual. Jackson (1965) postulated a marital quid pro quo whereby rules are established that dictate how mutual gratification, profits, and losses are balanced out. Sluzki and Beavin (1965) based their therapeutic approach on a typology of couple relationships that is grounded on the distribution of symmetrical (→ **symmetry**) and complementary (→ **complementarity**) aspects. According to Sager (1981), the various theoretical conceptualizations of couple relationships can be grouped together under the heading of a "contract model." This model posits that each marital relationship is based on a conscious or unconscious "contract" that determines who must perform what in the relationship, which expectations must be met by whom, and who receives what "reward" for meeting the terms of the contract.

In accord with such varying theoretical concepts, therapeutic methods will differ. For this reason intervention methods are difficult to categorize. It may be said, however, that a couples therapist is bound to fail if he or she enters into an alliance with only one of the partners. Also, the therapist must maintain an attitude of either → **multidirectional partiality** or → **neutrality.** In either case, it is necessary to determine whether the goal of therapy is to be the continuation or discontinuation of the relationship (→ **divorce therapy**). If the partners separate without freeing themselves from their mutual bond via appropriate operational → **mourning,** it is likely that both partners will carry over into any new relationships the same behavioral patterns that led to the insoluble conflicts and the splitting–up. It is also likely that such new relationships will be formed too quickly. Therapy makes possible an increased → **individuation** and differentiation for the relational partners.

Whereas the concept of "collusion" perceives a couple's existing conflicts to be the result of the individual life histories, therapists who work in a systemic manner consider the → **rules** of the couple's relationship to be largely independent of events prior to the relationship; it is the relational rules that often give rise to and foster pathological interaction (Jackson, 1965). This therapeutic approach, therefore, does not focus on working out the conflicts that stem from individual life histories but, rather, aims at changing the interactional rules of the relationship (→ **communication therapy,** → **strategic therapy,** → **systemic therapy**). Whatever the theoretical underpinnings of a therapeutic approach, there is general agreement that if a couple enters therapy with a clearly defined problem, this problem should be addressed first. However, it is also true that the ostensible problem that led the couple to seek therapy cannot be divorced from the overall context of the relationship. Furthermore, any solution of the problem will affect the structure of the entire relationship. An excellent example of this is → **sex therapy.**

When one views the literature of couples therapy with specific regard to the way the role of the therapist is understood, one finds two contrasting attitudes. Those therapists who derive their methods from individually oriented or psychoanalytic theories attempt, to a certain extent, to do individual therapy in the context of a couples relationship. These therapists concentrate and work on processes of → **transference** and → **countertransference,** which occur between the partners as well as between the couple and the therapist. These transference processes are then considered in the light of the individual life histories as well as in the context of the current problems.

The second approach is that of the system–oriented therapists who attempt to change the couple's relationship from a perspective meta to that relationship. System–oriented therapists avoid becoming part of the system, i.e., part of the pathological interaction. By remaining and intervening, as it were, from outside the system, the central problem that exists in all relationships, → **self–reference,** can be confronted and is more likely to be resolved.

Berman, E. M., & Lief, H. I. Marital therapy from psychiatric perspective: An overview. *American Journal of Psychiatry 132:* 583–592, 1975.

Framo, J. L. Marriage and marital therapy: Issues and initial interview techniques. In M. Andolfi & I. Zwerling (Eds.), *Dimensions of Family Therapy.* New York: Guilford Press, 1980, 49–71.

Gurman, A. S., & Rice, D. G. (Eds.). *Couples in conflict: New directions in marital therapy.* New York: Jason Aronson, 1975.

Jackson, D. D. Family rules: The marital quid pro quo. *Archives of General Psychiatry 12:* 589–594, 1965.

Jacobson, N. S. Behavioral marital therapy. In A. S. Gurman & D. P. Kniskern (Eds.), *Handbook of family therapy.* New York: Brunner/Mazel, 1981, 556–591.

Jacobson, N. S., & Margolin, G. *Marital therapy: Strategies based on social learning and behavior exchange principles.* New York: Brunner/Mazel, 1979.

Lederer, W., & Jackson, D. D. *Mirages of marriage.* New York: W. W. Norton & Co., 1968.

Martin, P. A. *A marital therapy manual.* New York: Brunner/Mazel, 1976.

Paul, N. L., & Paul, B. B. *A marital puzzle: Transgenerational analysis in marriage counseling.* New York: W. W. Norton & Co., 1975.

Rogers, C. *Becoming partners: Marriage and its alternative.* New York: Delacorte, 1972.

Sager, C. J. Couples therapy and marriage contracts. In A. S. Gurman & D. P. Kniskern (Eds.), *Handbook of family therapy.* New York: Brunner/Mazel, 1981, 85–130.

Sager, C. J., Kaplan, H. S., Gundlach, R. H., Kremer, M., Lenz, R., & Royce, J. R. The marriage contract. *Family Process 10:* 311–326, 1971.

Sluzki, C. E., & Beavin, J. Symmetry and complementarity: An operational definition and a typology of dyads. In P. Watzlawick & J. H. Weakland (Eds.), *The interactional view.* New York: W. W. Norton & Co., 1977.

Stanton, M. D. Marital therapy from a structural/strategic viewpoint. In G. P. Sholevar (Ed.), *The handbook of marriage and marital therapy.* New York: SP Medical and Scientific Books, 1981, 303–334.

Stuart, R. B. *Helping couples change: A social learning approach to marital therapy.* New York: Guilford Press, 1980.
Willi, J. *Couples in collusion.* New York: Jason Aronson, 1982. (German edition: *Die Zweierbeziehung.* Reinbek bei Hamburg: Rowohlt Verlag, 1975.)

CRISIS

In a crisis [Greek *krisis,* a turning point] situation, the internal and external adaptation (→ **adaptability**) of an individual or a system is disturbed. When previously successful adaptive mechanisms are insufficient to preserve stability or balance, new skills and a corresponding internal restructuring become necessary.

In his "crisis theory," Lindemann (1944) distinguished two types of disturbance of adaptation: emergency and crisis. One can cope with emergency situations by using accustomed methods; a crisis requires new patterns of behavior. From a cybernetic perspective, an emergency is regarded as an adaptation disturbance that can be mastered by first–order change; a crisis can only be overcome via second–order change (→ **change, first and second order**). Evolutionary processes in general can be understood as a succession of different crisis situations. This in in line with Erikson's (1959) conceptualization of the development of the individual within his or her social environment.

Analogous processes occur within family units. When change occurs in one family member, this inevitably leads to change in the ecosystem (→ **ecology**) of all the family members. These developmental processes and their related crises are therefore interconnected (→ **coevolution**). As Minuchin and Barcai (1972) have shown, therapeutic approaches can be derived from Lindemann's crisis theory. If therapists are able to induce a crisis, they create conditions for change within the family. The solution of such a crisis is only possible through discontinuous and sudden second–order change. This explains the astonishing results obtained by certain systemic interventions (→ **systemic therapy**).

In Thom's (1975) → **catastrophe theory,** adaptation to changed external conditions is regarded as the central force in evolution and in the development of the new structures (→ **morphogenesis**). It describes how systems can flip from one state of → **equilibrium** to another. Although Thom's theory was not developed with psychological or family processes in mind, it does present a possible formal definition of "crisis."

According to Capra (1982), the Chinese, who have always had an eminently dynamic world view and an acute sense of history, seem to have a profound understanding of the double–edged nature of crisis and the connection between crisis and change. Their term for crisis, "*wei–ji,*" is a combination of the characters for "danger" and "opportunity" (p. 21).

Andolfi, M., Angelo, C., Menghi, P., & Nicolò-Corigliano, A. M. *Behind the family mask: Therapeutic change in rigid family systems.* New York: Brunner/Mazel, 1983.

Capra, F. *The turning point.* New York: Bantam Books, 1982.

Erikson, E. H. Identity and the life cycle: Selected papers. *Psychological Issues, Monograph No. 1,* 1959.

Lindemann, E. Symptomatology and management of acute grief. *American Journal of Psychiatry 101:* 141–148, 1944.

Minuchin, S., & Barcai, A. Therapeutically induced family crisis. In C. J. Sager & H. S. Kaplan (Eds.), *Progress in group and family therapy.* New York: Brunner/Mazel, 1972, 322–329.

Rapoport, R. Normal crisis, family structure, and mental health. *Family Process 2:* 68–80, 1962.

Reiss, D. *The family's construction of reality.* Cambridge: Harvard University Press, 1981.

Thom, R. *Structural stability and morphogenesis.* Reading, Mass.: Benjamin, 1975.

* * * * * *

CRISIS FAMILY THERAPY

In crisis family therapy, intervention strategies are aimed at avoiding the hospitalization of the → **identified patient** and assisting the family in reducing or coping with current and recurrent stressors.

Various programs have tested the effectiveness of family therapy procedures in the resolution of acute crisis situations. They usually function in accord with the viewpoint that a crisis is an expression of a problem that involves all persons who are emotionally important to the patient. In these circumstances, the family interactional system is regarded as a significant resource. The intervention strategies aim at supporting the family in coping with the problem that precipitated contact with a clinic or hospital and in minimizing the need for hospitalization. The responsibility of each person for his or her actions is emphasized at the same time that each person receives emotional support. Medication may be prescribed for some or all of the family members in order to reduce tension and to alleviate symptoms. Selected family members are requested to carry out specific tasks aimed at introducing new problem–solving strategies into the family.

Some programs have a "hotline" open 24 hours a day. Other crisis intervention teams are only involved during the acute crisis, but usually they assure the family of their availability in any future crises. Other crisis family intervention programs have been oriented to the identification, anticipation, and prevention of recurrently stressful conditions, to reduced patient symptomatology, to diminished need for rehospitalization, and to improved family coping (Goldstein & Kopeikin, 1981). Another goal of crisis intervention is to provide care that is more cost–effective than psychiatric hospitalization of the identified patient. Another advantage of crisis family therapy is that it mitigates the chronicity of psychiatric problems. There are many published studies on the outcome of such crisis therapy, for example, those studies done at the Emergency Treatment Center of the Mental Research Institute in Palo Alto, California (see Everstine & Everstine, 1983). Sugarman and Masheter (1985) have reviewed the literature on family crisis intervention.

Everstine, D. S., Bodin, A. M., & Everstine, L. Emergency psychology: A mobile service for police crisis calls. *Family Process 16:* 281–292, 1977.

Everstine, D. S., & Everstine, L. *People in crisis*. New York: Brunner/Mazel, 1983.

Goldstein, M. J., & Kopeikin, H. S. Short– and long-term effects of combining drug and family therapy. In M. J. Goldstein (Ed.), *New developments in interventions with families of schizophrenics*. San Francisco: Jossey-Bass, 1981, 5–26.

Langsley, D. G., & Kaplan, D. M. *The treatment of families in crisis*. New York: Grune & Stratton, 1968.

Langsley, D. G., Pittman, F. S., Machotka, P., & Flomenhaft, K. Family crisis therapy—Results and implications. *Family Process 7:* 145–158, 1968.

Pittman, F. S. Managing acute psychiatric emergencies: Defining the family crisis. In D. Bloch (Ed.), *Techniques of family psychotherapy: A primer*. New York: Grune & Stratton, 1973, 99–107.

Pittman, F. S., DeYoung, C., Flomenhaft, K., Kaplan, D. M., & Langsley, D. G. Crisis family therapy. In R. J. Green & J. L. Framo (Eds.), *Family therapy: Major contributions*. New York: International Universities Press, 1981, 477–489.

Scott, D., & Starr, I. A 24-hour family oriented psychiatric and crisis service. *Journal of Family Therapy 3:* 177–186, 1981.

Sugarman, S., & Masheter, C. The family crisis intervention literature: What is meant by "family"? *Journal of Marital and Family Therapy 11:* 167–177, 1985.

Umana, R. F., Gross, S. J., & McConville, M. T. *Crisis in the family: Three approaches*. New York: Gardner Press, 1980.

* * * * * *

CYBERNETICS

The term "cybernetic" [Greek *kybernetes,* pilot, steersman] was coined by the mathematician Norbert Wiener in 1948 to encompass "the entire field of control and communication theory, whether in the machine or in

82

the animal" (p. 11). Cybernetics is concerned with scientific investigation of systemic processes of a highly varied nature, including such phenomena as regulation, information processing, information storage, adaptation, self–organization, self–reproduction, and strategic behavior. Within the general cybernetic approach, the following theoretical fields have developed: systems theory (→ **system**), → **control theory**, → **information theory**, → **communication theory**, → **game theory**, and decision theory.

Cybernetics is based on the supposition that the functions of control, regulation, information exchange, and information processing follow the same principles regardless of whether they are applied to machines, organisms, or social structures. Various aspects of cybernetic theory have been important in quite different areas of theoretical and practical research. The integration of these various aspects of cybernetics into a unified science of cybernetics was, for the most part, the work of mathematicians in the early 1940s. They accomplished this by restricting their investigations to the formal relationships and functions of behavior and by regarding these independently of the processes of energy transference and transformation. Gregory Bateson in particular realized the importance of cybernetics in the understanding and influencing of complex human relationships.

Within the realm of family therapy, the insights gained from cybernetics have caused fundamental questions to be asked about many epistemological presuppositions and certain diagnostic and therapeutic premises (→ **lineality**, → **circularity**). Here two phases can be distinguished. During the first phase, researchers were mainly concerned with how a sytem's stability could be maintained (→ **homeostasis**, → **morphostasis**). In the second phase the conditions of and requirements for change and creativity became the predominant issues (→ **change**, → **morphogenesis**). Maruyama (1963) spoke of the first phase, in which deviation–counteracting systems were given primary attention, as the "first cybernetics." Studies of deviation–amplifying mutual causal relationships are the "second cybernetics."

Ashby, W. R. *An introduction to cybernetics*. London: Methuen, 1956.
Bateson, G. Cybernetic explanation. *American Behavioral Scientist 10:* 29–32, 1967.
Bateson, G. *Steps to an ecology of mind*. New York: Ballantine Books, 1972.
Keeney, B. P. *Aesthetics of change*. New York: Guilford Press, 1983.
Klaus, G., & Liebscher, H. *Wörterbuch der Kybernetik* (4th revised ed.). Frankfurt: Fischer, 1979.
Maruyama, M. The second cybernetics: Deviation-amplifying mutual causal processes. *American Scientist 5:* 164–179, 1963.
Wiener, N. *Cybernetics, or control and communication in the animal and the machine* (2nd ed.). Cambridge: Massachusetts Institute of Technology Press, 1975. (2nd ed. originally published, 1954; 1st ed. originally published, 1948.)

* * * * * *

■ D ■

DELEGATION

The interpersonal processes described by Helm Stierlin as delegation refer to the double meaning of the Latin verb *"delegare"*: (1) to send forth and (2) to be entrusted with a mission. It implies that the delegated person, usually an adolescent, is both sent forth and yet bound to the family by the long leash of → **loyalty.** Delegated persons prove their loyalty by conscientiously fulfilling the mission they have been sent to accomplish, and the fulfillment of the appointed mission becomes the source of feelings of → **self–esteem.**

In terms of psychoanalytic concepts, one can distinguish between three kinds of missions according to whether they are designed to serve a delegator's (usually parental) id, ego, or superego. Missions on the id–level serve those elementary affective needs that the parents cannot satisfy themselves. The delegated one may be sent out to have sexual adventures, to experiment with drugs, generally to titillate the parents, and to experience a time of "storm and stress" that the parents, for whatever reasons, were not able to experience themselves. On the ego–level the delegated adolescent helps the parents to cope with the practical aspects of life, lends them support, fights their battles, and scouts out information for them.

In order to describe missions on the superego level, Freud's description of the characteristics of the superego (self–ideal, self–observation, and conscience) can be used as an orientation. If delegated persons are placed in the service of the parents' self–ideal, they must become famous athletes, scientists, artists, etc., which the parents were not able to become. If the mission is in the service of parental self–observation, delegates must incorporate into their personality the denied and rejected aspects of the parents' personalities so that parents can have these rejected aspects at a safe but observable distance. Delegates of this kind tend to be depressive or delinquent, a sort of garbage can for the unacceptable parental motivations, desires, needs, and characteristics. Finally, delegated adolescents help to assuage the consciences of their parents. As an example of this, Stierlin described the German teenagers who, in the framework of the *Aktin Sühne-zeichen* (Sign of Atonement Project), did heavy physical work in Israeli kibbutzim in order to expiate their parents' guilt as active or passive participants during the Nazi regime.

Delegations as described here often contain excessive and conflicting demands. In itself delegation is not necessarily pathological. On the contrary, delegation appears to be necessary to facilitate the development of a sense of life goals and direction in the growing child. Delegation becomes problematic when the demands placed on the child are not age–appropriate. Further, delegations cause difficulties when the child is thereby exposed to the conflict. One can differentiate between three types of conflict.

1. Conflict between two or more incompatible missions: The same child is asked at the same time to be a clinging, complaisant baby as well as a hard–boiled, successful artist.

2. Conflicts of loyalty: Often the mission of one delegator conflicts with that of another. In extreme cases, the child receives from each parent conflicting missions that invalidate or destroy the other parent.

3. Conflict resulting in irreconciliable differences of values between parental delegators and the surrounding social environment: A typical example of this is the parental demand: "Stay loyal to us. Don't ever leave us!" while society demands: "Become independent!" "Prove yourself!" "Make decisions!" "Carve a place for yourself in society!"

To recognize and unravel such conflicts is an essential task of family therapy. At times this proves to be a difficult task because delegations are often transmitted covertly, below the conscious level, in analogue rather than digital communication modes (→ **analogue/ digital communication**). Delegation can be transmitted to children at an early age by means of nonverbal signals, a type of "mood contaminant" described by behavior researchers. This gives rise to an internalized "life–program" or → **script.** This is not, however, a simple lineal transmissions of commands from parents to children. The entire process involves complex processes of internalization, exchange, and negotiation, which can in part be described by the psychoanalytic concepts of introjection, internalization, identification, and so on.

As the above–mentioned delegation phenomena expanded to become a central perspective of the Heidelberg Family Dynamic Concept, other relevant therapeutic aspects have been investigated. This further differentiation includes the concepts of the bound and the expelled delegate (→ **binding,** → **expelling**). Bound delegates must accomplish tasks that keep them in the center of the family's field of tension. Among such tasks is the mission of giving meaning to the life of an aging parent, to allow this parent to care for or even to sacrifice for the child. Further, a bound delegate may be given the task of continuing the life of a sibling who died at an early age, fulfilling the hopes and expectations that the parents had placed in the lost child. By doing this, the delegate enables the parents to avoid urgently needed grief work (→ **mourning**).

Expelled delegates suffer from other types of excessive demands. They are relatively loosely bound to their families. They experience at an early age parental aloofness and distance. They have to accommodate themselves to the fact that the small amount of attention or approval they will be granted has to be earned by fulfilling the perfectionistic expectations of their parents. Delegates of the expelling mode frequently suffer from psychosomatic illness or cancer; they have often been delegated the task of becoming uncomplaining, conforming, selfless personalities who, although they are expelled and rejected by their parents, tend to idealize them all the same.

Elements of delegation dynamics described here have been noted by other authors. Johnson (1949) developed the idea of the superego lacunae sanctioned by parents in their children. Klein (1946) introduced the concept of → **projective identification,** Richter (1960) that of the narcissistic projections of parents onto children. Wynne, (1965) mentions the "trading of dissociations"; other similar concepts include Dicks's (1967) and Willi's (1982) concept of → **collusion** as a form of reciprocal delegation. Delegation is also related to the concept of → **triangulation,** the inclusion of a third party into a dyad. A third party is required in a dyad either to stabilize or defuse the relationship. This is the case when a child is needed as a supplier of worry and concern, which helps parents avoid dealing with their explosive feelings of frustration and anger toward each other. Instead of discussing and working on their own problems and disappointed expectations, parents can haggle about each other's misguided child–rearing practices and use the child as evidence of each other's incompetence. A child triangulated in this manner is a multi–bound delegate.

Therapeutically, the recognition of delegation structures can lead to workable → **reframing** strategies. Children are then no longer seen as symptom carriers or as examples of ego or superego weakness, as lacking in control, easily led astray, immature, pathological, etc., but, rather, as performers of services or major sacrifices for their parents, or at least as helpers who deserve recognition for their deeds. This viewpoint often makes it possible for the family's → **epistemology** as a whole to be corrected.

An understanding of the delegation processes makes it comprehensible why an obedient, tractable delegate suddenly develops into a defiant, obstinate symptom bearer. The symptom bearer (for example, a girl suffering from anorexia nervosa) has discovered a weapon in the "over–accomplishment" of her task, a means of punishing the delegators; if such behavior does not bring approval, at least it serves to elicit constant attention and interest. It is, however, important to understand delegation processes as occurring not in a lineal (→ **lineality**) chain from delegator to delegate, but rather as unfolding in a circular fashion (→ **circularity**). This implies that the delegate often benefits from having a central role in the family, thus making it understandable that there will be resistance to giving up this role.

Bowen, M. A family concept of schizophrenia. In D. D. Jackson (Ed.), *The etiology of schizophrenia.* New York: Basic Books, 1960, 346–372.

Dicks, H. V. *Marital tensions: Clinical studies toward a psychological theory of interaction.* New York: Basic Books, 1967.

Johnson, A. M. Sanctions for superego lacunae of adolescents. In K. R. Eissler (Ed.), *Searchlights on delinquency: New psychoanalytic studies.* New York: International Universities Press, 1949.

Johnson, A. M., & Szurek, S. A. The genesis of antisocial acting out in children and adults. *Psychoanalytic Quarterly 21:* 323–343, 1952.

Klein, M. Notes on some schizoid mechanisms. *International Journal of Psychoanalysis 27:* 99–110, 1946.

Richter, H. E. Die narzisstischen Projektionen der Eltern auf das Kind. *Jahrbuch Psychoanalyse 1:* 62–81, 1960.

Ryckoff, I., Day, J., & Wynne, L. C. Maintenance of stereotyped roles in the families of schizophrenics. *American Medical Association Archives of General Psychiatry 1:* 93–98, 1959.

Shapiro, R. Adolescence and the psychology of the ego. *Psychiatry 26:* 77–87, 1963.

Shapiro, R. Action and family interaction in adolescence. In J. Marmor (Ed.), *Modern psychoanalysis.* New York: Basic Books, 1968, 454–475.

Stierlin, H. *Separating parents and adolescents: A perspective on running away, schizophrenia, and waywardness.* New York: Quadrangle, 1974.

Stierlin, H. *Delegation und Familie.* Frankfurt: Suhrkamp, 1978.

Stierlin, H., Rücker-Embden, I., Wetzel, N., & Wirsching, M. *The first interview with the family* (translated by S. Tooze). New York: Brunner/Mazel, 1980.

Willi, J. *Couples in collusion.* New York: Jason Aronson, 1982. (German edition: *Die Zweierbeziehung.* Reinbek bei Hamburg: Rowohlt Verlag, 1975.)

Wynne, L. C. Some indications and contra-indications for exploratory family therapy. In I. Boszormenyi-Nagy & J. L. Framo (Eds.), *Intensive family therapy: Theoretical and practical aspects, with special reference to schizophrenia.* New York: Harper & Row, 1965, 289–322.

Wynne, L. C., Ryckoff, I. M., Day, J., & Hirsch, S. I. Pseudo-mutuality in the family relations of schizophrenics. *Psychiatry 21:* 205–220, 1958.

* * * * * *

DETOURING OF CONFLICTS

This phrase describes a couple's attempt to avoid conflict by recruiting a third person, usually a child, to create a problem so that the couple can avoid focusing on their own difficulties.

Minuchin (1974) described detouring of conflicts as a type of → **rigid triad,** a situation in which the parents define the child as either "sick" or "bad." In "detouring–attacking," the parents attack the child as the source of family problems because the child is bad. From the perspective of an outside observer, the parents force the child into the → **role** of a → **scapegoat.** In "detouring–supportive" triads, the parents unite to protect a child who is defined as sick or weak (see Hoffman, 1981.) The behavioral problems of the children often have a stabilizing effect on the parents' relationship toward each other (→ **delegation**); in this way the parents are able to conceal their conflicts in their common concern for the well–being of their child.

Hoffman, L. *Foundations of family therapy: A conceptual framework for systems change.* New York: Basic Books, 1981.
Minuchin, S. *Families and family therapy.* Cambridge: Harvard University Press, 1974.

* * * * * *

DIACHRONIC/ SYNCHRONIC

Both terms are used to describe the arrangement of a structure with regard to the dimension of time. Historical developments, i.e., the *succession* or sequence of events over time, have a diachronic [Greek *dia* + *chronos,* through + time] structure. The concurrent (here and now) existence and relatedness of elements, i.e., the *contemporaneity* of events, exhibit a synchronic [Greek *syn,* together] structure.

The current interactional pattern of a family is to be understood as a synchronic structure; the family's history, as revealed through a → **multigenerational perspective,** is a diachronic structure. The distinction between diachronic and synchronic structural levels originated from linguistic theory. Lévi–Strauss was the first to apply these concepts to social → **structures.**

Lévi–Strauss, C. History and anthropology. In C. Lévi–Strauss, *Structural anthropology.* New York: Basic Books, 1963, 1–28. (a)
Lévi–Strauss, C. Structural analysis in linguistics and in anthropology. In C. Lévi–Strauss, *Structural anthropology.* New York: Basic Books, 1963, 29–53. (b)

* * * * * *

DIALECTICAL METHOD

The dialectical [Greek *dialektiké*, the art of discourse] method has as its objective the resolution of contradictions in thinking and being. It has a long tradition in Western intellectual history.

The dialectical method has become increasingly important to systemic and family–oriented therapists as they have explored the inherent contradictions in human → **relational reality.** The Greek philosophers who originated the method defined it as the art of making two contradicting doctrines appear plausible through adroit argumentation. Aristotle used the dialectical method as an intellectual tool with which truth could be distinguished from falsehood in commonly held beliefs.

In the Middle Ages, the dialectical method became more equated with formal logic. Kant (1781) spoke of the dialectical method as the "logic of appearances" (*Logik des Scheins*). The Kantian school of philosophy held it to be an attempt to arrive at knowledge by placing known concepts in relation to each other without appealing to experience.

Schelling (1800) was the first to explicitly combine the word "dialectic" with Fichte's (1794) concept of the three–stage dialectical progression of thesis, antithesis, and synthesis. Hegel (1807) further explicated the dialectical method by differentiating between dialectics as used in metaphysics or as an epistemological method. According to Hegel, the dialectical process is an ordered progression wherein thinking and being achieve identity. Hence, we note in dialectical processes the unfolding of laws that govern the evolution of concepts as well as of historical and social being.

Marx (1867) freed the dialectical concept from Hegel's idealistic application of it and regarded the concept as the key to interpreting economic and social processes. Engels (1882) contrasted the subjective, dialectical processes of understanding to those of an "objective dialectic of things–in–themselves." According to Engels, objective dialectical processes govern the patterns of nature and also of society. This concept of dialectical processes laid the foundation for so–called dialectical materialism.

In family theory and therapy, interpersonal reality often appears contradictory because reality can be described by a number of theoretical models. Each of these models, however, has its limitations, for example, our inability to go beyond the bounds of our own perception (→ **constructivism,** → **epistemology**), the problem of temporal structures (→ **diachronic/synchronic**), grammatically and socially conditioned → **punctuations,** and the confusion of → **logical types.** The dialectical method can be applied to point to and resolve these contradictions by using either the Hegelian method or any method that investigates and exposes the limitations of theoretical models of reality and clarifies the confusion of logical types. Following Hegel's method as presented in the *Phenomenology of Mind,* the interaction between "master and servant" presents a relational dialectic in which → **relational balance** can be construed, reciprocally created, or altered.

One can also speak of a therapeutic dialectic when it is a question of shaking up and reorienting the relational reality of a family or an individual, "turning the whole perspective about" as Wittgenstein (1958) said. This reorientation can take place with the help of new, often discordant information within the framework of the therapeutic techniques of → **circular questioning** and → **paradoxical intervention** (→ **reframing).**

Bopp, M. J., & Weeks, G. R. Dialectical metatheory in family therapy. *Family Process 23:* 49–61, 1984.

Engels, F. [1882] *Dialectics of nature.* New York: International Publishers, 1940.

Fichte, J. G. [1794] *The science of knowledge.* Cambridge: Cambridge University Press, undated.

Hegel, G. W. F. [1807] *The phenomenology of the mind, Vol. II.* London: Swann Sonnenschein, 1910.

Kant, I. [1781] *Critique of pure reason.* Garden City, L.I.: Doubleday, 1961.

Marx, K. [1867] *Capital: A critique of political economy.* London: Swann Sonnenschein, 1887.

Schelling, F.W. [1800] *System of transcendental idealism.* Charlottesville: University of Virginia Press, 1978.

Soper, P. H., & L'Abate, L. Paradox as a therapeutic technique: A review. In J. G. Howells (Ed.), *Advances in family psychiatry, Vol. II.* New York: International Universities Press, 1980, 369–384.

Stierlin, H. *Conflict and reconciliation.* New York: Science House, 1969.

Stierlin, H. *Das Tun des Einen ist das Tun des Anderen.* Frankfurt: Suhrkamp, 1971.

Stierlin, H. Reflections on the family therapy of schizo–present families. In H. Stierlin, L. C. Wynne, & M. Wirsching (Eds.), *Psychosocial intervention in schizophrenia: An international view.* Berlin: Springer–Verlag, 1983, 191–198.

Watzlawick, P. *The language of change: Elements of therapeutic communication.* New York: Basic Books, 1978.

Watzlawick, P., Weakland, J. H., & Fisch, R. *Change: Principles of problem formation and problem resolution.* New York: W. W. Norton & Co., 1974.

Weeks, G., & L'Abate, L. A bibliography of paradoxical methods in psychotherapy of family systems. *Family Process 17:* 95–98, 1978.

Weeks, G. R., & L'Abate, L. *Paradoxical psychotherapy: Theory and practice with individuals, couples, and families.* New York: Brunner/Mazel, 1982.

Wittgenstein, L. *Philosophical investigations.* Oxford: Basil Blackwell, 1958.

* * * * * *

DISCONFIRMATION/ DISQUALIFICATION

Disqualification is a communication mode that deprives one's own statements, or those of an interactional partner, of any clear meaning. If self–definition is the speaker's object, then disconfirmation has a negative effect on the development of personal → **identity.**

Disqualification is a communication technique that spares one from becoming involved in the → **communication** through the use of equivocal or contradictory statements and commitments. This technique is used to keep communication "up in the air" with regard to questions about a → **relationship,** for example: "Which of us is dominant?" "Do you love me?" "Who is closer to father and mother?" This technique is resorted to whenever a definition of relationship is to be avoided at all costs, for example, a marital relationship where one or both partners fear too much distance or too much → **closeness.** It also evades the question "Which one of us has lost (or won) the power play between us?" It thus avoids defining the positions of → **dominant/ inferior** in a relationship → **hierarchy.** As Watzlawick, Beavin, and Jackson (1967) noted, language presents us with a multitude of ways (→ **semantics**) to disqualify our own or other people's communications, for example, "self–contradictions, inconsistencies, subject switches, tangentializations, incomplete sentences, misunderstandings, obscure style or mannerisms of speech, the literal interpretations of metaphor and the metaphorical interpretation of literal remarks, etc." (p. 76).

When a family's predominant communication mode is that of disqualification, it points to an unwillingness or an inability to share a common focus of attention (→ **communication deviance**). It also highlights the limitations of the family's ability to solve problems (→ **consensus sensitivity**). Transactional disqualifications are especially prominent in families with a schizophrenic member, where they can be interpreted as an attempt to avoid definition of the relationship. This results in an absurd game where each player attempts to "win," although it is forbidden to "win" or to "lose." This is a game that never ends because the players are forced to maintain a high level of interactional tension that guarantees the continual repetition of the game. Players are enslaved to the game because of the illusion that as long as they keep playing, they might still win. At the same time it is forbidden to say openly that one wants to win or has won (Selvini–Palazzoli, Boscolo, Cecchin, & Prata, 1976).

In the context of such a game, disqualifications of the other are particularly effective in preventing the formation and confirmation of a mutually validated → **relational reality.** The consequence of this is that interpersonal → **boundaries** cannot be clearly established, with subsequent effects on → **self/object differentiation,** definition of self, and formation of identity (→ **enmeshment,** → **fusion,** → **undifferentiated family ego mass**).

Bateson, G., Jackson, D. D., Haley, J., & Weakland, J. H. Toward a theory of schizophrenia. *Behavioral Science 1:* 251–264, 1956.

Haley, J. An interactional description of schizophrenia. *Psychiatry 22:* 321–332, 1959.

Kaufmann, L. *Familie, Kommunikation und Psychose.* Bern: Verlag Hans Huber, 1972.

Laing, R. D. *The divided self.* London: Tavistock Publications, 1960.

Laing, R. D. Mystification, confusion, and conflict. In I. Boszormenyi–Nagy & J. L. Framo (Eds.), *Intensive family therapy: Theoretical and practical aspects.* New York: Harper & Row, 1965, 343–363.

Laing, R. D. *The politics of the family.* Toronto: Canadian Broadcast Corporation Publications, 1969. (a)

Laing, R. D. *The self and others: Further studies in sanity and madness.* London: Tavistock Publications, 1969. (b)

Searles, H. F. The effort to drive the other person crazy: An element in the aetiology and psychotherapy of schizophrenia. *British Journal of Medical Psychology 32:* 1–18, 1959.

Selvini–Palazzoli, M., Boscolo, L., Cecchin, G., & Prata, G. *Paradox and counterparadox: A new model in the therapy of the family in schizophrenic transaction* (translated by E. V. Burt). New York: Jason Aronson, 1978.

Singer, M. T., & Wynne, L. C. Thought disorder and family relations of schizophrenics: III. Methodology using projective techniques. *Archives of General Psychiatry 12:* 187–200, 1965. (a)

Singer, M. T., & Wynne, L. C. Thought disorder and family relations of schizophrenics: IV. Results and implications. *Archives of General Psychiatry 12:* 201–212, 1965. (b)

Singer, M. T., & Wynne, L. C. Principles for scoring communication defects and deviances in parents of schizophrenics: Rorschach and TAT scoring manuals. *Psychiatry 29:* 260–288, 1966.

Sluzki, C. E., Beavin, J., Tarnopolsky, A., & Verón, E. Transactional disqualifications: Research on the double bind. *Archives of General Psychiatry 16:* 494–504, 1967.

Watzlawick, P., Beavin, J. H., & Jackson, D. D. *Pragmatics of human communication: A study of interactional patterns, pathologies and paradoxes.* New York: W. W. Norton & Co., 1967.

Wynne, L. C., & Singer, M. T. Thought disorder and family relations of schizophrenics: I. A research strategy. *Archives of General Psychiatry 9:* 191–198, 1963. (a)

Wynne, L. C. & Singer, M. T. Thought disorder and family relations of schizophrenics: II. A classification of forms of thinking. *Archives of General Psychiatry 9:* 199–206, 1963. (b)

* * * * * *

DISENGAGEMENT

This term describes a type of family structure in which individual family members fail to form and maintain enduring relationships to each other.

Minuchin et al. (1967) described the concepts of → **enmeshment** and → **disengagement** in their research on slum families. Enmeshment and disengagement represent two opposite poles in the spectrum of strong and weak family cohesion. This description is consistent with Stierlin's (1974) differentiation between the interactional modes of → **binding** and → **expelling,** and the → **centripetal/ centrifugal patterns** operating in a family's developmental and → **individuation** processes.

Disengagement refers both to a process leading to marked isolation between family members and to the result of this process. In a more individually oriented psychological framework, the inability to enter into or maintain enduring relationships implies a disturbance in → **self/object differentiation** and → **object relations.** On the whole, families of this type show a lack of hierarchic structure and overly strong delineation of individual → **boundaries,** with limited opportunity for communication and mutual influence. In order to get one family member to react to another's behavior, a strong impact is often required. From the vantage point of the ambient social system, this type of family interaction may appear deviant or pathological. Such families are frequently labeled as "multi–problem" families. The concept of disengagement is similar to the concept of → **emotional cutoff.**

Aponte, H. Underorganization in the poor family. In P. J. Guerin (Ed.), *Family therapy: Theory and practice.* New York: Gardner Press, 1976, 432–448.

Minuchin, S. *Families and family therapy.* Cambridge: Harvard University Press, 1974.

Minuchin, S., Montalvo, B. G., Guerney, B., Rosman, B. L., & Schumer, F. *Families of the slums: An exploration of their structure and treatment.* New York: Basic Books, 1967.

Minuchin, S., Rosman, B. L., & Baker, L. *Psychosomatic families: Anorexia nervosa in context.* Cambridge: Harvard University Press, 1978.

Stierlin, H. *Separating parents and adolescents: A perspective on running away, schizophrenia, and waywardness.* New York: Quadrangle, 1974.

* * * * * *

DIVORCE THERAPY

The process that leads to the emotional and legal separation of a marital couple places a severe strain on each member of the family as well as on the entire family structure. Divorce therapy attempts to aid families to master this crisis situation. By investigating the "normal" phases of a separation process, divorce therapy focuses particularly on the well–being of the children and attempts to find acceptable, fair, and functional solutions for all the family members to the problems posed by divorce.

The problems in divorce families are similar to those observed in separation processes in general; the dynamics involved and the probability of pathological development are analogous to the processes of → **individuation** and → **mourning**. The specific phases of separation and divorce, as described by various authors (e.g., Bohannan, 1973; Kessler, 1975) can be summarized as follows: The initial phase is one of disillusionment, an increasing feeling of dissatisfaction. In this phase, the focus of attention is on the negative aspects of the relationship, and one tends to be overly critical of one's partner. If the partners are able to express their disappointments and are willing to share the responsibility for changing the situation, an improvement of the relationship is possible. If this does not succeed, a specific type of family pathology, → **relational stagnation,** is likely to develop and the relationship increasingly erodes. This state of affairs can last for years because a vague, diffuse hope that "things might get better" maintains the status quo. Fear of separation and fear of being alone prove to be stronger than the realization that the present situation is unsatisfactory, or even hopeless. The desire not to hurt anyone as well as consideration for the children's well–being can also lead to the denial of the status of the relationship.

This phase is usually followed by increased emotional distance, indifference, and, finally, the physical and spatial separation of the couple. At this point, the situation can no longer be denied, and the separation now has to be worked out emotionally. This process corresponds to a large extent to that which Kübler–Ross (1969) has described as the stages of mourning—denial and anger, the attempt to change the situation through action or compromise, depression, and final acceptance of loss. Once this process of mourning is complete, a second adolescence, an altered → **identity,** as it were, may be developed.

Divorce has many consequences for children: A parent who could serve as a figure of identification, as a model or a partner in the learning of gender roles, is missing; a figure of authority is lacking, which places the family → **hierarchy** in question; → **generational boundaries** may be blurred because only one parent is responsible for childrearing without the emotional and/or material support that a partner provides. Very often the social situation of the family changes. There is likely to be less income, a consequent decrease in the standard of living, and even social isolation if the culture in which the family is embedded stigmatizes divorce. If one or both spouses marry again, typical problem constellations are to be expected (→ **stepfamilies**).

Despite all of these consequences, it is not necessarily the case that divorce in every instance has negative effects on the children and their development. (For a survey of the literature, see Kaslow, 1981.) Divorce can also have positive effects upon the development of the children; it can resolve situations of massive → **binding** and lead to the dissolution of pathological triangles in which the child was responsible for deflecting parental conflicts (→ **triangulation**, → **rigid triad**, → **perverse triangle**, → **detouring of conflicts**).

At present there is no consensus as to the best method of dealing with problems in divorce. It is essential, however, that therapists be familiar with the stages of separation and divorce and the specific emotional problems related to them. They should also beware of "treating" one of the marital partners separately, for this can quickly lead to a new form of triangulation in which the therapist is drawn into a dysfunctional → **alliance** and risks becoming a substitute partner who helps the couple *sustain* a "terrible marriage." If one partner seemingly desires separation and the other does not, the therapist should avoid taking the vantage point of only one partner. A partitioning of roles between embattled couples is usually present, that is, there is a → **collusion** between the partners to oppose each other although they actually may be seeking a *joint* resolution of their ambivalence.

In the event that the marital partners do decide to divorce, it is the therapist's duty to help them to cope with their feelings of fear, guilt, and failure, and to help them to make constructive use of their experiences so that they can continue to develop as individuals and enter into new, more successful relationships. In efforts toward this end, therapists most likely will be guided by principles of their preferred → **model of family therapy** (→ **couples therapy**).

Under circumstances of transition and reciprocal blame, couples often are especially reluctant to accept "therapy," with its implications of illness and pathology. Therefore, a preferable mode of intervention is "consultation," in which the nature of the problem is identified and clarified (Wynne & Wynne, 1985). If the consultative focus is on the issue of cooperating in coparenting for the welfare of the children, rather than on past marital grievances, the intervention usually can be brief. This will prevent a situation in which the children become involved in conflicts of loyalty that, in the long run, rebound onto the parents in the form of guilt for having failed as parents.

Bohannan, P. The six stations of divorce. In M. E. Lasswell & T. E. Lasswell (Eds.), *Love, marriage, and family: A developmental approach.* Glenview, Ill.: Scott, Foresman & Co., 1973.

Framo, J. L. The friendly divorce. In J. L. Framo (Ed.), *Explorations in marital and family therapy: Selected papers of James L. Framo.* New York: Springer Publishing Co., 1982, 161–168.

Kaslow, F. W. Divorce and divorce therapy. In A. S. Gurman & D. P. Kniskern (Eds.), *Handbook of family therapy.* New York: Brunner/Mazel, 1981, 662–696.

Kessler, S. *The American way of divorce: Prescription for change.* Chicago: Nelson–Hall, 1975.

Kressel, K., Jaffee, N., Tuchman, B., Watson, C., & Deutsch, M. A typology of divorcing couples: Implications for mediation and the divorce process. *Family Process 19:* 101–116, 1980.

Kübler–Ross, E. *On death and dying.* New York: Macmillan Co., 1969.

Levinger, G., & Moles, O. C. (Eds.). *Divorce and separation: Context, causes, and consequences.* New York: Basic Books, 1979.

Wynne, A. R., & Wynne, L. C. At the center of the cyclone: Family therapists as consultants with family and divorce courts. In L. C. Wynne, S. H. McDaniel, & T. T. Weber, *The family therapist as systems consultant.* New York: Guilford Press, in press.

* * * * * *

DOMINANT/ INFERIOR

These terms refer to opposed positions and types of behavior that determine the pattern of a complementary (→ **complementarity**) relationship.

In a relationship that is founded upon inequality, one can differentiate between a dominant [Latin *dominus,* master] or superior (higher) positioning in a hierarchy and an inferior (lower) positioning in the same hierarchy. However, the allocation of positions in a hierarchy is questionable because, from a systemic point of view, the definition of who is passive or active, superior or inferior, or who really reacts in response to whom, is determined for the most part by processes of reciprocal → **punctuation.** One may ask, for example, who is dominant in a relationship in which the inferior partner *allows* the other to dominate, or even *manipulates* him or her into the position of

dominance. This question addresses the issues of the definition of →
relationship and → **power** within the family.

Watzlawick, P., Beavin, J. H., & Jackson, D. D. *Pragmatics of human communication: A study of interactional patterns, pathologies and paradoxes.* New York:
W. W. Norton & Co., 1967.
Watzlawick, P., Weakland, J. H., & Fisch, R. *Change: Principles of problem
formation and problem resolution.* New York: W. W. Norton & Co., 1974.

* * * * * *

DOUBLE BIND

The double bind is "a situation in which no matter what a person does, he
can't 'win' " (Bateson, Jackson, Haley, & Weakland, 1956, p. 251). The
concept is part of "a general communicational approach to the study of a
wide range of human (and some animal) behavior, including schizophrenia as one major case" (Bateson, Jackson, Haley, & Weakland, 1962,
p. 155).

In their original 1956 paper, Bateson et al. defined the necessary
ingredients for a double–bind situation:

1. Two or more persons. . . .
2. Repeated experience. . . .
3. A primary negative injunction. . . .
4. A secondary injunction conflicting with the first at a more abstract level, and
   like the first enforced by punishments or signals which threaten survival. . . .
5. A tertiary negative injunction prohibiting the victim from escaping from the
   field. . . .
6. Finally, the complete set of ingredients is no longer necessary when the victim
   has learned to perceive his universe in double bind patterns. (pp. 253–254)

In later publications, these ingredients and the "double–bind
theory" were clarified and modified. (See Sluzki & Ransom, 1976, and
Berger, 1978 for collections of relevant articles.) Bateson et al. (1962)
explicitly disavowed the nonsystemic concept of victim: "The most
useful way to phrase double bind description is not in terms of a binder
and a victim but in terms of people caught up in an ongoing system
which produces conflicting definitions of the relationship and consequent subjective distress" (p. 157). Another problem, noted by Sluzki
and Ransom (1976), is that the original presentation of brief examples
misleadingly gave the impression that double binding is primarily
synchronic, at one slice in time, while it is also crucial to recognize the
→ **diachronic** elements, the repetition of patterns through time. They

pointed out that "[f]ocusing on the moment while disregarding the historical sequence in which the moment is embedded has resulted in the use of the term 'double bind' frequently, and incorrectly, as a synonym for 'paradox' or 'incongruity between messages sent in different channels.' Although paradoxes and incongruities may befuddle and disorganize their recipients, they are not in themselves double binds" (p. 48).

Additionally, it is important to recognize the contextual elements in double binding: (1) the intense nature of the relationship between the persons involved; (2) the pressure to discriminate, to make a choice, whether to do so is feasible or not; and (3) the fact that the participants cannot, but must, comment (→ **metacommunication**) on the discrepant nature of the binding messages (Sluzki & Ransom, 1976, p. 47). The only possible escape from a double–bind situation is to proceed to a higher stage of abstraction, i.e., to metacommunicate about it. In a strict, definitional sense, the double–bind concept is applicable only when metacommunication is forbidden or impossible.

The foundation of the double–bind hypothesis was the formal analysis of communication structures following the approach developed by Bertrand Russell and Alfred North Whitehead between 1910 and 1913, in their theory of → **logical types.** According to Whitehead and Russell, one must differentiate semantically between two logical types: (1) concepts representing a class and (2) concepts representing the elements of a class. The higher logical type contains a proposition about the lower type. When two people interact, they must indicate clearly to which logical type their statements belong. For example, does a given action belong to the class of all actions that are games, or does it belong to the class of all actions that are non–games? At least two levels of communication are necessarily present in any interaction because one level demarcates and comments upon the other. The receiver of a message must be able to discriminate between these communication levels and the modes of communication related to those levels (→ **context marking**).

The double–bind hypothesis itself was developed by Gregory Bateson and his colleagues in 1956 during their research on communication structures in families with a member diagnosed as schizophrenic. They hypothesized that a person so diagnosed has difficulties in three areas of discrimination: (1) "assigning the correct communicational mode to the messages" one receives; (2) "assigning the correct communicational mode to those messages" one sends verbally or nonverbally; and (3) "assigning the correct communicational mode" to one's "own thoughts, sensations, and perceptions" (Bateson et al., 1956, pp. 252–253).

The relationship between double–bind phenomena and schizophrenia was described by Watzlawick, Beavin, and Jackson (1967) as follows:

Where double–binding is of long–lasting, possibly chronic duration, it will turn into a habitual and autonomous expectation regarding the nature of human relationships and the world at large, an expectation that does not require further reinforcement . . . The paradoxical behavior imposed by double–binding . . . is in turn of a double–binding nature, and this leads to a self–perpetuating pattern of communication. The behavior of the most overtly disturbed communicant, if examined in isolation, satisfies the clinical criteria of schizophrenia. (p. 215)

When discussing the relationship between double bind and schizophrenia, it is necessary to consider the context level and formal distinctions between logical types. With respect to the question of → **self/object differentiation,** individual (self) and interactional systems (dyad, family) belong to different logical types. The ability to discriminate between Self and Other is bound up with the ability to discriminate between logical classes (→ **category formation**). The inclusion of the level of context in the analysis of communication in double–bind situations reveals parallels with other family therapy concepts about schizophrenia, such as → **mystification,** → **fusion,** → **pseudomutuality,** → **rubber fence,** transactional disqualification (→ **disconfirmation**), as well as excessive or conflict–laden → **delegation.**

Bateson later pointed out that double–bind situations are not exclusive to schizophrenia. They occur in other communication contexts, in particular, literary or humorous ones, which often have paradoxical elements. What may be specific to the *schizophrenic* double–bind situation is that the paradox is not solved by humor or creative approaches. The insight that nonpathological forms of the double bind and creative or humorous restructuring are closely related led to the development of the *therapeutic* double bind. Within the framework of such therapy, Watzlawick et al. (1967) described how the client is given a prescription for behavior that "reinforces the behavior the patient expects to be changed, . . . implies that this reinforcement is the vehicle of change, and . . . thereby creates paradox because the patient is told to change by remaining unchanged. He is put into an untenable situation with regard to his pathology" (p. 241).

This approach can be regarded as a form of → **communication therapy** that specifically deals with the phenomenon of → **resistance.** The "resistant" family presents the therapist with a paradoxical message that simultaneously says, "Change us through therapy," and warns, "Don't you dare change us!" This of course is not a double bind in the stricter definition of the concept because the therapist is seldom vitally dependent upon the relationship. The therapist is, however, unable to respond simultaneously to both of the family's demands. By not resolving the therapeutic double bind, the therapist leaves the activity and the responsibility for change in the family's court (→ **paradoxical intervention**). The family may then make a discontinuous, creative, second–order → **change** (Wynne, 1976).

In summary, the double–bind hypothesis and the theory of logical types is of paramount importance in the field of family therapy. Interest in questions of → **epistemology**, the various conditions and stages of → **learning**, and context marking, was the inevitable consequence of research on double–bind situations. The first paper on the double bind (Bateson et al., 1956) marked the beginning of the application of the → **cybernetic** model, which incorporates the concepts of systems and communication theory into the study of family interactional styles. Bateson and colleagues were also the first to examine family → **homeostasis**. Since its introduction, the double–bind hypothesis in all its aspects has been subjected to minute criticism, a fact that has done little to diminish its actual importance. For an analysis of this debate, see Cronen, Johnson, and Lannamann (1982).

Bateson, G. *Steps to an ecology of mind*. New York: Ballantine Books, 1972.

Bateson, G., Jackson, D. D., Haley, J., & Weakland, J. H. Toward a theory of schizophrenia. *Behavioral Science 1:* 251–264, 1956.

Bateson, G., Jackson, D. D., Haley, J., & Weakland, J. H. A note on the double bind. *Family Process 2:* 154–161, 1962.

Berger, M. M. (Ed.). *Beyond the double bind: Communication and family systems, theories, and techniques with schizophrenics*. New York: Brunner/Mazel, 1978.

Cronen, V. E., Johnson, K. M., & Lannamann, J. W. Paradoxes, double binds, and reflexive loops: An alternative theoretical perspective. *Family Process 21:* 91–112, 1982.

Olson, D. H. Empirically unbinding the double bind: Review of research and conceptual reformulations. *Family Process 11:* 69–94, 1972.

Singer, M. T., & Wynne, L. C. Principles for scoring communication defects and deviances in parents of schizophrenics: Rorschach and TAT scoring manuals. *Psychiatry 29:* 260–288, 1966.

Sluzki, C. E., Beavin, J., Tarnopolsky, A., & Verón, E. Transactional disqualification: Research on the double bind. *Archives of General Psychiatry 16:* 494–504, 1967.

Sluzki, C. E., & Ransom, D. C. (Eds.). *Double bind: The foundation of the communicational approach to the family*. New York: Grune & Stratton, 1976.

Sluzki, C. E., & Verón, E. The double bind as a universal pathogenic situation. *Family Process 10:* 397–410, 1971.

Stierlin, H. The adaptation to the "stronger" person's reality. *Psychiatry 22:* 143–152, 1959.

Watzlawick, P. A review of the double bind theory. *Family Process 2:* 132–153, 1963.

Watzlawick, P., Beavin, J. H., & Jackson, D. D. *Pragmatics of human communication: A study of interactional patterns, pathologies and paradoxes*. New York: W. W. Norton & Co., 1967.

Weakland, J. H. The "double–bind" hypothesis of schizophrenia and three–party interaction. In D. D. Jackson (Ed.), *The etiology of schizophrenia*. New York: Basic Books, 1960, 373–388.

Whitehead, A. N. & Russell, B. *Principia mathematica* (3 vols.). Cambridge: Cambridge University Press, 1910–1913.

Wynne, L. C. On the anguish and creative passions of not escaping double binds: A reformulation. In C. E. Sluzki & D. C. Ransom (Eds.), *Double bind: The foundations of the communicational approach to the family.* New York: Grune & Stratton, 1976, 243–250.

Wynne, L. C., Ryckoff, I. M., Day, J., & Hirsch, S. I. Pseudo–mutuality in the family relations of schizophrenics. *Psychiatry 21:* 205–220, 1958.

* * * * * *

DRIVING CRAZY

"The effort to drive the other person crazy" was hypothesized by Searles (1959) as "an element in the aetiology and psychotherapy of schizophrenia." This is a form of behavior and/or communication that causes another person to experience extreme emotional conflict because it confuses and undermines the development of autonomy and has a detrimental effect on the other's sense of personal identity and positive self–image.

Driving the other person crazy, in Searles's (1959) use of the term, is similar to what Laing (1965) called → **mystification,** Singer and Wynne (1966) described as → **communication deviance,** Sluzki et al. (1967) as transactional disqualification, and Bateson et al. (1956) as → **double bind.** Persons exposed to these processes are unable to determine what kind of relationship they have with the other. Agreement regarding a mutual → **relational reality** is not possible; confidence in the reliability of one's emotional reactions and one's perception of the world is undermined; development of individual autonomy is hindered.

Searles regards the motives behind such efforts as a desire to destroy the other ("to murder psychologically") as well as the effort to externalize one's own internal threat of craziness in order to be rid of it. This corresponds to a certain type of → **delegation.** A child appealed to or delegated in this manner takes over the mission of fending off a threat from the family's past and of keeping the other family members safe from its curse. Searles believes that it is also an attempt to end an ambivalently symbiotic relationship that has become so tension–laden that one cannot gain any distance from it. The close relationship between the one who drives the other crazy and the one who is driven crazy must be understood in terms of the dynamics of → **fusion** and a symbiotic relationship. According to Searles, children who later become schizophrenic have from early childhood been used to satisfy the narcissistic needs of their parents. The child's aspirations toward → **autonomy** in this type of family structure have to be systematically invalidated and sabotaged (→ **identity**, → **individuation**). Searles remains largely faithful to a psychoanalytic framework even when he includes specific transactional patterns into his analysis. As with the concept of mystification, one can raise objections to the lineal (→ **lineality**), causal nature of this perspective. The reciprocal determinations of parental and child behavior are not sufficiently taken into consideration. For this reason, the therapeutic methods derived from this theory take the form of individual therapy. The point of view that one interactional partner is the victim and the other the victimizer does not accord with → **multidirectional partiality** or → **neutrality.**

Bateson, G., Jackson, D. D., Haley, J., & Weakland, J. H. Toward a theory of schizophrenia. *Behavioral Science 1:* 251–264, 1956.

Laing, R. D. Mystification, confusion, and conflict. In I. Boszormenyi–Nagy & J. L. Framo (Eds.), *Intensive family therapy: Theoretical and practical aspects.* New York: Harper & Row, 1965, 343–363.

Lidz, T., Cornelison, A. R., Terry, D., & Fleck, S. The intrafamilial environment of the schizophrenic patient: VI. The transmission of irrationality. *Archives of Neurology and Psychiatry 79:* 305–316, 1958.

Lidz, T., Fleck, S., & Cornelison, A. R. *Schizophrenia and the family.* New York: International Universities Press, 1965.

Searles, H. F. The effort to drive the other person crazy: An element in the aetiology and psychotherapy of schizophrenia. *British Journal of Medical Psychology 32:* 1–18, 1959.

Singer, M. T., & Wynne, L. C. Principles for scoring communication defects and deviances in parents of schizophrenics: Rorschach and TAT scoring manuals. *Psychiatry 29:* 260–288, 1966.

Sluzki, C. E., Beavin, J., Tarnopolsky, A., & Verón, E. Transactional disqualification: Research on the double bind. *Archives of General Psychiatry 16:* 494–504, 1967.

* * * * * *

ECOLOGY/ ECOSYSTEM

Ecology [Greek *oikos,* home, settlement, village] is the science or conceptualization that attempts to investigate and describe the reciprocal relationship between an organism and its environment. The fundamental tenet of ecology is that a survival unit never consists of an individual organism or species in a static environment, but, rather, that it is an ecological system, an entirety of all organisms in reciprocal relationships with one another and with their natural environment. Ecological systems develop according to the principles of → **coevolution.** Family therapy is ecological in that its intervention strategies attempt to modify the reciprocal relations between the individual and systems that are essential for the individual's survival (family, school, peer group, neighborhood, etc.).

The concept and definition of ecology as a relational system between interrelated organisms and their environment was developed by the English forestry expert A. G. Tansley (1935). However, some fundamental precursors of modern ecology research can already be detected in the "natural theology" of the 17th and 18th centuries. This natural theology posited a harmony and continued existence of the natural world on the basis of a dynamic balance resulting from the fight for survival among the various organisms (see Ellenberg, 1973; Gärtner, 1982; Stauffer, 1960).

The term "ecology" was introduced by Haeckel in 1866. Biologists, using the guidelines of the philosophy of → **holism,** considered what we today call an "ecological system" to be a higher–order organism. An aspect of ecological thought that has influenced family therapy theory is the insight that an organism does not have a lineal–causal relationship to its environment (→ **lineality**); every alteration within an ecological system will affect the members of that system. Gregory Bateson (1972) formulated this as follows: "The unit of survival—either in ethics or in evolution—is not the organism or the species but the largest system or 'power' within which the creature lives. If the creature destroys its environment, it destroys itself" (p. 332).

Therapy that regards itself as proceeding from the theory of ecological systems must therefore determine the relevant survival unit and take it into account during the therapeutic process; this unit may be the clinic, a patient's professional sphere, the community, etc. (→ **network therapy**). Such therapy must be based upon an ecological → **epistemology** (holism). The concept of ecology in family therapy is usually an extremely narrow one because it tends to be satisfied with consideration of only the social and economic aspects of ecological systems. Far more comprehensive is the ecosociological approach, which takes into consideration the reciprocal relationships between the phenomena of nature and social organizations.

Auerswald, E. H. Interdisciplinary versus ecological approach. *Family Process 7:* 202–215, 1968.
Bateson, G. *Steps to an ecology of mind.* New York: Ballantine Books, 1972.

Bronfenbrenner, U. Toward a theoretical model for the analysis of parent–child relationships in a social context. In J. C. Glidewell (Ed.), *Parental attitudes and child behavior*. Springfield, Ill.: Charles C. Thomas, 1961, 96–109.

Bronfenbrenner, U. Reality and research in the ecology of human development. *Proceedings of the American Philosophical Society 119:* 439–469, 1975.

Commoner, B. *The closing circle: Nature, man and technology*. New York: Alfred A. Knopf, 1971.

Ellenberg, H. Ziele und Stand der Ökosystemforschung. In H. Ellenberg (Ed.), *Ökosystemforschung*. Berlin: Springer–Verlag, 1973, 1–31.

Gärtner, E. Zum Stand der Ökosystemtheorie. *Argument 24:* 856–861, 1982.

Keeney, B. P. Ecosystemic epistemology: An alternative paradigm for diagnosis. *Family Process 18:* 117–129, 1979.

Margalef, R. *Perspectives in ecological theory*. Chicago: University of Chicago Press, 1968.

Renshaw, J. R. An exploration of the dynamics of the overlapping worlds of work and family. *Family Process 15:* 143–165, 1976.

Stauffer, R. Ecology in the long manuscript version of Darwin's "Origin of Species" and Linnaeus' "Oeconomy of Nature." *Proceedings of the American Philosophical Society 104:* 235–241, 1960.

Tansley, A. G. The use and abuse of vegetational concepts and terms. *Ecology 16:* 284–307, 1935.

* * * * * *

EGO PSYCHOLOGY/ EGO FUNCTION/ EGO ORGANIZATION

Ego psychology concerns itself with the development, structuring, and functioning of the ego. Ego is a theoretical construct defined in terms of its function, which is to insure the survival of the individual by organizing, integrating, and adapting (→ **adaptability**) internal/external perceptions and demands to the environment. One's capacity for → **self-organization** is determined to a great extent by one's interaction with his or her familial environment. Thus, there is a correlation, if not direct correspondence, between the theories of ego psychology and theories of family therapy; in both a developmental perspective is implied and the principles of → **coevolution** can be applied.

Modern ego psychology has its roots in Sigmund Freud's structural theory (1923), which differentiated between id, ego, and superego. According to Freud's theory, it is the task of the ego to protect the interests of the personality as a whole and to mediate between the conflicting demands of the id and the superego. The ego is an adaptive apparatus evolving in the ongoing discourse between the demands of the id and the necessities of adaptation to an external reality. Glover

(1939), following Freud, hypothesized that the "affective and memory traces" of early experience constitute ego–nuclei, which eventually join to form a coherent ego.

Anna Freud (1937) contributed to an understanding of the defense mechanisms of the ego, and this, in turn, led to a revision of psychoanalytic technique. The foundations of modern ego psychology were laid by Hartmann (1958, 1964) who posited that each individual is born with a matrix of largely undifferentiated genetic endowments. That which is denoted as the psychoanalytic ego and id cannot be distinguished at first because ego functions only develop in interaction with the external environment; the interaction between mother and child sets the stage for the unfolding of these genetic endowments.

In cooperation with Ernst Kris and Rudolf Lowenstein, Hartmann developed in numerous scientific articles the essential concepts of the processes that lead to the formation of psychic structures. Observation of children, particularly the research done by Spitz on "hospitalism" (1945) and "anaclitic depression," was a further major contribution to the development of ego psychology. Spitz's genetic field theory of ego development summarized his observations of the development of ego structures as a result of the dialogue between mother and child. Mahler and coworkers (Mahler, Pine, & Bergman, 1975) also relied on direct observations of mother and child interactions in the formation of a theory of normal child development. Within this theory, the four subphases of the process of separation/ → **individuation** are central.

An extensive survey and integration of the various theoretical perspectives in ego psychology can be found in Gertrude Blanck and Rubin Blanck (1974, 1979). Their theory of ego development concurs in part with the concepts of family therapy. Unlike Hartmann, these authors view the ego as not only determined through its adaptive function, but also through a specific aspect of this function, namely, the constant, ongoing process of organization and reorganization of internal (psychic) structures. Blanck and Blanck (1979) concluded "that the ego is better defined, not simply by its functions, but by its function*ing* as an organizer. From this it follows that ego *qua* ego *is* organizing process" (p. 18). The adult brings his or her inborn apparatus (potential) into the interaction with the environment "by using what it had provided as well as encompassing what it had omitted, having organized experience into representations of the result of the interaction" (p. 7). This concept of ego development as a process of self–organization corresponds to a large degree to the family therapy concept of coevolution and coindividuation as a process that involves the whole family.

The more one focuses upon the reciprocal relationship between intrapsychic organization (ego functions) and interpersonal organization (for example, family structures), the closer the interrelation between the practical, therapeutic applications of ego psychology and family therapy will be. The central question then remains how intrapsychic processes are converted into interactional processes, or, vice versa, how interactional forms such as therapeutic techniques can effect change in intrapsychic structures.

Blanck, G. *Ego psychology: Theory and practice.* New York: Columbia University Press, 1974.

Blanck, G., & Blanck, R. *Ego psychology II: Psychoanalytical development psychology.* New York: Columbia University Press, 1979.

Edelson, M. *Ego psychology, group dynamics, and the therapeutic community.* New York: Grune & Stratton, 1964.

Federn, P. *Ego psychology and the psychoses.* New York: Basic Books, 1952.

Freud, A. *The ego and the mechanisms of defense* (translated by C. Baines). London: Hogarth Press, 1937.

Freud, S. [1923] The ego and the id. *The standard edition of the complete psychological works of Sigmund Freud, Vol. XIX.* London: Hogarth Press, 1961, 12–59.

Glover, E. The psycho–analysis of affects. *International Journal of Psycho–analysis 20:* 299–307, 1939.

Hartmann, H. *Ego psychology and the problem of adaptation.* New York: International Universities Press, 1958.

Hartmann, H. *Essays on ego psychology.* New York: International Universities Press, 1964.

Hartmann, H., Kris, E., & Loewenstein, R. M. *Papers on psychoanalytic psychology.* New York: International Universities Press, 1964.

Mahler, M. S., Pine, F., & Bergman, A. *The psychological birth of the human infant: Symbiosis and individuation.* New York: Basic Books, 1975.

Spitz, R. A. Hospitalism: An inquiry into the genesis of psychiatric conditions in early childhood. *Psychoanalytic Study of the Child 1:* 53–74, 1945.

Spitz, R. A. Hospitalism: A follow–up report. *Psychoanalytic Study of the Child 2:* 113–117, 1946.

Spitz, R. *A genetic field theory of ego formation: Its implications for pathology.* New York: International Universities Press, 1959.

White, R. W. *Ego and reality in psychoanalytic theory.* New York: International Universities Press, 1963.

Winnicott, D. W. *The maturational processes and the facilitating environment.* New York: International Universities Press, 1965.

* * * * * *

EMOTIONAL CUTOFF

Murray Bowen introduced this concept to describe the strategy of dealing with the particularly strong (overt or covert) binding or fusing forces that link a person to one or more family members (usually in the family of origin). Emotional cutoff may manifest itself as the breaking off of all emotional ties, the search for physical distance from one's family, or a self–imposed isolation. In general, any situation is avoided in which strong emotional ties could reactivate emotional fusion. Emotional cutoff is an attempt to offset strong centripetal forces with strong centrifugal ones (→ **centripetal/ centrifugal patterns**).

If during an important early developmental stage a child experiences an emotional bond of unbearable closeness, it is probable that the child will sooner or later employ the mechanism of emotional cutoff. If one observes the history of a family through successive generations, one sees that the intensity of emotional cutoff is likely to increase. It presents a paradox in that it solves one problem only to create another. If one avoids all emotional contact in order to avoid transgenerational fusion, the fear of fusion is reduced, but the individuals concerned then become estranged and isolated from one another.

Within the framework of an individual psychological perspective, the use of emotional cutoff to solve the fear of fusion with another can be viewed as symptomatic of a narcissistic or schizoid personality disorder that stems from insufficiently developed → **self/object differentiation.** Emotional cutoff is the attempt to circumvent the fear of fusion with the other through avoidance and isolation, which is a pathological form of → **closeness/ distance** regulation. Emotional cutoff, however, does not solve fusion problems because the desire for intense relationships remains, ambivalently coupled with a fear of loss of self (Bowen, 1976). Therapeutically, one can only break through this vicious circle if one is able, in the context of joint family sessions, to increase the amount of contact between family members at the same time that one allows and encourages a greater measure of related → **individuation** or self/object differentiation.

Anonymous. Toward the differentiation of a self in one's own family. In J. Framo (Ed.), *Family interaction: A dialogue between family researchers and family therapists.* New York: Springer Publishing Co., 1972, 111–166.

Bowen, M. The use of family theory in clinical practice. *Comprehensive Psychiatry 7:* 345–374, 1966.

Bowen, M. Theory in the practice of psychotherapy. In P. J. Guerin (Ed.), *Family therapy: Theory and practice.* New York: Gardner Press, 1976, 42–90.

Bowen, M. *Family therapy in clinical practice.* New York: Jason Aronson, 1978.

Kerr, M. E. Family systems: Theory and therapy. In A. S. Gurman & D. P. Kniskern (Eds.), *Handbook of family therapy*. New York: Brunner/Mazel, 1981, 226–264.

* * * * * * *

EMOTIONAL DIVORCE

This term was coined by Murray Bowen to describe extreme emotional distance between interactional partners, usually married couples.

Emotional divorce generally remains consolidated and unchanged over a long period of time, and the interactional partners tend to exhibit symptomatic behavior (→ **relational stagnation**). Emotional divorce, however, can be a transitional phase in divorce situations (→ **divorce therapy**). In such situations, according to Bowen, the therapeutic goal should be to counteract the emotional divorce. If this goal is achieved, the couple is able to rekindle their attraction for one another and a "honeymoon atmosphere" frequently ensues.

The terms emotional divorce and → **emotional cutoff** are not always explicitly distinguished. It makes sense, however, to reserve the term emotional cutoff for families with disturbances in → **self/object differentiation** because such disturbances do not necessarily lead to emotional divorce.

Bohannan, P. The six stations of divorce. In M. E. Lasswell & T. E. Lasswell (Eds.), *Love, marriage, and family: A developmental approach*. Glenview, Ill.: Scott, Foresman & Co., 1973.

Bowen, M. The use of family theory in clinical practice. *Comprehensive Psychiatry 7:* 345–374, 1966.

Kaslow, F. W. Divorce and divorce therapy. In A. S. Gurman & D. P. Kniskern (Eds.), *Handbook of family therapy*. New York: Brunner/Mazel, 1981, 662–696.

Kessler, S. *The American way of divorce: Prescription for change*. Chicago: Nelson-Hall, 1975.

* * * * * *

ENACTMENT

Enactment is a technique applied in → **structural family therapy**. The family is induced to experience a new pattern of relating within the actual session.

Building upon the methods of Nathan Ackerman, Salvador Minuchin formally labeled, brought into the literature, and expanded the technique of enactment. After assessing the family pattern, the therapist restructures the interaction by bringing about an enactment of a new pattern. For example, a disengaged mother and daughter may be helped to talk together while the enmeshed father is blocked from the interaction. This is not simply assigned as a task, but is made to happen within the session itself. Thus the family has a new experience, the pre–existing structure is revised, and new options become available. The enacted pattern may then be assigned as a task to be enacted outside the session.

Enactment should be distinguished from "re–enactment." In the latter, a pre–existing pattern or problem is "staged" by the family at the request of the therapist. This provides the therapist with (a) diagnostic information, (b) a more vivid sense of what has been happening in the family, and (c) ideas as to how to intervene directly in the family's ongoing interactional patterns with a view toward changing them.

Aponte, H., & VanDeusen, J. Structural family therapy. In A. S. Gurman & D. P. Kniskern (Eds.), *Handbook of family therapy*. New York: Brunner/Mazel, 1981, 310–360.

Minuchin, S. *Families and family therapy*. Cambridge: Harvard University Press, 1974. (a)

Minuchin, S. Structural family therapy. In G. Caplan (Ed.), *American handbook of psychiatry. Vol. II, Child and adolescent psychiatry, sociocultural and community psychiatry* (2nd ed.). New York: Basic Books, 1974, 178–192. (b)

Minuchin, S., & Fishman, H. C. *Family therapy techniques*. Cambridge: Harvard University Press, 1981.

Minuchin, S., Montalvo, B. G., Guerney, B., Rosman, B. L., & Schumer, F. *Families of the slums: An exploration of their structure and treatment*. New York: Basic Books, 1967.

Minuchin, S., Rosman, B. L., & Baker, L. *Psychosomatic families: Anorexia nervosa in context*. Cambridge: Harvard University Press, 1978.

Stanton, M. D. Marital therapy from a structural/strategic viewpoint. In G. P. Sholevar (Ed.), *The handbook of marriage and marital therapy*. New York: SP Medical and Scientific Books, 1981, 303–334.

* * * * * *

ENMESHMENT

Enmeshment characterizes a family type or structure that exhibits a disturbance in the formation of interpersonal → **boundaries,** which, in these types of families, tend to be overly permeable. Members of the nuclear family seem unable to demarcate boundaries between themselves and vis–à–vis their families of origin. The roles of parent and child are not firmly established, change frequently and haphazardly, and an organizational structure and → **hierarchy** within the family are lacking.

Minuchin et al. (1967) took over the term enmeshment from Don Jackson and used it to describe an attribute of certain slum families. Since the publication of this study, the term has been used to characterize a particular type of family structure. Other → **family typologies** have used different terms to describe similar phenomena; among them are the concepts of → **binding,** → **undifferentiated family ego mass,** → **fusion,** and → **collective cognitive chaos.** These terms have been generally applied to families with a schizophrenic member.

Minuchin's structural analytic approach focuses on how family subsystems originate, how they interact with one another, and how (and if) roles within the family structure are defined and their corresponding functions performed. Enmeshed family members have extreme difficulty in defining roles and functions, and they are unable to structure their relationships. This type of confusion can be seen as a way to avoid direct confrontations and clarifications, which family members might feel are a threat to family unity. There is also a tendency in enmeshed families to nominate one person to act as a "peacemaker" whenever there is any impending threat of family conflict. (Minuchin's main examples of enmeshed families are cited in connection with studies of psychosomatic disorders such as anorexia nervosa.)

In contrast to enmeshment, → **disengagement** is characterized by the lack of binding relationships between family members. Within the framework of family typologies, disengagement and enmeshment can be described as extremes in the spectrum of family organizational forms. From a psychoanalytic perspective, both of these processes reflect a disturbance in → **individuation** or object relationships (→ **object relations theory**), with a concurrent disturbance of → **self/ object differentiation.** From an individual, psychological perspective, disengagement is an expression of a strong need for distance, sometimes going as far as → **emotional cutoff,** while enmeshment is a desire for fusion. In either case, one may speak of an imbalance of → **centripetal/centrifugal patterns** and/or a disturbance in → **closeness/ distance** regulation.

Hoffman, L. "Enmeshment" and the too richly cross-joined system. *Family Process 14:* 457–468, 1975.
Minuchin, S. *Families and family therapy.* Cambridge: Harvard University Press, 1974.

Minuchin, S., & Fishman, H. C. *Family therapy techniques.* Cambridge: Harvard University Press, 1981.
Minuchin, S., Montalvo, B. G., Guerney, B., Rosman, B. L., & Schumer, F. *Families of the slums: An exploration of their structure and treatment.* New York: Basic Books, 1967.
Minuchin, S., Rosman, B. L., & Baker, L. *Psychosomatic families: Anorexia nervosa in context.* Cambridge: Harvard University Press, 1978.

* * * * * *

ENTROPY/NEGENTROPY

Entropy is a rough measure of randomness and disorder, or the absence of pattern in the structuring of a system. Negative entropy, or negentropy, roughly refers to the degree of order or organization within a closed system.

The Second Law of Thermodynamics states that the entropy of a closed system will always increase toward a maximum, which is attained when equilibrium is reached. In thermodyamics, one speaks of an increase of entropy when systems change from less probable to more probable states. In the traditional thermodynamic theory of closed systems, this process is irreversible.

In → **information theory,** the concept of negentropy is used to describe the amount of organized, consistent information contained in a coded message; an increase of information implies a reduction of entropy. In other words, information and negentropy are essentially one and the same, as was posited by Shannon and Weaver (1949). However, their main concerns were quanta of information and the delivery of messages under controlled conditions—conditions not found in family interaction.

In DeBeauregard's (1961) refined definition, the relationship between negentropy and information entails the acquisition of knowledge or an increase in organizational capacity. Selvini–Palazzoli et al. (1980) refer to the above–mentioned research as the foundation of the strategy of → **circular questioning,** which involves the systematic introduction of information into chaotic family structures and, consequently, the improvement of the family's organizational capacity. Family interaction can initially appear to the therapist as totally chaotic or patternless. During the course of an interview, however, entropy may be reduced by increasing the amount of → **information.**

The concepts of entropy/negentropy may be used to understand a family's specific → **epistemology** (Selvini–Palazzoli et al., 1980). (See also → **morphogenesis,** → **fluctuation,** → **self–organization.**)

In applying the concept of entropy to communication, the greatest enemy of entropy has been said to be redundancy, the repetition of elements within a message that is indispensable for understandable communication. Entropy distorts communication, while negentropy and redundancy clarify.

With regard to the difficulties of transferring the concepts of physics to the realm of family therapy, we append here a personal communication from Wolf Beiglböck, a mathematician, who warns that it is "a dubious procedure . . . to apply the concepts of a science which have been moulded at a *high* level of reflexion onto another science, which is still in an early developmental stage." The entropic change, "dS = dQ/T, in other words the change of heat in relation to absolute temperature, is only comprehensible if one is able to conceive of the notion of absolute temperature. For physicists the crucial element of the equation is the apparently harmless 'T'. The science of physics needed two hundred years of hard work to understand this concept in closed systems, in other words, to realize the key importance of entropy when dealing with nonequilibrium processes; *an adequate theory of open systems still remains to be discovered.*" There are many "stipulations which must be fulfilled in order to apply the concept of entropy fruitfully in the natural sciences. Without some link to parameters which can be interpreted physically, entropy only becomes just another fashionable intellectual catchword. . . . Unfortunately, because the whole question is so difficult and because the concept of entropy only becomes comprehensible at a fairly advanced level of knowledge, the treatment of the notion in popular scientific literature, including popular literature on physics, is extremely sketchy for an outsider and irresponsibly creates a false impression of the subject."

Prigogine (1978), with somewhat similar implications, stated that "150 years after its formulation the second law of thermodynamics still appears to be more of a program than a well-defined theory in the usual sense, as nothing precise (except the sign) is said about the S [entropy] production. . . . This is one of the main reasons why the applications of thermodynamics were essentially limited to equilibrium processes" (p. 778). Although Prigogine goes on to discuss very recent progress in extending thermodynamic theory to nonequilibrium processes, the preliminary quality of the conclusions, even for thermodynamic systems, should provide a warning to family theorists to be cautious about making premature generalizations about family systems.

Bateson, G. *Steps to an ecology of mind.* New York: Ballantine Books, 1972.

Beiglböck, W. Personal communication, 1984.

DeBeauregard, O. Sur l'équivalence entre information et entropie. *Sciences 11* 51 ff., 1961.

Klein, M. Order, organization and entropy. *British Journal of Philosophical Science 4:* 158–164, 1953.

Prigogine, I. Order through fluctuation: Self-organization and social system. In E. Jantsch & C. Waddington (Eds.), *Evolution and consciousness: Human systems in transition.* Reading, Mass.: Addison-Wesley, 1976, 93–133.

Prigogine, I. Time, structure, and fluctuations. *Science 201:* 777–785, 1978.

Prigogine, I., & Stengers, I. *Order out of chaos: Man's new dialogue with nature.* New York: Bantam Books, 1984.

Rapoport, A. The promise and pitfalls of information theory. In W. Buckley (Ed.), *Modern systems research for the behavioral scientist: A sourcebook.* Chicago: Aldine Publishing Co., 1968, 137–142.

Selvini-Palazzoli, M., Boscolo, L., Cecchin, G., & Prata, G. Hypothesizing-circularity-neutrality: Three guidelines for the conductor of the session. *Family Process 19:* 3–12, 1980.

Shannon, C., & Weaver, W. *The mathematical theory of communication.* Urbana, Ill.: University of Illinois Press, 1949.

Sonne, J. C. Entropy and family therapy: Speculations on psychic energy, thermodynamics, and family interpsychic communication. In G. H. Zuk & I. Boszormenyi-Nagy (Eds.), *Family therapy and disturbed families.* Palo Alto: Science and Behavior Books, 1967, 85–95.

Szasz, T. Entropy, organization and the problem of the economy of human relationships. *International Journal of Psycho-analysis 36:* 289–297, 1955.

$$* \quad * \quad * \quad * \quad * \quad *$$

EPISTEMOLOGY

Epistemology [Greek *epistéme,* knowledge, theory of knowledge] designates a branch of philosophy that investigates the foundations, limits, methods, and validity of knowledge. As a science, epistemology is the study of how organisms think and arrive at decisions that determine behavior (Bateson, 1979). A number of family therapists also use this term to refer to the structure of knowledge or the knowledge of structure; hence, epistemology is often employed as a supraordinate term that encompasses → **paradigm/model/map.** (See also → **constructivism.**)

Epistemology is concerned with every aspect of the acquisition of knowledge. With regard to humans, it is concerned with the development of the structure of thought as well as the internal logic of emotional processes. The structure of knowledge of any organism can be seen as its model of the world and the frame of orientation for its behavior. The development of a model of the world is dependent upon the organism's communication with its environment, that is, the given structures and conditions of that world and the organism's potential for perceiving them. This is a dialectical process of internal and external adaptation. When one considers all the channels that flow into the formation of knowledge, perception, emotion, thought, and decision, it seems obvious, as Foerster (1974) stated in his "law of epistemological homeostasis," that the human nervous system is constructed to "compute" a *stable* reality. From an individual, psychological viewpoint, this may explain why family systems tend to avoid unstable conditions.

The problematic nature of the science of epistemology, however, shows itself in the fact that it is self–referent (→ **self–reference**), i.e., it refers back to itself when it tries to verify the foundations of (human) knowledge. Epistemology, nevertheless, has become of particular importance in family therapy. For example, schizophrenic thought disturbances are frequently an expression and consequence of epistemological errors that are, in turn, related to the interaction in "schizo–present" families (→ **communication deviance**, → **category formation**, → **logical types**).

Jean Piaget's research on "genetic epistemology" had produced fundamental insights into the nature of the development of the structure of human knowledge. Bateson (1972, 1979) brought epistemology to the attention of family therapists and introduced a systemic and cybernetic perspective into epistemological research. Bateson also was largely responsible for the fact that a major focus of family therapy research has been on the relationship between family interactional phenomena and epistemological errors or misperceptions. Bateson's major interest, however, was not family therapy as such but, rather, how mind and nature, which he saw as a unity, were related to one another.

Dell (1985) has differentiated five different ways in which Bateson used the word "epistemology"—as the theory of knowledge (the traditional philosophical usage); as paradigm (e.g., cybernetic, evolutionary, ecosystemic, and circular); as biological cosmology (referring to the properties of "mind"—"an aggregate of interacting parts or components . . . triggered by difference," Bateson, 1979, p. 92); as science (in which epistemology describes and explains the impossibility of objectivity); and as "character structure" (the habitual assumptions that specify how a person understands and relates to the world). Dell argues that with Bateson's epistemology there never was a clearly corresponding ontology, such as has been more explicitly developed by Maturana (1978) and Maturana and Varela (1980).

Auerswald (1985) has examined the congruence between Bateson's "evolutionary paradigm" that came from the study of the "living universe," the ecosystemic epistemology that emerged from the study of families in context, and the concepts of "new science" that emerged from the studies of Planck and Einstein of the inanimate universe. Auerswald distinguishes epistemology as "the rules used in thought by large groups of people to define reality," in other words, as the paradigm of paradigms, while the word "paradigm" itself denotes "a subset of rules that define a particular segment of reality" (Auerswald, 1985, p. 1).

Epistemological questions have become relevant for family therapy because the internal map or model of the world that an individual or family develops will determine how one acts, thinks, and feels, what symptoms occur, and whether and how one suffers. A goal of therapy is thus to understand the model of the world in question and to influence the → **reframing** of this model.

Auerswald, E. H. Families, change, and the ecological perspective. *Family Process 10:* 263–280, 1971.

Auerswald, E. H. Thinking about thinking in family therapy. *Family Process 24:* 1–12, 1985.

Bateson, G. *Steps to an ecology of mind.* New York: Ballantine Books, 1972.

Bateson, G. *Mind and nature: A necessary unity.* New York: E. P. Dutton, 1979.

Dell, P. F. The Hopi family therapist and the Aristotelian parents. *Journal of Marital and Family Therapy 6:* 123–130, 1980. (a)

Dell, P. F. Researching the family theories of schizophrenia: An exercise in epistemological confusion. *Family Process 19:* 321–335, 1980. (b)

Dell, P. F. Understanding Bateson and Maturana: Toward a biological foundation for the social sciences. *Journal of Marital and Family Therapy 11:* 1–20, 1985.

Foerster, H. von. Thoughts and notes on cognition. In P. L. Garvin (Ed.), *Cognition: A multiple view.* New York: Plenum Press, 1970, 25–48.

Foerster, H. von. Kybernetik einer Erkenntnistheorie. In W. D. Keidel, W. Handler, & M. Spring (Eds.), *Kybernetik und Bionik.* München-Wien: Oldenburg, 1974, 27–46.

Foerster, H. von. On constructing a reality. In P. Watzlawick (Ed.), *The invented reality.* New York: W. W. Norton & Co., 1984, 41–61.

Glaserfeld, E. von. An introduction to radical constructivism. In P. Watzlawick (Ed.), *The invented reality.* New York: W. W. Norton & Co., 1984, 17–40.

Guntern, G. Die kopernikanische Revolution in der Psychotherapie: Der Wandel vom psychoanalytischen zum systemischen Paradigma. *Familiendynamik 5:* 2–41, 1980.

Guntern, G. System therapy: Epistemology, paradigm and pragmatics. *Journal of Marital and Family Therapy 7:* 265–272, 1981.

Hampden-Turner, C. *Maps of the mind: Charts and concept of the mind and its labyrinths.* New York: Collier Books, 1981.

Hoffman, L. *Foundations of family therapy: A conceptual framework for systems change.* New York: Basic Books, 1981.

Keeney, B. P. Ecosystemic epistemology: An alternative paradigm for diagnosis. *Family Process 18:* 117–129, 1979.

Keeney, B. P. What is an epistemology of family therapy? *Family Process 21:* 153–168, 1982.

Keeney, B. P. *Aesthetics of change.* New York: Guilford Press, 1983.

115

Kuhn, T. S. *The structure of scientific revolutions.* Chicago: University of Chicago Press, 1962.
Maturana, H. R. Biology of language: The epistemology of reality. In G. A. Miller & E. Lenneberg (Eds.), *Psychology and biology of language and thought.* New York: Academic Press, 1978.
Maturana, H. R., & Varela, F. J. *Autopoiesis and cognition: The realization of living.* Boston: Reidel, 1980.
Morin, E. *Le paradigme perdu: La nature humaine.* Paris: Seuil, 1973.
Morin, E. *La méthode. I: La nature de la nature.* Paris: Seuil, 1977.
Piaget, J. *The language and thought of the child.* London: Routledge & Kegan Paul, 1952. (a)
Piaget, J. *The origins of intelligence in children.* New York: International Universities Press, 1952. (b)
Piaget, J. *Genetic epistemology* (translated by E. Duckworth). New York: Columbia University Press, 1970.
Piaget, J. *Biology and knowledge.* Chicago: University of Chicago Press, 1971.
Rapaport, D. (Ed.). *Organization and pathology of thought.* New York: Columbia University Press, 1951.
Riedel, R. *Biologie der Erkenntnis.* Hamburg: Parey, 1980.
Simon, F. B. *Der Prozess der Individuation: Über den Zusammenhang von Vernunft un Gefühlen.* Göttingen: Vandenhoeck & Ruprecht, 1984.
Watzlawick, P. *How real is real? Confusion, disinformation, communication.* New York: Random House, 1976.
Watzlawick, P. (Ed.). *The invented reality: How do we know what we believe we know? Contributions to constructivism.* New York: W. W. Norton & Co., 1984.

EQUIFINALITY/EQUIPOTENTIALITY

Similar to the distinction between phenotype and genotype in biology is the distinction between equifinality and equipotentiality [Latin *aequus,* equal; *finis,* end, goal; *potens,* able] in the development of systemic structures. In the case of equifinality, the same result is achieved although the starting position varies. In the case of equipotentiality, different final states and effects can be derived from the same starting point.

When one observes a system, structure, or function, one cannot necessarily make an inference regarding its past or future state from its present condition because the same initial conditions do not necessarily have the same effects. The reverse is also true: The same results do not have to have the same beginning conditions. This is an aspect of → **coevolution.** With regard to living systems in general and families in particular, the implication is that it is not possible to make deterministic predictions about developmental processes.

Bertalanffy, L. von. *General systems theory.* New York: George Braziller, 1968.

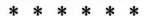

EQUILIBRIUM

Equilibrium (balance) is the maintenance of a stable condition within a system; changes within the system itself or disturbances from without are compensated for. Equilibrium thus implies merely the *relative* constancy of a system, condition, or structure for a certain period of time.

One particular form of equilibrium is → **homeostasis.** Systems that are capable of regaining lost balance or of reestablishing a new form of balance exhibit → **stability.** The propensity of a system or the elements of a system to maintain, lose and reestablish, or readjust to a new form of balance is dependent on all the elements of a system, as well as on those of another system that interacts with it. As Ashby (1956) has described it: "Formally: the whole is at a state of equilibrium if and only if each part is at a state of equilibrium in the conditions provided by the other part. (If there are several parts the last word is merely changed to 'parts')" (p. 83). This applies to families as well as to individual family members (→ **morphostasis,** → **morphogenesis,** → **coevolution**).

In recent years, Prigogine (1978) has introduced the important concept of *non*equilibrium as a source of order. He has shown that although irreversible processes contribute to → **entropy** when a closed thermodynamic system is near to equilibrium, the opposite occurs when the system is far from equilibrium; this nonequilibrium may discontinuously change to a "new type of order called dissipative structures" (→ **fluctuation**).

Stanton (1984) extends the concept of equilibrium across the extended family in his geodynamic balance theory. In the extended family, an overall balance is normally maintained in terms of function and hierarchy. The family attributes different valences or values to its various members and subsystems. When members of high valence or power are removed or compromised, for example, through death or illness, the imbalance during mourning becomes great, and other members or subsystems compensate or "move up" to fill in the void. Depending on how "drastic" the change and how functional the adaptation to it, the recalibration may or may not result in symptoms. It is hypothesized that sudden, unexpected loss of high valence members would be more likely to result in symptomatology than would be the expected loss of low valence members.

Ashby, W. R. *An introduction to cybernetics.* London: Methuen, 1956.
Bateson, G. *Steps to an ecology of mind.* New York: Ballantine Books, 1972.
Cannon, W. B. *Wisdom of the body.* New York: W. W. Norton & Co., 1932.
Jantsch, E. *The self-organizing universe.* Elmsford, N.Y.: Pergamon Press, 1980.

Klaus, G., & Liebscher, H. *Wörterbuch der Kybernetik* (4th revised ed.). Frankfurt: Fischer, 1979.

Miller, J. G. Living systems: The group. *Behavioral Science 16:* 302–398, 1971.

Miller, J. G. *Living systems.* New York: McGraw-Hill, 1978.

Prigogine, I. Time, structure, and fluctuations. *Science 201:* 777–785, 1978.

Stanton, M. D. Fusion, compression, diversion, and the workings of paradox: A theory of therapeutic/systemic change. *Family Process 23:* 135–167, 1984.

* * * * * *

ETHNICITY AND FAMILY THERAPY

Members of ethnic [Greek *ethnikos,* of a national group] groups tend to share certain characteristics deriving from a common national, cultural, geographic, and religious heritage. Ethnicity has been referred to as "a sense of commonality transmitted over generations by the family and reinforced by the surrounding community. It involves conscious and unconscious processes that fulfill a deep psychological need for identity and historical continuity" (McGoldrick & Garcia–Preto, 1984, p. 347). Ethnicity has special significance in countries, such as the United States, that serve as "melting pots" for various ethnic groups. With increasing contact between ethnic groups, there are challenges and/or problems with regard to an individual's and family's adaptation (→ **adaptability**), sense of → **identity,** related → **individuation,** as well as → **coevolution.** To cope with these challenges, special therapeutic considerations and interventions may be required.

Ethnicity determines to a large extent an individual's and family's model of the world (→ **paradigm/model/map**). It also accounts for profound differences in value systems as well as in patterns of emotional expression and communication. McGoldrick and Garcia–Preto (1984) noted that "certain groups, such as Italians and Hispanics, value emotional expressiveness. Words are used for drama, and physical expressions such as gesticulating, touching, and hugging are part of most close personal interactions. For some groups the sharing of sadness and grief is expected, and talking about problems is experienced as the best cure" (p. 354).

In contrast, McGill and Pearce (1982) describe the rugged individualism of Americans: "They tend to be good at self–reliance, self–sufficiency and self–control and rather less good at maintaining mutually giving relationships, tolerating dependency, and integrating and expressing an emotional experience. . . . In British–American families, one denies, carries on, and, above all, takes responsibility for one's problems by not complaining or not involving other people" (p. 458).

Ethnic issues are particularly prevalent in racial and cultural intermarriages. The greater the cultural differences between spouses, the more will there be a challenge to reconcile the differing emotional and communicational patterns, models, and value systems, as well as conflicting → **loyalty** and → **delegation.** Ethnic differences are also likely to profoundly affect the processes of → **separating parents and adolescents,** particularly in those families undergoing a cultural transition. For example, children of immigrant parents tend to absorb more easily the values and norms of their surrounding culture while their parents cling to those of their old culture.

"Link therapy," pioneered by Judith Landau, is an example of a special therapeutic technique required for some of these families. Such families appear unsuitable for more traditional approaches of family therapy mainly because of their fear of being exposed and because of rigid hierarchical structures that prevail in the extended family. In these families, it often is useful to train and coach a (generally asymptomatic) family member to function as a link therapist to his or her own family system. This person is selected by the therapist and the family. Another useful approach may be → **network therapy,** which assembles components of the larger system to work with a professional team in order to expose dysfunctional patterns and mobilize resources and support toward change. A therapist will also greatly profit from familiarity with the ethnic issues in question as well as some knowledge of → **sociolinguistics,** → **ethnomethodology,** and → **psychohistory.**

Falicov, C. J., & Karrer, B. M. Cultural variations in the family life cycle: The Mexican-American family. In E. A. Carter & M. McGoldrick (Eds.), *The family life cycle: A framework for family therapy.* New York: Gardner Press, 1980, 383–425.

Giordano, J., & Giordano, G. P. *The ethno-cultural factor in mental health: A literature review and bibliography.* New York: Institute on Pluralism and Group Identity of the American Jewish Committee, 1977.

Landau, J. Link therapy as a family therapy technique for transitional extended families. *Psychotherapeia 7:* 382–390, 1981.

Landau, J. Therapy with families in cultural transition. In M. McGoldrick, J., K. Pearce, & J. Giordano (Eds.), *Ethnicity and family therapy.* New York: Guilford Press, 1982, 552–572.

McGill, D., & Pearce, J. K. British families. In M. McGoldrick, J. K. Pearce, & J. Giordano (Eds.), *Ethnicity and family therapy.* New York: Guilford Press, 1982, 458–479.

McGoldrick, M., & Garcia–Preto, N. Ethnic intermarriage: Implications for therapy. *Family Process 23:* 347–364, 1984.

McGoldrick, M., Pearce, J. K., & Giordano, J. (Eds.). *Ethnicity and family therapy.* New York: Guilford Press, 1982.

Minuchin, S. *Family kaleidoscope.* Cambridge: Harvard University Press, 1984.

Minuchin, S., Montalvo, B. G., Guerney, B., Rosman, B. L., & Schumer, F. *Families of the slums: An exploration of their structure'and treatment.* New York: Basic Books, 1967.

Schwartzman, J. Creativity, pathology, and family structure: A cybernetic metaphor. *Family Process 21:* 113–128, 1982.

Speck, R. V., & Attneave, C. L. Social network intervention. In J. Haley (Ed.), *Changing families: A family therapy reader.* New York: Grune & Stratton, 1971, 312–332.

Speck, R. V., & Attneave, C. L. Social network intervention. In C. J. Sager & H. S. Kaplan (Eds.), *Progress in group and family therapy.* New York: Brunner/Mazel, 1972, 416–439.

Speck, R. V., & Attneave, C. L. *Family networks.* New York: Pantheon Books, 1973.

Spiegel, J. P. Cultural strain, family role patterns, and intrapsychic conflict. In J. G. Howells (Ed.), *Theory and practice of family psychiatry.* Edinburgh: Oliver & Boyd, 1968, 367–389.

Spiegel, J. P. *Transactions: The interplay between individual, family, and society* (edited by J. Papajohn). New York: Science House, 1971.

* * * * * *

ETHNOMETHODOLOGY

This term refers to fields of research within the social sciences, the goals of which are to study the relationship between patterns of speech or perception and specific social contexts. These approaches seek to clarify the prerequisites of so–called everyday knowledge. They are concerned with the interrelations between social, linguistic, and epistemological structures within the framework of a hermeneutic sociology (→ **paradigm/model/map,** → **epistemology,** → **semiotics,** → **syntax**).

This research is in line with the American pragmatic tradition and, in particular, with George Herbert Mead's (1934) work on symbolic interaction. The fundamental propositions (see Blumer, 1969) of symbolic interaction include:

1. People react to things according to the meaning these things hold for them.
2. Meaning is created within the context of social interaction.
3. The interpretation of meaning is constantly in the process of being modified.

According to Schütz (1962), the focus of this research is the everyday world in which a fully perceiving, adult person, surrounded by others, acts and experiences reality in a natural manner (Vol. I, p. 208). This everyday world is based on, and mediated through everyday communication processes. The structure and contextual determination of these communication processes remain, as a rule, unconscious.

Charles Sanders Peirce coined the term "indexical" to describe the situation–specific and situation–flexible character of such communication processes. Following this, Harold Garfinkel (1967) described the essential task of ethnomethodology as the investigation of the rational elements in indexical expressions and actions. Ethnomethodological research is directed toward the critical illumination of the self–evident nature of everyday experience. Ethnomethodologists attempt to view their own society much as a cultural anthropologist would view an exotic culture.

Research of this kind is important for family therapy in that it illuminates the central issues that interactional partners face when negotiating and validating a common → **relational reality.** Furthermore, ethnomethodology investigates the methodological problems involved in the attainment of knowledge about these negotiation and validation processes as well as explores the interactions involved in → **individuation** or → **self/object differentiation.**

Blumer, H. The methodological position of symbolic interactionism. In H. Blumer (Ed.), *Symbolic interactionism, perspective, and method.* New York: Prentice-Hall, 1969.

Garfinkel, H. *Studies in ethnomethodology.* Englewood Cliffs, N.J.: Prentice-Hall, 1967.

Garfinkel, H., & Sacks, H. *Contributions to ethnomethodology.* Bloomington: University of Indiana Press, 1973.

Habermas, J. *Theorie kommunikativen Handelns.* Frankfurt: Suhrkamp, 1981.

Mead, G. H. *Mind, self, and society.* Chicago: University of Chicago Press, 1934.

Peirce, C. S. *Collected papers* (6 vols.). Cambridge: Harvard University Press, 1931–1935.

Schütz, A. *Collected papers* (3 vols.). The Hague: Nijhoff, 1962–1966.

Weingarten, E., Sack, F., & Schenklein, J. (Eds.). *Ethnomethodologie: Beiträge zu einer Soziologie des Alltagshandelns.* Frankfurt: Suhrkamp, 1976.

EXPELLING

Expelling is one of the transactional modes described by Stierlin (1974). The expelling mode may be seen as the opposite of the binding mode. Both of these modes become evident in the context of → **separating parents and adolescents.** Like its opposite, the expelling mode is variously effective on different levels that can be approximated by the psychoanalytic concepts of an id level, an ego level, and a superego level.

If rejection takes place predominantly on the id level, emotional needs are insufficiently met. A cold and depriving atmosphere prevails; age–appropriate dependency needs are repelled. Children are forced into a premature, precocious, quasi–self–sufficiency. Reward and recognition are absent from family interaction, and the expelled members are denied the possibility of support and regressive relaxation. Expelling or lack of binding on the ego level can be defined as a lack of interest in and access to the "ego–world" of the other. Thoughts, perceptions, and feelings are withheld. The atmosphere tends to be restrictive, rigid, unemotional, and lacking in empathic participation. Expelling at the superego level implies a lack of enduring and significant ties of loyalty. Life seems to have no sense of direction.

Individuals who have been exposed to an expelling atmosphere may exhibit narcissistic and borderline disorders, as described by Kohut (1971) and Kernberg (1976). One also finds sociopathic characters, some types of severely neglected individuals, as well as certain chronically psychosomatic, severely ill individuals. (See Stierlin, 1974, and Wirsching and Stierlin, 1982, for a clinical description.) Expelling occurs frequently in → **stepfamilies** where children from former marriages are felt to be burdensome supernumeraries in the new family constellation.

On close inspection, expelling and binding stand in dialectic relationship to one another. An expelled child will seek ties and at the same time fear them. A bound–up child will seek to break away and at the same time fear to escape. Upon better acquaintance with a family of a bound–up child, it often transpires that the child was not really wanted. The child, however, made it possible for its parents to flee from an excessively binding family of origin into a feared marriage. This child will become in time an object of intense parental expulsion, even to the point of wishing the child dead. Such death fantasies provoke strong guilt feelings on the part of the parents. By a process of a reaction formation, these guilt feelings are turned into binding overprotection of the child. The more the child gives the parents a reason for concern, the greater becomes their desire to expel it. Hence the feelings of guilt and over–concern are also intensified. In this type of situation the child becomes all the more willing to supply a symptom, a problem, or an illness to justify parental overprotection. The extent to which expelling or binding are realized over time, and the manner in which this takes place, depend on the → **attribution** that comes into play at each particular point. Related concepts are → **disengagement,** disattachment, waywardness, isolation, and schizoid distancing.

Aichhorn, A. *Wayward youth: Psychoanalysis and correctional education, 10 introductory lectures*. New York: Whiting, 1935.

Blumberg, M. L. Child abuse and neglect. In S. Arieti & K. H. Brodie (Eds.), *American handbook of psychiatry, Vol. VII: Advances and new directions* (2nd ed.). New York: Basic Books, 1981, 172–186.

Kernberg, O. F. *Object relations theory and clinical psychoanalysis.* New York: Jason Aronson, 1976.

Kohut, H. *The analysis of the self. A systematic approach to the psychoanalytic treatment of narcissistic personality disorders.* New York: International Universities Press, 1971.

Minuchin, S., Montalvo, B. G., Guerney, B., Rosman, B. L., & Schumer, F. *Families of the slums: An exploration of their structure and treatment.* New York: Basic Books, 1967.

Stierlin, H. *Das Tun des Einen ist das Tun des Anderen.* Frankfurt: Suhrkamp, 1971.

Stierlin, H. *Separating parents and adolescents: A perspective on running away, schizophrenia, and waywardness.* New York: Quadrangle, 1974.

Wirsching, M., & Stierlin, H. *Krankheit und Familie.* Stuttgart: Klett-Cotta, 1982.

EXPRESSED EMOTION/AFFECTIVE STYLE

Expressed emotion (EE) is "an index of familial attitudes shown to be a powerful predictor of schizophrenic relapse" (Leff & Vaughn, 1985). EE scales assess the emotion expressed while a relative talks about a designated patient (who prototypically has recently had a schizophrenic breakdown). Criticism and emotional overinvolvement have been identified as the EE scales that are most highly predictive of later relapse. Affective style (AS) reflects "interpersonal analogs" of EE measured in direct family interaction with the patient present (Doane, West, Goldstein, Rodnick, & Jones, 1981).

The concept of expressed emotion (EE) has recently found a great deal of favor in psychiatric research and has stimulated major new family treatment approaches, especially with psychoeducational and behavioral components. The introduction of the EE concept was preceded by a series of studies on the impact of deinstitutionalization of psychiatric patients, primarily schizophrenics. Brown, Carstairs, and Topping (1958) found that English patients discharged to live with parents or spouses showed a higher readmission rate than those going elsewhere to live. In a second study, Brown, Monck, Carstairs, and Wing (1962) showed that if schizophrenic men went to live with relatives who showed "high emotional involvement" with them at the time of discharge, they were more likely to deteriorate and be readmitted during one–year follow–up.

In a third study (Brown, Birley, and Wing, 1972), the "emotional involvement" of relatives with patients was specified more precisely and the term "expressed emotion" was substituted. Using a technique developed by Brown and Rutter (1966), interviewers inquired of relatives, in a neutral, semi–structured, three–hour interview, about a patient family member's behavior during the three months before admission, and about the relative's feelings toward the patient. Ratings of the relative's feelings were based upon tone of voice and content and were successfully carried out with excellent interrater reliability. The most readily measurable component of expressed emotion in such interviews has been the number of critical comments. Global ratings of emotional overinvolvement and hostility/rejection also have been important indices, with warmth a less clear, more complex variable. Using the EE index, the thrust of prior findings was replicated and showed that high EE by relatives at the time of admission was strongly associated with symptomatic relapse nine months after discharge. Previous work impairment and behavioral disturbance predicted relapse only in association with high EE. However, if the patient spent less than 35 hours per week in contact with the relative, or if neuroleptic medication were used, the likelihood of relapse was reduced. These were interpreted as "protective" factors against the impact of high EE in a relative.

In another replication, by Vaughn and Leff (1976a, b), the interview, now called the Camberwell Family Interview (CFI), was shortened to about 1½ hours and the prior findings were confirmed. However, the findings were nonspecific for schizophrenia; a comparison group of depressives were found to be even more sensitive to criticism, which highly predicted relapse of depression. More recently, EE of relatives has also been found to be predictive of the course of illness of anorexia nervosa and of weight–maintenance in obese women (Leff & Vaughn, 1985).

In the first report of a major replication outside of England, Vaughn et al. (1984) obtained similar findings with "Anglo–American" schizophrenics and their relatives in southern California. Yet, in other cultural groups (especially in rural India), preliminary findings suggest that high EE occurs much less frequently and may not be strongly related to relapse.

Many other studies of clinical and contextual factors in relation to EE have now been carried out or are underway. Acute stressors in the form of threatening life events may precipitate schizophrenic relapse in unmedicated patients living in low EE homes (Leff & Vaughn, 1981, 1985). The stability of EE when the patient is in remission and the differences associated with family composition and living arrangements need further investigation. The impact of EE on young male schizophrenics living with their parents appears to be much greater than for older females living with a husband. Also, more detailed studies differentiating the components of EE are needed. Miklowitz,

Goldstein, and Falloon (1983) have shown that patients from emotionally overinvolved families were characterized by poorer premorbid adjustment and greater residual or deficit symptomatology at discharge than were patients from critical families. Another topic for future study is the degree to which analogs of EE in nonfamily environments are predictive of course of illness.

A number of family therapy approaches have been introduced with the goal of reducing stressful conditions, especially high EE in relatives, and thereby improving schizophrenic recovery. Goldstein (1981) has published reports of five such treatment programs. Goldstein and Kopeikin (1981) used crisis–oriented family therapy intended to reduce or prevent stress (not only stress in the form of EE). Berkowitz et al. (1981) combined information and group discussion with relatives of schizophrenics to modify family attitudes. Anderson, Hogarty, and Reiss (1980, 1981) developed a four–phase family intervention program that most distinctively included a psychoeducational "survival–skills" workshop. Snyder and Liberman (1981) and Falloon et al. (1981) used a behavioral family therapy approach, also with a psychoeducational component, with high EE families. Compared to a control group of patients given traditional individual therapy, those receiving family therapy had strikingly better outcomes in terms of florid relapse and target symptoms, social performance, family problem solving (observed in direct interaction), and family coping with everyday stressors (Doane, Falloon, Goldstein, & Mintz, 1985; Falloon, Boyd, & McGill, 1984). At present, there appears to be a consensus that these treatment approaches are effective, not only with high EE families but also with low EE families (Goldstein, 1984).

While EE is a measure of family member attitudes, rated in interviews about the patient, the concept of *affective style* (AS) assesses actual emotional behavior observed during direct intervention of family members with the patient present. Doane's scoring system includes ratings of benign and personal criticism, guilt induction, and critical and neutral intrusiveness (Doane et al., 1981, 1985). In studying AS and EE on the same sample, Miklowitz et al. (1984) found that parents with high EE also have more negative AS in direct interaction. Applying the AS measure in Falloon's family therapy study sample, Doane et al. (1985) found that AS is a highly accurate index that predicts patient and family functioning at follow–up and is influenced by family therapy in an expectable manner.

Studied in combination with parental → **communication deviance** (CD), a family affective style also has been found to predict disturbed versus benign, long–term outcomes of vulnerable adolescents (Doane et al., 1981; Goldstein, 1983; Goldstein & Doane, 1982). Further studies of interactive effects of CD, EE, AS, and other family measures are needed. Wynne (1984) has suggested a conceptual distinction: EE and AS appear more relevant to the attachment/caregiving phase of relational development, while CD is more associated with the development of attentional sharing, cognitive functioning, and language development, that is, with communication.

Anderson, C. M., Hogarty, G. E., & Reiss, D. J. Family treatment of adult schizophrenic patients: A psycho-educational approach. *Schizophrenia Bulletin 6:* 490–505, 1980.

Anderson, C. M., Hogarty, G. E., & Reiss, D. J. The psychoeducational family treatment of schizophrenia. In M. J. Goldstein (Ed.), *New developments in interventions with families of schizophrenics.* San Francisco: Jossey-Bass, 1981, 79–94.

Berkowitz, R., Kuipers, L., Eberlein-Frief, R., & Leff, J. Lowering expressed emotion in relatives of schizophrenics. In M. J. Goldstein (Ed.), *New developments in interventions with families of schizophrenics.* San Francisco: Jossey-Bass, 1981, 27–48.

Brown, G. W., Birley, J. L. T., & Wing, J. K. Influence of family life on the course of schizophrenic disorders: A replication. *British Journal of Psychiatry 121:* 241–258, 1972.

Brown, G. W., Carstairs, G. M., & Topping, G. Post-hospital adjustment of chronic mental patients. *Lancet 2:* 685–689, 1958.

Brown, G. W., Monck, E., Carstairs, G. M., & Wing, J. K. Influence of family life on the course of schizophrenic illness. *British Journal of Preventive and Social Medicine 16:* 55–68, 1962.

Brown, G. W., & Rutter, M. The measurement of family activities and relationships: A methodological study. *Human Relations 19:* 241–263, 1966.

Doane, J. A., Falloon, I. R. H., Goldstein, M. J., & Mintz, J. Parental affective style and the treatment of schizophrenia. *Archives of General Psychiatry 42:* 34–46, 1985.

Doane, J. A., West, K. L., Goldstein, M. J., Rodnick, E. H., & Jones, J. E. Parental communication deviance and affective style: Predictors of subsequent schizophrenic spectrum disorders in vulnerable adolescents. *Archives of General Psychiatry 38:* 679–685, 1981.

Falloon, I. R. H., Boyd, J. L., & McGill, C. W. *Family care of schizophrenia: A problem-solving approach to the treatment of mental illness.* New York: Guilford Press, 1984.

Falloon, I. R. H., Boyd, J. L., McGill, C. W., Strang, J. S., & Moss, H. B. Family management training in the community care of schizophrenia. In M. J. Goldstein (Ed.), *New developments in interventions with families of schizophrenics.* San Francisco: Jossey-Bass, 1981, 61–77.

Goldstein, M. J. (Ed.). *New developments in interventions with families of schizophrenics.* San Francisco: Jossey-Bass, 1981.

Goldstein, M. J. Family interaction: Patterns predictive of the onset and course of schizophrenia. In H. Stierlin, L. C. Wynne, & M. Wirsching (Eds.), *Psychosocial interventions in schizophrenia: An international view.* Berlin: Springer-Verlag, 1983, 5–19.

Goldstein, M. J. Family intervention programs. In A. S. Bellack (Ed.), *Treatment and care of schizophrenia.* New York: Grune & Stratton, 1984, 281–305.

Goldstein, M. J., & Doane, J. A. Family factors in the onset, course, and treatment of schizophrenic spectrum disorders: An update on current research. *Journal of Nervous and Mental Disease 170:* 692–700, 1982.

Goldstein, M. J., & Kopeikin, H. S. Short- and long-term effects of combining drug and family therapy. In M. J. Goldstein (Ed.), *New developments in interventions with families of schizophrenics.* San Francisco: Jossey-Bass, 1981, 5–26.

Kuipers, L. Expressed emotion: A review. *British Journal of Social and Clinical Psychology 18:* 237–243, 1979.

Leff, J., & Vaughn, C. The interaction of life events and relatives' expressed emotion in relapse of schizophrenia and depressive neurosis. *British Journal of Psychiatry 136:* 146–153, 1980.

Leff, J., & Vaughn, C. The role of maintenance therapy and relatives' expressed emotion in relapse of schizophrenia: A two-year follow-up. *British Journal of Psychiatry 139:* 102–104, 1981.

Leff, J., & Vaughn, C. *Expressed emotion in families: Its significance for mental illness.* New York: Guilford Press, 1985.

Miklowitz, D. J., Goldstein, M. J., & Falloon, I. R. H. Premorbid and symptomatic characteristics of schizophrenics from families with high and low levels of expressed emotion. *Journal of Abnormal Psychology 92:* 359–367, 1983.

Miklowitz, D. J., Goldstein, M. J., Falloon, I. R. H., & Doane, J. A. Interactional correlates of expressed emotion in the families of schizophrenics. *British Journal of Psychiatry 144:* 482–487, 1984.

Rutter, M., & Brown, G. W. The reliability and validity of measures of family life and relationships in families containing a schizophrenic patient. *Social Psychiatry 1:* 38–54, 1966.

Snyder, K. S., & Liberman, R. P. Family assessment and intervention with schizophrenics at risk for relapse. In M. J. Goldstein (Ed.), *New developments in interventions with families of schizophrenics.* San Francisco: Jossey-Bass, 1981, 49–60.

Vaughn, C. E., & Leff, J. P. The influence of family and social factors on the course of psychiatric illness: A comparison of schizophrenic and depressed neurotic patients. *British Journal of Psychiatry, 129:* 125–137, 1976. (a)

Vaughn, C. E., & Leff, J. P. The measurement of expressed emotion in the families of psychiatric patients. *British Journal of Social and Clinical Psychology 15:* 157–165, 1976. (b)

Vaughn, C. E., & Leff, J. P. Umgangsstile in Familien mit schizophrenen Patienten. In H. Katschnig (Ed.), *Die andere Seite der Schizophrenie.* München: Urban & Schwarzenberg, 1977, 181–194.

Vaughn, C. E., & Leff, J. P. Patterns of emotional response in relatives of schizophrenic patients. *Schizophrenia Bulletin 7:* 43–44, 1981.

Vaughn, C. E., Snyder, K. S., Jones, S., Freeman, W. B., & Falloon, I. R. H. Family factors in schizophrenic relapse: Replication in California of British research on expressed emotion. *Archives of General Psychiatry 41:* 1169–1177, 1984.

Wynne, L. C. The epigenesis of relational systems: A model for understanding family development. *Family Process 23:* 297–318, 1984.

* * * * * *

■ F ■

FAMILY CONSTELLATION/SIBLING CONFIGURATION

The comparative analysis of a large number of families resulted in the discovery that sibling position is frequently correlated with what appears to be typical personality characteristics, values, and ways of managing family internal and external relationships.

Walter Toman was one of the first to describe the relation of personality characteristics to family constellation. According to Toman (1976), first–born children tend to assume that they know what is "right" and "wrong," "good" and "bad." Often such children are not only required to help in the raising of younger siblings but also tend to be massively triangulated (→ **triangulation**) or delegated (→ **delegation**). Younger siblings are rarely pressed into the position of responsibility and hence are less often required to make family decisions. In Toman's opinion, the sibling position influences the choice of a mate and the rules that develop within a newly established family.

The marriage of two people who had different positions in their family constellations (therefore having different value orientations) can often result in a relationship in which the parents complement (→ **complementarity**) each other. The marriage of persons who had the same position in their sibling configurations often results in great emotional closeness and mutual identification; however, there is a likelihood of symmetrical (→ **symmetry**) escalation and rivalry for the sole possession of the former position.

In the family therapy field, Murray Bowen and his followers have been most obviously influenced by Toman's observations and ideas.

Bank, S., & Kahn, M. *The sibling bond.* New York: Basic Books, 1982.
Bowen, M. Theory in the practice of psychotherapy. In P. J. Guerin (Ed.), *Family therapy: Theory and practice.* New York: Gardner Press, 1976, 42–90.
Fishbein, H. D. Sibling set configuration and family dysfunction. *Family Process 20:* 311–318, 1981.
Hoover, C., & Franz, J.D. Siblings in the families of schizophrenics. *Archives of General Psychiatry 26:* 334–342, 1972.
Kempler, W., Iverson, R., & Beisser, A. The adult schizophrenic and his siblings. *Family Process 1:* 224–235, 1962.
Lidz, T., Fleck, S., Alanen, Y. O., & Cornelison, A. R. Schizophrenic patients and their siblings. *Psychiatry 26:* 1–18, 1963.
Toman, W. *Family constellation: Its effects on personality and social behavior* (3rd ed.). New York: Springer Publishing Co., 1976.

* * * * * *

FAMILY LIFE CYCLE

The concept of the family life cycle was first formulated in → **family sociology.** Since the early 1970s, nearly all family therapists have given major attention to this concept as a framework for diagnosis and treatment planning (→ **family typologies/dimensions**). Within the course of the family life cycle, transitional phases and crises are inevitable with exits and entries from the family. The individual life cycle fits like a cogwheel into the family life cycle. Hill (1970) has observed that researchers or clinicians who seek to generalize about families without taking developmental stage into account will encounter tremendous variance that they will not understand.

In 1948, Reuben Hill and Evelyn Duvall began conceptualizing family developmental tasks. In 1957, Duvall (1967) divided the family life cycle into eight stages organized around nodal events of exits and entries. Hill emphasized the intergenerational connectedness of the life cycle across at least three generations (Hill, 1964, 1970).

A methodologic problem in the study of the family life cycle is that there has not been a consensus about how many stages should be recognized. The family life cycle has been subdivided, by different authors, into 4 to 24 stages. A commonly used version involves five main stages: the newly married couple, the family with young children, the family with adolescents, launching children out of the family, and the family in later life. This may be subdivided further by the ages of the children and by the associated tasks of the family. For example, Fleck (1983) has divided families with young children into stages involving mother–infant nurturance and toddling. Other writers have made a distinction that emphasizes the age of the oldest child at each stage of the family life cycle, subdividing families with the oldest child up to 30 months, those with preschool children, and those with school children aged 6 to 13. In later life, the family life cycle can usefully be subdivided into a phase at the beginning of the empty nest to retirement, differing from the stage after retirement to the death of one's spouse. (For alternative variations for assessing the family life cycle, see Carter and McGoldrick, 1980; Duvall, 1967; Haley, 1973; Hill and Rodgers, 1964; and Grunebaum and Bryant, 1966).

Family life cycle stages have been recommended as an approach to → **family typologies,** with transition points regarded as times of potential → **crisis,** followed either by developmental stuckness or new movement. An example is the problem of delayed emancipation of the adolescent from the family of origin (Haley, 1973, 1980; Stierlin, 1974), often associated with → **marital schism/skew.**

With the current high frequency of divorce and remarried families, a modified family life–cycle schema often is needed to deal with the facts of single parenting and step–parenting. Carter and McGoldrick (1980) have outlined the life–cycle dislocations associated with divorce. The problems of these major exceptions as well as other arrangements, such as foster–parenting, the taking–over of child rearing by grandparents, etc., must be included in a comprehensive schema for assessing family life–cycle stages.

Another highly important issue is variability in the family life cycle associated with cultural differences (Falicov & Karrer, 1980), as well as the impact of migration and cultural transition on families and their therapy. These and other changes in the family life cycle can be examined using the technique of transitional mapping developed by Landau (1982). The transitional map is used as a graphic tool that expands the → **genogram** to include family life stages and relationships between family members and between the family and their context, and it highlights the family's repeating processes and patterns.

Despite the wide acceptance by family therapists of the hypothesis that dysfunction will predictably emerge at transition points in the family life cycle, very little empirical research of this idea has been carried out. Hadley et al. (1974) found a significant and positive relationship between symptom onset in a family member after the family developmental crisis of the addition (birth) or loss (death, separation) of a family member. However, for a substantial proportion of families, there were no family crises within nine months of symptom onset. "Healthy" coping by families needs to be examined in future studies along with symptoms.

The → **individuation** process and development of personal → **identity** also can be seen in terms of the entire family's → **coevolution.** As the child develops physically and psychologically, so the relational processes of the family, as a system, pass through epigenetic, developmental stages that may be out of synchrony with the "structural" entries and exits that mark change points in the family life cycle (Wynne, 1984). That is, the family life–cycle changes may take place when the emotional pattern between family members is not ready for change.

Barnhill, L. R., & Longo, D. Fixation and regression in the family life cycle. *Family Process 17:* 469–478, 1978.

Carter, E., & McGoldrick, M. (Eds.). *The family life cycle: A framework for family therapy.* New York: Gardner Press, 1980.

Combrinck-Graham, L. A developmental model for family systems. *Family Process 24:* 139–150, 1985.

Duvall, E. R. *Family development.* Philadelphia: J. B. Lippincott, 1967.

Erikson, E. H. Identity and the life cycle: Selected papers. *Psychological Issues, Monograph No. 1,* 1959.

Falicov, C. J., & Karrer, B. M. Cultural variations in the family life cycle: The Mexican-American family. In E. A. Carter & M. McGoldrick (Eds.), *The family life cycle: A framework for family therapy.* New York: Gardner Press, 1980, 383–425.

Fleck, S. A holistic approach to family typology and the axes of DSM-III. *Archives of General Psychiatry 40:* 901–906, 1983.

Grunebaum, H. U., & Bryant, C. M. The theory and practice of the family diagnostic: Theoretical aspects of resident education. *Psychiatric Research Reports 20:* 150–162, 1966.

Hadley, T. R., Jacob, T., Milliones, J., Caplan, J., & Spitz, D. The relationship between family developmental crisis and the appearance of symptoms in a family member. *Family Process 13:* 207–214, 1974.

Haley, J. *Uncommon therapy: The psychiatric techniques of Milton H. Erickson, M.D.: A casebook of an innovative psychiatrist's work in short-term therapy.* New York: W. W. Norton & Co., 1973.

Haley, J. *Leaving home: The therapy of disturbed young people.* New York: McGraw-Hill, 1980.

Hill, R. Methodological issues in family development research. *Family Process 3:* 186–204, 1964.

Hill, R. *Family development in three generations.* Cambridge: Schenkman, 1970.

Hill, R., & Rodgers, R. H. The developmental approach. In H. T. Christensen (Ed.), *Handbook of marriage and the family.* Chicago: Rand McNally, 1964, 171–211.

Landau, J. Therapy with families in cultural transition. In M. McGoldrick, J. K. Pearce, & J. Giordano (Eds.), *Ethnicity and family therapy.* New York: Guilford Press, 1982, 552–572.

Lidz, T. The life cycle: Introduction. In S. Arieti (Ed.), *American handbook of psychiatry, Vol. I: The foundations of psychiatry* (2nd ed.). New York: Basic Books, 1974, 241–251.

Olson, D. H., McCubbin, H. C., Barnes, H., Larsen, A., Muxen, M., & Wilson, M. *Families: What makes them work.* Beverly Hills: Sage Publications, 1983.

Solomon, M. A developmental, conceptual premise for family therapy. *Family Process 12:* 179–188, 1973.

Steinglass, P. The conceptualization of marriage from a systems theory perspective. In T. J. Paolino & B. S. McCrady (Eds.), *Marriage and marital therapy: Psychoanalytic, behavioral and systems theory perspectives.* New York: Brunner/Mazel, 1978, 298–365.

Stierlin, H. *Separating parents and adolescents: A perspective on running away, schizophrenia, and waywardness.* New York: Quadrangle, 1974.

Weeks, G., & Wright, L. Dialectics of the family life cycle. *American Journal of Family Therapy 7:* 85–91, 1979.

Wynne, L. C. The epigenesis of relational systems: A model for understanding family development. *Family Process 23:* 297–318, 1984.

* * * * * *

FAMILY LUNCH

Family lunch is a diagnostic and therapeutic tool used in the therapy of anorexia nervosa. A family meal is arranged and observed by the therapist. This gives the therapist an opportunity to observe family transactions, structural characteristics, and functional disturbances in this vital area of family life. The therapist further has the opportunity to intervene directly in the family's interactional → **pattern**(s).

The family lunch technique, developed by Salvador Minuchin (1971) in the treatment of anorexia nervosa, has three models that can be adjusted to the interactional patterns and developmental stage of the family in treatment (Rosman, Minuchin, & Liebman, 1975). The goal of Model One is to encourage the parents to assert themselves. The therapist requests that both parents in turn try and make their child eat. The therapist reminds the parents that they are responsible for making sure that their child receives sufficient nourishment. Hence, not illness, but authority and obedience are presented as the problems that need attention. As a rule, the parents are unsuccessful in this endeavor. As a result of the encouragement of the therapist and the parents' anger at their helplessness against the will (the mouth) of the child, the parents are able to join forces and establish a consistent attitude toward the child. When the parents are themselves no longer embattled, they are able to feed the child or the child begins spontaneously to feed itself.

In Model Two, the goal is to encourage the parents and the child in the formation of → **boundaries.** In the beginning of the session, as in the first model, the parents are enjoined to try to feed their child. These attempts usually are unsuccessful. Each parent is then asked in turn to act in a specific manner toward the child. One parent is asked to make the child eat by means of coaxing, flattering, begging, or appealing to the child's reason, or by any other means of "soft" pressure that occurs to the parent. The other parent is given the task of making the child eat by means of force, authoritative commands, and threats. It will finally become apparent to the parents how much power the apparently sick and helpless child has over them, and they will give up trying to control the child's eating habits. "The therapist then disengages the parents from further contact with the patient about food, making this into a private issue between patient and therapist" (Rosman et al., 1975, p. 847).

Model Three involves the attempt to neutralize family interaction around the topic of eating. The child is left to decide whether to eat or not. The therapist does not encourage engagement between parents and child on the topic of eating, and prevents the broaching of any subject that would focus attention on the child's eating habits.

The three models support and direct the confrontation between parents and children in quite different ways. The type of emotional experience created also differs in each of the three models. The choice of model depends on the therapist's estimation of the family's style, structure, and developmental level. In Models One and Two, a therapeutic → **crisis** is created in order to break up an overly rigid family structure. Model One is advantageous when dealing with younger and prepubescent children; it clarifies power struggles and enhances parental competence. Model Two is advantageous when dealing with adolescents whose struggle for autonomy and separation from the family need to be supported. In families whose structure appears to be more flexible, or in the event that the child has begun to eat again by itself, Model Three is appropriate.

In summary, these three models are capable of producing decisive change in family systems involved in life or death situations. The family lunch is a → **structural family therapy** intervention strategy, a special case of → **enactment** of family transactions whereby a specific family problem is "staged" during a therapeutic setting in order to derive an accurate diagnosis of family interaction patterns as well as to intervene directly in the ongoing interaction process.

Minuchin, S. "Anorexia nervosa: Interactions around the family table." Lecture given at the Institute of Juvenile Research, Chicago, 1971.

Minuchin, S. *Families and family therapy.* Cambridge: Harvard University Press, 1974.

Minuchin, S., & Fishman, H. C. *Family therapy techniques.* Cambridge: Harvard University Press, 1981.

Minuchin, S., Rosman, B. L., & Baker, L. *Psychosomatic families: Anorexia nervosa in context.* Cambridge: Harvard University Press, 1978.

Rosman, B. L., Minuchin, S., & Liebman, R. Family lunch session: An introduction to family therapy in anorexia nervosa. *American Journal of Orthopsychiatry 45:* 846–853, 1975.

* * * * * *

FAMILY MYTHS

Ferreira (1963) introduced and gave clinical examples of the concept of family myths, which often serve as family → **paradigms** either to maintain the family status quo (→ **homeostasis**) or to map out patterns of growth and directions for change at points of → **crisis.** Accordingly, such myths function for families in the same way that defense mechanisms function for individuals. One may differentiate between loosely and tightly woven myths.

Like other psychic and transactional phenomena, family myths are "over–determined." As Stierlin (1973) noted, family myths function concurrently as defense and as protective mechanisms. Defense mechanisms function largely within the family and come to the fore when family members jointly distort their → **relational reality** in order to avoid pain and conflict, and to deny, rationalize, or hide what they have done to one another. Protective mechanisms play a role in the family's interaction with the outside world and are used to keep outsiders out, or at least to keep them from gaining a clear picture of the family situation. To a certain extent the functions of defense and protection complement each other. If a family wants to deny its conflicts and problems to itself, it often will be necessary to sell these myths to the outside world.

According to Stierlin, the major family myths can be categorized as follows: (1) myths of harmony; (2) myths of forgiveness and atonement; and (3) rescue myths. Myths of harmony present a rosy picture of the family's past and present life, and they are in complete opposition to what an alert observer can "pick up" after only a few minutes contact with the family. They are particularly prevalent in families that exhibit a facade of pseudo–harmony (→ **pseudomutuality**), such as described by Wynne, Ryckoff, Day, and Hirsch (1958).

As a rule, myths of forgiveness and atonement have a more complicated structure. One observes processes of splitting, denial, idealization, and massive projection. The myth structure is such that one or more (living or dead) persons, inside or outside of the family, are made solely responsible for the predicament in which the family finds itself. In addition to any guilt of their own, such persons are also required to shoulder the guilt that other family members wish to be rid of. As delegates in the service of the family's superego, they atone for the guilt of the entire family (→ **delegation**).

Rescue myths are an extension of myths of forgiveness and atonement. A person outside the realm of the family, such as a therapist, is attributed magical powers and regarded as savior and benefactor, or, in another form of delegation, the person may be expected to achieve life goals that were not possible for a parent, sibling, or grandparent.

In therapy, the best strategy usually is to respect family myths and not to attack them directly, even if they appear to be dysfunctional. Whitaker often plays with myths and constructs fantasies about how family members can take mythic roles in order to help the family more.

134

This exaggeration of the positive aspects of the myth becomes a "psychotherapy of the absurd" (Whitaker, 1975), a version of → **paradoxical intervention.** As a result, the family may discontinuously abandon a dysfunctional myth. Other families are painfully barren of nurturant myths; they demythologize themselves and are "metaphorolytic" (Sonne, 1973). Such families may need help, perhaps through new rituals, in the construction of new myths.

Ferreira, A. J. Family myth and homeostasis. *Archives of General Psychiatry 9:* 457–463, 1963.
Ferreira, A. J. Family myths. In I. M. Cohen (Ed.), *Family structure, dynamics and therapy (Psychiatric Research Report No. 20).* Washington, D.C.: American Psychiatric Association, 1966, 85–90.
Sonne, J. C. *A primer for family therapists.* Moorestown, N.J.: The Thursday Press, 1973.
Stierlin, H. Group fantasies and family myths—Some theoretical and practical aspects. *Family Process 12:* 111–125, 1973.
Whitaker, C. A. Psychotherapy of the absurd: With a special emphasis on the psychotherapy of aggression. *Family Process 14:* 1–16, 1975.
Wynne, L. C., Ryckoff, I. M., Day, J., & Hirsch, S. I. Pseudo-mutuality in the family relations of schizophrenics. *Psychiatry 21:* 205–220, 1958.

* * * * * *

FAMILY SCULPTURE

Family sculpture is a diagnostic tool and therapeutic technique by which the relational patterns within the family can be spatially and concretely visualized and experienced. The types of interactional patterns that can be illustrated include the → **closeness/distance** of family members to one another, the structure of the family hierarchy, and the patterns of nonverbal communication.

The family sculpture technique was developed in the United States in the late 1960s by Duhl and associates (Duhl, Kantor, & Duhl, 1973). Papp (1976) and associates (Papp, Silverstein, & Carter, 1973), and Satir (1972) did much to make this technique popular. The family sculpture technique is related to psychodrama and offers the possibility of representing past and present family constellations without the limitations of lineal (→ **lineality**) and → **diachronic,** language–bound modes of expression. As a nonverbal visualization technique, it allows the synchronic representation of closeness and distance in the → **relational balance** of individual family members, and also the representation of the coalition (→ **alliance/coalition/alignment**) structures of the family and its → **hierarchy.**

The technique follows one of several procedures. A family member, sometimes a child who is not the focus of a family conflict, is asked to be the "sculptor" of the family. The "monitor," or therapist, guides the sculptor; the other members of the family or group are "actors" who lend themselves to portrayal of the sculptor's system; and others who are present observe and comment upon the process. Emotional distance and closeness are represented in spatial terms by asking the sculptor to place the family members in the room as he or she perceives their relationship to one another. After this "horizontal" representation has been visualized, the "vertical" dimension—the hierarchical structure of the family—is depicted. Those family members who are most assertive are placed "highest." The patterns of behaviors and relationships are further elucidated by "play acting" the body language of the other members: Who turns to whom? How do they look at each other? Which attitude do they assume?

The initially static aspect of family sculpture serves as a diagnostic tool. Because the sculpture defines the → **relationship** between family members, it also has a therapeutic function. Out of this static sculpture, a "family choreography" (Papp, 1976) can be developed. This gives the therapist an opportunity to intervene in a directive and modifying manner in the family's behavior sequences and relationship patterns (Schweitzer & Weber, 1982).

Another version of the family sculpture, "transitional sculpting," has been developed by Landau (1982, 1985). It is commonly used to clarify and alter the relationship between two extended family systems or subsystems in order to assist family members in negotiating a → **joining** and in resolving conflict. One member from each system serves as sculptor of his or her family of origin, one sculpting while the other watches. The initial sculpting is the scupltor's perception of his or her family's "real" structure. This is then followed by "fantasy" sculptures and a series of stages in which each sculptor "moves into" the other's sculpture. Finally, they negotiate the joining of their two original ("real") sculptures and participate in a debriefing. This method often leads to considerable insight about where the families are coming from and what change is possible.

In summary, a family sculpture is a spatial → **metaphor:** Information about the family is obtained and transmitted without requiring that there be linguistic competence; → **analogue communication** can address directly the experiential plane without the mediation of language.

Duhl, F. J., Kantor, D., & Duhl, B. S. Learning, space, and action in family therapy: A primer of sculpture. In D. Bloch (Ed.), *Techniques of family psychotherapy: A primer*. New York: Grune & Stratton, 1973.

Jefferson, C. Some notes on the use of family sculpture in therapy. *Family Process 17:* 69–76, 1978.

Landau, J. Therapy with families in cultural transition. In M. McGoldrick, J. K. Pearce, & J. Giordano (Eds.), *Ethnicity and family therapy.* New York: Guilford Press, 1982, 552–572.

Landau-Stanton, J. Adolescents, families and cultural transition: A treatment model. In M. D. Pravder Mirkin & S. L. Kolman (Eds.), *Handbook of adolescents and family therapy.* New York: Gardner Press, 1985, 363–380.

Papp, P. Family choreography. In P. J. Guerin (Ed.), *Family therapy: Theory and practice.* New York: Gardner Press, 1976, 465–479.

Papp, P., Silverstein, O., & Carter, E. Family sculpting in preventive work with "well families." *Family Process 12:* 197–212, 1973.

Satir, V. *Peoplemaking.* Palo Alto: Science and Behavior Books, 1972.

Schweitzer, J., & Weber, G. Beziehung als Metapher: Die Familienskulptur als diagnostische, therapeutische und Ausbildungstechnik. *Familiendynamik 7:* 113–128, 1982.

Simon, R. M. Sculpting the family. *Family Process 11:* 49–57, 1972.

* * * * * *

FAMILY SECRETS

Family secrets refer to those topics charged with intense feelings of fear, shame, and guilt. To speak openly about them is forbidden although, as a rule, the entire family knows about them. The taboo against revealing the secrets is primarily to avoid mortification and conflict.

The keeping of family secrets is a form of collective denial that is not necessarily pathological. Most families have a skeleton or two in the closet, and keeping them there is, within limits, functional. Family secrets can serve to protect the → **self–esteem** of the family members. Family secrets become a problem when they undermine mutual trust, inhibit dialogue, and distort reality in such a way that family → **adaptability** and development become restricted. This is the case when family secrets serve to uphold → **family myths.**

The content of family secrets, as Framo (1965) observed, usually has to do with the sexual life of the parents, illegitimate children, earlier marriages, etc. They are events or actions that society, in general, views as disgraceful, and whose disclosure would have painful consequences for the self–esteem of those involved.

As is the case with any family problem–solving strategies, the usefulness of the therapeutic strategy depends on the extent and the rigidity of its application. Experience in family therapy shows that it is not wise to try to "unearth" family secrets, nor is it helpful to view the guarding of them as resistance to therapy. The technique of → **circular questioning** has proven to be an effective method of "airing" the fantasies and fears of the family about the consequences of disclosing the secret while also respecting the family's desire to keep the secret. In this manner it becomes apparent what role the maintenance of the secret has in the family relational network and what consequences are feared if the secret were disclosed. Once these fears have been spoken about, the necessity of keeping the secret often disappears.

Framo, J. L. Rationale and techniques of intensive family therapy. In I. Boszormenyi-Nagy & J. L. Framo (Eds.), *Intensive family therapy: Theoretical and practical aspects.* New York: Harper & Row, 1965, 143–212.

Group for the Advancement of Psychiatry (GAP), Committee on the Family. *Treatment of families in conflict: The clinical study of family process.* New York: Science House, 1970.

Karpel, M. A. Family secrets: I. Conceptual and ethical issues in the relational contest. II. Ethical and practical considerations in therapeutic management. *Family Process 19:* 295–306, 1980.

Karpel, M. A., & Strauss, E. S. *Family evaluation.* New York: Gardner Press, 1983.

Napier, A. Y., & Whitaker, C. A. *The family crucible.* New York: Harper & Row, 1978.

Pincus, L., & Dare, C. *Secrets in the family.* New York: Pantheon Books, 1978.

* * * * * *

FAMILY SOCIOLOGY

Family sociology is a field of social sciences that studies the family as an institution, with special attention being given to historical, socioeconomic, and cultural conditions that shape family structures.

Because a human infant at birth is not capable of surviving by itself, it must be assumed that "family" is as old as human culture and, in some form, is part of human nature. An infant needs at least one parent (or person who is willing to act as a parental surrogate) to teach it survival skills. The structure of the family, however, and its functions beyond the ones strictly associated with the survival of progeny, show a great deal of cultural and social diversity (Lévi–Stauss, 1949; Malinowksi, 1944).

In the last few years, parallels between the development of family therapy and changes in the methodology of family sociology have become apparent. Psychodynamic and sociopsychological theories have come to the forefront in research, with a focus on viewing the family as an active, interactional network. Family sociology had previously restricted itself to questioning one family member about his or her family. "Nobody bothered about what happened when the family really came together" (Friedrich, 1977).

As clinical psychology began inquiry into the interactional styles of dysfunctional families, the hitherto unquestioned concept of a "normal family" began to totter. Research focus, which had formerly been content with a description of static structures and functions, shifted to a greater interest in the dynamics of ongoing family interactional patterns. Methods that had been developed to study exotic cultures were applied to the study of the culture and history of Western industrial society (→ **ethnomethodology,** → **sociolinguistics**). The actuality of families in an industrialized society proved a great deal more diverse than had been suggested by the normative concept of the "ideal" or "typical" family structure based on socially accepted values.

Sussman (1971), an American sociologist, catalogued the family structures currently found in the foremost industrial nations. Sussman's categories, as quoted by Friedrich (1977) are as follows:

1. The nuclear family (husband, wife, and children, living together in a single family household)
   1.1. Husband alone employed
   1.2. Both spouses employed
      1.2.1. Wife employed continually
      1.2.2. Wife employed intermittently
2. Marriage–partner family (spouses live alone together, without children, or children do not live at home)
   2.1. Husband alone employed
   2.2. Husband and wife employed
      2.2.1. Wife employed continually
      2.2.2. Wife employed intermittently
3. One–parent families (as a consequence of divorce, abandonment, or separation, usually with children of preschool and/or school age)
   3.1. Single parent employed
   3.2. Single parent unemployed
4. Single person household
5. Three–generation family (different possibilities of cohabitation in a single household of the family structures 1, 2, or 3)
6. Married couple in middle or advanced years, husband as "breadwinner," wife as housewife (children attending university or other occupational training, already employed, or married)
7. Extended families (nuclear families or unmarried relatives live in close geographical proximity and interact in a reciprocal system of exchange of goods and services)
8. Second–career families (wife seeks employment, anew, when the children go to school or leave home)

Experimental Family Structures:

1. Communal living arrangements
    1.1. Household containing more than one monogamous pair with children, sharing common resources, household appliances, and experiences (the socialization of children is a group endeavor)
    1.2. Household of adults and children—group marriage—as family structure (all adults are "married" to one another, the adults are "parents" of all the children)
2. An unmarried parent with children
3. Unmarried parenting couple with one child, either their own offspring or an informally adopted child

This catalogue makes it apparent that there is often a major discrepancy between that which is commonly conceived of as a "family" and the actual, existing forms of family structure. A similar discrepancy exists between the actuality and the notions of normality that underlie jurisdictional and/or legal concepts of a family. Because the problems that arise in families differ according to their different structures, the consideration of the relative dysfunctionality or functionality of a family's problem–solving strategies must be considered in the context of the family structure at issue. Yet, the plurality of family structures cannot be understood outside the context of their socioeconomic conditions.

In preindustrial society, the family was the smallest unit that insured economic survival. Men, women, and children worked together. This is still the case in some agricultural societies where children and parents work a farm together. The industrial revolution affected the economic function of the family unit by paying the individual worker for his or her labor. The effect of this on the family depended upon the socioeconomic class to which the family belonged (Thompson, 1966). The development of the family structure from a multigenerational, socioeconomic survival unit to the nuclear family, as we know it today, altered the role of the family. In the industrial society, the function of the family shifted toward insuring emotional and social survival and establishing a unit of joint consumption and resources. However, even these aspects of family functioning were taken over in part by larger, external institutions. The creation of a national social security system, for example, guaranteed the economic survival of the old and the sick. In contrast to many developing nations where a large number of offspring are required to insure survival of older individuals, the idea of "joint liability" for the needy was extended to society at large or to the state, and made largely independent of personal ties.

The structure of the family in the industrial era was further influenced by other factors. Birth control freed women from their tradition roles as child–rearers and homemakers. This altered the course of the individual life cycle as well as the → **family life cycle.** The role of the working mother affected the structure of the family → **hierarchy.** The relationship between man and wife became more equal, and the difference in roles decreased (Young & Willmott, 1973).

Family therapists must take into consideration these aspects of social reality in their diagnostic and therapeutic work. Ignoring the altered and shifting family structure can lead to the dangerous assumption, unthinkingly made by many therapists, that the norms of the middle–class are the norms by which families are to be judged as **healthy/ functional families.**

A great many problems that families present are the result of their socioeconomic background and must be understood in their social context. An example of this is the process of → **separating parents and adolescents.** In the preindustrial era, when the extended family was the unit of production, the adolescent's maturation process followed a different pattern from that found in the industrial era where each individual is held responsible for his or her own economic well–being. Accordingly, problems connected with the development of personal → **identity** cannot be restricted merely to the family and its structure, or to its habits of interaction and rules of behavior, but must be seen within the sociocultural and economic context in which the individual develops.

Burr, W. R., Hill, R., Nye, F. I., & Reiss, I. L. (Eds.). *Contemporary theories about the family* (2 vols.). New York: Free Press, 1979.

Demos, J., & Boocock, S. S. (Eds.). Turning points: Historical and sociological essays on the family. Chicago: University of Chicago Press, 1978. (Book form of *American Journal of Sociology 84, Suppl.,* 1978.)

Friedrich, H. Soziologie der Familie und Familientherapie. *Medizin–Mensch–Gesellschaft 2:* 201–208, 1977.

Gadlin, H. Private lives and public order: A critical view of the history of intimate relations in the United States. In G. Levinger & H. L. Rausch (Eds.), *Close relationships.* Amherst: University of Massachusetts Press, 1977, 33–72.

Gordon, M. (Ed.). *The American family in social-historical perspective.* New York: St. Martin's Press, 1973.

Kohn, M. D. *Class and conformity: A study in values.* Homewood, Ill.: Dorsey Press, 1969.

Laslett, P. (Ed.). *Household and family in past time.* Cambridge: Cambridge University Press, 1972.

Lévi-Strauss, C. Les structures élémentaires de la parenté. Paris: Presses Universitaires de France, 1949.

Malinowski, B. *A scientific theory of culture.* Chapel Hill: University of North Carolina Press, 1944.

Mead, G. H. *Mind, self, and society.* Chicago: University of Chicago Press, 1934.

Mogey, J. Sociology of marriage and family behavior, 1957–1968 (A trend report and bibliography). *Current Sociology 17:* 1–346, 1970.

Parsons, T., Bales, R. F., Olds, J., Zelditch, M., & Slater, P. E. *Family socialization and interaction process.* Glencoe, Ill.: Free Press, 1955.
Rosenberg, C. E. (Ed.). *The family in history.* Philadelphia: University of Pennsylvania Press, 1975.
Shorter, E. *The making of the modern family.* New York: Basic Books, 1975.
Sussman, M. Family systems in the 1970's: Analysis, policies, and programs. *Annals of the American Academy of Political and Social Science 396:* 180 ff., 1971.
Thompson, E. P. *The making of the English working class.* New York: Vintage Press, 1966.
Young, M., & Willmott, P. *The symmetrical family.* New York: Pantheon Books, 1973.

* * * * * *

FAMILY SOMATICS

Family somatics is an area of medical research that studies the interrelation of systemic family processes and individual, physical reactions to these processes. This concept is holistic in that it takes into consideration the physical, psychological, and social aspects of illness.

Since Weakland (1977) introduced the term "family somatics," psychosomatic medicine has been extended to include the study of psychological and family factors in physical and mental illness. The types of illness in which psychosocial influences have been established range from streptococcal infections to accident–proneness, and include such frequently occurring, chronic illnesses as disorders of the circulatory system and metabolism, heart disease, rheumatism, and cancer.

Wirsching and Stierlin (1982) have presented numerous examples of how the course of chronic disease is determined by the family relational system. The task that remains is to develop scientific models and therapeutic strategies that take these facts into account. An ecosystemic (→ ecology/ ecosystem) perspective would be advantageous in that it takes into consideration the indissoluble, coequal nature of physical and psychological processes. Body and environment are seen as intersecting → feedback loops. A number of dimensions can be distinguished that, in a state of continual interplay with one another, determine whether and how illness or health will prevail. Weiner (1977) described these dimensions as (1) biological organismic; (2) intrapsychic; (3) interpersonal; (4) sociocultural; and (5) physical-environmental.

The study of these dimensions requires appropriate observation methods and instruments. With the help of a → cybernetic, systemic model, the "translation rules" can be deciphered whereby cultural and social norms influence the interactional mode of a family, with concomitant effects on the intrapsychic experience and physical well–being of the individuals. This may be seen as a transformation process in which → **information** is reprocessed in various dimensions. Patterns of social adaptation and interpersonal relating are transposed into patterns of feeling and finally into the propensity toward illness or health. The following graph was adapted by Wirsching and Stierlin (1982, p. 31) from that used by Wynne, Singer, Bartko, and Toohey (1977); it is a simplified model of this complicated network of interrelations.

Model For The Study Of The Etiology, Manifestation, and Course of Illness

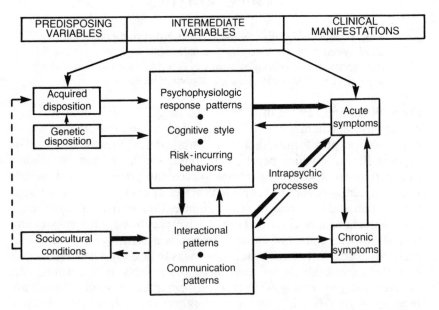

(Adapted from L.C. Wynne, M.T. Singer, J. Bartko, and M.L. Toohey, 1977)

Within this framework, strategic techniques allow direct intervention in the relational patterns of the family and thus influence the physical processes of the individual involved. Experience has shown that strategic interventions, even when applied over a relatively short span of time, are capable of producing lasting, positive change in the ongoing course of an illness. Hence, the study of family somatics is

143

becoming increasingly important for family therapists and practitioners of general medicine (→ **strategic therapy**, → **systemic therapy**), and for the new field of family systems medicine (Bloch, 1983).

Beavers, W. R. Hierarchical issues in a systems approach to illness and health. *Family Systems Medicine 1:* 47–55, 1983.

Bloch, D. A. Family systems medicine: The field and the journal. *Family Systems Medicine 1:* 3–11, 1983.

Doherty, W. J., & Baird, M. A. *Family therapy and family medicine: Toward the primary care of families.* New York: Guilford Press, 1983.

Engel, G. L. The need for a new medical model: A challenge for biomedicine. *Science 196:* 129–136, 1977.

Grolnick, L. A family perspective of psychosomatic factors in illness: A review of the literature. *Family Process 11:* 457–486, 1972.

Huygen, F. J. A., & Smits, A. J. A. Family therapy, family somatics, and family medicine. *Family Systems Medicine 1:* 23–32, 1983.

Jackson, D. D. Family practice: A comprehensive medical approach. *Family Process 7:* 338–344, 1966.

Minuchin, S., Rosman, B. L., & Baker, L. *Psychosomatic families: Anorexia nervosa in context.* Cambridge: Harvard University Press, 1978.

Penn, P. Coalitions and binding interactions in families with chronic illness. *Family Systems Medicine 1* (2): 16–25, 1983.

Richardson, H. *Patients have families.* New York: Commonwealth Fund, 1948.

Selvini-Palazzoli, M. *Self-starvation: From individual to family therapy in the treatment of anorexia nervosa.* New York: Jason Aronson, 1978.

Sperling, E. Beobachtungen in Familien mit chronischen Leiden. *Familiendynamik 8:* 32–47, 1983.

Stierlin, H. Psychosomatische Erkrankungen als Störung der Differenzierung—Integration: Ein Ausblick auf die "Familienpsychosomatik." *Familiendynamik 1:* 272–293, 1976.

Stierlin, H. Family dynamics in psychotic and severe psychosomatic disorders: A comparison. *Family Systems Medicine 1* (4): 41–50, 1983.

Weakland, J. H. "Family somatics"—A neglected edge. *Family Process 16:* 263–272, 1977.

Weiner, H. *Psychobiology of human disease.* Amsterdam: Elsevier, 1977.

White, M. Structural and strategic approaches to psychosomatic families. *Family Process 18:* 303–314, 1979.

Wirsching, M., & Stierlin, H. *Krankheit und Familie.* Stuttgart: Klett-Cotta, 1982.

Wynne, L. C., Singer, M. T., Bartko, J. L., & Toohey, M. L. Schizophrenics and their families: Recent research on parental communication. In J. M. Tanner (Ed.), *Developments in psychiatric research.* London: Hodder & Stoughton, 1977, 254–286.

* * * * * *

FAMILY TESTS

Family tests are standardized procedures for the evaluation of family relational processes. Such tests are sometimes used clinically as an aspect of consultation or treatment planning, and sometimes for the assessment of impasse or crisis situations during the course of marital or family therapy. They also are used in family therapy research for the evaluation of change from a baseline to various stages of outcome. Finally, apart from therapy, family tests are used in research on family processes that are associated with stages of the → **family life cyle,** with cultural variations, with the presence of psychiatric or physical illness in a family member, and in various studies in → **family sociology.**

The distinctive feature of a family "test" is that it is administered in a manner that is sufficiently consistent or standardized to facilitate comparisons between different families, and to assess change or stability in the same family at different points of time or under different circumstances. In family and marital therapy, family testing may be integrated fully into a consultative or therapeutic session, or the testing may be an explicitly demarcated portion of the work that precedes or is otherwise differentiated from the therapy proper.

Although certain procedures can be administered in the same way, or only slightly different ways, whether or not they are part of therapy or research, the testing *context* may be perceived by the family (and the tester) as significantly different, depending on what expectations are held about how the results will be used: "The family's construction of reality" (Reiss, 1981) about the nature of a testing context, unfolding in transaction with the researcher's expectations, is of paramount importance in the interpretation of findings (Sigafoos & Reiss, 1985).

Family tests can be broadly classified into methods that involve (1) the observation of direct interaction (transactions) between family members and (2) data collection from individual family members about their families or from which inferences about their families can be drawn.

Family interaction tests: Certain testing approaches are more readily integrated into a therapeutic framework than others. For example, the Structured Family Interview was designed by Watzlawick (1966) as a clinical tool, but data using his procedures have been coded and analyzed for use in many research programs (*cf.* Riskin & Faunce, 1972). The first of Watzlawick's test procedures—asking the family to discuss their "main problems"—is similar to the starting point of therapy. As a test, the problem discussion is tape–recorded and/or observed through a one–way window so that the interaction process can be rated or coded. One of the most common ways to structure the selection of problems to be discussed has been to adapt Strodtbeck's (1951) Revealed Differences technique. The ideas of individual family members are tapped first by interview or questionnaire. The tester then can select problems on which the family members have differences structured in accord with various → **alliances/ alignments/ coalitions** (for example, parents versus offspring, mother and son versus father, etc.). The family is then asked, as a whole and in subsystems, to discuss these problems for five to ten minutes each, sometimes with the instruction to try to reach agreement. This testing format can be elaborated (as with Watzlawick, 1966, and Doane, Goldstein, & Rodnick, 1981), or it can be simplified (as with Lewis et al., 1976, and Revenstorf et al., 1984). Ratings may be global and dimensionalized, as in the Beavers–Timberlawn Family Evaluation Scales (Beavers, 1977, 1981, 1983), or specific interaction sequences may be coded using one of numerous systems, such as those developed by Mishler and Waxler (1968), Gottman (1979), and Hahlweg et al. (1984).

A similar task that can be used both with families in therapy and with those who are "nonlabeled" is to ask them "to plan something together, something that you all could do together as a family" (Watzlawick, 1966, p. 258). Some tasks are more suitable for couples ("How did you meet?"), while others have a game–like quality, such as the Twenty Questions Test (Wild & Shapiro, 1977), the SIMFAM procedure (Straus & Tallman, 1971), and the Train Game (Ravich, 1969; Ravich & Wyden, 1974).

Another array of tasks depends upon observation of both verbal and nonverbal interaction. These procedures include those that are highly unstructured, such as the Family Free Play (Baldwin, Baldwin, & Cole, 1982), in which family members "spend time" together in a home–like setting with age–appropriate toys for the children. The use of nonverbal materials has been systematically explored in family art evaluation (Kwiatkowska, 1978). Similarly, nonverbal interaction can be observed in → **family sculpture,** which sometimes is carried out in a structured form that meets every criterion of a "test."

A procedure with structured instructions is the Consensus Rorschach in which a family or couple is asked to discuss and to reach agreement on Rorschach percepts; the Consensus Rorschach has been modified in several ways (Levy & Epstein, 1964; Loveland, 1967; Loveland, Wynne, & Singer, 1963; Wynne, 1968; and Willi, 1969). A computerized procedure in which contingent, structural interaction is highly monitored is the Card Sort Procedure (Reiss, 1981).

An extensive review and critique of quantifiable family interaction research in these and various other forms was published by Riskin and Faunce in 1972 and is still valuable; the numerous studies of more recent years have used earlier data collection procedures but have added innovative systems for coding sequences of interaction and data analysis (e.g., Gottman, 1979; Hahlweg & Jacobson, 1984; Walsh, 1982).

Family assessment from individual data: In contrast to the data obtained from observation of family interaction, test data are often collected from individual family members about their families. Fisher et al. (1985) have usefully made a distinction between such data that remain at an "individual" level and those that are combined into "relational" measures using a variety of statistical and conceptual approaches. The "individual" level data are obtained from only one family member, even though they may be *about* family relationships. The most widely used approach to family assessment is through self–report measures from which data can be analyzed in either individual or relational terms. Most family self–report measures are administered apart from therapy. An exception is the McMaster Family Assessment Device (FAD), which is a "screening" question-naire for obtaining information from individual family members on dimensions that are also assessed in the in–depth interviewing (Ep-stein, Baldwin, & Bishop, 1983) (→ **McMaster Model of Family Functioning**). Mann and Starr (1972) used a self–report questionnaire not only as an initial measure but also as a means of obtaining daily information about change during the course of therapy. This is then used to reinforce and help focus upon treatment goals.

Among the self–report measures that have been most frequently used in family research assessment are:

- Family Adaptability and Cohesion Evaluation Scale (FACES): Olson, Rus-sell, & Sprenkle (1983) (→ **Circumplex Model**)
- Family Environment Scale (FES): Moos & Moos (1981)
- Family–Concept Q Sort (FCQS): Van der Veen (1965)
- Family Assessment Measure (FAM): Skinner, Steinhauer, & Santa–Barbara (1983)
- Marital Adjustment Scale (MAS): Locke & Wallace (1959)
- Partnership Questionnaire (PFD): Hahlweg, Schindler, Revenstorf, & Bren-glemann (1984)

In a somewhat different self–report approach, family members fill out questionnaires in which they judge how the other family members perceive him or her:

- Interpersonal Perception Method (IPM): Laing, Phillipson, & Lee (1966)
- Giessen Test (GT): Beckmann & Richter (1975)

These data are analyzed with "relational" methods.

In earlier days of family research, projective tests were modified to have special relevance to family relationships but were administered to individual family members and interpreted in terms of individual attitudes, expressed explicitly or implicitly as projections, rather than as observable interaction. Such methods included the Family Relations Test (Anthony & Bene, 1957) and the Family Relations Indicator (Howells & Lickorish, 1968).

From a systemic perspective, most self–report methods fail to meet the criteria proposed by Rogers, Millar, and Bavelas (1985), who argue that a system–level method must "(a) focus on observable behavior; (b) provide sequential descriptions of those behaviors; and (c) be capable of describing system–level structurings that represent relational patterns" (p. 177). Family tests that meet these criteria mostly use the methods of sampling directly observed interaction.

Observation of tester–family member interaction: A final variety of family test methods involves individual data collection but focuses in a partially systemic manner on analogues of family relatedness; in these procedures, a tester or interviewer interacts with an individual family member (Wild et al., 1965). Singer and Wynne (1965) pointed out that procedures such as the Rorschach and the TAT are not suitable for the study of family relationships when they are used as projective tests; they are better used as a standardized means of obtaining communication samples in which the transactional impact of the speaker upon the listener (tester) can be assessed. This approach has been used in the study of → **communication deviance** in the Rorschach (Singer & Wynne, 1966), the TAT (Jones, 1977), and the Object Sorting Test (Wild, et al., 1965). Similarly, the Camberwell Family Interview (Vaughn & Leff, 1976) is an interview procedure conducted with individual family members (see → **expressed emotion**). The data thus obtained are not rated for the content of self–report but for the affective features that have been expressed about another family member (usually an → **identified patient**).

In summary, the diversity of family tests now available is considerable, but much work remains to be done in clarifying the meaning of the measures that are obtained. Constructs that appear to be similar but that are obtained by differing methods may be more method–specific than has been believed (Sigafoos et al., 1985). One of the more promising recent developments lies in more systemic approaches to the study of sequential patterns in family transactions (Hahlweg & Jacobson, 1984; Rogers et al., 1985)

Anthony, E. J., & Bene, E. A technique for the objective assessment of the child's family relationships. *Journal of Mental Science 103:* 541–555, 1957.

148

Baldwin, A. L., Baldwin, C. P., & Cole, R. E. Family Free-Play interaction: Setting and methods. *Parental pathology, family interaction, and the competence of the child in school. Monographs of the Society for Research in Child Development 47:* 36–44, 1982.

Beavers, W. R. *Psychotherapy and growth: A family systems perspective.* New York: Brunner/Mazel, 1977.

Beavers, W. R. A systems model of family for family therapists. *Journal of Marital and Family Therapy 7:* 299–307, 1981.

Beavers, W. R. Hierarchical issues in a systems approach to illness and health. *Family Systems Medicine 1:* 47–55, 1983.

Beckmann, D., & Richter, H. E. *Giessen-Test (GT): Ein Test für Individual– und Gruppendiagnostik* (2nd ed.). Bern: Huber, 1975.

Doane, J. A., Goldstein, M. J., & Rodnick, E. H. Parental patterns of affective style and the development of schizophrenia spectrum disorders. *Family Process 20:* 337–349, 1981.

Epstein, N. B., Baldwin, L. M., & Bishop, D. S. The McMaster Family Assessment Device. *Journal of Marital and Family Therapy 9:* 171–180, 1983.

Faunce, E. E., & Riskin, J. Family interaction scales: II. Data analysis and findings. *Archives of General Psychiatry 22:* 513–526, 1970.

Ferreira, A. J., & Winter, W. D. Family interaction and decision-making. *Archives of General Psychiatry 13:* 214–333, 1965.

Fisher, L., Kokes, R. F., Ransom, D. C., Phillips, S. L., & Rudd, P. Alternative strategies for creating "relational family data." *Family Process 24:* 213–224, 1985.

Gottman, J. M. *Marital interaction: Experimental investigations.* New York: Academic Press, 1979.

Hahlweg, K., & Jacobson, N. S. (Eds.). *Marital interaction: Analysis and modification.* New York: Guilford Press, 1984.

Hahlweg, K., Reisner, L., Kohli, G., Vollmer, M., Schindler, L., & Revenstorf, D. Development and validity of a new system to analyze interpersonal communication: Kategoriensystem für partnerschaftliche Interaktion. In K. Hahlweg & N. S. Jacobson (Eds.), *Marital interaction: Analysis and modification.* New York: Guilford Press, 1984, 182–198.

Hahlweg, K., Schindler, L., Revenstorf, D., & Brengelmann, J. C. The Munich marital therapy study. In K. Hahlweg & N. S. Jacobson (Eds.), *Marital interaction: Analysis and modification.* New York: Guilford Press, 1984, 3–26.

Howells, J. G., & Lickorish, J. *The family relations indicator.* Edinburgh: Oliver & Boyd, 1968.

Jones, J. E. Patterns of transactional style deviance in the TAT's of parents of schizophrenics. *Family Process 16:* 327–337, 1977.

Kwiatkowska, H. Y. *Family therapy and evaluation through art.* Springfield, Ill.: Charles C. Thomas, 1978.

Laing, R. D., Phillipson, H., & Lee, A. R. *Interpersonal perception: A theory and a method of research.* London: Tavistock Publications, 1966.

Levy, J., & Epstein, N. B. An application of the Rorschach test in family investigation. *Family Process 3:* 344–376, 1964.

Lewis, J. M., Beavers, W. R., Gossett, J. T., & Phillips, V. A. *No single thread: Psychological health in family systems.* New York: Brunner/Mazel, 1976.

Locke, H. J., & Wallace, K. M. Short-term marital adjustment and prediction tests: Their reliability and validity. *Journal of Marriage and Family Living 21:* 251–255, 1959.

Loveland, N. T. The relation Rorschach: A technique for studying interaction. *Journal of Nervous and Mental Disease 142:* 93–105, 1967.

Loveland, N. T., Wynne, L. C., & Singer, M. T. The Family Rorschach: A new method for studying family interaction. *Family Process 2:* 187–215, 1963.

Madanes, C. Predicting behavior in an addict's family: A communicational approach. In L. Wurmser (Ed.), *The hidden dimension.* New York: Jason Aronson, 1978, 368–380.

Madanes, C., Dukes, J., & Harbin, H. Family ties of heroin addicts. *Archives of General Psychiatry 37:* 889–894, 1980.

Mann, J., & Starr, S. The self-report questionnaire as a change agent in family therapy. *Family Process 11:* 95–105, 1972.

Mishler, E. G., & Waxler, N. E. *Interaction in families: An experimental study of family processes and schizophrenia.* New York: John Wiley & Sons, 1968.

Moos, R. H., & Moos, B. S. *Manual for the Family Environment Scale.* Palo Alto: Consulting Psychologist Press, 1981.

Olson, D. H., Russell, C. S., & Sprenkle, D. H. Circumplex Model of marital and family systems: VI. Theoretical update. *Family Process 22:* 69–83, 1983.

Ravich, R. A. The use of an interpersonal game-test in conjoint marital psychotherapy. *American Journal of Psychotherapy 23:* 217–229, 1969.

Ravich, R. A., & Wyden, B. *Predictable pairing.* New York: Wyden, 1974.

Reiss, D. *The family's construction of reality.* Cambridge: Harvard University Press, 1981.

Revenstorf, D., Hahlweg, K., Schindler, L., & Vogel, B. Interactional analysis of marital conflict. In K. Hahlweg & N. S. Jacobson (Eds.), *Marital interaction: Analysis and modification.* New York: Guilford Press, 1984, 159–181.

Riskin, J., & Faunce, E. E. An evaluative review of family interaction research. *Family Process 11:* 365–455, 1972.

Rogers, L. E., Millar, F. E., & Bavelas, J. B. Methods for analyzing marital conflict discourse: Implications of a systems approach. *Family Process 24:* 175–187, 1985.

Sigafoos, A., & Reiss, D. Rejoinder: Counterperspectives on family measurement: Clarifying the pragmatic interpretation of research methods. *Family Process 24:* 207–211, 1985.

Sigafoos, A., Reiss, D., Rich, J., & Douglas, E. Pragmatics in the measurement of family functioning: An interpretive framework for methodology. *Family Process 24:* 189–203, 1985.

Singer, M. T., & Wynne, L. C. Thought disorder and family relations of schizophrenics: III. Methodology using projective techniques. *Archives of General Psychiatry 12:* 187–200, 1965.

Singer, M. T., & Wynne, L. C. Principles for scoring communication defects and deviances in parents of schizophrenics: Rorschach and TAT scoring manuals. *Psychiatry 29:* 260–288, 1966.

Skinner, H. A., Steinhauer, P. D., & Santa-Barbara, J. The family assessment measure. *Canadian Journal of Community Mental Health 2:* 91–105, 1983.

Straus, M. A., & Tallman, I. SIMFAM: A technique for observational measurement and experimental study of families. In J. Aldous (Ed.), *Family problem solving.* Hinesdale, Ill.: Dryden Press, 1971.

Strodtbeck, F. Husband-wife interaction over revealed differences. *American Sociological Review 16:* 468–473, 1951.

Van der Veen, F. The parent's concept of the family unit and child adjustment. *Journal of Counseling Psychology 12:* 196–200, 1965.

Walsh, F. *Normal family processes*. New York: Guilford Press, 1982.

Watzlawick, P. A structured family interview. *Family Process 5:* 256–271, 1966.

Wild, C., & Shapiro, L. N. Mechanisms of change from individual to family performance in male schizophrenics and their parents. *Journal of Nervous and Mental Disease 165:* 41–56, 1977.

Wild, C. M., Singer, M. T., Rosman, B., Ricci, J., & Lidz, T. Measuring disordered styles of thinking. *Archives of General Psychiatry 13:* 471–476, 1965.

Willi, J. Joint Rorschach testing of partner relationships. *Family Process 8:* 64–78, 1969.

Winter, W. D., & Ferreira, A. J. (Eds.). *Research in family interaction: Readings and commentary*. Palo Alto: Science and Behavior Books, 1969.

Wynne, L. C. Consensus Rorschachs and related procedures for studying interpersonal patterns. *Journal of Projective Techniques and Personality Assessment 32:* 352–356, 1968.

$$* \quad * \quad * \quad * \quad * \quad *$$

FAMILY TYPOLOGIES/DIMENSIONS

A typology is an approach to classification or diagnosis in which distinctive, preferably mutually exclusive, patterns, groups, or types are identified. Typological approaches to classification contrast with dimensional approaches, but mixed models combining both typological and dimensional principles have also been attempted.

In Nathan Ackerman's last article in 1971, he voiced a long-standing concern in the family therapy field about the issue of family typologies and diagnosis, a concern that is still relevant:

The problem of family diagnosis confronts us with some curious contradictions. To all appearances, we are making swift progress in the development of family therapy, and yet we are experiencing a critical lag in the building of family diagnosis. In the mental health professions, there exists now a widespread bias against "labeling" people and families. Formal diagnosis of behavior is viewed by many as passé, a waste of time, and by a few it is even deemed harmful. Or, as others say, within the limits of present–day knowledge, a typology of families is simply not do–able.

Do–able or not, the sheer fact in clinical practice is that therapists inevitably draw judgment on the families they treat. They compare and contrast them. They draw meaningful clinical distinctions between them. They cannot help but do so. . . . The implied intent is to unshackle the interpretative function from the hobbling effects of the medical model of illness, to counteract scapegoating through psychiatric "labeling," and to avoid laying claim to a degree of accuracy we do not possess. Let us be very clear, however; *there is no way to sidestep the responsibility of conceptualizing and categorizing family types*. (p. 153; emphases added)

In more recent years, interest in family classification has grown for both research and economic reasons. Family therapy researchers are highly dissatisfied with using nonsystemic individual diagnosis, as in DSM–III, for grouping families. The first typologies in family therapy research used the medical model of diagnostic classification. Families were classified according to the symptomatology of the → **identified patient**, for example, "families of schizophrenics" or "families of alcoholics." Although such classifications provide an easy route to assembling a research sample, they clearly are not based upon distinctions that are primarily at the family system level of functioning.

Additionally, clinicians have hoped that a respectable classification of family or relational disorders might simultaneously be conceptually acceptable and economically reimbursable. (It has been said that the only diagnosis that could be agreed upon by all therapists is "acute reimbursable disorder.")

Wynne (1985) has surveyed family therapists and considered various possibilities for introducing a family classification system into the current American psychiatric nosology, DSM–III. Although the multiaxial approach of DSM–III offers some possibility of rapprochment between family therapists and individual–oriented diagnosticians, the DSM–III focus remains on "mental disorders," each conceptualized as a "syndrome or pattern that occurs in an individual" (DMS–III, 1980, p. 6). In any event, family therapists, theoreticians, and researchers have not yet resolved the problem of family classification in their own thinking, a task that presumably should precede "selling" a schema to other professionals.

Fisher (1977) valiantly attempted a classification of classifications: He organized the literature into five schemas according to (1) style of adaptation; (2) developmental family stage; (3) initial problem or diagnosis of the → **identified patient;** (4) family theme or dimension; and (5) types of marital relationship. From this review of 43 publications, Fisher than constructed his own typology—six clusters of family types that descriptively seem to fall together. He labeled these six clusters as constricted, internalized, object–focused, impulsive, childlike, and chaotic. Unfortunately, the criteria for identifying families belonging to each of these types have not been operationally specified and remain, for the most part, untried except by their original proponents.

More successfully, family therapists have described many typologies that have been of great value for theory development, although they are too abstract for use in empirical research or daily clinical practice. Keeney (1979) has discussed the difficulties of formulating "diagnosis" within the framework of → **cybernetics,** → **ecology,** and

→ **systems theory.** Bateson (1936) made an important early effort to examine data at three levels of → **abstraction,** beginning with "concrete," observed data, and concluding with an abstract, "diagnostic" typology. This was the distinction between → **symmetrical** and → **complementary** reciprocal relationships (Jackson, 1959; Sluzki & Beavin, 1965; Watzlawick, Beavin, & Jackson, 1967), derived from Bateson's concept of → **schismogenesis.**

Sometimes the distinction by Minuchin (1974) between → **enmeshment** and → **disengagement** is regarded as a two-class typology. Actually, Minuchin conceptualized families as falling along a continuum, not into typological classes, with families who have clear → **boundaries** falling between those who are enmeshed and those who are disengaged (→ **enmeshment,** → **disengagement**).

Kantor and Lehr (1975) described three major types of family systems—closed, open, and random. These basic types derive from three different models of → **homeostasis,** reflecting how the family maintains its → **boundaries:**

> In the closed family system, stable structures (fixed space, regular time, and steady energy) are relied upon as reference points for order and change. In the open family system, order and change are expected to result from the interaction of relatively stable evolving family structures (movable space, variable time, and flexible energy). In the random system, unstable structures (dispersed space, irregular time, and fluctuating energy) are experimented with as reference points for order and change. (p. 119; italics deleted)

Wertheim (1973) proposed a typology of family systems that built upon a classification along three dimensions: consensual → **morphostasis** (with a balanced distribution of intrafamilial → **power**); forced morphostasis (similar to → **pseudomutuality**); and induced → **morphogenesis** (the system's capacity for adaptive change in response to extra-systemic, e.g., therapeutic, intervention). Classifying each family as high or low on each dimension produced a grid of eight types of families, for example, an "open-integrated" system, high on consensual morphostasis, low on forced morphostasis, and high on induced morphogenesis.

Another kind of multidimensional grid approach to family typology has been proposed by Fleck (1983). He recommends a cross-sectional assessment of the family's present functioning in the four areas of leadership, boundaries, affectivity, and communication, combined with a longitudinal dimension in which problem-solving tasks change with each stage in the → **family life cycle.**

The difficulty of building concepts of change into family classifications has been formidable, despite efforts such as Wertheim's use of the concept of morphogenesis and Fleck's concept of change within the family life cycle. Hoffman (1981) sought a way of depicting the directions of discontinuous change within a typology. She suggested a series of platters or levels, with contrasting types of family functioning at each level, for example, Stierlin's typology of → **centripetal/ centrifugal** families at one level, and an anarchistic/authoritarian typology at the next level. In patterns of spiral movement, discontinuous second–order → **change** would take place by a leap to a new level of reorganization when a family became caught in an extreme form of first–level change, for example, in extreme centripetal functioning.

The preceding varieties of family classification, both typological and dimensional, are helpful in pointing to issues such as functional/ dysfunctional aspects of balance, for example, between → **closeness/ distance.** At the same time, the high degree of → **abstraction** of these classifications, and the consequent difficulties of converting these schemata into usable, reliable research instruments make all too obvious why it has been difficult for family therapists to agree upon any classification that they might actually use. In the light of these difficulties, it is surprising that a few approaches are nevertheless achieving a degree of acceptance by other than their originators. Each of the approaches is concerned both with conceptual issues that can contribute to their validity and with empirical methods that can be used reliably. These classificatory approaches have been described elsewhere in this volume: → **Beavers Systems Model,** → **McMaster Model of Family Functioning,** Olson's → **Circumplex Model,** and Reiss's Paradigm Model that includes a family typology of → **consensus sensitivity/ distance sensitivity/ environment sensitivity.** In addition, a number of → **family tests** lend themselves to the classification of families in potentially useful ways, especially those of Ravich (1969), Van der Veen (1965), Moos and Moos (1981), and Skinner, Steinhauer, and Santa–Barbara (1983). Bloom (1985) has recently conducted a factor analysis of self–report measures that revealed that 15 dimensions of family functioning could be subsumed under the three general headings of "relationship" (including family sociability, family idealization, and disengagement), personal growth (family emphasis on developmental processes), and system maintenance (structure and degree of control of family members with each other). Further studies on the overlap of family classificatory systems seems to be a major research task of the near future.

Ackerman, N. W. The growing edge of family therapy. *Family Process 10:* 143–156, 1971.

Bateson, G. *Naven: A survey of the problems suggested by a composite picture of the culture of a New Guinea tribe drawn from three points of view* (1st ed). Cambridge: Cambridge University Press, 1936.

154

Beavers, W. R. *Psychotherapy and growth: A family systems perspective*. New York: Brunner/Mazel, 1977.

Beavers, W. R. A systems model of family for family therapists. *Journal of Marital and Family Therapy 7:* 299–307, 1981.

Beavers, W. R., & Voeller, M. N. Family models: Comparing and contrasting the Olson Circumplex Model with the Beavers Systems Model. *Family Process 22:* 85–98, 1983.

Bloom, B. L. A factor analysis of self-report measures of family functioning. *Family Process 24:* 255–239, 1985.

DSM–III: Diagnostic and Statistical Manual of Mental Disorders (3rd ed.). Washington, D. C.: American Psychiatric Association, 1980.

Epstein, N. B., Baldwin, L. M., & Bishop, D. S. The McMaster Family Assessment Device. *Journal of Marital and Family Therapy 9:* 171–180, 1983.

Fishbein, H. D. The identified patient and stage of family development. *Journal of Marital and Family Therapy 8:* 57–61, 1982.

Fisher, L. On the classification of families: A progress report. *Archives of General Psychiatry 34:* 424–433, 1977.

Fleck, S. A holistic approach to family typology and the axes of DSM–III. *Archives of General Psychiatry 40:* 901–906, 1983.

Ford, F. R., & Herrick, J. A typology of families/Five family systems. *Australian Journal of Family Therapy 3:* 71–81, 1982.

Hoffman, L. *Foundations of family therapy: A conceptual framework for systems change*. New York: Basic Books, 1981.

Jackson, D. D. Family interaction, family homeostasis and some implications for conjoint family psychotherapy. In J. H. Masserman (Ed.), *Individual and familial dynamics*. New York: Grune & Stratton, 1959, 122–141.

Kantor, D., & Lehr, W. *Inside the family: Toward a theory of family process*. San Francisco: Jossey-Bass, 1975.

Keeney, B. P. Ecosystemic epistemology: An alternative paradigm for diagnosis. *Family Process 18:* 117–129, 1979.

Levant, R. Diagnostic perspectives on the family: Process, structural and historical contextual models. *American Journal of Family Therapy 11:* 3–10, 1983.

Minuchin, S. *Families and family therapy*. Cambridge: Harvard University Press, 1974.

Moos, R. H., & Moos, B. S. *Manual for the Family Environment Scale*. Palo Alto: Consulting Psychologist Press, 1981.

Olson, D. H., McCubbin, H. C., Barnes, H., Larsen, A., Muxen, M., & Wilson, M. *Families: What makes them work*. Beverly Hills: Sage Publications, 1983.

Olson, D. H., Sprenkle, D. H., & Russell, C. S. Circumplex Model of marital and family systems: I. Cohesion and adaptability dimensions, family types, and clinical applications. *Family Process 18:* 3–28, 1979.

Ravich, R. A. The use of an interpersonal game-test in conjoint marital psychotherapy. *American Journal of Psychotherapy 23:* 217–229, 1969.

Reiss, D. *The family's construction of reality*. Cambridge: Harvard University Press, 1981.

Skinner, H. A., Steinhauer, P. D., & Santa-Barbara, J. The family assessment measure. *Canadian Journal of Community Mental Health 2:* 91–102, 1983.

Sluzki, C. E., & Beavin, J. Symmetry and complementarity: An operational definition and a typology of dyads. In P. Watzlawick & J. H. Weakland (Eds.), *The interactional view*. New York: W. W. Norton & Co., 1977.

Van der Veen, F. The parent's concept of the family unit and child adjustment. *Journal of Counseling Psychology 12:* 196–200, 1965.

Watzlawick, P., Beavin, J. H., & Jackson, D. D. *Pragmatics of human communication: A study of interactional patterns, pathologies and paradoxes.* New York: W. W. Norton & Co., 1967.

Wertheim, E. S. Family unit therapy and the science and typology of family systems. *Family Process 12:* 361–376, 1973.

Wynne, L. C. A preliminary proposal for strengthening the multiaxial approach of DSM–III: Possible family-oriented revisions. In G. L. Tischler (Ed.), *Diagnosis and classification in psychiatry.* Cambridge: Cambridge University Press, in press.

* * * * * *

FEEDBACK LOOP/ FEEDBACK/ EVOLUTIONARY FEEDBACK

"Feedback is a method of controlling a system by reinserting into it the results of its past performance" (Wiener, 1954/1967, p. 84). Feedback loops and feedback structures are essential elements in cybernetic systems. In traditional family theory, negative (deviation–counteracting) feedback was conceptualized as regulating families and other systems (→ **homeostasis**), as a precondition for the survival of the system in a constantly changing environment. This formulation was more satisfactory for explaining → **stability** and → **morphostasis** than in understanding → **change,** especially discontinuous change. The concepts of positive (deviation-amplifying) feedback and evolutionary feedback, as well as → **morphogenesis,** → **coherence,** and → **coevolution,** have been advanced to correct "simple" feedback theories.

The self–corrective process whereby feedback counteracts deviation that goes beyond certain limits, opposing the direction of the initial change that produced the feedback, is usually called negative feedback. Bateson spoke of this as a "circular chain of causal events . . . such that the more of something, the less of the next thing in the circuit" (1972, p. 429). The simplest closed–loop control system, a servomechanism, involves a single feedback loop in which feedback is from a single point and correction from a single point. In multiple–loop systems, feedback can be initiated at more than one point in a process and corrections made from more than one point. Such systems are called "open" when interchange between a system and its context takes place.

Feedback control systems are actually quite ancient. Roman engineers maintained water levels for aqueduct systems by means of floating valves that opened and closed at specified levels. Dutch windmills of the 17th century were later examples, and the most famous example from the Industrial Revolution was James Watt's flyball governor (1769), a device that regulated steam flow to a steam engine in order to maintain constant engine speed despite a change in load. The first theoretical analysis of a closed-loop feedback system (Watt's governor) was published by James Clerk Maxwell in the 19th century, work that was soon generalized into → **control theory.**

Feedforward systems are open–loop control systems and were exemplified by the loom, invented by Jacquard in France in 1801; a set of punched cards programmed the patterns woven by the loom, but no information from the process was used to correct the machine's operation. The concept of "feedforward," which has been neglected in family theory but has been well-recognized by engineers and others, posits that change in a present condition is goal–directed in relation to an *anticipated* condition that is computed in accord with an inner model of the world (Rosen, 1979). See → **control theory** for comments on the clinical application for feedforward control theory.

With respect to living systems, Miller, Galanter, & Pribram (1960) proposed that the "unit we should use as the element of behavior" is "the feedback loop itself" (p. 27). However, living systems ordinarily have multiple feedback loops in a reciprocal, linked relationship to one another. The controlled variables can be influenced by a number of regulators. In the reciprocal relationship between these elements, it cannot be said which element is the regulator and which is regulated because each element of the system influences all the other elements (→ **circularity**). It is in this sense that Maruyama (1963) spoke of "mutual causal relationships" in complex feedback loops. He also described deviance–amplifying "mutual causal" processes that interact with deviance–counteracting processes. He showed that a loop with an even number of negative influences is deviation–amplifying (cumulative), while a loop with an odd number of negative influences is deviation–counteracting (compensatory). Unfortunately, the empirical applications of these theoretical deductions are limited. Closed–loop feedback systems can be empirically identified only in short interaction sequences of observed family interactions.

The ability of a system to survive (→ **adaptability**) depends upon what types of processes are available to the system and are balanced within it. In a milieu with relatively constant internal and external life conditions, negative feedback that compensates for disturbances and hinders change is structure–preserving. The reverse is the case in → **crisis** situations where adaptation to an extreme variation in the environment is required. In an environment in which extreme changes are taking place, stabilizing mechanisms threaten the survival of the system if they hinder the development and adaptation of the system to the changing circumstances of the environment. When established control mechanisms are no longer effective, new mechanisms must be sought (→ **trial–and–error method**). Positive feedback, in this view, is regarded as an essential element in shifting to a higher level of adaptability and → **self–organization** of systems (Klaus & Liebscher, 1979). Positive feedback structures that do not lead to a re–balancing of the system destroy the system; this phenomenon is called a "runaway" in the language of cybernetics.

From a metaperspective, Keeney (1983) argues that all feedback is negative: "What is sometimes called 'positive feedback' . . . is . . . a partial arc or sequence of a more encompassing negative feedback process. . . . Enlarging one's frame of reference enables the 'runaway' to be seen as a variation subject to higher orders of control" (p. 72).

From the perspective of a cybernetic model, a family can be viewed as a system of linked or overlapping feedback structures. The ability of the family to balance change and stability determines the developmental maturity and the "life conditions" of each member of the family (→ **healthy/ functional families**). Application of the abstract principles of feedback theory to family structures has a number of implications. Most importantly, the application of a circular model of causality takes into account that each family member influences every other family member. Hence, the behavior of each individual family member can only be explained and understood in the observation of the whole system (→ **context**). However, the concept of lineal causality (→ **lineality**) is also important in family theory because family → **power** and → **hierarchy** can only exist where the chances of family members influencing each other are unequal.

Evolutionary feedback: Most of the preceding discussion has concerned processes for maintaining the equilibrium of systems and for relatively gradual change. However, in recent years, considerable attention has been given to the concept of "evolutionary feedback," a term used by the physicist Prigogine (Dell & Goolishian, 1981; Hoffman, 1981; Nicolis & Prigogine, 1977; Prigogine, 1980). This concept modifies General System Theory, as developed by Bertalanffy (1968) and others, which applies to open systems at equilibrium or close to equilibrium. However, fluctuation may be amplified far from equilibrium under specific conditions. Prigogine (1978) showed that such states of chaotic nonequilibrium may evolve, in "evolutionary feedback," into new dynamic states called "dissipative structures" in physics and chemistry. At this point, "chaos gives rise to order" (Prigogine, 1978), and the fluctuations do not tend to bring the system back to its former state. Instead, the system mutates with discontinuous change (second–order), unlike the gradual change from relatively steady states that is expected when systems are near equilibrium. This evolutionary paradigm for thermodynamic systems has been conceptualized as relevant to the dramatic, seemingly discontinuous change that is observed at times in family therapy, for example, after certain → **paradoxical interventions.**

Earlier, prior to the work by Prigogine, a similar point of view was also discussed by Bateson when he modified his earlier noncybernetic views of → **schismogenesis** in order to account for discontinuous transformations of systems from one level to another. These processes are believed to take place with the introduction of a random element, and thus are inherently nonpredictable (Bateson, 1958).

Ashby, W. R. *Design for a brain.* London: Chapman & Hall, 1952.
Ashby, W. R. *An introduction to cybernetics.* London: Methuen, 1956.
Bateson, G. Epilogue, 1958. In G. Bateson, *Naven* (2nd ed.). Stanford, Cal.: Stanford University Press, 1958, 280–303.
Bateson, G. *Steps to an ecology of mind.* New York: Ballantine Books, 1972.
Bertalanffy, L. von. *General systems theory.* New York: George Braziller, 1968.
Cannon, W. B. *Wisdom of the body.* New York: W. W. Norton & Co., 1932.
Davies, P. C. W. *The runaway universe.* New York: Penguin Books, 1980.
Dell, P. F., & Goolishian, H. A. Order through fluctuation: An evolutionary epistemology for human systems. *Australian Journal of Family Therapy 2:* 175–184, 1981.
Elkaïm, M. From general laws to singularities. *Family Process 24:* 151–164, 1985
Elkaïm, M., Prigogine, I., Guattari, F., Stengers, I., & Dennebourg, J.-L. Openness: A round-table discussion. *Family Process 21:* 57–70, 1982.
Hoffman, L. Deviation-amplifying processes in natural groups. In J. Haley (Ed.), *Changing families: A family therapy reader.* New York: Grune & Stratton, 1971, 285–311.
Hoffman, L. *Foundations of family therapy: A conceptual framework for systems change.* New York: Basic Books, 1981.
Jackson, D. D. The question of family homeostasis. *Psychiatric Quarterly, Suppl. 31:* 79–90, 1957.
Keeney, B. P. *Aesthetics of change.* New York: Guilford Press, 1983.
Klaus, G., & Liebscher, H. *Wörterbuch der Kybernetik* (4th revised ed.). Frankfurt: Fischer, 1979.
Maruyama, M. The second cybernetics: Deviation-amplifying mutual causal processes. *American Scientist 5:* 164–179, 1963.
Miller, G. A., Galanter, E., & Pribram, K. H. *Plans and the structure of behavior.* New York: Henry Holt, 1960.
Nicolis, G., & Prigogine, I. *Self–organization in nonequilibrium systems: From dissipative structures to order through fluctuation.* New York: Wiley–Interscience, 1977.
Prigogine, I. Order through fluctuation: Self-organization and social system. In E. Jantsch & C. Waddington (Eds.), *Evolution and consciousness: Human systems in transition.* Reading, Mass.: Addison-Wesley, 1976, 93–133.
Prigogine, I. Time, structure, and fluctuations. *Science 201:* 777–785, 1978.
Prigogine, I. L'ordre a partir du chaos. *Prospective et Santé 13:* 29–39, 1980.

Rosen, R. Old trends and new trends in systems research: Ludwig von Bertalanffy Memorial Lecture. In *General systems research: A science, a methodology, a technology. Proceedings of the 1979 North American Meeting.* Louisville, Ky., 1979, 19–29.

Wender, P. H. Vicious and virtuous circles: The role of deviation-amplifying feedback in the origin and perpetuation of behavior. *Psychiatry 31:* 309–324, 1968.

Wiener, N. *The human use of human beings: Cybernetics and society* (2nd ed.). New York: Avon, 1967. (2nd ed. originally published, 1954.)

* * * * * *

FEMINIST THERAPY

This form of therapy evolved out of the feminist movement. The main focus is on how gender roles influence differing individual psychic development. The therapists view themselves as being partisan and politically engaged in furthering their clients' emancipation.

Feminist therapy developed in the late 1960s and early 1970s within the context of the feminist movement. The psychic suffering of women was viewed as deriving from social conditions prevailing in a patriarchal society. Consequently, women developed a therapy for women. The therapy has two major goals: first to foster an awareness of the social conditions and effects of differing gender roles, and, second, to initiate political action that could change these conditions. Gilbert (1980) concludes from the literature on feminist therapy that a central principle is that "the personal is political" (p. 248). An egalitarian, therapist–patient relationship is sought; feminist therapists are expected to present models for identification and a life plan that can help women to free themselves from societal constraints and to utilize their resources in accord with their needs. Compared with traditional therapies, feminist therapy also regards certain content areas as particularly important, especially wife battering, rape, pregnancy, menopause, childbirth, sexual orientation, → **power,** and → **justice.**

Family therapy and feminist therapy developed independently from each other and only recently the question has come up as to how and how much both might learn from the other (Goldner, 1985; Hare–Mustin, 1978; Libow, Raskin, & Caust, 1982; Women's Project in Family Therapy, 1982, 1983). From a systemic point of view, it became apparent that the concept of feminist therapy is based largely on unidirectional and unicausal thinking (→ **lineality**) and that it pays little attention to circular processes (→ **circularity**). The therapist

accepts and emphasizes her partiality. This contrasts with the usual →
neutrality of family therapists (→ multidirectional partiality).

Feminist therapists are correct in claiming that family therapists
so far have paid too little attention to the historical → context of
gender relationships. They criticize in particular → structural family
therapy for regarding as normative a family's patriarchal structure and
for aiming at the creation of a functional and clear–cut → hierarchy. If
this gender hierarchy is accepted and legitimatized as the status quo,
this status quo may then be equated with health and normality (→
healthy/ functional families).

Additionally, → systemic therapy has been criticized as containing biases against women. The notion of circular causality, with its
emphasis on neutrality, is interpreted by some systemic therapists to
mean that battered women, for example, are equally responsible with
abusing men for violent incidents. Bograd (1984) has noted that some
family therapists with a systems orientation "appear unwilling to
acknowledge that some battered women *are* innocent victims whose
sole 'collaboration' was standing within arm's reach of their husbands.
It is only recently that some clinicians have taken a more radical
position by stating that thinking systemically does not preclude the
position that the husband is solely accountable for the battering
incident" (p. 562). Before other treatment goals can be addressed, the
complete cessation of violence is regarded as "the primary goal of
clinical interventions with battered women and abusive men. . . . The
very structure of conjoint therapy takes the focus off the husband and
suggests that his battering is a problem of the couple . . . [I]ndividual
or group therapy with each spouse separately may produce more rapid
change. . . . [T]here are many ways of affecting and modifying a
system without treating the couple together: a potent systemic intervention is empowering a wife to obtain a legal order that requires her
husband to leave their home temporarily. . . . [Recent] family system
interventions now include structured separation as a crucial initial
stage in the conjoint therapy of battered women and abusive men" (pp.
565–566).

Feminist therapists also point out that some family therapists tend
to view the behaviors of mothers as being more pathogenic than that of
fathers (→ schizophrenogenic mothers). These mothers are being
viewed as emotionally overinvolved and enmeshed. This state of affairs,
however, results necessarily from a division of roles, sanctioned by
society, which allocates women in the family to expressive/affective
tasks and men to instrumental/adaptive ones (Parsons et al., 1955). As
a result of such role allocation, it becomes the mother's task to raise the
children and make this the main purpose of her life. Accordingly,
mothers hold center stage within the family while fathers remain

peripheral. It follows from this that the relations between mothers and children are qualitatively different than those between fathers and children. As long as the raising of children remains the central task of women, so long will the children (their thriving, development, and comportment) be of utmost importance for the → **identity** and the → **self–esteem** of mothers. Men, in contrast, may find more recognition and success in their professional lives. It is also true that most mothers tend to raise girls and boys differently, which accounts for a different development of self–identity.

Family therapists who share a systemic perspective cannot afford to disregard the wider social system in which a family is embedded. The social context of a sexist society in which men and women exert differing degrees of power also determines the → **rules** of a family. One cannot consider the individual members of a family as exchangeable elements of a system. Rather, the cultural–economic context codetermines which and how many options each member may have to change his or her behavior in a family. One needs to keep in mind that women presently have fewer and/or qualitatively different options than do men. A therapist who disregards this fact cannot be expected to practice multidirectional partiality.

Bograd, M. Family systems approaches to wife battering: A feminist critique. *American Journal of Orthopsychiatry 54:* 558–568, 1984.

Carter, E., Papp, P., Silverstein, O., & Walters, M. *Mothers and daughters, Monograph Series Vol. 1, No. 1.* Washington: Women's Project in Family Therapy, 1982.

Caust, B. L., Libow, J., & Raskin, P. A. Challenges and promises of training women as family systems therapists. *Family Process 20:* 439–447, 1981.

Chesler, P. *Women and madness.* New York: Doubleday, 1972.

Gilbert, L. A. Feminist therapy. In A. M. Brodsky & R. Hare-Mustin (Eds.), *Women and psychotherapy: An assessment of research and practice.* New York: Guilford Press, 1980, 245–265.

Gilligan, C. *In a different voice: Psychological theory and women's development.* Cambridge: Harvard University Press, 1982.

Gluck, N. R., Dannefer, E., & Milea, K. Women in families. In E. A. Carter & M. McGoldrick (Eds.), *The family life cycle: A framework for family therapy.* New York: Gardner Press, 1980, 295–327.

Goldner, V. Feminism and family therapy. *Family Process 24:* 31–47, 1985.

Gurman, A. S., & Klein, M. H. Marital and family conflicts. In A. M. Brodsky & R. Hare-Mustin (Eds.), *Women and psychotherapy: An Assessment of research and practice.* New York: Guilford Press, 1980, 159–188.

Hare-Mustin, R. T. A feminist approach to family therapy. *Family Process 17:* 181–194, 1978.

James, K., & McIntyre, D. The reproduction of families: The social role of family therapy? *Journal of Marital and Family Therapy 9:* 119–129, 1983.

Libow, J., Raskin, P., & Caust, B. Feminist and family systems therapy: Are they irreconcilable? *American Journal of Family Therapy 10:* 3–12, 1982.

Parsons, T., Bales, R. F., Olds, J., Zelditch, M., & Slater, P. E. *Family socialization and interaction process.* Glencoe, Ill.: Free Press, 1955.

Rich, A. *Of woman born: Motherhood as experience and institution.* New York: W. W. Norton & Co., 1976.

Wynne, L. C., & Frader, L. Female adolescence and the family: A historical view. In M. Sugar (Ed.), *Female adolescent development.* New York: Brunner/Mazel, 1979, 63–82.

* * * * * *

FIELD/ FIELD THEORY

The term "field," borrowed from the language of physics, is used in social psychology to denote the entirety of a process or situation perceived spatially or experientially. A perceiver structures the details of his or her perceptions into a coherent, perceptual field. Field theory posits, as does → **gestalt theory,** that the behavior and experience of an individual is configurally organized. The concomitant physiological processes are also assumed to be organized in configurations, e.g., → **patterns** of energy distribution or change. Viewed in this manner, field theory and gestalt theory can be considered to be concepts of → **epistemology.**

In family theory, gestalt theory, and social psychology, the concept of "field" is used as an → **analogue** to its usage in physics, where the term is defined as a continuous distribution of a quantity that is measurable in space and time. A field is located with a designation of coordinates in three spatial directions from a common point. When the measured property has magnitude but no direction, it is called a scalar. When it has direction, it is called a vector. The concept of vector is central in the formulations of Kurt Lewin (1935) who held, as do family theorists, that the context in which behavior occurs is of crucial importance. For Lewin, vector psychology was concerned with emotional forces having direction within the context of each person's "psychological life space" and the surrounding "social space." Lewin was concerned with symbolic or actual movement, or attempts at movement, from one region of the life space to another.

Lewin conceptualized tension and conflict as arising through imbalance in the emotional forces in the field, with the imbalance resulting in behavior that tends to restore equilibrium. Clearly, this formulation is similar to the concept of → **homeostasis** as used later in family theory. Lewin's formulations have been specifically used by Howells (1968), who spoke of "vector therapy," which is concerned with effecting changes in the pattern of the emotional forces "directed at individual family members, or at the family as a whole from the community and the culture" (p. 548). Stierlin's (1974) concept of → **centripetal/ centrifugal patterns** within the family also has links to field theory.

Stanton's (1984) "geodynamic balance theory of family process" is a more detailed and "modern" version of field theory. In Stanton's paradigm, people are viewed as traversing interpersonal orbits of → **closeness/ distance** among family members and between the family and "external systems" such as friendship networks, neighborhoods, and therapists. These orbits may be in phase with one another or run parallel but equidistant—keeping a constant distance. The extent to which two or more people have orbits that are both spatially close and parallel indicates the extent to which they might be considered enmeshed (→ **enmeshment**).

Thus, despite somewhat different terminologies, Lewin's field theory does correspond to important theoretical approaches in current systemic theory (→ **system/ systems theory**). Systemic theory gives greater emphasis to → **cybernetic** processes in social systems, whereas traditional field theory was more oriented to classical concepts of effects within force fields.

An essential similarity between field theory, gestalt theory, and more recent family therapy models is that subjective reality, or subjective models of the world (→ **paradigm/ model/ map**) are given full consideration. Individual as well as collective behavior is seen as being geared to this subjective reality. Thus, these three theoretical approaches also represent a constructivist (→ **constructivism**) theory of → **learning.**

Howells, J. G., & Lickorish, J. The family relations indicator. Edinburgh: Oliver & Boyd, 1968.

Lewin, K. A dynamic theory of personality. New York: McGraw-Hill, 1935.

Lewin, K. Principles of topological psychology. New York: McGraw-Hill, 1936.

Spitz, R. A genetic field theory of ego formation: Its implications for pathology. New York: International Universities Press, 1959.

Stanton, M. D. Fusion, compression, diversion, and the workings of paradox: A theory of therapeutic/systemic change. Family Process 23: 135–167, 1984.

Stierlin, H. Separating parents and adolescents: A perspective on running away, schizophrenia, and waywardness. New York: Quadrangle, 1974.

* * * * * *

FIRST INTERVIEW

The first interview plays a special role in family therapy. The major goals of the first interview are (1) diagnosis; (2) motivating family members to work on their problems; (3) drawing up of a therapeutic contract; and (4) setting the course for further therapeutic intervention. The strategies employed in the initial interview depend upon the treatment model that is applied (→ **models of family therapy**).

In the systemic family therapy model, the major task of the first interview is the formation of a hypothesis about the family dynamics; → **circular questioning** is the technique that best accomplishes this task. The interviewer proceeds to try out, validate, or reject hypotheses by means of this technique. If the therapist is able to understand the central aspects of the family's motivational dynamics and to introduce new perspectives, regardless of how confusing, seductive, or unsettling they may be, the family's motivation to continue therapy will be increased. Such motivation is of particular importance when the family's problems are chronic and a rigid, homeostatic situation prevails.

Framo, J. L. Marriage and marital therapy: Issues and initial interview techniques. In M. Andolfi & I. Zwerling (Eds.), *Dimensions of family therapy*. New York: Guilford Press, 1980, 49–71.

Franklin, P., & Prosky, P. A standard initial interview. In D. A. Bloch (Ed.), *Techniques of family psychotherapy: A primer*. New York: Grune & Stratton, 1973, 29–37.

Haley, J. *Strategies of psychotherapy*. New York: Grune & Stratton, 1963.

Haley, J. *Problem-solving therapy*. San Francisco: Jossey-Bass, 1976.

Selvini-Palazzoli, M., Boscolo, L., Cecchin, G., & Prata, G. Die erste Sitzung einer systemischen Familientherapie. *Familiendynamik 2:* 197–207, 1977.

Stierlin, H., Rücker-Embden, I., Wetzel, N., & Wirsching, M. *The first interview with the family* (translated by S. Tooze). New York: Brunner/Mazel, 1980.

Weber, T. T., McKeever, J. E., & McDaniel, S. H. A beginner's guide to the problem-oriented first family interview. *Family Process 24:* 1985.

* * * * * *

FLUCTUATION/ DISSIPATIVE STRUCTURES

Prigogine uses these terms to explain the spontaneous formation of structures in open systems. He describes how deviations from a relatively stable → **equilibrium** lead to new organizational forms (dissipative structures) with concomitant expenditure of energy. As applied to family systems by Dell and Goolishian (1981), it is *random* deviation from an original equilibrium that is the essential structuring factor, while non-equilibrium is the source of new order and organization, or "order through fluctuation" (Nicolis & Prigogine, 1977). Fluctuations in this sense are deviations from balanced conditions and lead to a progressive form of → **self-organization** by means of positive → **feedback loops.**

The application of Prigogine's concepts to social systems, such as families, is liable to misinterpretation. Prigogine's term "equilibrium" refers to the expenditure of energy. A dissipative structure consumes energy to maintain its structure. Thus, it is not to be equated with energetic (dynamic) equilibrium. However, as generally applied in cybernetics and family therapy, equilibrium refers to the maintenance of a structure (→ **morphogenesis**). Therefore, a steady supply of energy is the prerequisite for the equilibrium of a living system.

Although the transference of the concept of fluctuation to family organization involves a constant threat of conceptual confusion, what stands to be gained by the use of this concept is chiefly the recognition of the role of coincidence in the development of individuals and families. Whereas the concepts of equilibrium and → **homeostasis** lead one to think of behavior as goal–oriented, Prigogine's theory emphasizes the accidental character of change. Under certain conditions of disequilibrium, initially random behaviors can give the impetus for the formation of a new → **stability.** Fluctuations themselves are nothing more than trials and errors. In a constantly changing environment in which the system itself is involved in the processes of change, a fluctuation that was an error yesterday can be a success today. From the set of all possible fluctuations there thus develops, on the basis of chance *and* necessity, a new system of organization in accord with the principles of → **coevolution.**

The inherent danger in the use of the concept of fluctuation is that one can overlook or underestimate the unity of system and environment. The concept of equilibrium assumes that states of disequilibrium can be balanced out and disturbances adjusted by means of → **trial and error.** Whereas the concept of → **adaptability** situates the evolutionary impetus in the outside environment, the concept of fluctuation localizes this activity in the internal world of the system. Because we are dealing with circular processes (→ **circularity**), each of these concepts represents only one side of the coin.

The question as to whether the focus of creative activity lies within (in the structure) or without (in the environment) is largely ideological. If one places the focus of such activity within, one is easily led to the metaphysical concept of eternal "striving for higher things"; if one places the focus without, one runs the danger of seeing power and

166

control as being the only means of changing a system. It is probably more realistic to assume the "rule of cosmic laziness" (Russell, 1969, p. 25) in all those areas in which evolution plays a role, including families. This rule posits that everything a body (or system) does only occurs as a result of the imbalances occasioned by changes in its environment. As the reverse is also valid, and everything is interrelated with everything else, and processes that occur in time are not reversible, increasingly complex organizational forms do develop despite the phenomena of equilibrium. Only closed systems are able to maintain a state of equilibrium over a period of time. In family terms, this implies that lack of fluctuation and an over–emphasis on equilibrium will hinder the development of the family as well as the development of each family member.

Dell, P. F., & Goolishian, H. A. Order through fluctuation: An evolutionary epistemology for human systems. *Australian Journal of Family Therapy 2:* 175–184, 1981.

Fivaz, E., Fivaz, R., & Kaufmann, L. Agreement, conflict, symptom: An evolutionary paradigm. In R. Welter-Enderlin & J. Duss-von Werdt (Eds.), *Menschliche Systeme: Ein Rahmen für das Denken, die Forschung und das Handeln*. Zürich: Institut für Ehe und Familie, 1982, 140–178.

Glansdorff, P., & Prigogine, I. *Structure, stability and fluctuations*. London: Wiley, 1971.

Haken, H. *Synergetics: An introduction. Nonequilibrium phase transitions in physics, chemistry and biology* (2nd ed.). Berlin: Springer-Verlag, 1978.

Haken, H. *The signs of structure synergetics*. New York: Van-Nostrand Reinhold, 1984.

Nicolis, G., & Prigogine, I. *Self-organization in nonequilibrium systems: From dissipative structures to order through fluctuations*. New York: John Wiley & Sons, 1977.

Prigogine, I. Irreversibility as a symmetry breaking factor. *Nature 248:* 67–71, 1973.

Prigogine, I. Order through fluctuation: Self-organization and social system. In E. Jantsch & C. Waddington (Eds.), *Evolution and consciousness: Human systems in transition*. Reading, Mass.: Addison-Wesley, 1976, 93–133.

Prigogine, I. Time, structure, and fluctuations. *Science 201:* 777–785, 1978.

Prigogine, I. *From being to becoming: Time and complexity in the physical sciences*. San Francisco: Freeman, 1980.

Prigogine, I. Dialogue avec Piaget sur l'irréversibilité. *Archives de Psychologie 50:* 7–16, 1982.

Prigogine, I., & Stengers, I. *Order out of chaos: Man's new dialogue with nature*. New York: Bantam Books, 1984.

Russell, B. *The ABC of relativity* (3rd ed.). London: George Allen & Unwin, 1969.

* * * * * *

FREQUENCY OF SESSIONS

There are various opinions about the ideal frequency of therapeutic sessions, as well as the most effective spacing of the intervals between these sessions. These opinions differ according to the underlying → **models of family therapy** that are held by proponents of various schools of family therapy.

At one end of the spectrum, one finds the psychoanalytically oriented family therapists who believe that it is only possible to induce a profound and lasting change by means of protracted, reflective therapy that includes clarifying and working on the individual's personal and family life history, and analyzing the processes of transference, countertransference, and resistance. Accordingly, psychoanalytically oriented family therapy requires relatively frequent sessions, once a week or more often, as well as a relatively large number of sessions, about 50 or 60 in all, or more.

At the other end of the spectrum are located those therapy methods (e.g., → **systemic therapy** and → **brief therapy**) based on the concept of second–order → **change.** In systemic therapy, there are protracted intervals between therapy sessions, and a total of 10 to 12 sessions are usually considered to be sufficient. Originally, Selvini–Palazzoli et al. (1976) recommended one month as "the most opportune interval" in what they called "brief long therapy," that is, a small number of sessions spread out over one to two years. More recently, the Milan family therapists have worked with more variable time intervals. The impetus for change is generated during a systemic therapy session, but the "real change" is seen as taking place between the sessions; the system is given time to change. Such system–oriented theories are the basis of various approaches that advocate → **brief therapy.** (See also → **growth therapy.**)

de Shazer, S. *Patterns of brief family therapy: An ecosystemic approach.* New York: Guilford Press, 1982.

Selvini–Palazzoli, M. Why a long interval between sessions? The therapeutic control of the family-therapist suprasystem. In M. Andolfi & I. Zwerling (Eds.), *Dimensions of family therapy.* New York: Guilford Press, 1980, 161–169.

Selvini–Palazzoli, M., Boscolo, L., Cecchin, G., & Prata, G. Paradox and counterparadox: A new model for the therapy of the family in schizophrenic transaction. In J. Jørstad & E. Ugelstad (Eds.), *Schizophrenia 75: Psychotherapy, family studies, research.* Oslo: Universitetsforlaget, 1976, 283–294.

* * * * * *

FUSION/INTERSUBJECTIVE FUSION

Fusion is a condition of extreme → **binding** between two or more persons; it is a characteristic of pathologically close ("symbiotic") family systems. In such systems → **self/object differentiation** has been inadequately developed.

The term "intersubjective fusion" was coined by Boszormenyi–Nagy (1962, 1965) to denote family constellations in which subject–object positions have not been clearly negotiated. Dialogue in such families is not possible because the individuals are trapped in the web of an "amorphous We" (Boszormenyi–Nagy, 1965, p. 79). The term corresponds to a large extent to what other authors have described as → **undifferentiated family ego mass,** → **enmeshment,** → **pseudomutuality,** and symbiosis.

Boszormenyi–Nagy, I. The concept of schizophrenia from the perspective of family treatment. *Family Process 1:* 103–113, 1962.

Boszormenyi–Nagy, I. A theory of relationships: Experience and transaction. In I. Boszormenyi–Nagy & J. L. Framo (Eds.), *Intensive family therapy: Theoretical and practical aspects.* New York: Harper & Row, 1965, 33–86.

Mahler, M. *On human symbiosis and the vicissitudes of individuation. Vol. I, Infantile psychosis.* New York: International Universities Press, 1968.

Wynne, L. C., & Singer, M. T. Thought disorder and family relations of schizophrenics: II. A classification of forms of thinking. *Archives of General Psychiatry 9:* 199–206, 1963.

* * * * * *

◼ G ◼

GAME/STRATEGIC GAME

In everyday language, "game" defines a context (→ **context marking**) in which a distinction is made between "playing" and "being serious," between "fiction" and "reality." In mathematical game theory, "game" depicts the set of behaviors that are permissible in an interactional system. Strategic games differ from games of chance in that the result is not solely determined by coincidence.

A game can be seen as a model (→ **paradigm/model/map**). It is the sum of the → **rules** that are valid for an interactional system. Instances of such rules are: When A performs the activity of X, it is permissible for B to perform the activity Y; when B performs the activity Y, A is allowed to perform the activity Z, and so forth. Thus the games played in a system more or less describe its → **structure.**

There is a fundamental distinction to be made between two types of games within the framework of game theory. In "zero–sum games," only one player can win; the other loses. The sum of total wins and losses equals out at zero. In "non–zero–sum games," each player wins and loses to a certain extent. In the first type of game, the players have a competitive relation toward each other; in the latter type, they have a cooperative relationship. The formal distinction between these two types of games, however, may not always coincide with the short–term reality. For instance, if one is not capable of satisfying one's own needs, and another family member is required for the fulfillment of a need, strategic games are played. Every behavior in this context will be goal–directed and serve to gain a "profit." In a formally classified non–zero–sum game where one player profits 1% and the other player profits 99%, the player with a 1% profit will consider the game, *de facto*, as a zero–sum game because he or she, relatively speaking, has lost. The different game types, therefore, vary according to the perception of → **relational reality.** In a situation where a player experiences his or her relations to others as one of ongoing rivalry, there will be constant power struggles because of a fear of getting a bad deal, of being cheated, or of losing points. In another situation, one may maintain an attitude of cooperation and may fail to perceive real conflicts or even try to harmonize them away.

The differences between working and emotional relationships can be charted by using these two game models (Simon, 1983b). Games without rules for deciding when a player has won or lost or when the game is over are of necessity "games without end" (Simon, 1983a). Examples of this are → **malign clinch** and symmetrical escalation, in which both partners attempt to gain control over the relationship, but where there are no clearly defined and mutually agreed upon criteria for what constitutes having achieved this goal. Neither partner is willing to be placed in the inferior role, and neither is willing to give up the hope that he or she "still might win." Hence, the game never can be ended.

The concept of game in game theory is a neutral one that merely describes a behavior sequence that is goal–oriented. The everyday concept of "game" is evaluative in that it differentiates between "playing" and "being serious." If one overlooks this difference, confusion is likely to occur. This is often the case when psychoanalytically oriented therapists and systemically oriented therapists converse with one another. When the latter describe an interactional sequence as a "game," the former often will take this to mean a "game" in everyday language, i.e., that the persons involved are not seriously caught up in the events surrounding them but are merely "playacting."

Berne, E. *Games people play: The psychology of human relationships.* New York: Grove Press, 1967.

Haley, J. *Strategies of psychotherapy.* New York: Grune & Stratton, 1963.

Klaus, G., & Liebscher, H. *Wörterbuch der Kybernetik* (4th revised ed.). Frankfurt: Fischer, 1979.

Neumann, J. von, & Morgenstern, O. *Theory of games and economic behavior.* Princeton, N. J.: Princeton University Press, 1944.

Simon, F. B. Die Epistemologie des Nullsummen– und Nicht–Nullsummenspiels: Zur sozialen Logik von Individuationsstörungen. *Familiendynamik 8:* 341–363, 1983. (a)

Simon, F. B. Die Evolution unbewusster Strukturen. *Psyche 37:* 520–554, 1983. (b)

Watzlawick, P., Beavin, J. H., & Jackson, D. D. *Pragmatics of human communication: A study of interactional patterns, pathologies and paradoxes.* New York: W.W. Norton & Co., 1967.

* * * * * *

GAME THEORY

Game theory investigates conflict situations in strategic → **games,** largely with the help of mathematical methods. The tenets of game theory can also be applied in the analysis of interpersonal conflicts. Game theory is a specialized area of → **cybernetics.**

The founder of modern game theory is considered to be John von Neumann who, as early as 1928, published an article, "Towards a Theory of Social Games," which set forth fundamental ideas about the structure of strategic games. However, it was only after von Neumann and Oscar Morgenstern's joint publication in 1944 of *A Theory of Games and Economic Behavior* that the scientific world took notice of the theory. Today, game theory is used in mathematical analysis of conflict situations and interactions in many areas of science, e.g., in the evaluation of evolutionary (→ **coevolution**) processes (Eigen & Winkler, 1975) and the elucidation of the social behavior of animals in terms of their genetic determinants (Wickler & Seibt, 1977).

Game theory may be understood as a theory of interpersonal conflict and decision. The application of this to family processes is the result of the application of cybernetic concepts to these processes. The family is a system whose behavior is determined by family → **rules.** This behavior can be compared to a game in which all family members (the players) try to satisfy their individual needs or attain their individual goals. This striving for different needs and goals necessarily leads to conflict. Each individual family member must develop a → **strategy** in order to win or at least to keep losses minimal. Therapeutic methods can also be seen in the light of the game theory; the therapist must develop strategies to achieve therapeutic goals in the face of the individual's and/or family's → **resistance** to change (→ **strategic therapy**).

Eigen, M., & Winkler, R. *Laws of the game.* New York: Alfred A. Knopf, 1975.

Klaus, G., & Liebscher, H. *Wörterbuch der Kybernetik* (4th revised ed.). Frankfurt: Fischer, 1979.

Maynard Smith, J. *Evolution and the theory of games.* Cambridge: Cambridge University Press, 1982.

Neumann, J. von. Zur Theorie der Gesellschaftsspiele. *Mathematische Annalen 100*: 295–320, 1928.

Neumann, J. von, & Morgenstern, O. *Theory of games and economic behavior.* Princeton, N. J.: Princeton University Press, 1944.

Watzlawick, P., Beavin, J. H., & Jackson, D. D. *Pragmatics of human communication: A study of interactional patterns, pathologies and paradoxes.* New York: W. W. Norton & Co., 1967.

Wickler, W., & Seibt, U. Das Prinzip Eigennutz: Ursachen und Konsequenzen sozialen Verhaltens. München: Piper, 1977.

* * * * * *

172

GENERATIONAL BOUNDARIES

Generational boundaries are a special instance of the formation of →
boundaries. Boundary demarcations are of the utmost importance for
family functioning; they are the result of recognition and upholding of
the → **roles** within parental and child subsystems and the interactional
forms appropriate to these roles.

Most family therapists consider the blurring of generational boundaries and the resultant confusion of the family → **hierarchy** to be
dysfunctional. Representatives of structural therapy in particular have
as a therapeutic goal the active restructuring of the family system in
order that clear, but not overly rigid, generational boundaries can be
established. The blurring of generational boundaries is expressed in the
concepts of → **parentification,** → **perverse triangle,** → **rigid triad,** →
triangulation, and → **detouring of conflicts.**

The experience of family therapy suggests that children who hold
a position superior to their own parents in the family hierarchy, in
effect, assuming the status of their own grandparents, usually do so at
the cost of their own development. On the other hand, rigid generation
boundaries that allow no temporary role transposition also tend to be
pathogenic because the family is unable to function as an experimental
arena in which adult behavior can be learned. As is the case in all
boundary demarcation processes, a balance must be sought within the
family system between excessively open or closed interactional patterns. Such a balance enhances the developmental potential of the
individual because it supports adaptation to changing circumstances
while maintaining a stable frame of reference for behavior over clearly
defined periods of time. The strong complementary (→ **complementarity**) relationship that parents and small children have becomes more
symmetrical (→ **symmetry**) as children take on responsibilities that
make them more their parents' equals. In the course of the → **family
life cycle,** therefore, it is normal for generational boundaries to become
blurred at times, especially when the children themselves become
adult. A resumption and reversal of the old complementary relationship may ensue when aging parents become more dependent on their
own children.

Friedman, E. H. *From generation to generation: Family process in church and syna-
gogue.* New York: Guilford Press, 1985.
Haley, J. Toward a theory of pathological systems. In G. H. Zuk & I. Boszormenyi-
Nagy (Eds.), *Family therapy and disturbed families.* Palo Alto: Science and
Behavior Books, 1967, 11–27.
Hoffman, L. *Foundations of family therapy: A conceptual framework for systems
change.* New York: Basic Books, 1981.

Minuchin, S., Montalvo, B. G., Guerney, B., Rosman, B. L., & Schumer, F. *Families of the slums: An exploration of their structure and treatment.* New York: Basic Books, 1967.
Minuchin, S., Rosman, B. L., & Baker, L. *Psychosomatic families: Anorexia nervosa in context.* Cambridge: Harvard University Press, 1978.

* * * * * *

GENOGRAM

A genogram is a graphic representation of a multigenerational family constellation. Guerin and Pendagast (1976) call it "a roadmap of the family relationship system" that shows names, ages, dates of marriages, divorces, deaths, illnesses (including an → **identified patient**), key events, and other pertinent facts.

Genograms are widely used by family therapists both to provide an overview of the family system and to serve as a starting framework for inquiry about issues of → **alliance,** → **boundaries,** the context of → **networks,** and the → **family life cycle.**

The genogram may be extended to form a comprehensive "transitional map" that includes the "transitional position of the multigenerational family in society" and should include "the position of each individual and the family as a whole in life cycle stages, cultural origin, family form, and current status relative to other family members and the community" (Landau, 1982, p. 557). It is especially helpful in elucidating different rates of change of family subsystems, which can facilitate designing appropriate therapeutic interventions.

Guerin, P. J., & Pendagast, E. G. Evaluation of family system and genogram. In P. J. Guerin (Ed.), *Family therapy: Theory and practice.* New York: Gardner Press, 1976, 450–463.
Landau, J. Therapy with families in cultural transition. In M. McGoldrick, J. K. Pearce, & J. Giordano (Eds.), *Ethnicity and family therapy.* New York: Guilford Press, 1982, 552–572.
Lieberman, S. Transgenerational analysis: The genogram as a technique in family therapy. *Journal of Family Therapy 1:* 51–64, 1979.
Pendagast, E. G., & Sherman, L. A guide to the genogram family systems training. *The Family 5:* 3–14, 1977.
Stierlin, H., Wirsching, M., & Weber, G. How to translate different dynamic perspectives into an illustrative and experiential learning process: Role play, genogram and live supervision. In R. Whiffen & J. Byng-Hall (Eds.), *Family therapy supervision: Recent developments in practice.* New York: Grune & Stratton, 1982, 93–108.

* * * * * *

GESTALT/GESTALT THEORY

Wolfgang Köhler defined a "gestalt" as a unit or whole that stands out against its environment or background. The distinguishable elements of a gestalt are interdependent and, in their unified context, take on properties that cannot be ascribed to any single element but only to the configuration of the gestalt as a whole. This definition, which lays the foundation for gestalt theory and psychology, is almost identical to the concepts of → system and → structure in family therapy.

Gestalt psychology was developed by Wolfgang Köhler (1924, 1929), Kurt Koffka (1935), and Max Wertheimer (1950). These men opposed the tradition of reducing experience into fundamental elements and, instead, viewed wholes, systems, and organizational forms as the primary data of experience and behavior. In social psychology, Kurt Lewin's concept of → field/field theory is an extension of the holistic principles of gestalt psychology. Although gestalt psychology is indebted to the approaches of individual psychology, it has certain conceptual similarities to family theory and therapy. Formulations by the above–mentioned theorists on aspects of gestalt change anticipate certain insights in family theory on the importance of → change in structures (→ morphogenesis, → coevolution).

Gestalt theory is derived from gestalt psychology. Perls (1969a, b) and his associates (Perls, Hefferline, & Goodman, 1965), and Kempler (1973) describe the application of gestalt principles to the treatment of families. This type of therapy is a form of → growth therapy, which largely follows the principles of the encounter model (→ models of family therapy).

Bauer, R. Gestalt approach to family therapy. *American Journal of Family Therapy* 7: 41–45, 1979.
Kempler, W. *Principles of gestalt family therapy.* Los Angeles: Kempler Institute, 1973.
Koffka, K. *Principles of gestalt psychology.* New York: Harcourt, Brace, 1935.
Köhler, W. *Die physischen Gestalten in Ruhe und stationärem Zustand.* Erlangen: Philosophische Akademie, 1924.
Köhler, W. *Gestalt psychology.* New York: Liveright, 1929.
Lewin, K. *A dynamic theory of personality.* New York: McGraw-Hill, 1935.
Lewin, K. *Principles of topological psychology.* New York: McGraw-Hill, 1936.
Lewin, K. Field theory and experiment in social psychology: Conceptual methods. *American Journal of Sociology* 44: 868–896, 1939.
Perls, F.S. *Ego, hunger, and aggression.* New York: Random House, 1969. (a)
Perls, F.S. *Gestalt therapy verbatim.* Moab, Utah: Real People Press, 1969. (b)
Perls, F.S., Hefferline, R., & Goodman, P. *Gestalt therapy.* New York: Bell Publishing Co., 1965.

Wertheimer, M. Gestalt theory. *Social Research 11:* 78–99, 1944.
Wertheimer, M. Laws of organization in perceptual forms. In W. D. Ellis (Ed.), *A source book of gestalt psychology.* New York: Humanities Press, 1950, 71–88.

* * * * * *

GROWTH THERAPY

This term refers to types of therapy that are oriented toward the ideals and values of "humanistic psychology." Responsibility for one's actions, mutual acceptance and respect, and joint, cooperative solving of conflicts are important aspects of growth therapy.

The development of family therapy must be seen in conjunction with other contemporary social and cultural currents. Humanistic psychology and the various forms of therapy it has engendered have greatly influenced family therapists. Individual personal growth by means of therapeutic encounter is the goal of the encounter model (→ **models of family therapy**). The development of a stable feeling of personal worth (→ **self–esteem**) is only possible by means of communication between interactional partners who value each other as individuals. Hence, the goal of therapists of the humanistic or human potential movement is to create for their clients the experience of mutual esteem and respect in interpersonal interaction. Humanistic therapists believe that only by means of such experiences can the potential for individual growth be enhanced. Proponents of this movement are Boszormenyi–Nagy and Ulrich (1981) in their → **contextual therapy,** Paul (1967) in his → **mourning/operational mourning,** Satir (1964, 1972), whose form of therapy concentrates on the stabilization of the individual's feeling of self–esteem, and Whitaker (Whitaker & Keith, 1981) in his → **symbolic–experiential family therapy.** Bowen's (1978) school of family therapy can also be included as a more peripheral form of growth therapy.

The common goal of all growth–oriented therapies (→ **psychoanalytically oriented family therapy**) is to resolve emotional entanglements within the family and to promote individual differentiation and ego–strength of all family members. This approach is based on a → **multigenerational perspective** that posits that persons who remain bound to their families of origin by unresolved conflicts tend to "recruit" a third person, usually a member of the third generation (a child), to resolve or mitigate these conflicts (→ **parentification,** → **triangulation**). It is the task of the therapist, as an initiator of dialogue,

176

to break up deadlocked interactional patterns and to encourage the process of family–wide → **individuation.**

Beavers, W. R. *Psychotherapy and growth: A family systems perspective.* New York: Brunner/Mazel, 1977.
Boszormenyi-Nagy, I., & Ulrich, D. N. Contextual family therapy. In A. S. Gurman & D. P. Kniskern (Eds.), *Handbook of family therapy.* New York: Brunner/Mazel, 1981, 159–186.
Bowen, M. *Family therapy in clinical practice.* New York: Jason Aronson, 1978.
Friedman, E. H. *From generation to generation: Family process in church and synagogue.* New York: Guilford Press, 1985.
Kaplan, M. L., & Kaplan, N. R. Individual and family growth: A gestalt approach. *Family Process 17*: 195–205, 1978.
Kempler, W. *Experimental psychotherapy within families.* New York: Brunner/Mazel, 1981.
Napier, A. Y., & Whitaker, C. A. *The family crucible.* New York: Harper & Row, 1978.
Paul, N. L. The role of mourning and empathy in conjoint marital therapy. In G. H. Zuk & I. Boszormenyi-Nagy (Eds.), *Family therapy and disturbed families.* Palo Alto: Science and Behavior Books, 1967, 186–205.
Satir, V. *Conjoint family therapy: A guide to theory and technique.* Palo Alto: Science and Behavior Books, 1964.
Satir, V. Symptomatology: A family production. Its relevance to psychotherapy. In J. G. Howells (Ed.), *Theory and practice of family psychiatry.* Edinburgh: Oliver & Boyd, 1968, 663–670.
Satir, V. *Peoplemaking.* Palo Alto: Science and Behavior Books, 1972.
Whitaker, C. A., & Keith, D. V. Symbolic-experiential family therapy. In A. S. Gurman & D. P. Kniskern (Eds.), *Handbook of family therapy.* New York: Brunner/Mazel, 1981, 187–225.

* * * * * *

■ **H** ■

HARMONIZING

Harmonizing is a conflict–avoiding mechanism employed by individuals and families whereby a picture of total harmony is maintained and existing conflicts between individual family members are filtered out of awareness.

The opposite of harmonizing is the emphasizing of conflict whereby minor, everyday disagreements are magnified and there is a risk of permanent dissolution of the relationship. Both of these conflict–

management strategies evolve against the background of a disturbance in → **self/object differentiation** wherein impairment of harmony is perceived as a dire threat to the relationship while harmony itself becomes synonymous with fusion. In both cases, family members are only able to express feelings in one emotional area: in harmonizing, only love, tenderness, and concern, in emphasizing of conflict, only hostility, anger, and rejection. The more extreme forms of → **pseudomutuality/pseudohostility** are found in families with a schizophrenic member. Massive harmonizing attempts and denial of conflict characterize many families in which there are psychosomatic disturbances, particularly where there is an anorexic family member (→ **consensus sensitivity**).

Minuchin, S., Rosman, B. L., & Baker, L. *Psychosomatic families: Anorexia nervosa in context*. Cambridge: Harvard University Press, 1978.
Wynne, L. C., Ryckoff, I. M., Day, J., & Hirsch, S. I. Pseudo-mutuality in the family relations of schizophrenics. *Psychiatry 21:* 205–220, 1958.

* * * * * *

HEALING THROUGH ENCOUNTER

In this therapeutic model, experiential encounter between family members and between members of different generations is the central issue. The therapist initiates and sustains the encounter. The term "healing through encounter" was coined by the therapist Hans Trüb (1971) to characterize the relationship between therapist and client.

This model posits that encounter in the sense of positive → **mutuality** is blocked. Family members are at the same time in a situation of → **enmeshment** *and* are estranged from one another. Experiences of betrayal and injustice are topics that must be avoided in the family dialogue, otherwise feelings of guilt, shame, and fear would become intolerable. For this reason, it is the therapist's central task to initiate a dialogue with a view to creating trust between the family members and promoting an encounter about these forbidden topics. Such topics include → **family myths,** → **family secrets**, disappointed expectations, and justice withheld. The family therapist gets the family to pledge to "Try as best you can to talk to each other about things that you previously have not been able to talk about." As a consequence of the active, empathic action of the family therapist, the encounter between the estranged and deeply divided family members is set in motion. In the course of therapy, more and more essential layers of hidden conflict can be probed and covert conflicts brought out into the open, resulting in reconciliation and reunification of the family members, including the parents of the parents (the third generation).

This fundamental strategy of family therapy was first formulated by Boszormenyi-Nagy and Spark (1973). The family therapy that Napier and Whitaker present in their book, *The Family Crucible* (1978), can be viewed as an example of the "healing through encounter" model. Such therapy does not make use of the basic rule of psychoanalysis although it has some similarity to psychoanalytic therapy. Encounter therapy is less concerned to bring unconscious material to the conscious level than to enhance experience through the discussion of topics that are consciously avoided. As in psychoanalysis, the central goal of change may be tackled in relatively frequent sessions. This is in contrast to the model of healing through system change (→ **systemic therapy**), which usually spaces the sessions at longer intervals, for example, four weeks (→ **frequency of sessions**, → **models of family therapy**).

Boszormenyi-Nagy, I., & Spark, G. M. *Invisible loyalties: Reciprocity in intergenerational family therapy*. New York: Harper & Row, 1973.
Buber, M. [1923] *I and thou*. New York: Scribner's, 1958.
Napier, A. Y., & Whitaker, C. A. *The family crucible*. New York: Harper & Row, 1978.
Stierlin, H., Rücker-Embden, I., Wetzel, N., & Wirsching, M. *The first interview with the family* (translated by S. Tooze). New York: Brunner/Mazel, 1980.
Trüb, H. *Heilung durch Begegnung*. Stuttgart: Klett, 1971.

* * * * * *

HEALTHY/FUNCTIONAL FAMILIES

The concepts of health and normality cannot be defined simply or unequivocally for individuals or families. Offer and Sabshin (1966) differentiated four perspectives of normality: as health (reasonable absence of illness and distress), as utopia (ideal), as statistical average, and as transactional system involved in change processes over time. The fourth of these perspectives, which is probably most congenial to family therapists, may better apply to the term "functional families" rather than to "healthy" or "normal" families.

Dysfunctional families inevitably receive more attention from therapists than functional families. Recently, however, clinicians and family therapy theorists have taken an increased interest in the question of how functional and dysfunctional families differ. Therapeutic experiences as well as the scientific observation of symptom–free, "non–labeled" families over a period of years promise some answers to this question (Riskin, 1976), and essential differences in these two types of families have already been discovered. Differences are apparent in the areas of problem–solving strategies, emotional climate of the family, the ability to change during the course of the → **family life cycle,** the ability to balance → **closeness/distance** in the intrafamily relationships, and the formation of functional → **generational boundaries.** Obviously, the socioeconomic, community, and cultural contexts of families have to be taken into account in any assessment of what is called functional, healthy, or normal. An excellent comprehensive overview of conceptualizations about healthy family functioning has been assembled by Walsh (1982).

According to Satir (1964) as well as Riskin and McCorkle (1979), even families that function well solve problems with varying degrees of success and require varying amounts of time to do so. Functional families, however, avoid crippling or fixating their interactional processes. Conflicts often have a positive effect in functional families insofar as they encourage necessary developmental changes. Existing problems need not be located in an individual by naming a → **scapegoat.** According to Weakland et al. (1974), functional families are able to relinquish problem–solving strategies that have proven to be ineffective, and to develop creatively new strategies. This is in contrast to dysfunctional families that attempt to solve their problems by repeating unsuccessful strategies, by blaming, by emotional overreaction, or simply by denying that any problem exists. The "solutions" of dysfunctional families often become the problem (Watzlawick et al., 1974).

Reiss (1981) has found that "normal" families, "free of serious psychopathology," are generally "environment sensitive" and show qualities of mastery, cooperation, and openness to fresh experience. Also, environment–sensitive families function high on the dimension of "configuration," which, operationally, is "the contribution that the family, working as a group, makes to the problem's solution. . . . Family problem–solving effectiveness would represent the additional contribution the family group makes to whatever the individuals could achieve by acting separately" (Reiss, 1981, p. 73).

Wynne (1984) has approached the issue of "healthy" family functioning from a developmental, epigenetic standpoint. The processes of → **mutuality** are the processes of positively valued re–engagement and reshaping over time of relatedness, triggered by divergence and conflict, growth and aging, and discontinuities in individual and family life cycles. Mutuality builds upon the developmental phase of *joint* problem solving, a concept that was derived differently but is similar to Reiss's formulation of family problem–solving effectiveness. In Wynne's model, communication is the stage of relational development prior to joint problem solving. Wynne, Jones, and Al–Khayyal (1982) have operationalized the concept of healthy communication in a scoring system used with a → **family test,** the Consensus Family Rorschach (Loveland, Wynne, & Singer, 1963).

Beginning at the earliest developmental phase of attachment/ caregiving (Bowlby, 1969; Wynne, 1984), the issue of → **relational balance** between closeness and distance is paramount. This balance is determined in part by an optimal ratio between → **centripetal/ centrifugal patterns** in the family, and by the type and degree of related individuation or → **self/object differentiation.** During development, family members face a continuing task of reorienting and redefining their relationships to one another (→ **coevolution**). While the necessary restructuring of the family relationship network demands flexibility and the ability to adapt to changing circumstances, → **stability** is also necessary in order to maintain a reliable frame of reference within the family. In a functional family, stability and flexibility are balanced and have to be constantly renegotiated (→ **morphogenesis,** → **morphostasis**).

From 1955 to 1964, Westley and Epstein (1969) conducted a large study of college students and their families in Montreal, with the goal of relating emotional health of individuals to family functioning. Their most important finding was that positive emotional health of the children was closely related to a warm and supportive marital relationship, which did not necessarily depend on the parents being emotionally healthy as individuals.

Epstein and his coworkers (Epstein, Bishop, & Baldwin, 1982) delineated partly overlapping and partly differing dimensions of family functioning within three task areas: the Basic Task Area, which is concerned with supplying the family's instrumental, material needs; the Developmental Task Area, related to the life cycle; and the Hazardous Task Area, which reflects a family's ability to cope with unforeseen crises. For a family to function in a healthy manner, all three task areas must be handled effectively (→ **McMaster Model of Family Functioning**).

Olson et al. (1983) have studied normative functioning in 1,140 families from a stratified, randomly selected sample in seven stages of the family life cycle. Working within the → **Circumplex Model** with questionnaire data, they found major differences in the kind of marital and family strengths that were emphasized in the various stages of the family life cycle.

From the observation of characteristic communication patterns in dysfunctional families, Satir (1964) posited a number of communication rules that she believes will guarantee family functionality:

1. Transactions that are begun are also ended.
2. Questions are clearly asked and clearly answered.
3. Hostility and conflict are recognized and interpreted.
4. Family members are aware of themselves and of how they are perceived by others.
5. Each member is able to express differing opinions about each other and to communicate the hopes, fears, and expectations each has with regard to the interactional partners.
6. Difference of opinion is allowed.
7. Individual family members are able to choose between a number of behavioral alternatives. Each family member is able to learn from experience and to reject obsolete models.
8. The messages family members send to one another are clearly stated, and the corresponding behavior is congruent to the message; there exists minimal difference between the feelings manifested and the messages communicated. Thus, as few covert messages as possible are sent.

This type of functional communication style, which exhibits problem–solving abilities, capacity for internalization, and balancing between distance and closeness, makes related individuation possible.

A number of studies show that functional families exhibit a clear hierarchical organization with unequivocal, but not impermeable generational boundaries. In dysfunctional families, one observes with regularity a blurring of generational boundaries, with a suspension of hierarchical organization and the formation of pathological → **triangulation.** Finally, functional families characteristically are able to deal with problems about family → **justice** and the balancing of the family → **ledger of merits** in such a way that a positive mutuality is achieved (*cf.* Boszormenyi–Nagy & Spark, 1973).

In summary, Beavers (1977) presents a number of attributes that characterize a functional family:

1. A common system of values that can be religious in a traditional sense, but not necessarily so.
2. A concern for one another, an investment in the well–being of each member, an enhancement rather than a devaluation of one another, yet without foregoing the ability to delineate boundaries and to assert individual independence.
3. A large range of feelings, such as tenderness, joy, sorrow, hostility, etc., that allows for conflict, confrontation, and dispute, that is, the kind of interaction that tends to clear the air and lead to solutions.

182

4. A willingness to trust, to believe that people within and outside of the family are generally well–meaning and not rejecting and hostile.
5. A chance for dialogue that allows each to tune into what another is feeling and yet to maintain and express one's own position—a dialogue that strives for fairness, justice, and reconciliation.

Barcai, A. Normative family development. *Journal of Marital and Family Therapy 7:* 353–359, 1981.
Barnhill, L. Healthy family systems. *Family Coordinator 28:* 94–100, 1979.
Beavers, W. R. *Psychotherapy and growth: A family systems perspective.* New York: Brunner/Mazel, 1977.
Boszormenyi-Nagy, I., & Spark, G. M. *Invisible loyalties: Reciprocity in intergenerational family therapy.* New York: Harper & Row, 1973.
Bowlby, J. *Attachment and loss. Vol. I, Attachment.* New York: Basic Books, 1969.
Epstein, N. B., Bishop, D. S., & Baldwin, L. M. McMaster Model of family functioning: A view of the normal family. In F. Walsh (Ed.), *Normal family processes.* New York: Guilford Press, 1982, 115–141.
Ferreira, A. J., & Winter, W. D. Information exchange and silence in normal and abnormal families. *Family Process 7:* 251–276, 1968.
Ferreira, A. J., Winter, W. D., & Poindexter, E. J. Some interactional variables in normal and abnormal families. *Family Process 5:* 60–75, 1966.
Fisher, B. L., Giblin, P. R., & Hoopes, M. H. Healthy family functioning: What therapists say and what families want. *Journal of Marital and Family Therapy 8:* 273–284, 1982.
Hansen, C. Living in with normal families. *Family Process 20:* 53–75, 1981.
Jackson, D. D. The myth of normality. In P. Watzlawick & J. H. Weakland (Eds.), *The interactional view.* New York: W. W. Norton & Co., 1977, 157–163.
Kantor, D., & Lehr, W. *Inside the family: Toward a theory of family process.* San Francisco: Jossey-Bass, 1975.
Lewis, J. M., Beavers, W. R., Gossett, J. T., & Phillips, V. A. *No single thread: Psychological health in family systems.* New York: Brunner/Mazel, 1976.
Loveland, N. T., Wynne, L. C., & Singer, M. T. The Family Rorschach: A method for studying family interaction. *Family Process 2:* 187–215, 1963.
Mishler, E. G., & Waxler, N. E. The sequential patterning of interaction in normal and schizophrenic families. *Family Process 14:* 17–50, 1975.
Offer, D., & Sabshin, M. *Normality: Theoretical and clinical concepts of mental health* (revised ed.). New York: Basic Books, 1974.
Olson, D. H., McCubbin, H. C., Barnes, H., Larsen, A., Muxen, M., & Wilson, M. *Families: What makes them work.* Beverly Hills: Sage Publications, 1983.
Reiss, D. *The family's construction of reality.* Cambridge: Harvard University Press, 1981.
Reiss, D. The working family: A researcher's view of health in the household. *American Journal of Psychiatry 139:* 1412–1420, 1982.
Riskin, J. "Non-labeled" family interaction: Preliminary report on a prospective study. *Family Process 15:* 433–439, 1976.
Riskin, J., & McCorkle, M. E. "Nontherapy" family research and change in families: A brief clinical research communication. *Family Process 18:* 161–162, 1979.
Satir, V. *Conjoint family therapy: A guide to theory and technique.* Palo Alto: Science and Behavior Books, 1964.
Stabenau, J. R., Tupin, J., Werner, M., & Pollin, W. A comparative study of families of schizophrenics, delinquents, and normals. *Psychiatry 28:* 45–59, 1965.

Walsh, F. *Normal family processes: Implications for clinical practice.* New York: Guilford Press, 1982.

Watzlawick, P., Weakland, J. H., & Fisch, R. *Change: Principles of problem formation and problem resolution.* New York: W. W. Norton & Co., 1974.

Weakland, J. H., Fisch, R., Watzlawick, P., & Bodin, A. M. Brief therapy: Focused problem resolution. *Family Process 13:* 141–168, 1974.

Westley, W. A., & Epstein, N. B. *The silent majority.* San Francisco: Jossey-Bass, 1969.

Wynne, L. C. The epigenesis of relational systems: A model for understanding family development. *Family Process 23:* 297–318, 1984.

Wynne, L. C., Jones, J. E., & Al-Khayyal, M. Healthy family communication patterns: Observations in families "at risk" for psychopathology. In F. Walsh (Ed.), *Normal family processes: Implications for clinical practice.* New York: Guilford Press, 1982, 142–164.

* * * * * *

HIERARCHY

The concept of hierarchy has a threefold meaning in family therapy. First, it describes the function of → **power** and its structures in families. To this aspect of hierarchy belongs the differentiation of → **roles** for parents and children as well as of boundaries between generations (→ **generational boundaries**). Second, it refers to the organization of → **logical types,** or logical hierarchies, in which a lower order of logical types is an element within a higher order. Third, there is a hierarchy of increasingly inclusive → **system** levels. In this sense, an individual family member is a system that is logically subordinate to the system of the family in the same way that a family is subordinate to the system "community," and the community to the system "society" (Engel, 1977, 1980; Hoffman, 1981, pp. 54–56).

Family therapists such as Haley (1967), Madanes (1980), and Minuchin et al. (1967) see clear and unequivocal internal family hierarchy as the prerequisite for a family's functionality (→ **structural family therapy,** → **strategic therapy**). These authors base their theories in part on therapeutic experience and normative ideas about what a healthy family is (→ **healthy/functional families**). The reversal of the parent–child roles (→ **parentification**) is generally regarded as pathological. To clarify and correct incongruities in the family hierachy is hence of great importance (Madanes, 1978, 1980). A therapist needs to put the parents "in the driver's seat" (Minuchin, 1974). As described by Madanes and Haley (1977), one of the fundamental dimensions along which family therapists differ is in their emphasis on equality versus

184

hierarchy, that is, whether to regard participants as having equal status and power or to be concerned with hierarchical differences, especially generational.

The maintenance of a recursive network of logical hierarchies, which implies the discrimination of logical types, is of prime importance with regard to the treatment of schizophrenic thought disturbance (Bateson et al., 1956; Haley, 1955). The possibility of a correlation between particular disturbances in the family's hierarchical structure and schizophrenic thought disturbances must be taken into consideration (→ **category formation**).

Hofstadter (1979) has described the phenomenon of "strange loops" that occurs "whenever, by moving upwards (or downwards) through the levels of some hierarchical system, we unexpectedly find ourselves right back where we started. . . . Sometimes I use the term *Tangled Hierarchy* to describe a system in which a *Strange Loop* occurs" (p. 10). See → **logical types** for a discussion of the untangling of strange loops.

Bateson, G. Double bind, 1969. In G. Bateson, *Steps to an ecology of mind*. New York: Ballantine Books, 1972, 271–278.

Bateson, G., Jackson, D. D., Haley, J., & Weakland, J. H. Toward a theory of schizophrenia. *Behavioral Science 1:* 251–264, 1956.

Boszormenyi-Nagy, I., & Spark, G. *Invisible loyalties: Reciprocity in intergenerational family therapy*. New York: Harper & Row, 1973.

Engel, G. L. The need for a new medical model: A challenge for biomedicine. *Science 196:* 129–136, 1977.

Engel, G. L. The clinical application of the biopsychosocial model. *American Journal of Psychiatry 137:* 535–544, 1980.

Haley, J. Paradoxes in play, fantasy, and psychotherapy. *Psychiatric Research Reports 2:* 52–58, 1955.

Haley, J. *Strategies of psychotherapy*. New York: Grune & Stratton, 1963.

Haley, J. Toward a theory of pathological systems. In G. H. Zuk & I. Boszormenyi-Nagy (Eds.), *Family therapy and disturbed families:* Palo Alto: Science and Behavior Books, 1967, 11–27.

Hoffman, L. *Foundations of family therapy: A conceptual framework for systems change*. New York: Basic Books, 1981.

Hofstadter, D. R. *Gödel, Escher, Bach: An eternal golden braid*. New York Basic Books, 1979.

Keeney, B. P. *Aesthetics of change*. New York: Guilford Press, 1983.

Madanes, C. Predicting behavior in an addict's family: A communicational approach. In L. Wurmser (Ed.), *The hidden dimension*. New York: Jason Aronson, 1978, 368–380.

Madanes, C. The prevention of rehospitalization of adolescents and young adults. *Family Process 19:* 179–191, 1980.

Madanes, C. *Strategic family therapy*. San Francisco: Jossey-Bass, 1981.

Madanes, C., & Haley, J. Dimensions of family therapy. *Journal of Nervous and Mental Disease 165:* 88–98, 1977.

Minuchin, S. *Families and family therapy*. Cambridge: Harvard University Press, 1974.

Minuchin, S., Montalvo, B. G., Gurney, B., Rosman, B. L., & Schumer, F. *Families of the slums: An exploration of their structure and treatment.* New York: Basic Books, 1967.

Minuchin, S., Rosman, B. L., & Baker, L. *Psychosomatic families: Anorexia nervosa in context.* Cambridge: Harvard University Press, 1978.

* * * * * *

HOLISM

In this philosophical–epistemological school of thought, all aspects of reality—including inanimate matter, the animate–physical, and the psychic—form a unit and a whole. From this point of view, there can be said to exist a holistic school of medicine as well as of psychotherapy, which includes family and systemic therapy.

The essential concepts of holism were formulated in the 1920s by the Boer general and prime minister, Jan Christian Smuts, in his book *Die holistische Welt* (1938), in which he referred to an organizational principle inherent in nature. According to Smuts, only in the observation of the whole is it possible to grasp the tendency of nature to develop organizational forms of ever–increasing complexity. In this, he anticipated many of the concepts of systemic thought (→ **coevolution,** → **epistemology,** → **paradigm/model/map**). A holistic approach refutes the belief that wholes can be analyzed by the reductionistic methods of science, which attempt to reach a conclusion about the nature and behavior of the whole from a knowledge of the characteristics and behavior of the parts.

Arthur Koestler and John Raymond Smythies (1969), Marilyn Ferguson (1980), and Fritjof Capra (1982) have surveyed the application of a holistic perspective in various areas of science.

Capra, F. *The turning point.* New York: Bantam Books, 1982.

Ferguson, M. *The aquarian conspiracy.* Los Angeles: J. P. Tarchner, 1980.

Koestler, A., & Smythies, J. R. *Beyond reductionism: New perspectives in the life sciences.* New York: Macmillan Co., 1969.

Smuts, J. C. *Die holistische Welt.* Berlin: Metzner, 1938.

* * * * * *

HOMEOSTASIS

Homeostasis [Greek *homois*, similar; *stasis*, stand still] is the relatively steady internal state of a system that is maintained through self–regulation.

The concept of homeostasis was introduced into physiology in 1932 by Walter B. Cannon to explain the relative constancy of certain physiological dimensions, such as the constancy of the body temperature of mammals in the face of changing temperature in the external environment. In awe, Cannon (1932) stated:

When we consider the extreme instability of our bodily structure, its readiness for disturbance by the slightest application of external forces and the rapid onset of its decomposition as soon as favoring circumstances are withdrawn, its persistence through many decades seems almost miraculous. The wonder increases when we realize that the system is open, engaging in free exchange with the outer world, and that the structure itself is not permanent but is being continuously broken down by the wear and tear of action, and as continuously built up again by processes of repair.

The ability of living beings to maintain their own constancy has long impressed biologists. The idea that disease is cured by natural powers, by a *vis medicatrix naturae,* an idea which was held by Hippocrates (460–377 B.C.), implies the existence of agencies which are ready to operate correctively when the normal state of the organism is upset. More precise references to self–regulatory arrangements are found in the writings of modern physiologists. Thus the German physiologist, Pflüger, recognized the natural adjustments which lead toward the maintenance of a steady state of organisms when (1877) he laid down the dictum, "The cause of every need of a living being is also the cause of the satisfaction of the need." Similarly, the Belgian physiologist, Léon Fredericq, in 1885, declared, "The living being is an agency of such sort that each disturbing influence induces by itself the calling forth of compensatory activity to neutralize or repair the disturbance. . . .

The constant conditions which are maintained in the body might be termed *equilibria.* That word, however, has come to have fairly exact meaning as applied to relatively simple physico–chemical states, in closed systems, where known forces are balanced. The coordinated physiological processes which maintain most of the steady states in the organism are so complex and so peculiar to living beings—involving, as they may, the brain and nerves, the heart, lungs, kidneys and spleen, all working cooperatively—that I have suggested a special designation for these states, *homeostasis.* The word does not imply something set and immobile, a stagnation. It means a condition—a condition which may vary, but which is relatively constant.

It seems not impossible that the means employed by the more highly evolved animals for preserving uniform and stable their internal economy (i.e., for preserving homeostasis) may present some general principles for the establishment, regulation and control of steady states, that would be suggestive for other kinds of organization —even social and industrial—which suffer from distressing perturbations. Perhaps a comparative study would show that every complex organization must have more or less effective self–righting adjustments in order to prevent a check on its functions or a rapid disintegration of its parts when it is subjected to stress. (pp. 20–25)

Ashby (1952) extended this concept to → **cybernetic** → **systems** in general. There are certain systems that are capable of compensating for certain changes in the environment while maintaining relative stability in their own structures (→ **morphostasis**). In addition to morphostatic mechanisms, in which the structure remains relatively constant, there also exist mechanisms in which → **equilibrium** is maintained because a new equilibrium is achieved (→ **change, first and second order**) through changes in the form or content of the internal structure (→ **morphogenesis**).

Spiegel (1954) appears to have been the first to apply the term homeostasis when characterizing the doctor–patient relationship as a transactional system. Jackson (1957) was the first to apply the concept to family systems. Unlike Cannon, Jackson applied the term primarily to describe pathological mechanisms and systems. These pathological systems were characterized by excessive rigidity, a lack of flexibility, and limited potential for development.

Considering the difficulties in defining the concept of homeostasis and the realization that family systems cannot be adequately described if the focus is only on system *maintenance* while the aspects of system *change* are ignored, it has been debated of late whether the concept of homeostasis should be applied in family theory and therapy at all (→ **self–organization**).

Dell (1982) has criticized Jackson's concept that "the family is a rule–governed system" (1965) on the grounds that Jackson was regarding rules as not intrinsic to the system's function, but as homeostatic mechanisms imposed on the system. Similarly, Dell (1982) regards Cannon's concept of self–regulation as flawed on the grounds that if the self regulates the self, what regulates the aspect of the self that is doing the regulating? Dell proposes the concept of fit or → **coherence** as conceptually preferable to homeostasis.

Ashby, W. R. *Design for a brain*. London: Chapman & Hall, 1952.
Ashby, W. R. *An introduction to cybernetics*. London: Methuen, 1956.
Bateson, G. *Steps to an ecology of mind*. New York: Ballantine Books, 1972.
Cannon, W. B. *Wisdom of the body*. New York: W. W. Norton & Co., 1932.
Dell, P. F. Beyond homeostasis: Toward a concept of coherence. *Family Process 21:* 21–41, 1982.
Elkaïm, M. Von der Homöostase zu offenen Systemen. In J. Duss-von Werdt & R. Welter-Enderlin (Eds.), *Der Familienmensch*. Stuttgart: Klett-Cotta, 1980, 150–155.

Ferreira, A. J. Family myth and homeostasis. *Archives of General Psychiatry 9:* 457–463, 1963.

Gray, W., Duhl, F., & Rizzo, N. *General systems theory and psychiatry.* Boston: Little, Brown & Co., 1969.

Jackson, D. D. The question of family homeostasis. *Psychiatric Quarterly, Suppl. 31:* 79–90, 1957.

Jackson, D. D. Family interaction, family homeostasis and some implications for conjoint family psychotherapy. In J. H. Masserman (Ed.), *Individual and familial dynamics.* New York: Grune & Stratton, 1959, 122–141.

Jackson, D. D. The study of the family. *Family Process 4:* 1–20, 1965.

Jantsch, E. *The self-organizing universe.* Elmsford, N. Y.: Pergamon Press, 1980.

Klaus, G., & Liebscher, H. *Wörterbuch der Kybernetik* (4th revised ed.). Frankfurt: Fischer, 1979.

Miller, J. G. Living systems: The group. *Behavioral Science 16:* 302–398, 1981.

Miller, J. G. *Living systems.* New York: McGraw-Hill, 1978.

Speer, D. C. Family systems: Morphostasis and morphogenesis, or "Is homeostasis enough?". *Family Process 9:* 259–278, 1970.

Spiegel, J. P. The social roles of doctor and patient in psychoanalysis and psychotherapy. *Psychiatry 17:* 369–376, 1954.

Wertheim, E. S. Family unit therapy and the science and typology of family systems. *Family Process 12:* 361–376, 1973.

Wertheim, E. S. The science and typology of family systems II. Further theoretical and practical considerations. *Family Process 14:* 285–309, 1975.

* * * * * *

HYPNOTHERAPY

This is a form of directive, therapeutic communication based on a strictly complementary relationship (→ **complementarity**). The hypnotherapist induces a trance state in the client, placing the client in a position to use his or her own creative problem–solving abilities. The various hypnotherapeutic methods aim at the creation and stabilization of complementary client–therapist relationships either by means of circumventing the client's → **resistance** or by making resistance appear to be fruitless. Within the framework of this complementary relationship, the therapist is able to implant suggestions that alter pathology in the client's interpretative and behavioral schemata (→ **reframing**).

Hypnosis has become increasingly interesting for family therapists because it can be viewed in conjunction with questions regarding the development of the structures of human knowledge (→ **epistemology**) as well as the influence these structures have on interpersonal communication and individual behavior. If an individual's symptomatology makes sense in the → **context** of family interaction, there must exist a corresponding conscious or unconscious interpretative schema in that individual (→ **paradigm/model/map**). Hence, it is not objective reality that sustains the symptoms, but rather a person's subjective image of reality. From this perspective, therapy must aim at changing the client's subjective world view. The study of hypnotherapy as well as other forms of therapeutic communication has advanced the understanding of unconscious information processing, thereby making it possible to influence these unconscious processes therapeutically (→ **neurolinguistic programming**, → **psycholinguistics**).

Considerations of this sort preoccupied Gregory Bateson and the Palo Alto group. The → **double–bind** theory of schizophrenia developed by this research group is based on the tenets of a → **communication theory,** which owes much to the hypnotherapeutic approach. An exact analysis of the methods of the hypnotherapist Milton Erickson (Erickson & Rossi, 1979; Erickson, Rossi, & Rossi, 1976) played a central role in the development of this research (Haley, 1963, 1973). It may be said that Erickson's hypnotherapy, intermingled with the theoretical considerations of Bateson and colleagues, laid the central foundations for communication theory and → **communication therapy.**

Hypnotherapy progresses in a series of stages. In one approach, after the initiation of a trance state, the "utilization" phase is introduced, during which the client and the therapist tackle the problem previously explored in the pre–trance stage. It is left to the client to find the solution to his or her problem. In contrast to the widespread belief about and prejudice against hypnosis, the therapist does not directly influence the problem–solving process. Rather, the hypnotist initiates a search process until the client has found an acceptable solution. In the trance state, the client is questioned about the possibly positive aspects of the symptom that the client finds consciously disturbing. This → **positive connotation** on the symptom frees the client to employ his or her "creative self" to search for alternatives that retain these positive aspects.

After this, the "part of the person" that is responsible for the symptom is asked if the chosen alternative to the symptom is acceptable. In this way, an internal dialogue is initiated between the two sides of the ambivalence that characterizes a symptom. The goal of this strategy is to find a new behavior that can take over the adaptive functions of the symptom while discarding the suffering that the original symptom entails. Once this goal is achieved, a post–hypnotic suggestion is given that will cause the new behavior to manifest itself on the next occasion where it is needed. The therapist therefore uses a → **dominant** position to mobilize the client's innate problem–solving abilities. It is less that the symptoms are removed than that the range of behavior choices is expanded. There exists a marked similarity between these goals and methods and those of → **systemic therapy,** → **strategic therapy,** and communication therapy in general.

Bandler, R., & Grinder, J. *Patterns of the hypnotic techniques of Milton H. Erickson, M.D., Vol. I.* Cupertino, Cal.: META Publications, 1975. (a)

Bandler, R., & Grinder, J. *The structure of magic, Vol. I.* Palo Alto: Science and Behavior Books, 1975. (b)

Erickson, M. H., & Rossi, E. *Hypnotherapy: An exploratory casebook.* New York: Irvington, 1979.

Erickson, M. H., Rossi, E., & Rossi, S. *Hypnotic realities: The induction of clinical hypnosis and forms of indirect suggestion.* New York: Irvington, 1976.

Grinder, J., & Bandler, R. *The structure of magic, Vol. II.* Palo Alto: META Publications, 1976.

Grinder, J., & Bandler, R. *Trance-formations: Neuro-linguistic programming and the structure of hypnosis.* Moab, Utah: Real People Press, 1981.

Grinder, J., Delozier, J., & Bandler, R. *Patterns of the hypnotic techniques of Milton H. Erickson, M.D., Vol. II.* Cupertino, Cal.: META Publications, 1977.

Haley, J. *Strategies of psychotherapy.* New York: Grune & Stratton, 1963.

Haley, J. *Uncommon therapy: The psychiatric techniques of Milton H. Erickson, M. D.: A casebook of an innovative psychiatrist's work in short-term therapy.* New York: W. W. Norton & Co., 1973.

Ritterman, M. K., *Using hypnosis in family therapy.* San Francisco: Jossey-Bass, 1983.

Zeig, J. (Ed.). *A teaching seminar with Milton H. Erickson.* New York: Brunner/Mazel, 1980.

* * * * * *

HYPOTHESIS FORMATION

Within the framework of → **systemic therapy,** the formation of hypotheses is a necessary step in the preparation of therapeutic interventions. The formation, confirmation, and disconfirmation of hypotheses are methods of ordering, from a perspective of circular causality (→ **circularity**), all the information one has about a family.

The conscious or unconscious formation of hypotheses is the foundation for action in general, including therapeutic interaction. The continual formulation and reformulation of "circular" hypotheses, however, are characteristic of systemic family therapy. Systemic family therapy is based on → **cybernetic** or circular concepts of interaction, which often stand in contradiction to the structure of language and, hence, the structure of thought. From a cybernetic perspective, it is of utmost importance to view a family problem from as many vantage points as possible and also to question all tacit assumptions. The → **identified patient's** symptom often proves to be a brilliant move in the family's ongoing → **game.** This view of a symptom is in opposition to the negative connotation a symptom might have in the framework of everyday psychology because a symptom often has enormous, positive value for the family. The careful preparation of circular hypotheses can allow therapists to escape the → **lineality** of their own thoughts and enable them to develop intervention strategies that do justice to the circularity of the family's interactional processes (→ **paradigm/model/map**).

Bentovim, A. Toward creating a focal hypothesis for brief focal family therapy. *Journal of Family Therapy 1:* 125–136, 1979.
Haley, J. Ideas which handicap therapists. In M. M. Berger (Ed.), *Beyond the double bind: Communication and family systems, theories, and techniques with schizophrenics.* New York: Brunner/Mazel, 1978, 65–82.
Penn, P. Circular questioning. *Family Process 21:* 267–280, 1982.
Selvini-Palazzoli, M., Boscolo, L., Cecchin, G., & Prata, G. Hypothesizing-circularity-neutrality: Three guidelines for the conductor of the session. *Family Process 19:* 3–12, 1980.

IDENTIFIED PATIENT/SYMPTOM BEARER

This is the family member who presents, or is presented as the main symptom–bearer in the family.

The symptomatology or problem behavior of the identified or index patient usually is the primary reason for a family's initial contact with a therapeutic facility. The identified patient, however, is not necessarily that family member whom an objective observer would view as the person with the most, or the most conspicuous problems. From a systemic viewpoint, individual pathology is only comprehensible within the context of family interaction. For example, the illness of an adolescent can hinder changes in the context of the → **family life cycle,** and prevent the necessary cycle of → **separating parents and adolescents.** The processes of a family–wide → **coindividuation** become blocked and the painful steps toward separation are evaded.

Symptoms can also have an important function in other phases of family development. Parental conflicts can be diverted onto the child (→ **detouring of conflicts**, → **triangulation**), or the child can be used as a → **scapegoat** or delegate (→ **delegation**) in regulating the parents' needs for → **closeness/distance**. The function of symptoms is contradictory. On the one hand, symptoms serve to maintain a pathological form of → **homeostasis**; on the other hand, they offer the family an opportunity for change (the identified patient's symptoms having led the family into therapy). If individual symptoms are not recognized as an expression of the entire family structure and are treated only as an individual problem, there is a danger of → **symptom shift**, wherein the homeostatic function of the symptom will be taken on by another family member.

Bursten, B. Family dynamics, the sick role, and medical hospital admissions. *Family Process 4:* 206–216, 1965.

Byng-Hall, J. Symptom bearer as marital distance regulator: Clinical implications. *Family Process 19:* 355–365, 1980.

Erikson, K. T. Patient role and social uncertainty—a dilemma of the mentally ill. *Psychiatry 20:* 263–274, 1957.

Fishbein, H. D. The identified patient and stage of family development. *Journal of Marital and Family Therapy 8:* 57–61, 1982.

Richardson, H. *Patients have families.* New York: Commonwealth Fund, 1948.

Satir, V. Symptomatology: A family production. Its relevance to psychotherapy. In J. G. Howells (Ed.), *Theory and practice of family psychiatry.* Edinburgh: Oliver & Boyd, 1968, 663–670.

Vogel, E. F., & Bell, N. W. The emotionally disturbed child as the family scapegoat. In E. F. Vogel & N. W. Bell (Eds.), *The family.* Glencoe, Ill.: Free Press, 1960, 412–427.

* * * * * *

IDENTITY/SELF-DEFINITION

Identity is the feeling of being someone who, despite changing circumstances, physical states, and relationships, remains constant—in other words, exhibits continuity and coherence.

The work of Erik H. Erikson (1950, 1956, 1959, 1968) in particular emphasizes the importance of the feeling of identity in the context of psychoanalytic thought. The concept of identity is closely linked to the concepts of self and → **individuation**. In the framework of family theory and therapy, this concept is of particular importance with regard to experiences undergone by schizo–present families. In these families, the development of a feeling of identity as well as → **self/object differentiation** was shown to be largely dependent upon communication and interaction processes.

Erikson pointed out that the concept of identity is practically synonymous with what various authors have depicted as "Self." George Herbert Mead (1934) speaks of "self–concept"; Harry Stack Sullivan (1953b) of "self–system"; Paul Schilder (1951), Paul Federn (1952), and others, of "fluctuating experience of self"; Heinz Hartmann (1950) and Edith Jacobson (1954) of "Self"—to mention only the most important of these authors. According to Erikson (1959), three interdependent processes determine the development of identity: "1. the process of organismic organization of bodies within the time–space of the life–cycle (evolution, epigenesis, libido development, etc.); 2. the process of the organization of experience by ego synthesis (ego space–time, ego defenses, ego identity, etc.); 3. the process of the social organization of ego organisms in geographic–historical units (collective space–time, collective life plan, ethos of production, etc.)" (p. 48).

An individual's perception of self centers on the personal unity of self and the intrasystemic perception of physical being, as well as the extrasystemic perception of forms of social organization. The development of an identity (individuation) may be seen as a continual working out of a definition of self (Watzlawick, Beavin, & Jackson, 1967). Not only is a concept of self and objects as bodies with continuity and coherence worked out, but also the rules that govern behavior.

Feeling or definition of self is an aspect of an internal map (→ **paradigm/model/map**) by which individuals orient their lives. This internal map is a subjective model of the world that is, for the most part, charted and transmitted within one's family of origin. To the extent that new experiences change this model of the world, one's definition of self is also changed. In the context of a normal, individual life cycle, this inevitably occurs as a result of a → **crisis.**

That which is denoted as the identity of an individual, family, or group in the terminology of social psychology is, from the perspective of systemic theory, a phenomenon of → **coherence.** Specific elements— be they idiosyncrasies, behaviors, or relationships—develop together in the dimension of time; in other words, they have a common history and can be separated from other phenomena of everyday reality (→ **boundaries,** → **system,** → **coevolution,** → **script**).

Anonymous. Toward the differentiation of a self in one's own family. In J. Framo (Ed.), *Family interaction: A dialogue between family researchers and family therapists.* New York: Springer Publishing Co., 1972, 111–166.

Arieti, S. *The intrapsychic self: Feeling, cognition, and creativity in health and mental illness.* New York: Basic Books, 1967.

Bateson, G. *Steps to an ecology of mind.* New York: Ballantine Books, 1972.

Erikson, E. H. *Childhood and society.* New York: W. W. Norton & Co., 1950.

Erikson, E. H. The problem of ego identity. *Journal of the American Psychoanalytic Association 4:* 56–121, 1956.

Erikson, E. H. Identity and the life cycle: Selected papers. *Psychological Issues, Monograph No. 1,* 1959.

Erikson, E. H. *Identity, youth and crisis.* New York: W. W. Norton & Co., 1968.

Federn, P. *Ego psychology and the psychoses.* New York: Basic Books, 1952.

Fogarty, T. F. Systems concepts and the dimensions of self. In P. J. Guerin (Ed.), *Family therapy: Theory and practice.* New York: Gardner Press, 1976, 144–153.

Hartmann, H. Comments on the psychoanalytic theory of the ego. *Psychoanalytic Study of the Child 5:* 74–95, 1950.

Hartmann, H. *Essays on ego psychology.* New York: International Universities Press, 1964.

Hofstadter, D., & Dennet, D. (Eds.). *The Mind's I: Fantasies and reflections on self and soul.* New York: Penguin Books, 1981.

Jacobson, E. The self and the object world. *Psychoanalytic Study of the Child 9:* 75–127, 1954.

Kagan, J., & Moss, H. A. *Birth to maturity: A study in psychological development.* New York: John Wiley & Sons, 1962.

Karpel, M. A. Individuation: From fusion to dialogue. *Family Process 15:* 65–82, 1976.

Kegan, R. *The evolving self: Problems and process in human development.* Cambridge: Harvard University Press, 1979.

Kernberg, O. F. *Object relations theory and clinical psychoanalysis.* New York: Jason Aronson, 1976.

Kohut, H. *The analysis of the self. A systematic approach to the psychoanalytic treatment of narcissistic personality disorders.* New York: International Universities Press, 1971.

Kohut, H. *The restoration of the self.* New York: International Universities Press, 1977.

Mead, G. H. *Mind, self, and society.* Chicago: University of Chicago Press, 1934.

Schilder, P. *The image and appearance of the human body.* New York: International Universities Press, 1951.

Selman, R. L. *The growth of interpersonal understanding: Developmental and clinical analyses.* New York: Academic Press, 1980.

Simon, F. B. *Der Prozess der Individuation: Über den Zusammenhang von Vernunft und Gefühlen.* Göttingen: Vandenhoeck & Ruprecht, 1984.

Sullivan, H. S. *Conceptions of modern psychiatry: The first William Alanson White Memorial Lectures* (2nd ed.). New York: W. W. Norton & Co., 1953. (a)

Sullivan, H. S. *The interpersonal theory of psychiatry.* New York: W. W. Norton & Co., 1953. (b)

Watzlawick, P., Beavin, J. H., & Jackson, D. D. *Pragmatics of human communication: A study of interactional patterns, pathologies and paradoxes.* New York: W. W. Norton & Co., 1967.

* * * * * *

INDIVIDUATION/RELATED
INDIVIDUATION/COINDIVIDUATION

From the vantage point of family dynamics, concepts about individuation and differentiation mainly apply to the formation of individual (→ identity) and psychic → boundaries. One can say that animate beings have been striving toward higher levels of individuation for about a billion years; this process entails the danger of hypo–individuation as well as hyper–individuation. Related individuation, according to Stierlin et al. (1980), is a general principle whereby a higher level of individuation both demands and makes possible a correspondingly higher level of relatedness. This concept highlights the necessity (task) of reconciliation faced by all higher life forms, especially human beings. As a rule, this task includes a family–wide coindividuation in which each family member determines the conditions for the individuation of the other members.

Hyper–individuation is characterized by a delineation of boundaries that are too impermeable and rigid; independence becomes isolation, separation becomes hopeless loneliness, and all exchange with others terminates. Hypo–individuation, which somewhat overlaps with the concepts of → binding and fusion, is characterized by the failure to demarcate boundaries; the boundaries between self and others are too diffuse, permeable, or brittle. Loss of individuation through fusion with or absorption by stronger organisms becomes a threat. Each step toward further individuation entails new demands with respect to communication and reconciliation. At given times, and in a certain manner, otherwise solid and protective boundaries must open up; separation and mutuality, individuation and solidarity, autonomy and dependence, must be reconciled with one another. This process leads to ever–increasing complexity in relationship structures and the processes of development, and it provides the conditions that make coindividuation and → coevolution possible. Heinz Werner's (1957a) "Principle of Differentiation and Integration" proposed that, in the course of any type of development, a condition of relative globality and limited differentiation will resolve itself into a state of increasing differentiation, articulation, and hierarchical integration.

Related individuation is a concept developed during the Heidelberg Family Therapy Institute's research on family dynamics. As applied to human beings, it refers to the ability to differentiate one's internal world into clearly articulated feelings, needs, expectations, internal and external perceptions, and so forth. This highly differentiated, internal world must then be marked off from the external world, particularly with regard to the ideas, needs, expectations, and demands of others. The ability to achieve definition and demarcation of self is especially important and at the same time put to the greatest test in human relationships that are characterized by or based upon closeness and empathy (→ **self/object differentiation**). Generally speaking, one can say that the concept of related individuation refers to a greater extent to cognitive processes, while the concept of binding emphasizes affective and/or libidinous elements. It must be said, however, that a differentiation between affect and libido will always be difficult (→ **affect logic**).

In the practice of family therapy, one encounters three types of dysfunctional or limited individuation, which can be understood as subcategories of hyper–individuation and hypo–individuation: (1) symbiotic fusion in which one's own experience, one's feeling of self, one's gender role or occupational role becomes merged with those of another; (2) a rigid, autistic detachment from others that often has mistrustful, paranoid overtones; and (3) an ambivalent switching between the extremes of fusion and detachment.

Information about the quality and level of a couple's or family's individuation can be obtained by listening to their dialogue. As a rule, the more developed the degree of related individuation is, the greater will be the quality of positive → **mutuality.** The literature on family therapy has generated many terms to describe families with disturbed or limited individuation. Until recently, the phenomenon of hypo–individuation was in the forefront of discussion. A list of terms to describe this phenomenon include: Bowen's (1961) → **undifferentiated family ego mass** and self–differentiation deficiency, Wynne's (1965) → **collective cognitive chaos,** Reiss's (1971) → **consensus sensitivity,** Boszormenyi–Nagy's (1965) → **fusion,** Minuchin et al.'s (1967) → **enmeshment,** and Karpel's (1976) description of forms of disturbed individuation in the relationship of couples. Hypo–individuation is also related to Wynne et al.'s (1958) concepts of → **pseudomutuality/ pseudohostility,** as well as to the concept of binding.

In the area of psychoanalysis, there are links between the concepts of "individuation–separation" (Mahler, 1968) and Jacobson's (1954) term "self/object differentiation." Here, an understanding of schizophrenic disturbances plays an important role (see Schulz & Kilgalen, 1969; Stierlin, 1959). The processes of individuation and coindividuation can also be understood as forms of → **self–organization** of psychic structures of individual family members within their reciprocal relationships to one another (→ **ego psychology,** → **object relations theory**).

It needs to be mentioned that the concept of individuation plays a central role in the analytical psychology of C. G. Jung: "Individuation means becoming a single, homogeneous being, and, in so far as 'individuality' embraces our innermost, last, and incomparable uniqueness, it also implies becoming one's own self" (Jung, 1959, p. 143).

A related term of "pseudo–individuation" was developed by Stanton and associates (1978) to denote behavior that appears to indicate individuation but that also serves to keep the person displaying it in an infantile and dependent state, such as the addict who, when intoxicated, appears both "distant" (individuated) and helpless or dependent (hypo–individuated).

Boszormenyi–Nagy, I. A theory of relationships: Experience and transaction. In I. Boszormenyi–Nagy & J. L. Framo (Eds.), *Intensive family therapy: Theoretical and practical aspects*. New York: Harper & Row, 1965, 33–86.

Bowen, M. The family as the unit of study and treatment. *American Journal of Orthopsychiatry 31:* 40–60, 1961.

Jacobson, E. The self and the object world. *Psychoanalytic Study of the Child 9:* 75–127, 1954.

Jung, C. G. In V. S. de Laszlo (Ed.), *The basic writings of C. G. Jung*. New York: Modern Library, 1959.

Karpel, M. A. Individuation: From fusion to dialogue. *Family Process 15:* 65–82, 1976.

Mahler, M. *On human symbiosis and the vicissitudes of individuation. Vol. I, Infantile psychosis*. New York: International Universities Press, 1968.

Mahler, M. S., Pine, F., & Bergman, A. *The psychological birth of the human infant: Symbiosis and individuation*. New York: Basic Books, 1975.

Minuchin, S., Montalvo, B. G., Guerney, B., Rosman, B. L., & Schumer, F. *Families of the slums: An exploration of their structure and treatment*. New York: Basic Books, 1967.

Reiss, D. Varieties of consensual experience: I. A theory for relating family interaction to individual thinking. *Family Process 10:* 1–28, 1971. (a)

Reiss, D. Varieties of consensual experience: II. Dimensions of a family's experience of its environment. *Family Process 10:* 28–35, 1971. (b)

Reiss, D. Varieties of consensual experience: III. Contrasts between families of normals, delinquents, and schizophrenics. *Journal of Nervous and Mental Disease 152:* 73–95, 1971. (c)

Schulz, C. G., & Kilgalen, R. K. *Case studies in schizophrenia*. New York: Basic Books, 1969.

Sears, R. R., Rau, L., & Alpert, R. *Identification and child rearing*. Stanford: Stanford University Press, 1965.

Simon, F. B. *Der Prozess der Individuation: Über den Zusammenhang von Vernunft und Gefühlen*. Göttingen: Vandenhoeck & Ruprecht, 1984.

Stanton, M. D., Todd, T. C., Heard, D. B., Kirschner, S., Kleiman, J. I., Mowatt, D. T., Riley, P., Scott, S. M., & Van Deusen, J. M. Heroin addiction as a family phenomenon: A new conceptual model. *American Journal of Drug and Alcohol Abuse 5:* 125–150, 1978.

Stierlin, H. The adaptation to the "stronger" person's reality. *Psychiatry 22:* 143–152, 1959.

Stierlin, H. Aspects of relatedness in the psychotherapy of schizophrenia. *Psychoanalytic Review 51:* 355–364, 1964.

Stierlin, H. *Psychoanalysis and family therapy: Selected papers*. New York: Jason Aronson, 1977.

198

Stierlin, H. Family dynamics in psychotic and severe psychosomatic disorders: A comparison. *Family Systems Medicine 1* (4): 41–50, 1983.

Stierlin, H., Rücker-Embden, I., Wetzel, N., & Wirsching, M. *The first interview with the family* (translated by S. Tooze). New York: Brunner/Mazel, 1980.

Werner, H. *Comparative psychology of mental development* (revised ed.). New York: International Universities Press, 1957. (a)

Werner, H. The concept of development from a comparative and organismic point of view. In D. B. Harris (Ed.), *The concept of development*. Minneapolis: University of Minnesota Press, 1957, 125–148. (b)

Winawer, H. The Heidelberg concept: An introduction to the work of Helm Stierlin and his associates. *Family Systems Medicine 1* (4): 36–40, 1983.

Wynne, L. C. Some indications and contra-indications for exploratory family therapy. In I. Boszormenyi-Nagy & J. L. Framo (Eds.), *Intensive family therapy: Theoretical and practical aspects, with special reference to schizophrenia*. New York: Harper & Row, 1965, 289–322.

Wynne, L. C. The epigenesis of relational systems: A model for understanding family development. *Family Process 23:* 297–318, 1984.

Wynne, L. C., Ryckoff, I. M., Day, J., & Hirsch, S. I. Pseudo-mutuality in the family relations of schizophrenics. *Psychiatry 21:* 205–220, 1958.

* * * * * *

INFORMATION

For various practical and theoretical reasons, the concept of information [Latin *informare,* to form, to shape] needs to be more clearly defined than is usually the case in everyday speech. Information is not synonymous with "meaning." The amount of information does not specify the content value, truthfulness, or purposes of the information. The amount of information in a statement is a measure of how much the statement reduces the number of possible outcomes, that is, how much it increases → **negentropy.**

Wherever information is exchanged, one can speak of a communication system. The amount of information that the behavior of one interactional partner has for another depends first of all on whether both have access to the same → **code** and, secondly, on the quality of transmission. A code determines whether and to what extent interactional partners can communicate with one another, and whether a communication system can be maintained. Information is not an inherent, static attribute of some object, but an aspect of interaction between a "sender" and a "receiver." Thus, Gregory Bateson's (1979) definition of information is "any difference that makes a difference" (p. 250). The reaction to information depends on whether interactional partners recognize a difference *as* a difference; if so, information can be said to be created (→ **information theory**).

In family therapy, the manner in which a family deals with information is a decisive factor in diagnosis and therapy. The introduction of information into a system (be it individual or family) has the potential of changing that system. Rigid family systems have at their disposal mechanisms that allow them to ignore new information. An excellent example of this is the → **rubber fence** phenomenon. Further, all forms of → **resistance** can be seen as an attempt to exclude or depreciate information. If differences are not acknowledged as such, they cannot make a difference. Therapy, therefore, can only be effective when the therapist succeeds in getting the family to use available information to reorganize itself. One way to achieve this is the use of → **circular questioning,** which systematically promotes the awareness of differences within the family.

Bateson, G. Cybernetic explanation. *American Behavioral Scientist 10:* 29–32, 1967.
Bateson, G. *Steps to an ecology of mind.* New York: Ballantine Books, 1972.
Bateson, G. *Mind and nature: A necessary unity.* New York: E. P. Dutton, 1979.
Klaus, G., & Liebscher, H. *Wörterbuch der Kybernetik* (4th revised ed.). Frankfurt: Fischer, 1979.
Selvini-Palazzoli, M., Boscolo, L., Cecchin, G., & Prata, G. Hypothesizing-circularity-neutrality: Three guidelines for the conductor of the session. *Family Process 19:* 3–12, 1980.
Shannon, C., & Weaver, W. *The mathematical theory of communication.* Urbana, Ill.: University of Illinois Press, 1949.

* * * * * *

INFORMATION THEORY

This is an area in the field of → **cybernetics** wherein formal aspects of information transmission, processing, and storage are examined by means of mathematical methods.

Information theory in its current form was pioneered by Shannon and Weaver (1949). Information theory does not concern itself with the content of communicational processes, but focuses instead on the formal aspects of these processes. As applied in family therapy, this analytical procedure has shed new light on interpersonal processes (→ **communication theory,** → **analogue/digital communication,** → **entropy/negentropy**).

Bateson, G. Cybernetic explanation. *American Behavioral Scientist 10:* 29–32, 1967.
Klaus, G., & Liebscher, H. *Wörterbuch der Kybernetik* (4th revised ed.). Frankfurt: Fischer, 1979.
Rapoport, A. The promise and pitfalls of information theory. In W. Buckley (Ed.), *Modern systems research for the behavioral scientist: A sourcebook.* Chicago: Aldine Publishing Co., 1968, 137–142.
Shannon, C., & Weaver, W. *The mathematical theory of communication.* Urbana, Ill.: University of Illinois Press, 1949.
Wiener, N. *Cybernetics, or control and communication in the animal and the machine* (2nd ed.). Cambridge: Massachusetts Institute of Technology Press, 1975. (2nd ed. originally published, 1954; 1st ed. originally published, 1948.)

* * * * * *

INNER OBJECTS

Within the framework of psychoanalytic theory, objects are defined essentially by their functions; they permit a conceptual understanding of relationships or interchanges between intrapsychic and transactional processes. Thus, family and systemic processes can also be described with this concept.

According to Stierlin (1970), inner objects perform three central functions in psychoanalysis:

1. They serve as an internal frame of reference. In this sense they are best depicted as object representations, the more or less exact copies (within the psyche) of external objects. The ability to represent external objects internally requires, among other things, memory and the ability to symbolize; without it, we would not be able to find our bearings in external reality.

2. Inner objects serve as guideposts for the conduct of present and future interpersonal relationships. In this extended sense of the concept, an inner object is best described as an "imago." An imago may serve as a standard against which one measures one's choices among external objects. For instance, a young woman may be unconsciously governed in her choice of a marital partner by an inner object that bears the characteristics of her father. Inner objects, therefore, guide the course of our relationships much as a gyroscope unerringly keeps a ship at sea on its course. (Stierlin notes the "gyroscopic function" of inner objects, which also possesses a dynamic, directive element.)

3. Inner objects contribute to the relative autonomy of the individual. They create the possibility of increased independence by allowing the individual to enter into a relationship with aspects of himself or herself. Inner objects thus constitute internal resources and are at the same time the prerequisites for an internal dialogue. It is for this reason that Stierlin speaks of the *autonomy-promoting* function of inner objects.

These three functions of inner objects are interdependent and overlap to a great extent with the functions of the ego (→ **ego psychology/ego functions/ego organization**). Disturbances of these functions manifest themselves in various forms of individual and family pathology, accompanied by disturbances of the process of → **individuation.** Disturbances of individual functioning of inner objects can have varying consequences depending on prevailing → **relational modes** and the tasks related to individual development and the → **family life cycle.** This is particularly apparent in the process of → **separating parents and adolescents.**

Fairbairn, W. *Psychoanalytic studies of the personality.* London: Tavistock Publications, 1952.

Guntrip, H. *Schizoid phenomena, object-relations and the self.* New York: International Universities Press, 1969.

Kernberg, O. F. *Object relations theory and clinical psychoanalysis.* New York: Jason Aronson, 1976.

Modell, A. H. *Object love and reality: An introduction to a psychoanalytic theory of object relations.* New York: International Universities Press, 1968.

Spitz, R. A. Genèse des premières relations objectales. *Revue Française de Psychoanalyse 28,* 1954.

Stewart, R. H., Peters, T. C., Marsh, S., & Peters, M. J. An object-relations approach to psychotherapy with marital couples, families, and children. *Family Process 14:* 161–178, 1975.

Stierlin, H. The functions of "inner objects." *International Journal of Psycho-analysis 51:* 321–329, 1970.

Winnicott, D. W. Transitional objects and transitional phenomena. In D. W. Winnicott, *Collected papers: Through paediatrics to psycho-analysis.* New York: Basic Books, 1958, 229–242.

ISOMORPHISM

Isomorphism [Greek *isos,* equal; *morphe,* form, configuration] is a precise mathematical concept borrowed by systems theorists. Hofstadter (1979) notes that the word "applies when two complex structures can be mapped onto each other, in such a way that to each part of the structure there is a corresponding part in the other structure, where 'corresponding' means that the two play similar roles in their respective structures" (p. 49). The copy "preserves all the information in the original theme, in the sense that the theme is fully recoverable from any of the copies." Isomorphism, therefore, is "an information–preserving transformation" (p. 9).

The concept of isomorphism helps generate hypotheses about essential aspects of human thought and communication processes. Structures (e.g., the relational field of a therapist) gain a special significance when they are isomorphic with respect to other structures (e.g., the relational field of an → **identified patient** or a family). Given that the essential task of family therapists is to understand and influence structures and → **patterns,** therapists must decide to what extent patterns of behavior and communication are isomorphic in, for example, a nuclear family, the parents' families of origin, the therapeutic system (family plus therapists), the treatment team subsystem, and the families of origin of the therapists. In terms of practical therapeutic work, the concept of isomorphism is of particular importance within the framework of the → **binocular theory of change** (de Shazer, 1982), in consultation to family therapists (Penn & Sheinberg, 1985), and in the therapeutic technique of → **reframing.**

In responding to criticisms of general system theory, Bertalanffy (1968) commented that "the use of 'analogy' (isomorphism, logical homology)—or, what amounts to nearly the same, the use of conceptual and material models—is not a half-poetical play but a potent tool in science. Where would physics be without the analogy or model of 'wave' . . . ?" Bertalanffy argues that "[i]t is commonplace in cybernetics that systems which are *different materially* . . . may be *formally identical,*" that "the researcher has to work out the common structure (flow diagram), and [that] this may be of incomparable value" (p. 20; emphases added).

Bertalanffy, L. von. General systems theory—A critical review. In W. Buckley (Ed.), *Modern systems research for the behavioral scientist: A sourcebook.* Chicago: Aldine Publishing Co., 1968, 11–30.

de Shazer, S. *Patterns of brief family therapy: An ecosystemic approach.* New York: Guilford Press, 1982.

Hofstadter, D. R. *Gödel, Escher, Bach: An eternal golden braid.* New York: Basic Books, 1979.

Penn, P., & Sheinberg, M. Is there therapy after consultation? A consultation map in five steps. In L. C. Wynne, S. H. McDaniel, & T. T. Weber (Eds.), *The family therapist as systems consultant.* New York: Guilford Press, in press.

■ J ■

JOINING/WORKING ALIANCE/THERAPEUTIC SYSTEM

Joining refers to a specific form of working relationship between therapist and family members. In the context of this alliance, the therapist "joins" the family in order to facilitate changes in the family structure (→ **structural family therapy**).

The therapist gains acceptance of and admittance into the family by acknowledging and promoting the family's strengths, by respecting the family's existing hierarchies and value systems, by supporting the family subsystems, and by confirming each individual's feeling of self–worth. The therapist thus becomes, in a sense, a part of the family. In his or her socially acknowledged role as an expert, the therapist then proceeds to take over the leadership within the family. In this role, the therapist is able to change the rules that govern the family system. The therapist can support different family members at different times, or can deliberately upset their → **relational balance.** If these strategic maneuvers are done in rapid succession, one speaks of the "stroke and kick" method. In any event, the therapeutic goal is to break up rigid patterns and to create new experiences. The therapist must join the family because "outside" intervention will be resisted. According to Minuchin et al. (1978), "The therapist has to join the field of stabilized family interactions in order to observe them. He must gain experiential knowledge of the controlling power that the system exerts. Only then can he challenge the family interactions with any knowledge of the range of thresholds that the system can tolerate" (p. 94).

This method of joining is usually less explicitly described by other authors, but it is characteristic of family therapy in general. As a rule, if a stable alliance between therapist and family is not achieved, any interventions aimed at changing the structure of the family will remain unsuccessful, and contact between the two parties breaks off after the first interview. This state of affairs can be explained conceptually in a number of ways. From a systemic perspective, the family system is capable of change only when it is receptive to information that challenges or changes existing structures. In order for this to take place, a therapist–family system must be superimposed. In such a system, the socially established authority of the therapist creates a pre–condition for the family and therapist to come together.

Whether the authority of the therapist is accepted and whether its

204

potential for change is effective are determined to a great extent by the course of the → **first interview,** as well as by the competence and empathy of the therapist in that interview. In the first interview, the therapist must establish a bond with the family and initiate a working relationship with each individual family member. In conjunction with the method of joining, the therapist can place the family in a therapeutic → **double bind,** which makes it impossible for the family to miss the next session. Selvini–Palazzoli and her colleagues (1980) find it effective to use a questioning strategy that constantly surprises and holds the attention of the family members, but at the same time gives them the feeling of having been understood. All family therapists agree that establishing a stable alliance with the family is a prerequisite for successful therapy. Although very few therapists have been able to describe accurately what exactly it is that they do, family therapy researchers agree that top priority should be given to investigation of the process dimension of the therapeutic alliance. Methods for doing so are emerging in current research, with helpful leads from individual psychotherapy research (Bordin, 1979).

Bordin, E. S. The generalizability of the psychoanalytic concept of the working alliance. *Psychotherapy: Theory, Research and Practice 16:* 252–260, 1979.
Minuchin, S. *Families and family therapy.* Cambridge: Harvard University Press, 1974.
Minuchin, S., Rosman, B. L., & Baker, L. *Psychosomatic families: Anorexia nervosa in context.* Cambridge: Harvard University Press, 1978.
Selvini-Palazzoli, M., Boscolo, L., Cecchin, G., & Prata, G. Hypothesizing-circularity-neutrality: Three guidelines for the conductor of the session. *Family Process 19:* 3–12, 1980.

* * * * * *

JUSTICE

Justice—or, more precisely, the just distribution of a family's resources—is a central issue in family relationships. These resources can be material, such as money and property, or intangible, such as love, recognition, status, and security. One may thus speak of material and immaterial resources that become the subject of an ongoing "equity dialogue."

As a rule, parents initially decide about the distribution of resources. They can pass on wealth and status (e.g., of a family name) and, thus, affect the family as well as the family in relation to its environment.

Parents may also give the immaterial resources of love, recognition, and protection. The distribution of resources, however, can also operate in the other direction; through its laughter, growth and development, joy in life, and affection, a child can give its parents a vital measure of happiness. Decades later, the child as adult will determine to some extent its parents' happiness by a willingness to show or to withhold both varieties of resources. This represents a dynamics of distribution that is vertical, for example, extends throughout a number of generations, *and* horizontal in that it also occurs between members of the same generation, for example, marriage partners and siblings (→ **multigenerational perspective**).

The dynamics of distribution, whether horizontal or vertical, are related to questions regarding each family member's debits and credits, or obligations and claims within the family's → **ledger of merits** (Boszormenyi–Nagy & Spark, 1973). These questions remain vital throughout the lives of the members of a family. According to Boszormenyi–Nagy, as long as the family exists, so does the active accounting in its ledger of merits. This ledger is a record of the good and the bad one has received or not received, the good and the bad one has dealt out or has withheld; and the accounts often remain open throughout a succession of generations. The concept of account–keeping has the same motivational force behind it for family behavior that the drive to satisfy instinctual needs has in psychoanalytic theories. The ledger of merits is the basis for and the expression of a never–ending equity dialogue, and a final settlement of accounts may take several generations (→ **contextual therapy**).

Therapeutic attempts to effect an equity dialogue and a settlement of accounts presents a problem because of the difficulty of defining the nature of the material and immaterial resources to be distributed (→ **power**). Therapeutic and everyday experience shows that material and immaterial resources are often interfused with one another in the consciousness of the family. On a symbolic level, money and property can represent love, recognition, and security; they can also represent the opposite, a bad conscience and a poor substitute for lack of love, recognition, and concern. What constitutes a desirable resource, therefore, is determined not only by its just or unjust distribution, but also by one's perception of its value.

The same problem exists with regard to the concepts and claims of entitlement and indebtedness, which may be perceived and evaluated differently by different family members. These perceptions and evaluations are for the most part internalized (unconscious), but they are active in the determination of what is considered to be the just or unjust distribution of family resources, what is considered to be a debt "already settled" or still "owing." This accounting system and perception of specific value is part of the family's → **epistemology,** which guides as well as limits its sense of fairness and justice (→ **relational ethics**). Experience in family therapy shows that in disturbed families, individual perceptions about justice are in irreconcilable conflict with each other, and an equity dialogue is long overdue. This deadlock can develop into a tragic drama of continuous retribution, and the ability of the therapist to perceive and influence the course of this drama will call for ethical sensitivity and the skillful use of → **multidirectional partiality.**

Boszormenyi–Nagy, I. Loyalty implications of the transference model in psychotherapy. *Archives of General Psychiatry 27:* 374–380, 1974. (a)
Boszormenyi–Nagy, I. Ethical and practical implications of intergenerational family therapy. *Psychotherapy Psychosomatics 24:* 261–268, 1974. (b)
Boszormenyi–Nagy, I., & Spark, G. M. *Invisible loyalties: Reciprocity in intergenerational family therapy.* New York: Harper & Row, 1973.
Boszormenyi–Nagy, I., & Ulrich, D. N. Contextual family therapy. In A. S. Gurman & D. P. Kniskern (Eds.), *Handbook of family therapy.* New York: Brunner/Mazel, 1981, 159–186.
Stierlin, H. *Delegation und Familie.* Frankfurt: Suhrkamp, 1978.
Stierlin, H., Rücker-Embden, I., Wetzel, N., & Wirsching, M. *The first interview with the family* (translated by S. Tooze). New York: Brunner/Mazel, 1980.

* * * * * *

■ L ■

LEARNING/STAGES OF LEARNING

Learning may be understood as the assimilation and task–oriented storage of information. Of importance are the → **logical types** of the assimilated information; a series of stages, a logical hierarchy in learning has been posited, which is determined by the logical type of the learned material. The stages in learning correspond to the abstract sequence from "learning" to "learning to learn."

In 1942, in his work on deutero–learning, Bateson (1972, pp. 159–176) made the distinction between *"proto–learning"* (primary learning) and *"deutero–learning"* (secondary learning) in an attempt to describe how the learning experiences in one context can be transposed to another context. This, of course, makes learning more economical and leads to quicker results. Irrespective of the actual material to be learned, what one learns is more or less *the capacity to learn in the process of learning.* Learning is thus accomplished simultaneously on a number of levels; these levels, however, differ in their logical typology and, thus, in their degree of abstraction. In the process of learning, rules for further learning are established and a form of generalization takes place.

In his later work, Bateson (1972, pp. 279–308) expanded his logical classification of the process of learning by introducing the concepts of Learning 0, Learning I, Learning II, Learning III, and Learning IV. *Learning 0* refers to changes that occur in a system when the simplest assimilation of information about an external event takes place. For example, an event is given a meaning that remains constant: The ringing of a church bell a specific number of times denotes a specific hour of the day. The direct linkage of event and meaning does not need to be constantly corrected once it has been learned. If the linkage does alter, then learning of a higher category, Learning I, takes place.

Learning I is what is commonly understood as "learning" in experimental psychology laboratories. It refers to specific changes in stimulus response or perception brought about by → **trial and error.** A stimulus represents an internal or external signal and is situated within a specific → **context.** The stimulus is no longer an isolated phenomenon but, rather, the signal for a specific context of meaning. This is thus a form of → **metacommunication,** which induces a preliminary selection from among all the many possible ways of responding. This → **context marking** makes it possible to apply previous experience in similar contexts to the current situation. The dog in Pavlov's experiment, for example, did not initially salivate in Context A (the ringing of a bell). In Context B, after the bell is rung, the dog is presented with food, and it naturally salivates in the presence of nourishment. Context A and B are thus linked, and the dog salivates upon hearing the bell. The different contexts are classified, or logically typologized, according to the criterion "food presented" or "no food presented." It is no longer necessary to analyze each situation anew because a context has been marked and a selection of adequate behaviors are already present. Thus, behavior becomes more economical.

Learning II is learning on a higher logical plane. It also is referred to as "deutero–learning," "set–learning," or "learning to learn." In Learning II, the marked context (of Learning I) becomes modified through processes of trial and error. An individual has at his or her disposal a supply of contexts and matching context markings, as well as patterns of responses to such contexts (stimuli) as reward, punishment, and so forth. This marking of contexts is based upon a specific →

punctuation. "Subjective" punctuation is what the layman refers to as a person's "character." Specific behavior of self or others can be defined as being either stimulus or response to stimulus. The time sequence construed from this leads to stimulus–response chains that become context–specific. A change in punctuation, that is, a redefinition of what is a stimulus and what is a response (or what is cause and what is effect) takes place at the level of Learning II. The *manner* in which events are punctuated is the result of type–II Learning.

To recapitulate, learning always takes place in a context, and the learners are themselves part of that context. In Learning 0, learners perceive only those aspects of the context that lie outside their own spheres. In Learning I, learners are able to locate themselves in relation to external events. In Learning II, learners are able to change that relation.

Learning III may be understood as a change that may take place as a result of Learning II. It takes place on a metalevel and, hence, belongs to a higher logical type. Learning III questions the premises of established punctuation processes in communication sequences. It is doubtful whether this type of learning can be adequately expressed by means of traditional language because language itself conveys punctuation patterns that denote type–II Learning. The practice of Zen, with its paradoxes and imperatives, places all forms of punctuation in question. Bateson considered the symptoms usually labeled psychotic as the attempts at type–III Learning. In → **double–bind** situations, type–III learning is necessary.

Learning IV is only possible where the biological prerequisites for learning can be changed. Thus, Learning IV cannot be expected to take place on the individual plane, but rather at the level of a species undergoing genetic changes. Here the ontogenetic potentiality for learning (in the development of the individual) has reached its limits and phylogenetic mechanisms (in the development of the species) become active.

In that learning at any level is always defined as change, there exists a correlation between the stages of learning and the stages of → **change.** Learning within one stage is generally first–order change, in other words, change in the structure itself does not occur. Learning at the next higher stage implies second–order change and, therefore, an attendant change in structure. Learning processes in individuals and the physical evolutionary development of a species are both stochastic processes. Stochastic processes involve the selection, via reinforcement and elimination, of random changes that are of significance for the survival of the species. On the level of the individual, this involves behavior selection and the construction of a subjective → **epistemology** as the foundation of information assimilation and processing (→

information, → information theory, → communication theory, → paradigm/model/map).

If one views learning as a process of structure formation in a system (regardless of whether these are mental or material structures), then learning with its ever–increasing levels of abstraction is the realization of the principles of → **self–organization.** The development of the world's mind (the world's learning process) is then equivalent to the concept of → **coevolution** (see Bateson, 1979).

Bandura, A. *Social learning theory*. Englewood Cliffs, N.J.: Prentice-Hall, 1974.
Bateson, G. *Steps to an ecology of mind*. New York: Ballantine Books, 1972.
Bateson, G. *Mind and nature: A necessary unity*. New York: E. P. Dutton, 1979.
Guntern, G. Das syngenetische Programm und seine Rolle in der Verhaltenssteuerung. In J. Duss-von Werdt & R. Welter-Enderlin (Eds.), *Der Familienmensch*. Stuttgart: Klett-Cotta, 1980, 97–115.
Piatelli-Palmarini, M. (Ed.). *Language and learning: The debate between Jean Piaget and Noam Chomsky*. London: Routledge & Kegan Paul, 1980.

* * * * * *

LEDGER OF MERITS

According to Ivan Boszormenyi–Nagy, a "ledger of merits" is an accounting system that develops overtly or covertly in groups (usually in families). On the basis of these accounts, a just balance between individual "debits" and "merits" is negotiated across generations.

Boszormenyi–Nagy coined the term "ledger of merits" in an attempt to express metaphorically the importance of the human desire for justice. If a family member sacrifices personal interests and personal potential for another or for the good of the family, he or she feels entitled to and will expect to be repaid for this sacrifice. If this debt is not paid by the beneficiary generation, the next generation is often called upon to "cancel the debt." Thus, such patterns of behavior as → **parentification** are passed on from one generation to the next. The model of the family–wide attempt at or actual balancing of merits over the course of generations is the foundation of Boszormenyi–Nagy's → **contextual therapy.** This model contains some problematic suppositions about the lineal (→ **lineality**) nature of causality; yet the idea that an individual's symptoms are an expression of his or her → **loyalty** toward the family and are, therefore, to be valued as a positive contribution (→ **positive connotation**), does correspond to a circular concept of causality (→ **circularity**).

Boszormenyi–Nagy, I., & Krasner, B. R. Gruppenloyalität als Motiv für politischen Terrorismus. *Familiendynamik 3:* 199–208, 1978.
Boszormenyi–Nagy, I., & Krasner, B. R. Trust-based therapy: A contextual approach. *American Journal of Psychiatry 137:* 767–775, 1980.
Boszormenyi–Nagy, I., & Spark, G. M. *Invisible loyalties: Reciprocity in intergenerational family therapy.* New York: Harper & Row, 1973.
Boszormenyi–Nagy, I., & Ulrich, D. N. Contextual family therapy. In A. S. Gurman & D. P. Kniskern (Eds.), *Handbook of family therapy.* New York: Brunner/Mazel, 1981, 159–186.

* * * * * *

LEFT/RIGHT HEMISPHERES OF THE BRAIN/LATERALITY

Neurological research has demonstrated laterality in the performance of cognitive tasks by the left and right hemispheres of the brain. The left hemisphere (dominant in right–handed persons) translates perceptions into logical and syntactical representations, that is, it is specialized for verbal and analytic tasks, for language, and for language–bound thought. The right hemisphere (nondominant in right–handed persons) is specialized for spatial and synthetic tasks, for the comprehension of complex associations, patterns, forms, and structures. These different functions (left hemisphere = analytical–dissection; right hemisphere = synthetic–wholistic) correspond to modalities of → **analogue/digital communication**).

Investigations of persons who have lost the connection between the brain hemispheres ("split–brain patients") because of an operation or accident have shown that each brain hemisphere has differing functions in the areas of human perception and behavior. (See Gazzaniga, 1970; Kimura, 1973; Sperry, 1970; and Walsh, 1978, as well as overviews in Hoppe, 1975; Popper and Eccles, 1977; and Watzlawick, 1978). The results of these investigations have been applied in both psychoanalytic theory and → **communication theory.** The activities or functions of the right hemisphere are, phenomenologically speaking, those that Freud described as "primary process," and those of the left hemisphere correspond to what he called "secondary process." From the perspective of communication theory, it can be assumed that the comprehension of analogue communication forms is essentially the task of the (usually) nondominant hemisphere, whereas digital—and in particular language—communication is processed in the (usually) dominant side of the brain. Both parts of the normal brain are connected, so that digital and analogue information is integrated.

The "Two Brain Theory" has become popular in the field of psychotherapy because it offers a speculative formulation of the processes of empathy and intuition. Each side of the brain breaks down the circularity of reciprocal relationships (between parts and wholes) differently and arrives at different conclusions from the same objective facts (Simon, 1984). However, because the schematic classification of isolated perceptual functions into "parts" and "wholes" represents a logical absurdity (each *is* the prerequisite of the other), one should view these neurological findings as indicating nothing more than a different orientation in the overall unfolding of information processing.

Certainly, one of the reasons why these neurological findings have resonated in family therapy discussions is that they appear to provide biological answers to questions about → **epistemology.** The difference between thinking and feeling, → **lineality** and → **circularity,** individual–oriented thinking and system–oriented thinking, language and gesture, insight and empathy, "head and heart," is often uncritically regarded as being equivalent to the difference in the functions of the brain hemispheres.

The rational tradition of the Enlightenment was based on a lineal view of cause–and–effect relationships, in other words, left–brain thinking. As the dangerous limitations of narrowly lineal models became apparent, there was the temptation to overcorrect, to use the incompleteness of the lineal models of thought as proof of the failure of rationality, and to replace rationality with irrationality. This was especially apparent in the fields of art (Dadaism) and literature (symbolist poetry, stream–of–consciousness "fiction"), as well as in the revived interest in Oriental mysticism (Zen). In the less esthetic spheres, models based on right–brain thinking, with its emphasis on a wholistic approach (→ **holism**), did provide a needed corrective to the analytic–dissecting mode of left–brain thinking. Both models of thought, however, are based on partial views of reality. It is just as irrational to give primacy to the language–bound left hemisphere as it is to give primacy to the "speechless" (so to speak) but pattern–perceptive right hemisphere; both must be brought together in synthesis.

Gazzaniga, M. S. *The bisected brain.* New York: Appleton-Century-Crofts, 1970.
Hoppe, K. Die Trennung der Gehirnhälften. *Psyche 29:* 929–940, 1975.
Kimura, D. The asymmetry of the human brain. *Scientific American 228:* 70–80, 1973.
Popper, K., & Eccles, J. *The self and its brain: An argument for interactionism.* New York: Springer Publishing Co., 1977.
Simon, F. B. *Der Prozess der Individuation: Über den Zusammenhang von Vernunft und Gefühlen.* Göttingen: Vandenhoeck & Ruprecht, 1984.

Sperry, R. Perception in the absence of neocortical commisures. *Research Publication of the Association of Nervous and Mental Disease 48:* 123–138, 1970.
Springer, S. P., & Deutsch, G. *Left brain, right brain.* New York: Freeman, 1981.
Walsh, K. *Neuropsychology.* Edinburgh: Livingstone, 1978.
Watzlawick, P. *The language of change: Elements of therapeutic communication.* New York: Basic Books, 1978.

* * * * * *

LINEALITY/LINEAL CAUSALITY/LINEARITY

These terms designate certain forms of causal relationships and/or mathematical relations.

A causal relationship is called lineal when feedback processes are not involved, in other words, when the cause–and–effect sequence does not lead back to the starting point. The lineal nature of cause and effect is generally held to be self–evident, a fact that is reflected in everyday language. In the literature on family therapy, this presupposition is widely denoted as "lineal causality." The concept leads to confusion, however, when one works on the basis of a → **cybernetic** model. With reference to the cybernetic model, which is oriented toward a mathematical model, Bateson (1979) describes linearity and lineality: "*Linear* is a technical term in mathematics describing a relationship between variables such that when they are plotted against each other on orthogonal Cartesian coordinates, the result will be a straight line. *Lineal* describes a relation among a series of causes or arguments such that the sequence does not come back to the starting point. The opposite of *linear* is *nonlinear*. The opposite of *lineal* is *recursive*" (p. 228).

Everyone is familiar with linear, mathematical graphs that plot the variables "X" and "Y" so that an increase (or decrease) in one involves a constant and proportional increase (or decrease) in the other. Both variables are dependent upon each other with regard to quantitative change, and this change is continuous. Responses of a system to the input of information may be either linear—directly proportional to the input, or nonlinear—variable to the input. Biological systems almost always show nonlinear responses. Discontinuous change, which occurs in second–order → **change** is nonlinear, (→ **nonlinearity**). Nonlinear relationships are not, however, necessarily discontinuous.

The conceptual counterpart of "lineality" is → **circularity,** in which the relationship of the progression of causes is such that the initial cause is also affected by the progression itself. Cybernetic models attempt to analyze these circular processes and to grasp the reciprocal relationships between cause and effect.

An important issue in psychotherapy is whether concepts of circular causality or lineal causality are more appropriate. This issue is the subject of heated debate between proponents of family or systemic schools of therapy on the one hand and individual–oriented therapists on the other. According to the latter, the life–history of the individual is of paramount importance, and this view often goes hand in hand with an exclusively lineal notion of causality. The question of → **power** and emancipation (→ **autonomy/emancipation**) is also important. Both of these phenomena seem more or less bound to a lineal view of causality and, hence, appear to stand in contradiction to a circular conception of causality. The confusion that arises is very likely the result of the fact that lineal causality and circular causality can only be understood by different processes of abstraction. *Lineality* represents an abstraction in terms of the effect of *present or synchronic* relationships; circularity is an abstraction in terms of *past (historical) or diachronic* relationships (→ **diachronic/synchronic**). Circular and lineal notions of causality thus represent two points of view that need to be seen together in order to complete the picture.

One must bear in mind that no circular relationships exist within the dimension of "present time" as a factor of human experience; but all diachronic (i.e., successive) effects do have a lineal relationship to each other. When one "recognizes" situations as being similar, circularity becomes possible. The present can then be evaluated and measured against experiences of the past, and these experiences can be modified. In the relationships of people with each other (for example, in a family), past experiences and expectations based on these experiences can be confirmed and/or changed in the present with regard to interpersonal relationships. This means a feedback effect ensues and outmoded thinking or behavior can be corrected (→ **learning**).

Cybernetics does not view all relationships within a system as being circular. It is important to differentiate between "control," which uses feedback to check out values, and "piloting," in which a one–directional relation exists (see Klaus & Liebscher, 1979, p. 769 ff.). If one blurs the distinction between the two types of relationship, it becomes difficult to grasp the complexity of such central topics in psychology and family therapy as → **justice** in the family or power relationships. In employing circular causality as a model, it is easy to assume that each condition affects every other condition in an equal manner. This is not the case. Many interpersonal relationships are reflected more accurately by a "piloting" model than they are by a circular model. This fact raises important questions of interpersonal ethics that often are extremely difficult to answer.

214

Bateson, G. *Mind and nature: A necessary unity.* New York: E. P. Dutton, 1979.
Klaus, G., & Liebscher, H. *Wörterbuch der Kybernetik* (4th revised ed.).
Simon, F. B. Linearität und Puritanismus: Das Selbstverständnis des Therapeuten und die Verwirrung des "Kausalitäts"-Begriffs. *Familiendynamik 8:* 309–312, 1983.

* * * * * *

LOGICAL TYPES

According to the theory of Logical Types, proposed by Alfred North Whitehead and Bertrand Russell (1910–1913), one must distinguish between a class (set) and the elements of the class. A statement that refers to a class manifests a higher level of abstraction—in other words, is of a higher logical type—than does a statement that refers to the elements of a class or set. This distinction is of particular importance when two statements are so presented that it cannot be determined from the outset whether reference is being made to the class as a whole or to an element of the class. The word "man" can refer to an individual being; it can also refer to a class, the class of all human beings. In the latter case, the concept of "man" is located at a higher level of abstraction and corresponds to a higher logical type.

The differentiation of logical types as proposed by Whitehead and Russell in their "Theory of Logical Types" is of major importance in the field of human communication research. The fact that statements belong to different logical types and can refer either to a class as a whole or to an element of the class means that they can be used to comment upon each other (→ **metacommunication**). A statement about a class is equally valid for any single element of that class. For example, what is stated as being valid for human beings as members of a species (class) must be valid for each individual member of the species. Logical typologizing leads to a hierarchy of valid statements where the lower order of logical type is contained in the higher order of logical type.

In the event that logical types become compounded with one another, i.e., the level of validity is not distinguishable, a paradox inevitably results. This can be illustrated by the paradox of Epimenides the Cretan: "Cretans always lie." Epimenides was making a concrete statement and, at the same time, a statement about all his statements (higher logical type). If the statement "Cretans [i.e., I too] always lie" is valid, then the concrete statement, the sentence itself (lower logical type) is invalid. The paradox is generated by the fact that the class (statement regarding all statements) is an element of itself, and therefore self–referent (→ **self–reference**).

Just as concepts exhibit different logical types, so that which is described by them can also be classified into different types. Correspondingly, all elements of a system can be viewed as (sub)systems, which then can be differentiated into logical types, as can the term "system" itself, according to whether it refers to a system as a whole or to a part–system. It must be remembered, however, that the allocation to logical types is done by an observer or speaker, and that such types are not innately characteristic of the systems being observed or the terms being used. What we are dealing with here is a method of structuring knowledge that helps to preclude self–reference when such self–reference is out of place.

The Theory of Logical Types became important for the field of family therapy research when Gregory Bateson and his coworkers (1956) applied the theory in their research on families with a schizophrenic member. They observed that in these families, messages and behavioral imperatives that were mutually exclusive were simultaneously transmitted at different logical levels. This investigation resulted in the → **double–bind** theory of schizophrenia (→ **context,** → **context marking,** → **communication theory,** → **communication therapy**).

Because the Theory of Logical Types was so central in the development of Batesonian epistemology, recent challenges to the formulation raise complex questions about how other concepts should be re–formulated. Spencer–Brown (1973), Cronen, Johnson, and Lannamann (1982), de Shazer (1982), and Keeney (1983) are among those who have vigorously objected to the theory. Indeed, Spencer–Brown (1973) reports that when he showed Russell in 1967 that the theory was unnecessary, Russell "was delighted. The theory was, he said, the most arbitrary thing he and Whitehead had ever had to do, not really a theory but a stopgap, and he was glad to have lived long enough to see the matter resolved" (pp. viii–ix). A basic difficulty was that the theory was an attempt to deal with self–reflexive loops that neglected a temporal dimension. Such "Strange Loops" (Hofstadter, 1979), exemplified in Escher's "Drawing Hands" (see p. 216a), are "strange" and created a "tangled hierarchy" only "when what you presume are clear hierarchical levels take you by surprise and fold back in a hierarchy–violating way. ... A simple tangle, like feedback, doesn't involve violations of presumed level distinctions. An example is when you're in the shower and you wash your left arm with your right, and then vice versa. There is no strangeness to the image. Escher didn't choose to draw hands drawing hands for nothing! Events such as two arms washing each other happen all the time in the world, and we don't notice them particularly. I say something to you, then you say something back to me. Paradox? No; our perceptions of each other didn't involve a hierarchy to begin with, so there is no sense of strangeness" (p. 691). Hofstadter states that the "seeming paradox" in the "Drawing Hands" lithograph is that the "level" of Escher himself drawing the hands is invisible. We fall for the illusion by forgetting the existence of Escher.

In the concept of the double bind, directly derived from the Theory of Logical Types, schizophrenics were depicted as unable, or unwilling, to step outside the family communication system. In this failure of metacommunication, they become "trapped" and confused by the illusion of a *seeming* paradox. The experience of being in a double bind is linked to *their construction of reality,* not by an "objective" reality, which does not exist. Bateson (1972) and Wynne (1976), among others, have described the creativity, humor, and zest associated with discovering that a different reality can be created through a different → **punctuation** of experience. Indeed, as Keeney (1983) points out, the "successful elimination of logical mistyping would result in a flat and stagnant experiential world" (p. 31).

Bateson, G. *Steps to an ecology of mind.* New York: Ballantine Books, 1972.
Bateson, G. *Mind and nature: A necessary unity.* New York: E. P. Dutton, 1979.
Bateson, G., Jackson, D. D., Haley, J., & Weakland, J. H. Toward a theory of schizophrenia. *Behavioral Science 1:* 251–264, 1956.
Cronen, V. E., Johnson, K. M., & Lannamann, J. W. Paradoxes, double binds, and reflexive loops: An alternative theoretical perspective. *Family Process 21:* 91–112, 1982.
de Shazer, S. Some conceptual distinctions are more useful than others. *Family Process 21:* 71–84, 1982.
Haley, J. Paradoxes in play, fantasy, and psychotherapy. *Psychiatric Research Reports 2:* 52–58, 1955.
Hofstadter, D. R. *Gödel, Escher, Bach: An eternal golden braid.* New York: Basic Books, 1979.
Keeney, B. P. *Aesthetics of change.* New York: Guilford Press, 1983.
Spencer-Brown, G. *Laws of form.* New York: Bantam Books, 1973.
Whitehead, A. N., & Russell, B. *Principia mathematica* (3 vols.). Cambridge: Cambridge University Press, 1910–1913.
Wynne, L. C. On the anguish and creative passions of not escaping double binds: A reformulation. In C. E. Sluzki & D. C. Ransom (Eds.), *Double Bind: The foundations of the communication approach to the family.* New York: Grune & Stratton, 1976, 243–250.

* * * * * *

LOYALTY

Loyalty is a feeling of solidarity and commitment that unifies the needs and expectations of a social unit (for example, the family) and "the thinking, feelings and motivations of each member" (Boszormenyi–Nagy, & Spark, 1973, p. xix).

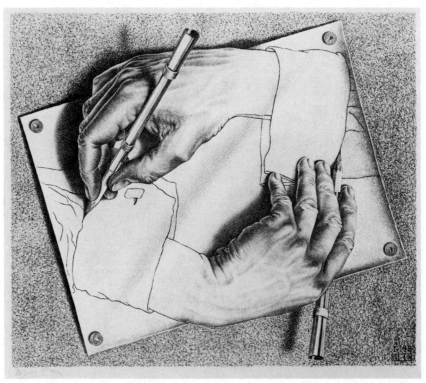

(*Drawing Hands* (lithograph, 1948) by M. C. Escher)

The concept of loyalty is central in → **contextual therapy** as developed by Boszormenyi–Nagy. Loyalty implies → **binding** and has an ethical dimension. The concept of loyalty makes understandable the continuity and → **coherence** of families during the course of successive generations, and how patterns of behavior, value systems, and missions become hallowed family traditions—as well as how these same patterns can become dysfunctional.

Within Boszormeny–Nagy's complex theory of the structure of relationships, the concept of loyalty means more than an individual acting responsibly toward another person (the "object of loyalty"). Rather, the individual is viewed as being embedded in a multiperson, loyalty network. Within the context of this structured network, it is demanded of each person that he or she comply with the expectations and obligations of the group. This idea is founded on what Martin Buber (1957) called "the order of the human world," within the framework of which such things as trust, merit, legacy, and fulfillment are far more important than the " 'psychological' functions of 'feeling' and 'knowing' " (Boszormenyi–Nagy & Spark, 1973, p. 37).

The therapeutically relevant dynamics of groups, particularly of families, become more transparent as soon as one discovers who is bound to whom in overt or covert loyalty and what this means for those so bound. Such loyalty often expresses itself in behavior that is self–destructive and unhealthy. A grown daughter can express her loyalty to her aging mother by reverting to a state of immaturity, illness, and dependence where she is in need of nursing care herself. Or a daughter can prove her covert loyalty to her father by ridiculing her own husband, and ruining her marriage, thereby showing her father that he is the only man who means anything to her.

Etymologically, the word "loyalty" is derived from the French word *loi* (law) and hence implies lawful or legal behavior. On the level of a system (family, group, etc.), loyalty can be understood as the expectation of adherence to certain → **rules** and the threat of expulsion should these rules be transgressed. On the level of the individual this includes "identification with the group, genuine object relatedness with other members, trust, reliability, responsibility, dutiful commitment, faithfulness, and staunch devotion" (Boszormenyi–Nagy & Spark, 1973, p. 42). Thus viewed, the psychic structure of an individual is an internalization of loyally accepted expectations and percepts. Loyalty is therefore the key to the understanding of → **delegation** and consequent derailments. Conflicting missions, for instance, are often the result of "a legacy of divided loyalty." Individuals and systems then reveal themselves as held together by multigenerational, motivational structures in which the concept of "merit" plays the same significant role that the concept of instinctual drive plays in psychoanalytic

218

theory. Through the fulfillment of obligations and the credit that an individual achieves for the family, he or she in turn is bestowed with the right to make demands on other family members. In the course of the generations, a → **ledger of merits** is set up and this ledger becomes the yardstick for the family's idea of → **justice** within the family. Thus, the concept of loyalty attempts to take account of ethical and moral dimensions, within which the needs of the individual in a multiperson network can be gauged and given their due (→ **relational ethics**).

Boszormenyi–Nagy, I. Loyalty implications of the transference model in psychotherapy. *Archives of General Psychiatry 27:* 374–380, 1974.
Boszormenyi–Nagy, I., & Krasner, B. R. Gruppenloyalität als Motiv für politischen Terrorismus. *Familiendynamik 3:* 199–208, 1978.
Boszormenyi–Nagy, I., & Krasner, B. R. Trust-based therapy: A contextual approach. *American Journal of Psychiatry 137:* 767–775, 1980.
Boszormenyi–Nagy, I., & Spark, G. M. *Invisible loyalties: Reciprocity in intergenerational family therapy.* New York: Harper & Row, 1973.
Buber, M. Guilt and guilt feelings. *Psychiatry 20:* 114–129, 1957.

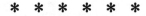

■ M ■

MALIGN CLINCH

This concept refers to an advanced state of progressive, symmetrical (→ **symmetry**) escalation between two or more relational partners.

This term, with its obvious analogy to the sport of boxing, was introduced into family therapy literature by Helm Stierlin. One speaks of a clinch when two opponents, entangled in each other's grasp and fired by the spirit of the fight, continue to flay wildly at each other although neither one is able to gain any decisive advantage. In a physical clinch, the → **strategies** and tactics that reflect the opponents' ideas, goals, experiences, and life histories are as if obliterated. What remains is two masses of undifferentiated muscle pounding at each other. In a "relational clinch" the weapons are not the fists but, rather, the strategies developed by the two opponents to devalue the adversary. Among the weapons in this arsenal are "making–the–other–helpless" and "making–the–other–feel–guilty" by resorting to symptoms or masochistic behaviors. Other weapons include mutual → **mystifica-**

tion, the construction of → **double binds** (relational traps), the avoidance of any definition of → **relationship,** and the evasion of a leadership role and personal responsibility.

The metaphor of the clinch also opens up certain therapeutic analogies. In a boxing match the referee breaks up the clinch. To separate the struggling opponents, he must intervene actively and energetically; he must literally use his own weight. This weighty, active response again sets the deadlocked opponents in motion, and gives the individuals back their obliterated identities, strategies, and motivations—and room to develop again. Similarly, a therapist with a couple or family must, in the face of a malign clinch, apply the weight of his or her personality and authority in order to break it up and allow the opponents to differentiate their values and motivations once again. In this sense the family therapist is a "clinch breaker" and a "dialogue facilitator." The metaphor of the clinch makes evident, however, the divided feelings the therapist is bound to elicit; for as long as the clinch exists, neither opponent can be "knocked out," and the contact between them is close and intensive at the same time that it is hostile and distant. Once the clinch is dissolved, the danger of losing increases, as does that of winning and losing contact altogether.

Stierlin, H. Status der Gegenseitigkeit: Die fünfte Perspektive des Heidelberger familiendynamischen Konzepts. *Familiendynamik 4:* 106–116, 1979.
Stierlin, H. Der Therapeut Schizophrener als Dialogpartner und Dialogermöglicher. In R. Battegay (Ed.), *Herausforderung und Begegnung in der Psychiatrie.* Bern: Huber, 1981, 145–154.
Stierlin, H. Der misslungene Dialog. In H. Stierlin (Ed.), *Delegation und Familie.* Frankfurt: Suhrkamp, 1982, 164–185.
Stierlin, H., Rücker-Embden, I., Wetzel, N., & Wirsching, M. *The first interview with the family* (translated by S. Tooze). New York: Brunner/Mazel, 1980.

* * * * * *

MARITAL SCHISM/MARITAL SKEW

Lidz, Cornelison, Fleck, and Terry (1957) described marital schism and marital skew as two patterns of marital interaction observed in the parents of adolescent and young adult schizophrenics. Marital schism is "severe chronic disequilibrium and discord"; with marital skew, relative equilibrium is achieved, but with family life distorted by shared "aberrant conceptualizations" as husband and wife attempt to complement each other sufficiently to maintain marital harmony.

Lidz et al (1957) formulated the concepts of marital schism and skew as deficits in fulfilling the requisites for successful marriage that had been proposed by Parsons et al. (1955): "reciprocal interrelating roles with each other and ... with their children; ... mutual trust and effective communication; ... the need ... not to confuse or blur distinctions between parents and children" (Lidz et al. 1957, p. 242). While Lidz et al. explicitly disavowed seeking to "establish a direct etiological relationship" between disturbed marriages and schizophrenia in an offspring, they found in these marriages a number of features that were "theoretically adverse" to "normal" development of a child.

In marital schism, the spouses failed to achieve role reciprocity. Each tried to coerce the other to conform to his or her expectations, but were met by defiance. There was chronic undercutting of the worth of one partner to the children by the other partner, together with mutual distrust of one another's motivations.

In marital skew, serious psychopathology of one partner dominated the home, but the other went along with the this partner's "distorted ideation," masking potential conflict and "creating an unreal atmosphere in which what was said and admitted differed from what was actually felt and done" (p. 246). The offspring in these families grow up in a family environment that deviates greatly from the rest of the "real" world. The necessity of adapting to this social environment is associated with a disturbance in the child's orientation toward accepted cultural traditions and symbols of society, and the child's cognitive development is likely to be impaired.

Both marital patterns are usually associated with a blurring of → **generational boundaries** and pathological forms of parent–child coalition (→ **alliance,** → **triangulation,** → **rigid triad,** → **perverse triangle**). In marital schism, one observes a symmetrical (→ **symmetry**) fight for dominance, which can only be resolved by involving a third party. This third party is the child who often then takes on the role of the → **identified patient.** If the child enters into a coalition with one of the parents, he or she is then in the position of deciding the outcome of the fight, and thus has the power that is hierarchically inappropriate. Developing schizophrenic symptoms gives the child the opportunity to take and yet not to take this role. The validity of the child's decision in favor of one of the parents is, as it were, made ambiguous by the offspring's bizarre behavior.

By continuing in marital schism, parents remain in alliance at a distance. The → **relational balance** between → **closeness/distance** is lacking, and the parents cannot move to a higher level of related → **individuation.** The need for distance usually can be explained by the fact that both partners are still strongly bound (→ **binding**) to their families of origin; too close a relationship to the spouse would cause a conflict of → **loyalty** with respect to the parents' own parents. The "marital feud" allows the spouses to engage in an intensive relationship with each other, while at the same time denying that this is so (→ **pseudohostility**).

By means of the allocation of a rigidly defined strong and weak role in the relationship, the spouses are able to complement and confirm one another; the weak partner confirms the other's strength, the strong partner the other's weakness. In this situation, both rely on one another and both are equally dependent. Furthermore, in this distribution of roles, each obtains the power to keep the other in the relationship. The strong partner lives in the security that the weak partner cannot live without him or her; the weak, helpless partner can be assured that he or she will not be left to face the world alone. In this manner, the partners are able to avoid conflict (→ **pseudomutuality**).

Lidz, T. *The origin and treatment of schizophrenic disorders.* New York: Basic Books, 1973.

Lidz, T., Cornelison, A. R., Fleck, S., & Terry, D. The intrafamilial environment of schizophrenic patients: II. Marital schism and marital skew. *American Journal of Psychiatry 114:* 241–248, 1957.

Lidz, T., Cornelison, A. R., Terry, D., & Fleck, S. The intrafamilial environment of the schizophrenic patient: VI. The transmission of irrationality. *Archives of Neurology and Psychiatry 79:* 305–316, 1958.

Lidz, T., Fleck, S., & Cornelison, A. R. *Schizophrenia and the family.* New York: International Universities Press, 1965.

Parsons, T., Bales, R. F., Olds, J., Zelditch, M., & Slater, P. E. *Family, socialization and interaction process.* Glencoe, Ill.: Free Press, 1955.

*　*　*　*　*　*

McMaster Model of Family Functioning

This is a problem–oriented systems model of family functioning developed by Nathan B. Epstein and his coworkers (see references). Its concepts evolved from studies of both normal and clinical populations; they are intended to define family health and pathology. "Health" is largely equated with "normality" (→ **healthy/functional families**).

Epstein, Bishop, and Baldwin (1982) assume that "a primary function of today's family unit is to provide a setting for the development and maintenance of family members on the social, psychological, and biological levels" (p. 118), in basic instrumental tasks, developmental tasks associated with normative transitions of the life cycle, and tasks arising with crises such as illness, job change, and so on. The model takes a multidimensional approach to understanding family patterns of

(1) problem solving; (2) communication; (3) roles; (4) affective responsiveness; (5) affective involvement; and (6) behavior control. Each dimension is defined as ranging from "most ineffective" to "most effective." It is assumed that "most ineffective" functioning in any of these dimensions can contribute to clinical symptomatology, whereas "most effective" functioning in all dimensions optimizes physical and emotional health.

Recently, the McMaster Family Assessment Device (FAD) (Epstein, Baldwin, & Bishop, 1983) has been developed as a screening device to evaluate families on these six dimensions, plus a scale of "general functioning." The psychometric properties of the FAD were assessed on 503 individuals. Persons from families with clinical problems were significantly differentiated from persons whose families did not present themselves for clinical care.

The McMaster Clinical Rating Scale (CRS) has now been developed for use by clinicians to parallel and validate the questionnaire assessment with the FAD. These scales are intended for application in comparisons of a range of families and in treatment outcome studies. Epstein, Bishop, and Baldwin (1982) have discussed similarities and differences of the McMaster Model and the → **Beavers Systems Model,** Reiss's Paradigm Model (→ **consensus sensitivity**), Olson's → **Circumplex Model,** Moos's Family Environment Scale (→ **family tests**), and Van der Veen's Family Concept Test (→ **family tests**).

Epstein, N. B. Concepts of normality or evaluation of emotional heatlh. *Behavioral Science 3:* 335–343, 1958.

Epstein, N. B., Baldwin, L. M., & Bishop, D. S. The McMaster Family Assessment device. *Journal of Marital and Family Therapy 9:* 171–180, 1983.

Epstein, N. B., & Bishop, D. S. Problem-centered system therapy of the family. In A. S. Gurman & D. P. Kniskern (Eds.), *Handbook of family therapy.* New York: Brunner/Mazel, 1981, 444–482.

Epstein, N. B., Bishop, D. S., & Baldwin, L. M. McMaster Model of family functioning: A view of the normal family. In F. Walsh (Ed.), *Normal family processes.* New York: Guilford Press, 1982, 115–141.

Epstein, N. B., Bishop, D. S., & Levin, S. The McMaster Model of family functioning. *Journal of Marriage and Family Counseling 4:* 19–31, 1978.

Epstein, N. B., Levin, S., & Bishop, D. S. The family as a social unit. *Canadian Family Physician 22:* 1411–1413, 1976.

* * * * * *

METACOMMUNICATION

Metacommunication [Greek *meta,* among, in the midst of, between, after, according to] is communication about communication.

Failure to distinguish between communication and metacommunication inevitably results in paradoxes because these two forms of communication belong to different → **logical types.** In the area of interpersonal interaction, metacommunication always serves to mark the → **context** (→ **context marking).** This context determines how behavior is to be understood and evaluated. Whether two interactional partners are merely "playing" the role of adversaries, or whether they are "serious," and the situation may involve possible life–and–death combat, can only be clarified through metacommunication. All available forms of communication can be utilized as modalities of metacommunication on the interpersonal level. This means that any type of communicational behavior—language, gesture, facial expression, and so forth—has the ability to comment upon the information being sent. Bateson (1955) and his coworkers (Bateson et al., 1956) first called attention to the enormous importance of differentiating communication and metacommunication in interpersonal interaction. The formulation of the → **double–bind** theory of schizophrenia is partly based on this discovery. This theory describes the consequences of the simultaneous transmission of mutually exclusive messages and behavioral imperatives on the levels of communication and metacommunication.

Bateson, G. A theory of play and fantasy. *Psychiatric Research Reports 2:* 39–51, 1955.

Bateson, G., Jackson, D. D., Haley, J., & Weakland, J. H. Toward a theory of schizophrenia. *Behavioral Science 1:* 251–264, 1956.

Cronen, V. E., Johnson, K. M., & Lannamann, J. W. Paradoxes, double binds, and reflexive loops: An alternative theoretical perspective. *Family Process 21:* 91–112, 1982.

Haley, J. Paradoxes in play, fantasy, and psychotherapy. *Psychiatric Research Reports 2:* 52–58, 1955.

Watzlawick, P., Beavin, J. H., & Jackson, D. D. *Pragmatics of human communication: A study of interactional patterns, pathologies and paradoxes.* New York: W. W. Norton & Co., 1967.

* * * * * *

METAPHOR

Metaphor [Greek *metaphora,* a transferring to one word the sense of another; from *metapherein: meta,* over + *pherein,* to bear] refers to a turn of speech that is used in a figurative, nonliteral sense. Although a metaphor is a "figure of speech," it has much in common with → **analogue communication;** in both there is an analogy between the evoked image and that which it is intended to express.

The use of metaphors in therapy allows one to offer, linguistically, interpretations that are vividly linked to concrete experiences. Accordingly, dream symbols with their associative, analogy–based dynamics can be understood as a highly metaphorical language (see Simon, 1982). Symptoms also can be viewed as metaphors (see Madanes, 1984). Metaphors are particularly suited to portraying specific aspects of relationships. Unlike normal, denotative language, which always translates synchronic structures into diachronic ones (→ **diachronic/ synchronic**), the multiple layers of simultaneous associations evoked by metaphors makes possible a representation of synchronic structures.

Examples of the use of metaphors in family therapy are → **story telling** and the use of → **family sculpture.** In story telling, a tale is told that exhibits a similar structure to the history of the family or the individual concerned. In family sculpture, emotional relationships, in particular those involving the need for closeness and distance, are portrayed in spatial terms.

In the framework of → **hypnotherapy** and → **neurolinguistic programming,** metaphors are used as a sort of reverse technique of dream interpretation. Whereas in traditional psychoanalytic procedure the imagery of a dream (an analogue communication mode) is translated into the structure of everyday language (a digital mode of communication), the strategy of hypnotherapy and neurolinguistic programming is to exclude any rational interpretation and to induce a direct change of the underlying imagery. The common denominator of both techniques is the postulation of representational systems (→ **psycholinguistics**) in which experiences are combined in a primary process manner not dictated by the logic of language. The goal of both psychoanalytic techniques and suggestive methods that intervene indirectly on a symbolic level is to decipher and then to change these images or narratives when they have become dysfunctional.

Andolfi, M., Angelo, C., Menghi, P., & Nicolò-Corigliano, A. M. *Behind the family mask: Therapeutic change in rigid family systems.* New York: Brunner/Mazel, 1983.
Bandler, R., & Grinder, J. *Patterns of the hypnotic techniques of Milton H. Erickson, M.D., Vol. I.* Cupertino, Cal.: META Publications, 1975. (a)

Bandler, R., & Grinder, J. *The structure of magic, Vol. I*. Palo Alto: Science and Behavior Books, 1975. (b)
Cade, B. Some uses of metaphor. *Australian Journal of Family Therapy 3:* 135–140, 1982.
Erickson, M. H., & Rossi, E. *Hypnotherapy: An exploratory casebook*. New York: Irvington, 1979.
Erickson, M. H., Rossi, E., & Rossi, S. *Hypnotic realities: The induction of clinical hypnosis and forms of indirect suggestion*. New York: Irvington, 1976.
Gordon, D. *Therapeutic metaphors: Helping others through the looking glass*. Cupertino, Cal.: META Publications, 1978.
Grinder, J., & Bandler, R. *The structure of magic, Vol. II*. Palo Alto: META Publications, 1976.
Grinder, J., & Bandler, R. *Trance-formations: Neuro-linguistic programming and the structure of hypnosis*. Moab, Utah: Real People Press, 1981.
Grinder, J., Delozier, J., & Bandler, R. *Patterns of the hypnotic techniques of Milton H. Erickson, M. D., Vol. II*. Cupertino, Cal.: META Publications, 1977.
Madanes, C. *Behind the one-way mirror: Advances in the practice of strategic therapy*. San Francisco: Jossey-Bass, 1984.
Simon, F. B. Semiotische Aspekte von Traum und Sprache: Strukturierungsprinzipien subjektiver und intersubjektiver Zeichensysteme. *Psyche 36:* 673–699, 1982.
Zeig, J. (Ed.). *A teaching seminar with Milton H. Erickson*. New York: Brunner/Mazel, 1980.
Zeig, J. *Ericksonian approaches to hypnosis and psychotherapy*. New York: Brunner/Mazel, 1982.

* * * * * *

MODELS OF FAMILY THERAPY

Models that guide therapeutic endeavors with families contain implicit or explicit concepts about what makes a family functional or dysfunctional; as such, they are the expression and consequence of particular → **paradigms** and, in turn, → **epistemologies.**

Models of family therapy can be classified from various perspectives. The classification principle used in Heidelberg locates differing models of family therapy along an axis of ideal types. The three models of the Heidelberg Classification System—Healing through Encounter (encounter model), Healing through System Change (systemic model), and Healing through Active Restructuring (structural model)—while in part mutually exclusive, do offer certain possibilities for intermodel integration and many opportunities for experimentation with innovative models of therapy. For example, the active support as well as directive challenge of selected family members (such as is practiced by Minuchin in → **structural family therapy**) may appear to obstruct system–wide → **paradoxical intervention** at the end of the session. Yet, certain elements of the structural model can be integrated into a systemic intervention strategy, for example, by prescribing rituals at the end of the session. Experienced therapists can also integrate the encounter model into → **systemic therapy** according to the type of problem the family presents, the particular phase in the individual and → **family life cycles,** and the type of relational structure in the family.

Another classificatory principle was recently introduced by Stanton (1984) as part of his "geodynamic balance" theory. In this formulation, therapeutic approaches or techniques fall within one of two general categories: "diversion" or "compression." Diversion approaches are those that aim at directly breaking up or shifting family coalitions or patterns through blocking, unbalancing, confronting, or substituting—thereby working against the prevailing interpersonal/ family patterns or structures. Examples are structural therapy, prob- lem–centered therapy, behavioral techniques, reality therapy, ration- al–emotive therapy, and the go–between approach. In contrast, com- pression approaches are directed toward increasing or intensifying an existent pattern—pushing or compressing it—to a point of counterac- tion. For example, people may be encouraged to "do more of what you are doing," whether it is to intensify a compulsive act or to visit a grave if they are undergoing prolonged bereavement. Paradoxical tech- niques, implosive therapy, provocative therapy, reversals, returning home, grief work, and reaffiliation therapy are all examples of a compression dynamic. Stanton postulates that diversion and compres- sion approaches take different but complementary directions in chang- ing the interpersonal orbits that family members traverse.

In 1977, Madanes and Haley delineated seven dimensions along which models of family therapy can be compared: (1) emphasis on the past or on the present; (2) use of interpretation versus therapeutic directives for action in the session or between sessions; (3) basic goal of resolving the presenting problem versus emphasizing growth of the family (and therapist); (4) use of a formal method of treatment applied to every case versus a specific procedure for each family or problem; (5) emphasis on units of one, two, or three people; (6) emphasis on quality of status between family members versus concerns with hierar- chy and power issues in the family; and (7) analogical versus digital ways of describing behavior and communication. Madanes and Haley then evaluated schools of therapy with respect to their approach on each of these dimensions. They compared psychodynamic, experien- tial, extended–family, behavioral, structural, and strategic approaches to family therapy. Interestingly, there appears to have been shifts in approaches since this paper was published in 1977, and the distinctions between schools are now less clear—probably because ideas have changed and have been partially integrated into previously opposed approaches.

The *Handbook of Family Therapy,* edited by Gurman and Kniskern (1981) distinguishes 13 models or schools of family therapy that are identified either with various schools of individual therapy (psychoanalysis, behavioral therapy, gestalt therapy, and so forth) or with innovative (founding) personalities such as Ivan Boszormenyi–Nagy, Murray Bowen, Jay Haley, and Salvador Minuchin. Doherty et al. (1984, 1985) analyzed these 13 models according to their emphases on the dimensions of inclusion (boundaries, commitment, belonging, autonomy), control (influence, power, decision making), and intimacy (self–disclosure, friendship, in–depth personal sharing). First, they categorized each model's major concepts on each of the three dimensions, and then they estimated the relative emphasis on each dimension or issue in the chapters of the *Handbook.* A final conceptual analysis was reached after feedback from the authors: "Four models had a primary emphasis on inclusion: Structural [Aponte & VanDeusen], Bowen [Kerr], Contextual [Boszormenyi–Nagy & Ulrich], and Functional [Barton & Alexander]. Four had a primary emphasis on control: Strategic [Stanton], Interactional [Bodin], Problem–Centered [Epstein & Bishop], and Behavioral [Jacobson]. Five emphasized intimacy as their primary area: Open Systems Group–Analytic [Skynner], Couples Contracts [Sager], Family of Origin [Framo], Symbolic–Experiential [Whitaker & Keith], and Integrative [Duhl & Duhl]" (Doherty, Colangelo, Green, & Hoffman, 1985, p. 301). Additionally, secondary emphases often were important. For example, structural family therapy showed a strong emphasis on control (power) in addition to the primary focus on inclusion (boundaries), but placed only tertiary emphasis on intimacy. The comparisons by Doherty et al. (1985) reveal interesting areas of overlap between current family therapy models at the same time that differences continue. Perhaps in future research the process and outcomes of family therapy can be compared when the model of therapy fits or does not fit the problem or concerns of the family.

As family therapy comes of age, there are increasing attempts to achieve both conceptual and clinical integration of the various models—or at least some understanding of their differences and similarities. Given the fact that many differing models serving many different purposes can be constructed, the prospects for any "grand integration" is rather dim but has been successfully proposed for related models such as structural therapy, systemic therapy, and → **strategic therapy.**

Colapinto, J. On model integration and model integrity. *Journal of Strategic and Systemic Therapies 3* (3): 38–42, 1984.

Doherty, W. J., & Colangelo, N. The family FIRO model: A modest proposal for organizing family treatment. *Journal of Marital and Family Therapy 10:* 19–29, 1984.

228

Doherty, W. J., Colangelo, N., Green, A. M., & Hoffman, G. S. Emphases of the major family therapy models: A family FIRO analysis. *Journal of Marital and Family Therapy 11:* 299–303, 1985.

Farrelly, F., & Brandsma, J. *The beginnings of provocative therapy.* Cupertino, Cal.: META Publications, 1974

Gurman, A. S., & Kniskern, D. P. (Eds.). *Handbook of family therapy.* New York: Brunner/Mazel, 1981.

Hoffman, L. *Foundations of family therapy: A conceptual framework for systems change.* New York: Basic Books, 1981.

Keeney, B. P., & Ross, J. M. *Mind in therapy: Constructing systemic family therapies.* New York: Basic Books, 1985.

Madanes, C., & Haley, J. Dimensions of family therapy. *Journal of Nervous and Mental Disease 165:* 88–98, 1977.

Pinsof, W. Integrative problem-centered therapy: Toward the synthesis of family and individual psychotherapies. *Journal of Marital and Family Therapy 9:* 19–36, 1983.

Ritterman, M. K. Paradigmatic classification of family therapy theories. *Family Process 16:* 29–48, 1977.

Rohrbaugh, M. The strategic systems therapies: Misgivings about mixing the models. *Journal of Strategic and Systemic Therapies 3* (3): 28–32, 1984.

Sluzki, C. E. Process, structure and world views: Toward an integrated view of systemic models in family therapy. *Family Process 22:* 469–476, 1983.

Stanton, M. D. Strategic approaches to family therapy. In A. S. Gurman & D. P. Kniskern (Eds.), *Handbook of family therapy.* New York: Brunner/Mazel, 1981, 361–402.

Stanton, M. D. Fusion, compression, diversion, and the workings of paradox: A theory of therapeutic systemic change. *Family Process 23:* 135–167, 1984.

Stierlin, H., Rücker-Embden, I., Wetzel, N., & Wirsching, M. *The first interview with the family* (translated by S. Tooze). New York: Brunner/Mazel, 1980.

Winawer, H. The Heidelberg concept: an introduction to the work of Helm Stierlin and his associates. *Family Systems Medicine 1* (4): 36–40, 1983.

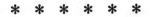

MORPHOGENESIS

Morphogenesis [Greek *morphe,* form; *genesis,* generation] refers to the formation and development of structures in a system.

The concept of morphogenesis was introduced into cybernetics by Maruyama (1960). It describes the phenomenon whereby positive, deviation–amplifying feedback, by exaggerating a minimal deviation (change) in the system, can induce a disproportionately large change in that same system (→ **equilibrium,** → **homeostasis,** → **change,** → **stability,** → **coevolution,** → **self–organization**).

The long–term functionality of a family depends, as does every system, on the extent to which the system's structures are capable of change (→ **adaptability**). Without the ability to change, the potentiality for the development of individuals and families is limited. Inevitable changes will occur in the individual and → **family life cycle** and will lead to unavoidable crisis situations that will require new definitions of → **relationship.** Normal adaptation crises occur, for example, when a child is born and, later, when the child becomes autonomous and separates from the parents. These crises can only be mastered if the family is capable of changing its → **relational balance.** Functionality requires a continual reestablishment of balance between structural change and structural stability (→ **morphostasis**).

Hoffman, L. Deviation-amplifying processes in natural groups. In J. Haley (Ed.), *Changing families: A family therapy reader.* New York: Grune & Stratton, 1971, 285–311.

Maruyama, M. Morphogenesis and morphostasis. *Methods 12:* 251–296, 1960.

Speer, D. C. Family systems: Morphostasis and morphogenesis, or "Is homeostasis enough?". *Family Process 9:* 259–278, 1970.

Thom, R. *Structural stability and morphogenesis.* Reading, Mass.: Benjamin, 1975.

Wertheim, E. S. Family unit therapy and the science and typology of family systems. *Family Process 12:* 361–376, 1973.

Wertheim, E. S. The science and typology of family systems II. Further theoretical and practical considerations. *Family Process 14:* 285–309, 1975.

* * * * * *

MORPHOSTASIS

Morphostasis [Greek *morphe,* form; *stasis,* stand still] is the ability of a system to maintain its structure in a changing environment.

This concept is similar to that of → **homeostasis.** Both refer to the way in which a system eliminates disturbances and is able to maintain a particular structure (→ **coherence**). The essential mechanisms that enable the system to do this are negative → **feedback loops.**

Early theories of family therapy accentuated this aspect of family systems above all others. This was in line with clinical experience with families that tended predominantly to maintain a status quo, and whose structural → **adaptability** was limited. This structural rigidity went hand in hand with a high level of pathology and symptomatic behavior in individual family members. Accordingly, early family therapists saw their primary task as breaking up such homeostatic structures. Today, it is generally assumed that pathological or dysfunctional families are also able, via processes of → **morphogenesis,** to change their structures themselves. A constant balancing between morphogenesis and morphostasis appears to be the optimal structural condition. This revised view has also changed therapuetic intervention strategies. Interventions are now less oriented toward the removal of what were considered pathological, morphostatic mechanisms, and more oriented toward strengthening morphogenetic mechanisms (→ **stability**, → **coevolution**).

Maruyama, M. Morphogenesis and morphostasis. *Methods 12:* 251–296, 1960.
Speer, D. C. Family systems: Morphostasis and morphogenesis, or "Is homeostasis enough?". *Family Process 9:* 259–278, 1970.
Thom, R. *Structural stability and morphogenesis*. Reading, Mass.: Benjamin, 1975.
Wertheim, E. S. Family unit therapy and the science and typology of family systems. *Family Process 12:* 361–376, 1973.
Wertheim, E. S. The science and typology of family systems II. Further theoretical and practical considerations. *Family Process 14:* 285–309, 1975.

* * * * * *

MOURNING/ OPERATIONAL MOURNING

This refers to the emotional ability to cope with losses and separations. Blockage and denial of the need for mourning account for various pathological reactions within the family.

The concept "operational mourning" was introduced by Norman Paul to describe "a corrective mourning experience" instituted during therapy (Paul & Grosser, 1965). Such mourning experiences are able to dissolve blockage in family developmental processes that result from incomplete or "bogged–down" processes of mourning. In Paul's opinion, the denial of painful feelings over the death of a close family member can have effects extending over many generations. In such instances, the loss is not "digested," nor is the structure of the family reestablished to offset the loss; what happens is that a substitute is found for the lost object. Very often the family member who later develops into the → **identified patient** is delegated (→ **delegation**) to comfort the family for the loss. Thus, in the context of a symbiotic relationship, a pathological balance is maintained in which the formation of individual → **identity** and familial → **individuation** is disturbed.

Sigmund Freud (1917, 1926) referred to mourning and separation anxiety as essential and critical factors in human development. Bowlby's work (see references) and that of Erich Lindemann (1944) confirmed the importance of the affective working out of loss and separation from the beloved object. Using the insights of these authors and others, Paul (1967) assigned denial of mourning reactions to a central position in the maintenance of pathological homeostasis in family systems. In many families with psychotic or neurotic members, Paul regarded unfinished mourning processes as the background to and an essential element of disturbed individuation processes (Paul, 1978; Paul & Grosser, 1965; Paul & Paul, 1975).

The therapeutic techniques applied as a result of these insights aim at forcefully breaking up blocked mourning processes within the framework of therapeutic sessions or activities involving the entire family. The therapist attempts to stimulate the expression of feelings associated with loss, even if the actual event took place fifty years previously. In this process, children witness, often for the first time, intense emotional expression on the part of their parents. As a result of this experience, a feeling of affective unity and continuity is created for the family unit. The therapist assures the family members that the experience of grief is normal, thereby counteracting the denial of death, which is a fundamental feature of Western civilization. The painful and liberating feelings mobilized in this manner are also usually linked to expressions of hostility and anger toward the lost object. Kübler–Ross (1969) described this as one of the stages of the mourning process. After a first phase, characterized by denial, there follows a phase in which anger and rage predominate. Experience in family therapy shows that feelings related to the blocked processes of mourning are often directed toward other family members. When these feelings have been clarified, they can be redirected. Williamson (1978) has described a method for → **individuation** from a dead former parent by having clients visit the parental grave and completing the mourning process.

Fear of loss and fear of separation in families suffering from blocked mourning processes often result in extreme manifestations of → **binding.** Therapeutic experience has shown that families going through the processes of operational mourning advance through developmental stages similar to those described by Bowlby (1961a) for children going through the process of separation. When a family is willing to accept the loss and the related feelings of grief, its members are free from the necessity of constantly fighting against change. On an affective level, the family → **epistemology** can then be changed and related → **individuation** becomes possible once the homeostatic mechanisms preventing the → **coevolution** of all family members are overcome (→ **homeostasis**). Similar processes are found in divorce situations (→ **divorce therapy**).

232

Bowlby, J. Separation anxiety. *International Journal of Psycho-analysis 41:* 89–113, 1960.
Bowlby, J. Process of mourning. *International Journal of Psycho-analysis 42:* 317–340, 1961. (a)
Bowlby, J. Separation anxiety: A critical review of the literature. *Journal of Child Psychology and Psychiatry 1:* 251–269, 1961. (b)
Bowlby, J. *Attachment and loss. Vol. II, Separation: Anxiety and anger.* New York: Basic Books, 1973.
Bowlby, J. *Attachment and loss. Vol. III, Loss.* New York: Basic Books, 1980.
Freud, S. [1917] Mourning and melancholia. *The standard edition of the complete psychological works of Sigmund Freud, Vol. XIV.* London: Hogarth Press, 1957, 243–258.
Freud, S. [1926] Inhibitions, symptoms and anxiety. *The standard edition of the complete psychological works of Sigmund Freud, Vol. XX.* London: Hogarth Press, 1959, 87–172.
Kübler-Ross, E. *On death and dying.* New York: Macmillan Co., 1969.
Lindemann, E. Symptomatology and management of acute grief. *American Journal of Psychiatry 101:* 141–148, 1944.
Paul, N. L. The role of mourning and empathy in conjoint marital therapy. In G. H. Zuk & I. Boszormenyi-Nagy (Eds.), *Family therapy and disturbed families.* Palo Alto: Science and Behavior Books, 1967, 186–205.
Paul, N. L., & Grosser, G. H. Operational mourning and its role in conjoint family therapy. *Community Mental Health Journal 1:* 339–345, 1965.
Paul, N. L., & Paul, B. B. *A marital puzzle: Transgenerational analysis in marriage counseling.* New York: W. W. Norton & Co., 1975.
Pincus, L. *Death and the family: The importance of mourning.* New York: Pantheon Books, 1974.
Pincus, L. Verdrängte Trauer. *Familiendynamik 3:* 269–276, 1978.
Williamson, D. S. New life at the graveyard: A method of therapy for individuation from a dead former parent. *Journal of Marriage and Family Counseling 4* (1): 93–101, 1978.

* * * * * *

MULTIDIRECTIONAL PARTIALITY

Multidirectional partiality (Boszormenyi–Nagy, 1966) is an attitude that allows a therapist to empathize with each family member, to recognize the merits of each, and to take sides because of these merits. Thus, the therapist makes a remedial distribution of → **justice** and can convey to each member in turn a sense of personal worth. The foundation for multidirectional partiality is a dialectical approach to relationships whereby every judgment about a relational position will be offset, sooner or later, by a respective judgment about the position of the relational partner (→ **dialectical method**).

Boszormenyi–Nagy regards this therapeutic attitude, derived from psychoanalysis, as the foundation of his approach (→ **contextual**

therapy). However, because all family members are the objects of multidirectional partiality, changes in the family's relations are facilitated. The therapist empathizes with each family member in turn and encourages the others in their perceptions of violations of interactional justice. This both promotes the family's wish for fairness and heightens the desire for reconciliation and a balancing of the family's → **ledger of merits**. Besides this empathy with individual suffering and merit in the family's history and current situation, the multidirectional therapist is expected to detect growth potentials, positive forces, and resources of which the family is unaware. Awareness and reinforcement of these positive attributes are important apsects of balance within the family system.

Multidirectional partiality must be distinguished from the concept of → **neutrality** in the systemic therapy model. Though there is an empathic *attitude* toward all family members, the neutral therapist will show partisanship for none rather than show partisanship for all of them individually. This is done to insure maintenance of a metaposition toward the family interaction.

Boszormenyi-Nagy, I. A theory of relationships: Experience and transaction. In I. Boszormenyi-Nagy & J. L. Framo (Eds.), *Intensive family therapy: Theoretical and practical aspects.* New York: Harper & Row, 1965, 33–86.

Boszormenyi-Nagy, I. From family therapy to a psychology of relationships: Fictions of the individual and fictions of the family. *Comprehensive Psychiatry 7:* 408–423, 1966.

Boszormenyi-Nagy, I. Loyalty implications of the transference model in psychotherapy. *Archives of General Psychiatry 27:* 374–380, 1974.

Boszormenyi-Nagy, I., & Krasner, B. R. Trust-based therapy: A contextual approach. *American Journal of Psychiatry 137:* 767–775, 1980.

Boszormenyi-Nagy, I., & Spark, G. M. *Invisible loyalties: Reciprocity in intergenerational family therapy.* New York: Harper & Row, 1973.

Stierlin, H., Rücker-Embden, I., Wetzel, N., & Wirsching, M. *The first interview with the family* (translated by S. Tooze). New York: Brunner/Mazel 1980.

* * * * * *

MULTIGENERATIONAL PERSPECTIVE/ FAMILIES OF ORIGIN/ MULTIGENERATIONAL THERAPY

The interactional patterns of a nuclear family often prove to have been prefigured and established in the parents' families of origin. Emotional and social disorders can thus be seen as the expression of problems that have been developed and passed on over the course of many generations. A multigenerational perspective does not, for example, view the mother of a schizophrenic child as responsible for the child's schizophrenia; the mother is merely one "player" in a long line of "players" in other generations. Specific rules and values of the family system have been established during the course of the family → **coevolution.** In certain situations, the rules and values can result in conflict, tension, and strain, which give rise to symptoms. With this in mind, it often makes sense to include the grandparents in therapy, either for diagnostic reasons or to change the relational patterns of the family.

The multigenerational perspective has been especially important in the works of Boszormenyi–Nagy (Boszormenyi–Nagy & Spark, 1973) and Bowen (1976, 1978). Bowen focuses on specific family mechanisms of → **self/object differentiation.** He has been able to show how similar mechanisms of → **projective identification** have come into effect over a number of generations. This is the case when parents make demands upon their children although these demands are actually directed toward their own parents. It is also the case when parents call their children to account for something that was done to them (the parents) by their own parents. Within the context of a therapeutic session, the merits, demands (entitlements), and debts of each family member can be clarified and then directed to the correct addressee. In this school of therapy, encounter and reconciliation between generations is the central issue (→ **justice,** → **relational ethics,** → **delegation**).

Boszormenyi-Nagy, I. Ethical and practical implications of intergenerational family therapy. *Psychotherapy Psychosomatics 24:* 261–268, 1974.

Boszormenyi-Nagy, I., & Spark, G. M. *Invisible loyalties: Reciprocity in intergenerational family therapy.* New York: Harper & Row, 1973.

Bowen, M. Theory in the practice of psychotherapy. In P. J. Guerin (Ed.), *Family therapy: Theory and practice.* New York: Gardner Press, 1976, 42–90.

Bowen, M. *Family therapy in clinical practice.* New York: Jason Aronson, 1978.

Framo, J. L. Family of origin as a therapeutic resource for adults in marital and family therapy: You can and should go home again. *Family Process 15:* 193–210, 1976.

Friedman, E. H. *From generation to generation: Family process in church and synagogue.* New York: Guilford Press, 1985.

Kerr, M. E. Family systems: Theory and therapy. In A. S. Gurman & D. P. Kniskern (Eds.), *Handbook of family therapy.* New York: Brunner/Mazel, 1981, 226–264.

Kramer, J. R. *Family interfaces: Transgenerational patterns.* New York: Brunner/Mazel, 1985.

Paul, N. L. Now and the past: Transgenerational analysis. *International Journal of Family Psychiatry 1:* 235–248, 1980.

Paul, N. L., & Paul, B. B. *A marital puzzle: Transgenerational analysis in marriage counseling.* New York: W. W. Norton & Co., 1975.

Stierlin, H. Toward a multigenerational therapy. In H. Stierlin, *Psychoanalysis and family therapy: Selected papers.* New York: Jason Aronson, 1977, 323–342.

Whitaker, C. A., & Keith, D. V. Family therapy as symbolic experience. *International Journal of Family Psychiatry 1:* 197–208, 1980.

235

Whitaker, C. A., & Keith, D. V. Symbolic-experiential family therapy. In A. S. Gurman & D. P. Kniskern (Eds.), *Handbook of family therapy:* New York: Brunner/Mazel, 1981, 187–225.

* * * * * *

MULTIPLE FAMILY THERAPY

In its simplest form, multiple family therapy consists of meeting of three or more families gathered together to discuss common problems. Usually one or more members of each family have been identified as needing psychiatric, legal, or social assistance. This form of therapy combines features of family therapy and group therapy.

The first use of therapeutic groups in which patients and their parents met together was described by Abrahams and Varon (1953). These authors focused primarily on the symbiotic relationship of presumptively → **schizophrenogenic mothers** and their schizophrenic daughters. During the 1950s and 1960s a number of clinicians led patient–family meetings in inpatient settings as an adjunct to treatment, and to help families tolerate severely disturbed behavior in the patients. However, the creation of multiple family therapy in the present–day sense is usually credited to H. Peter Laqueur. Although Laqueur did not describe his work in a publication until 1962 (Laqueur & LaBurt, 1962), he had initiated this approach ten years earlier as part of an effort to establish a therapeutic community in a state hospital setting (see Jones, 1953).

In 1951, Laqueur had begun having group meetings of families in order to offer them factual information about the patient's illness and about problems that might be encountered on the patient's return to the home environment. He also held separate group meetings with the patients, but noted that these separate meetings produced mutual distortion and suspicion between the patients and families about what was taking place. Therefore, he initiated joint meetings of patients and their families in which hostilities and mutual suspicions were ventilated, and the therapist provided a good deal of education and explanation (Laqueur & LaBurt, 1962). In many ways, this work was similar to the psychoeducational approaches introduced later by Anderson et al. (1980) and others in an effort to reduce family → **expressed emotion** and parental feelings of being blamed.

After conjoint family therapy with one family at a time was becoming established as a treatment approach, Laqueur continued to treat several families together because of a shortage of state hospital therapists. He believed that the multiple family approach was not only expedient, but also that it had therapeutic advantages in inducing changes within a shorter period of time. By using participant family members in cotherapist roles, the presence of other families seemed to stimulate active efforts by these hospitalized patients in their struggles toward self–differentiation; "a patient or a relative may identify with a member of another family . . . and learn by analogy with much less anxiety than is usually associated with such learning" (Laqueur, 1972, p. 403). Sharing the problems of a hospitalized schizophrenic, members of other families, as "cotherapists," help to decipher the semantically distorted family → **code.** Also, interfamily competition leads to internal changes in family → **power** structures and behavior. Laqueur's groups were kept "open," meaning that new families could join at any time. Families in different phases of the change process exchange experiences, support one another, and alleviate each other's fears (→ **healthy/ functional families**).

Laqueur described a typical progression of phases of multiple family therapy:

1. The newly arrived family and/or the index patient appear relieved; anxiety recedes as do the symptoms of the index patient.
2. The original fears of the patient return and general resistance increases. With the help of the families who have been in therapy longer, it is usually possible to reduce these fears and the resistance of the patient and family.
3. Significant changes take place. The patients and their families gain insight into their problems, and at the same time they learn to deal with these problems.

In summary, multiple family therapy represents one of the few methods of applying the principles of → **systems/ systemic theory** with families with a hospitalized member (Laqueur, 1972) (also see → **bifocal family therapy**). With full recognition of the clinical and community context, an effort is made to involve the whole family.

Abrahams, J., & Varon, E. *Maternal dependency and schizophrenia: Mothers and daughters in a therapeutic group, A group analytic study.* New York: International Universities Press, 1953.

Anderson, C. M., Hogarty, G. E., & Reiss, D. J. Family treatment of adult schizophrenic patients: A psycho-educational approach. *Schizophrenia Bulletin 6:* 490–505, 1980.

Blinder, M., Colman, A., Curry, A., & Kessler, D. MFGT: Simultaneous treatment of several families. *American Journal of Psychiatry 19:* 559–569, 1965.

Jones, M. *The therapeutic community: A new treatment method in psychiatry.* New York: Basic Books, 1953.

Laqueur, H. P. Mechanisms of change in multiple family therapy. In C. J. Sager & H. S. Kaplan (Eds.), *Progress in group and family therapy.* New York: Brunner/Mazel, 1972, 400–415.

Laqueur, H. P. Multiple family therapy: Questions and answers. In D. A. Bloch (Ed.), *Techniques of family psychotherapy: A primer.* New York: Grune & Stratton, 1973, 75–85.

Laqueur, H. P., & LaBurt, H. A. The therapeutic community on a modern insulin ward. *Journal of Neuropsychiatry 3:* 139–149, 1962.

Laqueur, H. P., LaBurt, H. A., & Morong, E. Multiple family therapy: Further developments. In J. Haley (Ed.), *Changing families: A family therapy reader.* New York: Grune & Stratton, 1971, 82–95.

Leichter, E., & Schulman, G. L. Multi-family group therapy: A multidimensional approach. *Family Process 13:* 95–110, 1974.

McFarlane, W. R. Multiple-family therapy in the psychiatric hospital. In H. T. Harbin (Ed.), *The psychiatric hospital and the family.* New York: SP Medical and Scientific Books, 103–129, 1982.

McFarlane, W. R. Multiple family therapy in schizophrenia. In W. R. McFarlane (Ed.), *Family therapy in schizophrenia.* New York: Guilford Press, 1983, 141–172.

Paul, N. L., & Bloom, J. Multiple family therapy: Secrets and scapegoating in family crisis. *International Journal of Group Psychotherapy 20:* 37–47, 1970.

Reiss, D., & Costell, R. The multiple family group as a small society: Family regulation of interaction with nonmembers. *American Journal of Psychiatry 134:* 21–24, 1977.

Strelnick, A. H. Multiple family group therapy: A review of the literature. *Family Process 16:* 307–325, 1977.

MULTIPLE IMPACT THERAPY

This intervention strategy was developed for families with delinquent adolescents. It is derived from procedures applied in the field of social work.

A multidisciplinary team (usually consisting of a social worker, a psychologist, a psychiatrist, and advanced students in these various fields) intervenes forcefully in a number of areas of a family system over a period of two days. Several family and individual sessions take place. This procedure attempts to resolve the acute family crisis as well as to influence long–term change in the family's structure, functions, and models (MacGregor, 1967; Richie, 1960).

MacGregor, R. Multiple impact therapy with families. *Family Process 1:* 15–29, 1962.

MacGregor, R. Progress in multiple impact theory. In N. W. Ackerman, F. L. Beatman, & S. N. Sherman (Eds.), *Expanding theory and practice in family therapy.* New York: Family Service Association of America, 1967, 47–58.

Richie, A. Multiple impact therapy: An experiment. *Social Work 5:* 16–21, 1960.

* * * * * *

MUTUALITY

Mutuality is a reciprocal relationship that takes either a positive or negative form of spiraling give–and–take (Stierlin). The concept also has been used to characterize a phase of development in relational systems (Wynne).

In *Conflict and Reconciliation* (1969) and *Das Tun des Einen ist das Tun des Anderen (The Doing of the One Is the Doing of the Other)*, published in 1971, Stierlin describes the concepts of positive and negative mutuality. Positive mutuality is the "process of spiraling mutual growth and need fulfillment" (Stierlin, 1969, p. 110), with movement toward the encompassing of ever further and deeper aspects of the personalities of the interactional partners. In Hegelian terms, the movement of relationship is a movement toward mutual recognition: "I am validated in the other and the other is validated in me." This process is accomplished by complicated forms of duplicating that take place in self–awareness, that is, one must first lose oneself in order to find oneself in the other. This in turn involves a reciprocal demarcation of boundaries and reconciliation with the other that leads in each instance to higher levels of related → **individuation.** An ongoing dialogue is essential in order for this process to occur.

Dialogue understood in this manner is, as Spitz (1965) described it, a dialogue of action and response. This dialogue takes place within the context of a dyad, and in the form of circular feedback processes that are mutually stimulating. This dialogue is in turn influenced by the manner in which certain → **relational balances** change and make themselves felt within the framework of the developing relationship. Dialogue is an important concept in Buber's *I and Thou* (1923), and in Hegel's fundamental work, *The Phenomenology of Mind* (1807).

In contrast to positive mutuality, negative mutuality expresses itself through a lack of movement, a lack of real dialogue, and a mutual depreciation between dyadic partners. Relationships of this type may end in → **schismogenesis,** either → **complementary** or → **symmetrical.**

In a series of papers since 1958, Wynne has used the term "mutuality" with a meaning somewhat similar to what Stierlin (1969) calls "positive mutuality." Wynne, Ryckoff, Day, and Hirsch (1958) formulated a theory of relatedness in which mutuality was a main "solution" to the dilemma of needing to resolve both the problems of striving for relatedness and striving for a sense of personal identity (→ **individuation**): "[E]ach person brings to relations of genuine mutuality a sense of his own meaningful, positively–valued identity, and, out of experience or participation together, mutual recognition of identity develops, including a growing recognition of each other's potentialities and capacities. . . . Genuine mutuality, unlike pseudo–mutuality, not only tolerates divergence of self–interests, but thrives upon the recognition of such natural and inevitable divergence" (p. 207).

More recently, Wynne (1984) has elaborated upon the concept of mutuality as a developmental phase, building epigenetically upon the relational processes of attachment/caregiving, communicating, and joint problem solving. Dysfunctions of miscarried solutions that develop instead of mutuality are → **pseudomutuality/ pseudohostility,** which have some features in common with Stierlin's concept of negative mutuality.

Buber, M. [1923] *I and thou.* New York: Scribner's, 1958.
Hegel, G. W. F. [1807] *The phenomenology of the mind, Vol. II.* London: Swann Sonnenschein, 1910.
Spitz, R. A. *The first year of life: A psychoanalytic study of normal and deviant development of object relations.* New York: International Universities Press, 1965.
Stierlin, H. *Conflict and reconciliation.* New York: Science House, 1969.
Stierlin, H. *Das Tun des Einen ist das Tun des Anderen.* Frankfurt: Suhrkamp, 1971.
Stierlin, H. Status der Gegenseitigkeit: Die fünfte Perspektive des Heidelberger familiendynamischen Konzepts. *Familiendynamik 4:* 106–116, 1979.
Wynne, L. C. Methodological and conceptual issues in the study of schizophrenics and their families. *Journal of Psychiatric Research 6 (Suppl. 1):* 185–199, 1968.
Wynne, L. C. The epigenesis of relational systems: A model for understanding family developments. *Family Process 23:* 297–318, 1984.
Wynne, L. C., Ryckoff, I. M., Day, J., & Hirsch, S. I. Pseudo-mutuality in the family relations of schizophrenics. *Psychiatry 21:* 205–220, 1958.

$$* \quad * \quad * \quad * \quad * \quad *$$

MYSTIFICATION

As defined by Laing, mystification is the "misdefinition of the issues" (1969a, p. 27). It means "both the *act* of mystification and the *state* of being mystified." To mystify in the active sense is "to befuddle, cloud, obscure, mask whatever is going on, whether this be experience, action, or process, or whatever is 'the issue' " (1965, p. 344).

The term "mystification" was originally used by Karl Marx in 1867 (Marx, 1887) to describe the distortion and camouflage of facts that one class (the exploiters) uses to make and keep another class (the exploited) docile. The exploiters often succeed in convincing the exploited that these exploitations are actually forms of charity. According to Marx, the ensuing confusion leads the exploited to identify with their exploiters. It can even lead to the exploited being grateful for their own (unperceived) exploitation. In such instances, the exploiters need not fear any rebellion by the exploited.

Laing (1965) borrowed the term to describe a similar situation that occurs vividly in the families of schizophrenics, but he noted that a "certain amount of mystification occurs in everyday life" (1965, p. 345). He describes this concept as follows:

> The theoretically ultimate extreme of mystification is when the person (p) seeks to induce in the other (o) confusion (not necessarily recognized by o) as to o's whole experience (memory, perceptions, dreams, fantasy, imagination), processes, and actions. The mystified person is one who is given to understand that he feels happy or sad regardless of how he feels he feels, that he is responsible for this or not responsible for that regardless of what responsibility he has or has not taken upon himself. Capacities, or their lack, are attributed to him without reference to any shared empirical criteria of what these may or may not be. His own motives and intentions are discounted or minimized and replaced by others. His experience and actions generally are construed without reference to his own point of view. There is a radical failure to recognize his own self–perception and self–identity. (1965, p. 350)

Mystification is a transpersonal means of reinforcing one's security through → **disconfirmation** of the → **autonomy,** → **identity,** and perhaps differing views held by others. Laing described a close correlation between his conceptualization of mystification and earlier concepts in the family literature such as → **pseudomutuality,** → **driving crazy,** and imperviousness (Lidz et al., 1958). The active component of mystification is essentially synonymous with → **communication deviance.** Laing believed that mystification overlapped but was not synonymous with the → **double-bind** concept. "The essential distinction is that the mystified person, in contrast to the double–bound person, may be left with a relatively unequivocal 'right' way to experience and to act. This right thing to experience or right way to act may entail, from our viewpoint as investigators and therapists, a betrayal of the person's potentialities for self–fulfillment, but this may by no means be felt by the person himself" (1965, p. 353).

Laing's mystification concept belongs to a relatively early stage of family theory and therapy, which was mostly bound to a lineal concept of causality (→ **lineality**). It is now generally believed that the communication tactics described by Laing are characteristic of the communication style of many families with a schizophrenic member. However, the classification of the roles of "victim" (→ **identified patient**) and "victimizer" (parents) is in contradiction to the nature of circular causality (→ **circularity**), which determines to a great extent what occurs in families. From the perspective of the intervening therapist, the positing of a victim–culprit relationship leads inevitably to the therapist's identification with the victim. This attitude makes work with the entire family system nearly impossible because attitudes of → **neutrality** and → **multidirectional partiality,** so vital in therapy, are more or less ruled out.

Bateson, G., Jackson, D. D., Haley, J., & Weakland, J. H. Toward a theory of schizophrenia. *Behavioral Science 1:* 251–264, 1956.

Laing, R. D. Mystification, confusion, and conflict. In I. Boszormenyi-Nagy & J. L. Framo (Eds.), *Intensive family therapy: Theoretical and practical aspects.* New York: Harper & Row, 1965, 343–363.

Laing, R. D. *The politics of the family.* Toronto: Canadian Broadcast Corporation Publications, 1969. (a)

Laing, R. D. *The self and others: Further studies in sanity and madness.* London: Tavistock Publications, 1969. (b)

Laing, R. D., & Esterson, A. *Sanity, madness, and the family. Vol. I, Families of schizophrenics.* London: Tavistock Publications, 1964.

Lidz, T., Cornelison, A. R., Fleck, S., & Terry, D. The intrafamilial environment of schizophrenic patients: VI. The transmission of irrationality. *Archives of Neurology and Psychiatry 79:* 305–316, 1958.

Marx, K. [1867] *Capital: A critique of political economy.* London: Swann Sonnenschein, 1887.

Wynne, L. C., Ryckoff, I. M., Day, J., & Hirsch, S. I. Pseudo-mutuality in the family relations of schizophrenics. *Psychiatry 21:* 205–220, 1958.

* * * * * *

■ N ■

NETWORK THERAPY

This form of therapeutic intervention is used with larger social systems. Relatives, friends, neighbors, involved professionals, and other persons who appear relevant to the problem family are involved in the therapeutic process. Because this involves a large number of people (the average size of a network group of a typical, urban middle–class family is about 40 people), a qualified therapeutic team is required.

Network therapy was developed by Speck and Attneave. It considers itself to be in the tradition of various tribal cultures (very likely dating back to prehistorical times) in which the entire tribe met in periods of crisis to seek common solutions to tribal problems. For many of these cultures, tribal meetings were an occasion for the healing of the sick.

The basic idea of such therapy is to rediscover and systematically

242

use the healing power of rituals and myths, which in primitive societies generated a feeling of mutual bonding between group members. The methods applied to achieve this have their source for the most part in experiences of so–called "group cultures." An acute crisis situation, e.g., delinquent behavior or schizophrenic decompensation of a family member, brings the family into contact with the intervention team. After a discussion of the presenting problem, the family is asked to invite all relevant persons to their home. The family system is thus expanded to components of the → ecosystem, and the → context of the family (metacontext of the → identified patient) is made visible.

The goals of the intervention team are to question rigid patterns of relationship and behavioral sequences, to loosen old ties, and to establish new bonds, in other words, to change the structures of perception and consciousness as well as the organizational schemata of the entire social network. With the help of nonverbal exercises and rituals, the intervention leader is able to change rigid patterns of behavior, to correct perceptions of experiences, and to establish new relationships. A so–called "system effect" (more accurately, network effect) is thus created through predominantly nonverbal expressions of community and belonging. Speck and Attneave (1972) compared this effect with what happened every night in Preservation Hall in New Orleans when the jazz bands of the Dixieland era started improvising:

> The audience of habituées and tourists begins the evening relatively unrelated to one another, at separate tables, and in couples or small groups. Under the mystical, religious, tribal, hypnotic, musical spell they become closely knitted together. They sit tightly pressed. The small group boundaries dissolve. They clap, sway, beat out rhythms, and move their bodies in a united complex response. The group mood is a euphoric high, and the conventional bonds dissolve. New relationships melt away the conventional barriers of status, generation, territory and sex. Young white women, lower–class black men, older spinsters, and hippie youths recognize a mutuality and express it in gesture, contact, and verbal expressions. (p. 434).

In the large group sessions of network intervention, something similar occurs. An experience of fusion is initiated on the affective level, old boundaries (particularly those of the problem family) are broken up, and the feeling of unity leads to the creation of new ways to solve problems. Because of the multiple resources offered by the new, higher–order system, the family's problem no longer seems unresolvable. Not only the context of the illness (the family) but also the family's own context (the superordinate social network) is changed and the definition of the illness itself is modified. It is a true ecosystemic (→ ecology/ecosystem) approach.

To induce a change of this type and to bring it to a successful conclusion, the intervention team must possess sufficient experience in dealing with large groups. This requires, among other things, a willingness to come to terms with one's own role as therapist and the expectations involved in this role, as well as a high degree of sensitivity for the correct timing of intervention strategies in group process. A variation of this procedure is work done with peer groups and institutions, where the roles of therapists, consultants, and trainers in group dynamics begin to merge.

The great advantage of this type of intervention is the fact that individuals are not removed from their reference group and, in such a group, they can relate the experiences they have had in the therapeutic setting to their everyday world. The identified patient's entire, real, everyday social system has gone through the therapeutic experience with him or her.

An alternative developed by Judith Landau (1981, 1982) is to meet with an extended family or a network only once in order to select a "link therapist" from the family to be trained and coached to be the therapist to his or her own family system. This method is both cost–effective and brief and also serves to empower the family and remove the therapy label. It can be used where families are not accessible to therapists for geographic, economic, or cultural reasons.

Attneave, C. L. Therapy in tribal settings and urban network intervention. *Family Process 8:* 192–210, 1969.

Auerswald, E. H. Interdisciplinary versus ecological approach. *Family Process 7:* 202–215, 1968.

Auerswald, E. H. Thinking about thinking about health and mental health. In G. Caplan (Ed.), *American handbook of psychiatry, Vol. 2: Child and adolescent psychiatry, sociocultural and community psychiatry* (revised ed.). New York: Basic Books, 1974, 316–338.

Erickson, G. D. A framework and themes for social network intervention. *Family Process 23:* 187–198, 1984.

Halevy-Martini, J., Hemley-van der Velden, E. M., Ruhf, L., & Schoenfeld, P. Process and strategy in network therapy. *Family Process 23:* 521–533, 1984.

Landau, J. Link therapy as a family therapy technique for transitional extended families. *Psychotherapeia 7:* 382–390, 1981.

Landau, J. Therapy with families in cultural transition. In M. McGoldrick, J. K. Pearce, and J. Giordano (Eds.), *Ethnicity and family therapy.* New York: Guilford Press, 1982, 552–572.

Rueveni, U. Network intervention with a family in crisis. *Family Process 14:* 193–203, 1975.

Speck, R. V., & Attneave, C. L. Social network intervention. In J. Haley (Ed.), *Changing families: A family therapy reader.* New York: Grune & Stratton, 1971, 312–332.

Speck, R. V., & Attneave, C. L. Social network intervention. In C. J. Sager & H. S. Kaplan (Eds.), *Progress in group and family therapy.* New York: Brunner/Mazel, 1972, 416–439.

Speck, R. V., & Attneave, C. L. *Family networks.* New York: Pantheon Books, 1973.

Speck, R. V., & Rueveni, U. Network therapy—A developing concept. *Family Process 8:* 182–191, 1969.

244

Trimble, D., & Kliman, J. Community network therapy: Strengthening the networks of chronic patients. *International Journal of Family Psychiatry 2:* 269–290, 1981.

* * * * * *

NETWORKS

The linkage of effects in the dimensions of time and space can be conceptualized as a → **structure** in the form of a network. The concept of a network of effects is applicable to events, sequences, and functions in various areas of reality. For example, the neuronal activity within the brain can be viewed as a network of effects, and can be analyzed by means of mathematical models (Kleene, 1956; McCulloch & Pitts, 1943). The social behavior of an individual in relation to his or her environment can also be viewed as a network of effects (→ **structuralism**).

The investigation of the structure of networks provides a formal framework for the integration of social and biological data. In family therapy, the concept of networks is usually used in a more restricted sense to refer to the family's social environment, that is, the world of work, school, neighborhood, etc. In this sense, → **network therapy** goes beyond the boundaries of the nuclear family and even the extended family and attempts to include the ecosystem (→ **ecology/ ecosystem**). Even when the social environment and the persons who comprise it are not directly involved in the therapeutic process, the therapist must consider them in relation to the → **context** of symptom formation.

A vast literature on social networks dates especially from the pioneering work of Elizabeth Bott (1957). Earlier writers, especially in anthropology and sociology, used other terms such as "kindred." Bott used the term network "to describe a set of social relationships for which there is no common boundary" (p. 59). That is, each person is, as it were, in touch with a number of people, some of whom are directly in touch with each other and some of whom are not. Thus, a network is *not* a → **system,** for which a defining feature is a → **boundary.**

In considering the context of families, various investigators have studied the size and quality of social networks in relation to family and patient functioning. The work of Pattison and associates (1975) has shown that "healthy" persons have 20 to 30 persons in their psychosocial networks, whereas neurotic patients have only 10 to 12 people; psychotics have only 4 or 5 people, usually family members. Small network size may be a premorbid characteristic in some but not in all cases of mental illness. A factor in decline in network size after the onset of mental illness appears to be the absence of reciprocity in relationships between the → **identified patient** and other persons (Westermayer & Pattison, 1981).

The concept of social networks is "more connotatively neutral and more structurally oriented" (Hammer, 1981, p. 45) than the concept of "social supports," which is important in clinical planning about the resources available to individual patients and families. Beels (1981) has defined "social supports" to be "whatever factors there are in the environment that promote a favorable course of the illness" (p. 60). Some patients deteriorate when social connections disappear; others are overwhelmed by emotionally overinvolved or critical persons in the environment (→ **expressed emotion/ affective style**). Earlier hypotheses had proposed that parents with high expressed emotion would be more isolated from effective social supports, but Anderson and associates (1984) recently showed that families that are internally overinvolved are also more involved with their networks and are not isolated.

Adams, B. Interaction theory and the social network. *Sociometry 30:* 64–78, 1967.

Anderson, C. M., Hogarty, G., Bayer, T., & Needleman, R. Expressed emotion and social networks of parents of schizophrenic patients. *British Journal of Psychiatry 144:* 247–255, 1984.

Beels, C. C. Social support and schizophrenia. *Schizophrenia Bulletin 7:* 58–72, 1981.

Bott, E. *Family and social networks.* London: Tavistock Publications, 1957.

Hammer, M. Social supports, social networks, and schizophrenia. *Schizophrenia Bulletin 7:* 45–57, 1981.

Kleene, S. C. Representation of events in nerve nets and finite automata. In C. E. Shannon & J. McCarthy (Eds.), *Automata studies.* Princeton, N. J.: Princeton University Press, 1956, 3–41.

McCulloch, W. S., & Pitts, W. H. A logical calculus of ideas immanent in nervous activity. *Bulletin of Mathematical Biophysics 5:* 115–133, 1943.

Parsons, T., Bales, R. F., Olds, J., Zelditch, M., & Slater, P. E. *Family, socialization and interaction process.* Glencoe, Ill.: Free Press, 1955.

Parsons, T., & Fox, R. Illness, therapy and the modern urban American family. *Journal of Social Issues 8:* 31–44, 1953.

Pattison, E. M., DeFrancisco, D., Wood, P., Frazier, H., & Crowder, J. A psychosocial kinship model for family therapy. *American Journal of Psychotherapy 132:* 1246–1251, 1975.

Speck, R. V., & Attneave, C. L. *Family networks.* New York: Pantheon Books, 1973.

Tolsdorf, C. C. Social networks, support, and coping: An exploratory study. *Family Process 15:* 407–417, 1976.

Westermeyer, J., & Pattison, E. H. Social networks and mental illness in a peasant society. *Schizophrenia Bulletin 7:* 125–134, 1981.

* * * * * *

NEUROLINGUISTIC PROGRAMMING

This form of therapy, founded by Bandler and Grinder, applies to the methods of → **hypnotherapy** and some aspects of → **communication theory,** → **epistemology,** and → **psycholinguistics.** It is based on the concept of unconscious representational systems in which past, subjective experiences of individuals take the form of internal programs that differ from individual to individual.

Each individual has preferred modalities or levels of sensory experience, e.g., auditory, visual, or kinesthetic. These modalities make an imprint on the individual's experience even before language has structured the experience. The language that the individual then uses remains closely linked with the imprinted, chosen sensory modality. Thus, interpersonal communication is successful (or unsuccessful) to the extent that interactional partners are able to adjust to each other's preferred sensory modalities. This is of particular importance for communication between therapist and patient.

Bandler and Grinder (see reference list) arrived at their therapeutic methods by analyzing the nonverbal → **analogue communication** of therapists and their clients. They discovered incongruities in communication behavior when differing messages were sent on levels of communication that corresponded to various levels of sensory perception. If the incongruities of these messages can be demonstrated, conclusions can then be drawn about the manner in which an identified patient not only "draws" but also "colors in" his or her "internal map" (→ **paradigm/ model/ map**). The therapist who wishes to change this internal map (→ **reframing**) must know its colors. An indication of the preferred sensory mode can be gained from the kind of speech an individual uses. A person who prefers the visual mode uses such terms as: "I can picture that," "I see," "that is clear," etc. An auditive person will use such expressions as "loud," "I hear you," "harmonious," etc. A person oriented toward the kinesthetic mode will choose such expresses as "pressure," "tension," and "feeling."

The following is an example of unsuccessful interaction between a visually oriented client and a kinesthetically oriented therapist:

> *Client:* "My husband just doesn't see me as a valuable person."
> *Therapist:* "How do you feel about that?"
> *Client:* "What?"
> *Therapist:* "How do you feel about your husband's not feeling you're a person?"
> *Client:* "That's a hard question. I just don't know."

The therapist later said he felt frustrated because this woman was resisting and giving him a hard time (Bandler & Grinder, 1979, p. 16).

Grinder's and Bandler's theories belong to the field of psycholinguistics, which concerns itself with the relationship between language and unconscious psychic structures. Their therapeutic methods are a further development and a variation of communication therapy approaches. However, their formidably technical term, "neurolinguistic programming," is not conceptually new; it is a systematic description of what good therapists do intuitively, and poor therapists never learn: the ability to make the client feel understood (→ **joining**).

Bandler, R., & Grinder, J. *Patterns of the hypnotic techniques of Milton H. Erickson, M. D., Vol. I.* Cupertino, Cal.: META Publications, 1975. (a)

Bandler, R., & Grinder, J. *The structure of magic, Vol. I.* Palo Alto: Science and Behavior Books, 1975. (b)

Bandler, R., & Grinder, J. *Frogs into princes.* Moab, Utah: Real People Press, 1979.

Bandler, R., & Grinder, J. *Tranceformation.* Moab, Utah: Real People Press, 1981.

Bandler, R., & Grinder, J. *Reframing: Neurolinguistic programming and the transformation of meaning.* Moab, Utah: Real People Press, 1982.

Dilts, R. B., Grinder, J., Bandler, R., Delozier, J., & Cameron-Bandler, J. *Neurolinguistic programming, Vol. I.* Cupertino, Cal.: META Publications, 1979.

Grinder, J., & Bandler, R. *The structure of magic, Vol. II.* Palo Alto: META Publications, 1976.

Grinder, J., & Bandler, R. *Trance-formations: Neuro-linguistic programming and the structure of hypnosis.* Moab, Utah: Real People Press, 1981.

Grinder, J., Delozier, J., & Bandler, R. *Patterns of the hypnotic techniques of Milton H. Erickson, M. D., Vol. II.* Cupertino, Cal.: META Publications, 1977.

Lankton, S. *Practical magic: The clinical applications of neuro-linguistic programming.* Cupertino, Cal.: META Publications, 1979.

* * * * * *

NEUTRALITY

This is the preferred attitude of a therapist toward all the members of a family in → **systemic therapy.** Used with → **circular questioning,** this attitude prevents the therapist from being drawn into "family games," from being tempted to enter a coalition with one or more family members, or from being "brought around" to acting in certain ways within the family system. No family member is given the opportunity to feel that he or she has a special relationship to the therapist. The therapist maintains the same degree of → **closeness/ distance** to each family member and, thus, stays on the level of → **metacommunication** during therapy. In this

248

sense, neutrality is not so much an internal attitude as a "technical maneuver" that enables the therapist to maintain the role of authority with all the members of the family.

The concept of neutrality, described by Selvini–Palazzoli and her team (1980), attempts to do justice to the fact that families are in possession of a number of strategies that aim at "chipping away" the therapist's authority, at trying to use the therapist as a stabilizing element within the family structure and thereby thwarting the therapist's attempts to change the family. This danger always presents itself when the therapist allows the family to pull him or her down to the level where "we are all just equals." In order to maintain the role of the expert, i.e., an effective metaposition in regard to the family and its problems, a therapist must remain neutral and relatively calm in the face of stormy events and emotionally harrowing reports by members of the family. Neutrality in no way prohibits the therapist from having empathy for the actors in the family drama. On the contrary, it makes a special type of empathy possible, an empathy that takes the form of circular questioning, rather than a reaction toward the momentary behavior of any particular family member. A well–coordinated team will insure a consistent attitude of neutrality. Some of the team members work with the family directly while others observe the session from behind a one–way mirror. A therapist being observed and supervised by the other team members runs less risk of being enticed by the family to "join the system." (The concept of neutrality in family therapy must be differentiated from the concept of → **multidirectional partiality,** which is a psychodynamically oriented procedure that tries to institute a dialogue between family members.)

Penn, P. Circular questioning. *Family Process 21:* 267–280, 1982.
Selvini-Palazzoli, M., Boscolo, L., Cecchin, G., & Prata, G. Hypothesizing-circularity-neutrality: Three guidelines for the conductor of the session. *Family Process 19:* 3–12, 1980.
Tomm, K. One perspective on the Milan systemic approach: Part I. Overview of development, theory and practice. *Journal of Marital and Family Therapy 10:* 113–125, 1984. (a)
Tomm, K. One perspective on the Milan systemic approach: Part II. Description of session format, interviewing style and interventions. *Journal of Marital and Family Therapy 10:* 253–271, 1984. (b)

* * * * * *

Nonlinearity/Step Function

In mathematics and in the context of → **cybernetics,** nonlinearity refers to a relationship between variables that does not form a straight line in a right–angled, Cartesian system of coordinates. Its opposite is linearity (→ **lineality/ linearity**), where change in one variable effects a proportional change in another variable. Besides continuous nonlinear relationships, there exist discontinuous nonlinear relationships that are called step functions in mathematics. These form the mathematical counterpart of what is denoted in systems theory as second–order change (→ **change, first and second order**).

Nonlinearity is exhibited in all instances of positive → **feedback** where a deviation exponentially reinforces itself. An example of this is the population explosion. Discontinuous changes that cause a system to switch from one behavioral mode to another correspond to mathematical step functions. An example of this is the manner in which the gears and the transmission of an automobile function. In first gear, speed is limited to a certain level; when this level is reached, one must shift to a higher gear to increase speed further, in other words, to induce change. This shifting of gears is bound up with the activation of other internal structures (gear mechanisms) of the system. We have, in short, a recalibration of the system. The fact that change can take place on a number of levels, in a nonlinear manner, is an essential prerequisite in the understanding of the effects achieved by certain family therapy interventions. All forms of → **brief therapy** are based on the concept of nonlinearity, i.e., on the insight that more effort does not necessarily imply better results (→ **stability**).

Watzlawick, P., Beavin, J. H., & Jackson, D. D. *Pragmatics of human communication: A study of interactional patterns, pathologies and paradoxes.* New York: W. W. Norton & Co., 1967.

■ O ■

OBJECT RELATIONS THEORY

This psychoanalytic theory of human relationships, developed by Fairbairn (1952), has influenced various concepts of family therapy. Fairbairn posits that every individual has a fundamental need for satisfactory object relationships, and that this need will shape future behavior. He regards the development of personality as largely equivalent to the establishment of a system of → **inner objects.** The manner in which these objects are internally represented and → **self/object differentiation** is structured, largely determines how an individual feels, thinks, and relates to others. The functions of these inner objects can be understood as an aspect of ego functions (→ **ego psychology**), which are important in the development of individual → **autonomy.**

The psychology of object relations and the psychology of Self are sometimes considered to be distinct from one another in psychoanalytic theory; however, they represent a functional unity. By means of the construction of "object representations" and "object images," on the one hand, and "self–representations" and "self–images," on the other hand, each individual develops an internalized *model* of human relationships (→ **paradigm/ model/map**). The decisive factor is not the static images themselves but the manner in which these images are related to one another. Kernberg (1976) attempted to integrate these two theoretical spectra within psychoanalytic theory.

According to Fairbairn, inner objects develop as the result of early frustrations. Because the mother is not capable of satisfying all the relational needs of the infant and the child is unable to change reality, the child introjects the frustrating aspects of the mother. This in general then forms the foundation of the child's future interpersonal expectations and relationships. During the child's development, these internalized objects (or object representations) can be modified, split, or fused with aspects of self–representation (Mahler, 1968). If new levels of related → **individuation** are to be achieved, inner objects and the Self must be constantly reexamined and reintegrated (altered). If this process of change is unsuccessful, new relationships will be seen, evaluated, and structured in the light of old models, for instance, when an adult retains a childlike view of his or her parents who obviously have changed over the course of time. Such parents then become objects of intrafamilial → **transference,** which needs to be differentiated from extrafamilial transference that is directed toward an outsider, e.g., a therapist (Stierlin, 1977).

Therapists who work within the encounter model attempt to confront families with real and internalized objects in order to achieve an internal family dialogue in which disappointed expectations can be articulated, conflicts brought into the open, and reconciliation processes initiated. These procedures, derived from psychoanalysis, mainly support the development of differentiation and integration of inner objects. The aim is to achieve an enhanced and more astute perception of Self and of reference persons that is not principally determined by the mechanisms of → **projective identification** (→ **growth therapy**).

Fairbairn, W. *Psychoanalytic studies of the personality.* London: Tavistock Publications, 1952.

Guntrip, H. *Schizoid phenomena, object-relations and the self.* New York: International Universities Press, 1969.

Jacobson, E. The self and the object world. *Psychoanalytic Study of the Child 9:* 75–127, 1954.

Kernberg, O. F. *Object relations theory and clinical psychoanalysis.* New York: Jason Aronson, 1976.

Mahler, M. *On human symbiosis and the vicissitudes of individuation. Vol. I, Infantile psychosis.* New York: International Universities Press, 1968.

Slipp, S. *Object relations: A dynamic bridge between individual and family treatment.* New York: Jason Aronson, 1984.

Spitz, R. A. Genèse des premières relations objectales. *Revue Française de Psychanalyse 28,* 1954.

Stewart, R. H., Peters, T. C., Marsh, S., & Peters, M. J. An object-relations approach to psychotherapy with marital couples, families, and children. *Family Process 14:* 161–178, 1975.

Stierlin, H. Familientherapeutische Aspekte der Übertragung und Gegenübertragung. *Familiendynamik 2:* 182–197, 1977.

Winnicott, D. W. *The maturational processes and the facilitating environment.* New York: International Universities Press, 1965.

* * * * * *

■ P ■

PARADIGM/ MODEL/ MAP

The term "paradigm" has gained wide usage in family therapy and theory in part because family therapists have regarded the emergence of the family therapy field as a "paradigmatic shift," a concept developed by

Thomas S. Kuhn (1962). It is noteworthy that Kuhn used the term to describe phenomena that he regarded as specific in the development of science. He defined paradigms as "universally recognized scientific achievements that for a time provide model problems and solutions to a community of practitioners" (p. x). Over the years, the term has sometimes been used in accord with Kuhn's formulation, and at other times more casually. The terms "model" and "map" (or internal map) can be viewed as conceptually nested within the broader concept of paradigm, while the term paradigm can be regarded as constituent of the larger term → epistemology.

Kuhn was particularly concerned with major paradigms of science, such as the contributions of Aristotle, Copernicus, Galileo, Newton, and Einstein. Two essential characteristics of such achievements, according to Kuhn, were that they were "sufficiently unprecedented to attract an enduring group of adherents away from conflicting models of scientific activity" and were "sufficiently open–ended to leave all sorts of problems for the redefined group of practitioners to resolve" (p. 10). In Kuhn's terminology, models spring from coherent traditions of research within any given paradigm. He notes that "the road to a firm research consensus is extraordinarily arduous" and that "it remains an open question what parts of social science have yet acquired such paradigms at all" (p. 15). Since 1962, when Kuhn made these formulations, many family therapists would like to think that they have in fact now traveled the road to paradigmatic consensus. It is reassuring to note Kuhn's statement that a paradigm "need not, and in fact never does, explain all the facts with which it can be confronted" (p. 18).

Keeney (1979) proposed that the paradigm that has evolved in the family field is based upon → cybernetics, → ecology, and → systems theory, and that it be called "ecosystemic epistemology." It also has been called a Batesonian paradigm. With the seeming recognition of this "systemic" paradigm, however labeled, it is interesting that purifications and clarifications, not clearcut criticisms, of the paradigm have become increasingly common (Cronen, Johnson, & Lannamann, 1982; Dell, 1982, 1985; de Shazer, 1982; Elkaïm, 1985). Indeed, Kuhn's formulation predicts that such dissatisfactions will emerge as a paradigm becomes the "object for further articulation and specification under new or more stringent conditions" (p. 22). Among the "new conditions" since the late 1970s that are of increasing concern to family therapists are observations about discontinuous change, → self-organization/ autopoiesis, and the extension of family therapy into work with culturally diverse groups and networks (Minuchin, 1984; Walters, 1985). The complexity of studying family relationships following divorce and remarriage makes boundaries of family systems difficult to redefine, and even makes the applicability of the system concept questionable.

Ironically, as a paradigm becomes regarded as satisfactory to more and more people and provides a framework within which more and more puzzles can be solved, the paradigm can "insulate the community from those socially important problems that are not reducible to the puzzle form, because they cannot be stated in terms of the conceptual and instrumental tools that the paradigm supplies" (Kuhn, p. 37; see also Schwartz & Perrotta, 1985). A paradigm provides criteria for those problems that seem to have solutions while the paradigm is still taken for granted. However, when anomalous findings start to emerge in the course of studies within a paradigm, the novelty of such anomalies is at first resisted. "By insuring that the paradigm will not be too easily surrendered, resistance guarantees that scientists will not be lightly distracted and that the anomalies that led to paradigm change will penetrate existing knowledge to the core" (Kuhn, p. 55).

It is probably too soon to decide whether the recent revisions (?challenges) to the systemic, Batesonian paradigm are going to be replaced shortly by a genuinely newer paradigm or whether the Batesonian paradigm is merely undergoing internal refinements. (See *Family Process,* 1982 and *The Family Therapy Networker 9* (4), 1985 for examples of this controversy.) For example, de Shazer (1982b) and Cronen, Johnson, and Lannamann (1982) sharply criticize the theory of Logical Types, which was a significant starting point for Bateson's formulations. Similarly, Dell (1982) speaks of Bateson's failure to formulate an ontology comparable to Maturana's contribution. However, it is not quite clear whether these challenges to Bateson are a revision of Bateson or a proposed new paradigmatic shift away from Bateson. It also may be that Kuhn's concept of revolutionary paradigm shifts is found only in exceptional circumstances. Kuhn's critics from the fields of philosophy and the history of science do in fact challenge him on this point. For example, Hofstadter (1979) states: "The Kuhnian theory that certain rare events called 'paradigm shifts' mark the distinction between 'normal' science and 'conceptual revolutions' does not seem to work, for we can see paradigm shifts happen all throughout the system, all the time" (p. 660).

Reiss's Family Paradigm: Reiss (1981) has used Kuhn's concept of paradigm "metaphorically" as a concept applicable to specific families rather than to science. He speaks of the "*family paradigm* as a central organizer of its shared constructs, sets, expectations, and fantasies about its social world" (p. 2). In analogy to Kuhn's paradigms of science, Reiss concludes that families construe their social world as having properties that within the family are not subject to dispute, and that specify how their world is to be investigated, what conclusions are permissible, and how further explorations of the world will be shaped. The family paradigm is manifest not only in the family's patterns of daily living, but also in its mode of functioning in ambiguously structured laboratory tests (Sigafoos & Reiss, 1985).

Models and Maps: At times the term "model" is used interchangeably with paradigm, but Kuhn's usage suggests that it may be preferable to use "models" as constituent sets of ideas within paradigms. Further, the term "map" can be regarded as the application of a model to a specific situation. Thus, a therapist can use a "model" of treatment to construct a "map" for interventions with a specific family. It should be noted that the terms map and mapping have been widely used as far back as Lewin's formulations of field theory (1935), and by a number of therapists: Bloch (1973), de Shazer (1982a), Kantor & Lehr (1975), Landau (1982), Minuchin (1974), and Satir, Stachowiak, and Taschman (1975) have emphasized mapping concepts in planning therapy. De Shazer (1982a) has drawn upon the concepts of Heider (1946) in order to apply balance theory to the mapping of therapeutic interventions, particularly in specifying the procedures of Milton Erickson. Minuchin (1974) used the concept of "a structural map" to organize clinical material and to formulate hypotheses for treatment planning. In contrast to the → **genogram,** which shows demographic data and kinship ties, Minuchin's maps show coalitions (→ **alliance**), conflicts, → **boundaries,** and other structural features relevant to treatment issues. He also spoke of the family's own map or organizational scheme, using the term somewhat as Reiss uses the term family paradigm. Still more comprehensively, the "transitional mapping" described by Landau (1982) is a graphic tool for identifying stages of the → **family life cycle,** family relationships inside and outside the family, and the family's repeating processes and patterns.

In general, the concept of "internal map" refers to the subjective experience or frame of reference used by individuals or family systems that helps make their behavior comprehensible to themselves. This process involves cognitive selection and processes of → **abstraction.** Changes in an internal map involve changes in behavior and are associated in family therapy with → **reframing.**

Auerswald, E. H. Thinking about thinking in family therapy. *Family Process 24:* 1–12, 1985.

Bateson, G. *Mind and nature: A necessary* unit. New York: E. P. Dutton, 1979.

Bloch, D. A. The clinical home visit. In D. A. Bloch (Ed.), *Techniques of family psychotherapy: A primer.* New York: Grune & Stratton, 1973, 39–45.

Coyne, J. C., Denner, B., & Ransom, D. C. Undressing the fashionable mind. *Family Process 21:* 391–396, 1982.

Cronen, V. E., Johnson, K. M., & Lannamann, J. W. Paradoxes, double binds, and reflexive loops: An alternative theoretical perspective. *Family Process 21:* 91–112, 1982.

Dell, P. F. Beyond homeostasis: Toward a concept of coherence. *Family Process 21:* 21–41, 1982.

Dell, P. F. Understanding Bateson and Maturana: Toward a biological foundation for the social sciences. *Journal of Marital and Family Therapy 11:* 1–20, 1985.

de Shazer, S. *Patterns of brief family therapy: An ecosystemic approach.* New York: Guilford Press, 1982. (a)

de Shazer, S. Some conceptual distinctions are more useful than others. *Family Process 21:* 71–84, 1982. (b)

Elkaïm, M. From general laws to singularities. *Family Process 24:* 151–164, 1985.

Elkaïm, M., Prigogine, I., Guattari, F., Stengers, I., & Denebourg, J.-L. Openness: A round-table discussion. *Family Process 21:* 57–70, 1982.

Hampden-Turner, C. *Maps of the mind: Charts and concept of the mind and its labyrinths.* New York: Collier Books, 1981.

Heider, F. Attitudes and cognitive organization. *Journal of Psychology 21:* 107–112, 1946.

Hoffman, L. *Foundations of family therapy: A conceptual framework for systems change.* New York: Basic Books, 1981.

Hofstadter, D. R. *Gödel, Escher, Bach: An eternal golden braid.* New York: Basic Books, 1979.

Kantor, D., & Lehr, W. *Inside the family: Toward a theory of family process,* San Francisco: Jossey-Bass, 1975.

Keeney, B. P. Ecosystemic epistemology: An alternative paradigm for diagnosis. *Family Process 18:* 117–129, 1979.

Keeney, B. P., & Sprenkle, D. H. Ecosystemic epistemology: Critical implications for the aesthetics and pragmatics of family therapy. *Family Process 21:* 1–19, 1982.

Kuhn, T. S. *The structure of scientific revolutions.* Chicago: University of Chicago Press, 1962.

Landau, J. Therapy with families in cultural transition. In M. McGoldrick, J. K. Pearce, & J. Giordano (Eds.), *Ethnicity and family therapy.* New York: Guilford Press, 1982, 552–572.

Lewin, K. *A dynamic theory of personality.* New York: McGraw-Hill, 1935.

Maturana, H. R., & Varela, F. J. *Autopoiesis and cognition: The realization of living.* Boston: Reidel, 1980.

Minuchin, S. *Families and family therapy.* Cambridge: Harvard University Press, 1974.

Minuchin, S. *Family kaleidoscope.* Cambridge: Harvard University Press, 1984.

Morin, E. *Le paradigme perdu: La nature humaine.* Paris: Seuil, 1973.

Reiss, D. *The family's construction of reality.* Cambridge: Harvard University Press, 1981.

Satir, V., Stachowiak, J., & Taschman, H. A. *Helping families to change.* New York: Jason Aronson, 1975.

Schwartz, R., & Perrotta, P. Let us sell no intervention before its time. *Family Therapy Networker 9* (4): 18–25, 1985.

Sigafoos, A., & Reiss, D. Rejoinder: Counterperspectives on family measurement: Clarifying the pragmatic interpretation of research methods. *Family Process 24:* 207–211, 1985.

Simon, F. B. *Der Prozess der Individuation: Über den Zusammenhang von Vernunft und Gefühlen.* Göttingen: Vandenhoeck & Ruprecht, 1984.

Tolman, E. G. Cognitive maps in rats and men. *Psychological Review 55:* 189–208, 1948.
Walters, M. Where have all the flowers gone? *Family Therapy Networker 9* (4): 38–41, 1985.
Watzlawick, P. (Ed.). *The invented reality: How do we know what we believe we know? Contributions to constructivism.* New York: W. W. Norton & Co., 1984.

* * * * * *

PARADOXICAL INTERVENTION

This therapeutic technique plays a particularly important role in → **communication therapy,** → **strategic therapy,** and → **systemic therapy.** The patient or the family is exposed to contradictory instructions. A situation is created that cannot be resolved by means of logic, but only by creatively changing one's internal map of the world (→ **paradigm/ model/ map**), or through second–order → **change.**

When a therapist instructs a patient or a family to hold onto a symptom, the therapist, in effect, takes control of the therapeutic system. If the symptom continues to be present, this can be regarded as the result of compliance with the instructions of the therapist. If the symptom disappears, therapy has been successful. A patient who wishes to be rid of the symptom, but yet shows → **resistance** to any therapeutic efforts toward change, can be freed from this paradoxical situation by means of a "counterparadox" (Selvini–Palazzoli et al., 1978). The patient can only resist therapy by giving up the symptom, or can only maintain the symptom by giving up the resistance. Paradoxical instructions aim at invalidating the pathogenic paradoxes that patients have constructed from their own → **epistemology.** They are especially necessary where interactional partners mutually reinforce each other's rigidly maintained lineal (→ **lineality**) patterns of argument and are in danger of ending up in a → **malign clinch.**

The → **double–bind** theory describes the relational traps and dilemmas that result in such instances, particularly in those families with a schizophrenic member. Paradoxical interventions as techniques of resolving such situations have been described by a number of authors, especially by Erickson (Erickson & Rossi, 1975; Haley, 1973). The advocacy of various authors (see the reference list) for the use of paradoxical techniques is founded on the belief that the client and family make use of the symptom in some way, in other words, that the symptom is functional in the individual's or family's → **adaptability.**

Haley (1967, 1976) has attempted to analyze and describe the prerequisites for a paradoxical intervention. The problem must first be clearly defined. Change must be clearly stipulated as the goal of the therapeutic relationship. The therapist then works out a plan that challenges the perspective in which the symptom has been viewed. On the basis of this plan, the therapist gives a paradoxical instruction (→ **symptom prescription**), for example, by telling the family that they can only change by staying the way they are, or that they can only stay the way they are by changing.

Rohrbaugh et al. (1981) has identified three types of paradoxical interventions: prescribing, restraining, and positioning operations. In the prescribing strategy, the therapist instructs the family members to engage in the specific behavior to be eliminated. When restraining, the therapist discourages change and may even deny that change is possible. In paradoxical positioning, the therapist accepts and exaggerates a position that the patient or problem has taken.

By not matching the typical expectations of the family vis–à–vis a therapeutic role, for example, by requesting the family *not* to change, the therapist forces them to take a counterposition. The family can then abandon the false alternative that either everything must change or that everything must remain as it is. Instead of these two dead–end alternatives, a third solution may be found, a solution that the therapist will not always know in advance. Paradoxical interventions force the family to develop new, creative approaches to old problems, which may lead them to adopt new forms of → **individuation.** (See also → **reframing,** → **positive connotation.**)

Erickson, M. H., & Rossi, E. Varieties of double bind. *American Journal of Clinical Hypnosis 17:* 143–157, 1975.

Fisher, B. L., Giblin, P. R., & Hoopes, M. H. Healthy family functioning: What therapists say and what families want. *Journal of Marital and Family Therapy 8:* 273–284, 1982.

Frankl, V. E. Paradoxical intention: A logotherapeutic technique. *American Journal of Psychotherapy 14:* 520–535, 1960.

Frankl, V. E. *Psychotherapy and existentialism: Selected papers on logotherapy.* New York: Washington Square Press, 1967.

Haley, J. *Strategies of psychotherapy.* New York: Grune & Stratton, 1963.

Haley, J. (Ed.). *Advanced techniques of hypnosis and therapy: The selected papers of Milton H. Erickson, M. D.* New York: Grune & Stratton, 1967.

Haley, J. *Uncommon therapy: The psychiatric techniques of Milton H. Erickson, M. D.: A casebook of an innovative psychiatrist's work in short-term therapy.* New York: W. W. Norton & Co., 1973.

Haley, J. *Problem–solving therapy.* San Francisco: Jossey-Bass, 1976.

Haley, J. *Ordeal therapy.* San Francisco: Jossey-Bass, 1984.

Madanes, C. *Strategic family therapy.* San Francisco: Jossey-Bass, 1981.

Papp, P. The Greek chorus and other techniques of paradoxical therapy. *Family Process 19:* 45–57, 1980.

258

Papp, P. *The process of change.* New York: Guilford Press, 1983.
Raskin, D. E., & Klein, Z. E. Losing a symptom through keeping it: A review of paradoxical treatment techniques and rationale. *Archives of General Psychiatry 33:* 548–555, 1976.
Rohrbaugh, M., Tennen, H., Press, S., & White, L. Compliance, defiance and therapeutic paradox: Guidelines for strategic use of paradoxical interventions. *American Journal of Orthopsychiatry 51:* 454–467, 1981.
Selvini-Palazzoli, M., Boscolo, L., Cecchin, G., & Prata, G. *Paradox and counterparadox: A new model in the therapy of the family in schizophrenic transaction* (translated by E. V. Burt). New York: Jason Aronson, 1978.
Soper, P. H., & L'Abate, L. Paradox as a therapeutic technique: A review. *International Journal of Family Counseling 5:* 10–21, 1977.
Stanton, M. D. Fusion, compression, diversion, and the workings of paradox: A theory of therapeutic/systemic change. *Family Process 23:* 135–167, 1984.
Watzlawick, P. *The language of change: Elements of therapeutic communication.* New York: Basic Books, 1978.
Watzlawick, P., Beavin, J. H., & Jackson, D. D. *Pragmatics of human communication: A study of interactional patterns, pathologies and paradoxes.* New York: W. W. Norton & Co., 1967.
Watzlawick, P., Weakland, J. H., & Fisch, R. *Change: Principles of problem formation and problem resolution.* New York: W. W. Norton & Co., 1974.
Weakland, J. H., Fisch, R., Watzlawick, P., & Bodin, A. M. Brief therapy: Focused problem resolution. *Family Process 13:* 141–168, 1974.
Weeks, G. R., & L'Abate, L. A bibliography of paradoxical methods in psychotherapy of family systems. *Family Process 17:* 95–98, 1978.
Weeks, G. R., & L'Abate, L. *Paradoxical psychotherapy: Theory and practice with individuals, couples, and families.* New York: Brunner/Mazel, 1982.
Wynne, L. C. Paradoxical interventions: Leverage for therapeutic change in individual and family systems. In J. S. Strauss, M. Bowers, T. Downey, S. Fleck, S. Jackson, & I. Levine (Eds.), *Psychotherapy of schizophrenia.* New York: Plenum Press, 1980, 191–202.

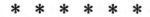

PARENTIFICATION

Parentification is the assumption or assignment (→ **attribution/ labeling**) of the parental role by or to one or more children in a family system. It involves a form of role reversal that is related to a disturbance of → **generational boundaries.**

Most authors on family therapy believe that an important prerequisite for the functioning of a family (→ **healthy/ functional families**) is the maintenance of a family → **hierarchy,** which implies that the parent and child subsystems are clearly delineated. In families with parentified children, one can assume that the parents' needs were not met by their own parents, and that the wishes for fulfillment of these needs have now been transferred to their own children. Parentification is thus a form of → **delegation.** In a sense, the children take on the role of the grandparents.

There exist, however, differing views about the meaning of parentification. Minuchin (1974) and other proponents of → **structural therapy** generally view parentification in a negative light because they regard hierarchy structures in families as normative. Therapists of this school therefore aim at consolidating generational boundaries and putting the parents "back in the driver's seat." Boszormenyi–Nagy (1962, 1965), one of the first authors to describe the effects of parentifying role assignments, does not consider parentification as such to be pathological or pathogenic. He considers it to be more important that the assumption of the parental role by the child be justly "reimbursed" by a balancing–out of the family's → **ledger of merits.** In his opinion, parentification is pathological only when it remains "unrewarded" or "under–rewarded" in the context of the family's system of values (→ **justice**) (Boszormenyi–Nagy & Spark, 1973).

Within the course of the → **family life cycle,** the degree of dysfunction in parentification must certainly be carefully weighed. Whereas parentification of a very young child is normally the exception (or only takes place in the clear context of a child playfully "trying out" the parental role), parentification in later stages of life becomes legitimate as the aging parents are in increasing need of care and the adult child is necessarily placed in the position of taking on a quasi–parental role.

Boszormenyi-Nagy, I. The concept of schizophrenia from the perspective of family treatment. *Family Process 1:* 103–113, 1962.

Boszormenyi-Nagy, I. A theory of relationships: Experience and transaction. In I. Boszormenyi-Nagy & J. L. Framo (Eds.), *Intensive family therapy: Theoretical and practical aspects.* New York: Harper & Row, 1965, 33–86.

Boszormenyi-Nagy, I., & Spark, G. M. *Invisible loyalties: Reciprocity in intergenerational family therapy.* New York: Harper & Row, 1973.

Framo, J. L. Rationale and techniques of intensive family therapy. In I. Boszormenyi-Nagy & J. L. Framo (Eds.), *Intensive family therapy: Theoretical and practical aspects.* New York: Harper & Row, 1965, 143–212.

Minuchin, S. Structural family therapy. In G. Caplan (Ed.), *American handbook of psychiatry, Vol. II, Child and adolescent psychiatry, sociocultural and community psychiatry* (2nd ed.). New York: Basic Books, 1974, 178–192.

Parsons, T., Bales, R. F., Olds, J., Zelditch, M., & Slater, P. E. *Family, socialization and interaction process.* Glencoe, Ill.: Free Press, 1955.

Schmideberg, M. Parents as children. *Psychiatric Quarterly, Suppl. 22:* 207–218, 1948.

Zuk, G. H., & Rubinstein, D. A review of concepts in the study and treatment of families of schizophrenics. In I. Boszormenyi-Nagy & J. L. Framo (Eds.), *Intensive family therapy: Theoretical and practical aspects.* New York: Harper & Row, 1965, 1–31.

* * * * * *

PATTERN

Pattern, one of the most fundamental concepts in theories of family systems, implies an ordered sequence or connection of events. It refers to a functional entity whose parts can be differentiated from one another. Its meaning overlaps with that of other concepts such as → **structure** and → **gestalt.** In the concept of "pattern," the psychology of perception, → **system/ systems theory,** gestalt theory, and → **field theory** meet on common ground.

The concept of "pattern" was particularly important in the work of Bateson (1979). According to Bateson, we all think with the help of "patterns which connect," which he regarded as an "aesthetic" concept. In his final work, he viewed "mental processes" as essentially the formation and realization of patterns. In line with the concept of → **logical types,** patterns must be distinguished from "patterns of patterns," or metapatterns. In the process of → **learning,** patterns are progressively superimposed. Here, Bateson was not referring to static patterns but to "patterns in time," i.e., "stories." The development of epistemological structures no less than the development of material structures should accordingly be understood as a process of → **coevolution,** → **epistemology,** and → **rules.**

Stanton (1984), in his geodynamic balance theory, has proposed that family patterns can be seen as a complex of the "interpersonal orbits" of the various members, sequentially moving both together and apart, with their various moves and countermoves constituting a complete family sequence or pattern.

Pattern recognition, an important concept in the family experiments of Reiss (1967), has been described by Hofstadter (1979) as a fundamental issue in problem solving. He states that "the elusive sense for patterns which we humans inherit from our genes involves all the mechanisms of representation of knowledge, including nested contexts, conceptual skeletons and conceptual mapping, slippability, descriptions and meta–descriptions and their interactions, fission and fusion of symbols, multiple representations (along different dimensions and different levels of [→] **abstraction**), default expectations, and more" (p. 674).

Bateson, G. *Steps to an ecology of mind.* New York: Ballantine Books, 1972.
Bateson, G. *Mind and nature: A necessary unity.* New York: E. P. Dutton, 1979.
Hofstadter, D. R. *Gödel, Escher, Bach: An eternal golden braid.* New York: Basic Books, 1979.
Reiss, D. Individual thinking and family interaction: II. A study of pattern recognition and hypothesis testing in families of normals, character disorders and schizophrenics. *Journal of Psychiatric Research 5:* 193–211, 1967.

Stanton, M. D. Fusion, compression, diversion, and the workings of paradox: A theory of therapeutic/systemic change. *Family Process 23:* 135–167, 1984.

* * * * * *

PERVERSE TRIANGLE

This refers to a pathological relationship structure between three persons, in which two persons on different hierarchical levels form a coalition (→ **alliance/ coalition/ alignment**) against the third. This alliance typically takes the form of an overstepping of → **generational boundaries,** with one parent and a child in coalition against the other parent.

The term "perverse triangle" was introduced by Haley in 1967. According to Haley, such triangulated structures in social systems invariably result in the formation of symptoms, violence, and the destruction of the system. With regard to families, the most serious aspect of this constellation appears to be a disregard for generational boundaries, which places the family → **hierarchy** in jeopardy. This leads to confusion regarding the validity or invalidity of the family → **rules** because an authority figure who could enforce these rules cannot be relied upon. Because the existence of this coalition is typically denied, confusion inevitably results as to what is "real" or "unreal" (→ **mystification**). The process of → **separating parents and adolescents** becomes particularly difficult because discussion about and demarcation from parental authority is not possible (→ **triangulation,** → **rigid triad,** → **relationship**). In Haley's view, the classic Oedipal situation, as defined in psychoanalysis, is nothing other than a special kind of perverse triangle.

Haley, J. Toward a theory of pathological systems. In G. H. Zuk & I. Boszormenyi-Nagy (Eds.), *Family therapy and disturbed families.* Palo Alto: Science and Behavior Books, 1967, 11–27.

* * * * * *

POSITIVE CONNOTATION/ POSITIVE INTERPRETATION/ NOBLE ASCRIPTION

Positive connotation refers to a family therapist's positive evaluation of behavior that usually would be regarded as pathological or "sick." Positive connotation is an essential element of → **strategic therapy,** →

systemic therapy, and → **hypnotherapy.** It aims at changing the family's value system and, hence, the family's model of the world (→ **paradigm/ model/ map**). When the meaning and the evaluation of a behavior changes, family members must necessarily react in a different manner toward this behavior; → **games** without end, or self–perpetuating interaction cycles can thus be dissolved. The term "positive interpretation" was coined by Soper and L'Abate (1977) and is a generic term for this technique.

The concept of positive connotation is based on the insight that every symptom and every form of pathological behavior fulfills (among other things) a stabilizing function; the recognition and positive evaluation of this is the first step toward its dissolution. Accordingly, in the context of the strategic therapy model, methods were developed early to prescribe symptoms (→ **symptom prescription**) and to reframe (→ **reframing**) the family's evaluation of symptoms and behaviors. An important feature of this approach, as described by Stanton, Todd, and their associates (1982), is the tendency of the therapist to ascribe positive motives to clients; in this way, any semblance of criticism and/or confrontation is avoided and → **resistance** can be obviated because "we are referring here to the practice of . . . assuming—or at least conveying to the family—that everything that everybody does is for good reason and is understandable. This applies to even the most 'destructive' of their behaviors. We have termed such therapeutic moves as 'ascribing noble intentions' or 'noble ascriptions' " (p. 125). This technique was developed in work with families of addicts in which family defensiveness was so high that conventional → **joining** techniques were inadequate.

From a systemic perspective, in which every element of a system has a bearing upon the function and the rules of functioning of the entire system, it has been shown that symptoms have indeed a positive, stabilizing effect on the whole family. On the basis of this insight Selvini-Palazzoli, Boscolo, Cecchin, and Prata (1980) decided that not only the behavior of the symptom carrier should be positively connoted, but also the behavior of all members of the family; otherwise the danger exists that the therapists could abandon their → **neutrality** and involuntarily revert to a lineal (→ **lineality**) model of causality. As is the case with other forms of → **paradoxical intervention,** the positive connotation of a symptom must be linked with a scrupulously undertaken → **hypothesis formation** about the circular causes of a family's interaction patterns (→ **circularity**).

de Shazer, S. *Patterns of brief family therapy: An ecosystemic approach.* New York: Guilford Press, 1982.

Erickson, M. H., & Rossi, E. *Hypnotherapy: An exploratory casebook.* New York: Irvington, 1979.

Erickson, M. H., Rossi, E., & Rossi, S. *Hypnotic realities: The induction of clinical hypnosis and forms of indirect suggestion.* New York: Irvington, 1976.

Selvini-Palazzoli, M., Boscolo, L., Cecchin, G., & Prata, G. Hypothesizing-circularity-neutrality: Three guidelines for the conductor of the session. *Family Process 19:* 3–12, 1980.

Soper, P. H., & L'Abate, L. Paradox as a therapeutic technique: A review. In J. G. Howells (Ed.), *Advances in family psychiatry, Vol. II.* New York: International Universities Press, 1980, 369–384.

Stanton, M. D., & Todd, T. C. Structural family therapy with drug addicts. In E. Kaufman & P. Kaufman (Eds.), *The family therapy of drug and alcohol abuse.* New York: Gardner Press, 1979, 55–69.

Stanton, M. D., Todd, T. C., & Associates. *The family therapy of drug abuse and addiction.* New York: Guilford Press, 1982.

POWER

This is an often applied and frequently controversial concept in the field of family therapy. From a rigorously cybernetic point of view, power can be conceptualized as follows: A's power over B shows itself in A's ability to define a context in which a *relatively* lineal relationship between cause and effect is established (or represented) between A and B's behavior. This relationship can be limited in time or restricted to certain areas of relational → **complementarity.**

The structure of power and struggle for power have been described in the literature on family therapy since its very beginnings. All authors on family therapy are of the opinion that questions of power are an essential aspect of family dynamics, and "everyone knows what power is, until you ask them" (Cromwell & Olson, 1975, p. 3). The problem that presents itself when one attempts to develop a conclusive definition of power is a problem that exists for the social sciences in general. The question is of concern to clinicians because an understanding of the → **circularity** of family interactions makes untenable any naive, lineal (→ **lineality**) concepts of cause and effect. When it is unclear who does what to whom, or where interactional circles have their beginnings, or which → **rules** determine the behavior of interactional partners, then the traditional definitions of power, as they have been applied in the social sciences until now, lose their meaning.

The literature on power in families demonstrates that practically every author has his or her own definition of power. For example, some authors believe that any type of social behavior is in some way an exercise of power, and that every social relationship is based on the attempt to balance power. Accordingly, the social system is seen as an organization of power structures (Hawley, 1963). Other authors use such terms as "influence," "control," "authority," "dominance," "self–assertion," and "the ability to decide," synonymously with the concept of power. The question is also largely unresolved as to whether power implies the actual influence exerted on one person by another, or whether all that is required is the possibility that one can exert it and has the ability to do so. Further unclarified questions are: Is it something one aspires to or not? Is power overt, covert, or both? Is the person in power the one who decides, or is it the person who is seen to be active? Is power a process or is it the result of a process? In any event, it can be said that power is an aspect of a relationship more than it is a characteristic of any one individual. As a characteristic of a system, power can be understood as "the (potential or actual) ability of an individual to change the behavior of other members of a social system" (Cromwell & Olson, 1975, p. 5).

According to Lewin's (1939) Field Theory (→ **field/ field theory**), power corresponds to the ratio of the maximum force (that A can exert over B) to the maximum resistance (that B is able to oppose to that force). Even in the event that A does not effect a change in B, the potential that A has to do so is understood as power (Cartwright, 1959, p. 198). In the further development of Lewin's theory, it was posited that, in order to be effective, A's power resources must accord with B's motivation. A's power rests on the characteristics that make A suitable for satisfying B's needs (Wolfe, 1959, p. 100). This view is based on theories of social exchange wherein interaction is viewed as an exchange process based on a cost–benefit assessment. A's power over B is dependent on the extent to which A can determine what benefits B can gain from the interaction, which means nothing more than that the power of one interactional partner is founded on the dependence of the other (Emerson, 1962, p. 194; Harsanyi, 1962a, b; Holm, 1969).

Resource Theory, a further variation on this thesis, is based on three propositions:

1. Each individual constantly strives to satisfy his or her needs and to attain his or her goals.
2. Most of these individual needs are satisfied through social interaction with other persons or groups.
3. These interpersonal interactions revolve essentially around a constant exchange of "resources" that serve to satisfy individual needs (Wolfe, 1959, p. 100). In such relationships, power devolves upon the person with the best resources for satisfying individual or group needs.

The concept of power in Decision Theory is also based on the concept of exchange processes. When one interactional partner is attuned to the system of values of the other and is in a position to influence the decisions of the other (who has no way of obtaining an equal "benefit" in the interaction), then the power of the first is equivalent to his or her ability to influence the decision of the second (Beckman–Brindley & Tavormina, 1978; Dahl, 1968; March, 1966; Pollard & Mitchell, 1972).

The surveys of Riskin and Faunce (1972) and Glick and Haley (1971) showed that, despite the theories outlined above, there then existed no generally accepted theory of power processes in families. Clinical concepts such as escalation in symmetrical relationships (→ symmetry) or → malign clinch describe important aspects of circularity in power interactions. The situation is even more complex in cut–and–dried power status situations, i.e., complementary and conflict–free relationships, than it is when there is a constant struggle for power. Often the essential point is not who decides, but rather who decides who will do the deciding. Thus, differing → logical types of decision are involved that are then negotiated or challenged on various levels of overt and covert communication.

Within the framework of a systemic approach, which posits the circularity of all interactional processes, it is nearly impossible to determine power relationships unequivocally; all action rebounds upon the actor in one way or another. Bateson (1972) commented: "Perhaps there is no such thing as unilateral power. After all, the man 'in power' depends on receiving information all the time from the outside. He responds to that information just as much as he 'causes' things to happen" (p. 486). There are, however, differences in the degree to which action affects the initiator; not all interactions will have the same effect on its participants. If one takes account of each interactional partner's subjective evaluation of an interaction, then A's behavior toward B can indeed be seen as a lineal–causal power relationship, especially when the partners "profit" from an exchange process. If A is able to effect a change in B's behavior, and risks little in doing so, this certainly has a retroactive influence on A. This influence can be negative, of no importance, or even positive. The "exchange rate" upon which the interaction is based is a function of the context in which it takes place.

An example of the complexity of power positions within the family is the parent–child relationship. As a rule, as the child's → autonomy increases, the parents' power over the child decreases. The newborn child is totally dependent upon the person assuming caretaking functions toward it. In order that the infant may survive, the caretaker must take charge of all those functions that the infant cannot perform. Yet, even an infant has some power over its parents. By crying at night, the infant offers the parents a "negative exchange benefit"—to obtain a night's undisturbed sleep, the parents are induced to attend to the infant's needs. How much power the infant has over the parents depends on the parents' system of values. A mother who likes to consider herself a "good mother" will allow the infant to have more power over her than someone who is largely indifferent to this title. In a certain sense, the infant is allowed to "decide" whether the parents are equal to this self–appointed task or not.

A further way in which children gain power over their parents is in their ability to satisfy the needs of their parents. These needs can be the long unsatisfied parental wishes and desires actually directed toward the parents' own parents (→ **multigenerational perspective**, → **parentification**, → **delegation**), or the need to project (→ **projective identification**) the positive or negative aspects of one's concept of self (→ **identity**) onto the child in order to rid oneself of them or to have them realized by proxy. A child who is delegated to refurbish the parents' waning feelings of self–worth, to realize the parents' ego–ideal, has a strong power position vis–à–vis its parents.

A clinical example will illustrate the role that context plays in interpersonal power relationships. When a man decides to leave his wife after twenty years of marriage to live with a younger woman, the wife's power resources lie in the positive or negative benefits she receives in exchange for her husband's behavior. These, however, are determined by the contexts. If she wishes to prevent her husband from leaving her, she can demand so much alimony that a separation becomes difficult for purely financial reasons. Or she can demand custody of the children, making separation difficult for emotional reasons. Besides these legally defined "exchange conditions," she can also appeal to her husband's individual code of ethics and morals. If, for example, the wife becomes depressed and needs medical treatment for this condition, the definition of the context has been radically changed; the husband no longer is separating from a healthy wife, but rather from a suffering person in need of help. In this context, his behavior will then be appraised differently by his social environment and by himself. He might decide not to leave his wife until she is "well" again. She, however, "must not" get well, for if she does, he will leave her. An interaction circle has been consolidated that cannot be dissolved by itself. Thus, in the assessment of power relationships within the family, the social frame of reference must always be kept in mind—the objective factors that affect the situation and the effect that they have on the family (→ **feminist therapy**).

The existence of power relationships in the family is not pathological in itself. Quite the reverse: Power relationships are necessary for the socialization process of children. In fact, some authors consider power relationships to be centrally important for family functioning (→ **structural therapy**, → **healthy/ functional families**). For example, Haley (1976) has stated that power is a "central issue in human life" and that he tries to "view a power struggle as a product of the needs of a system rather than the needs of a person" (p. 78). On the other hand, Keeney (1982) argued that acceptance of the concept of power is nonsystemic and non–Batesonian, and he cites Bateson's statement that "power corrupts most rapidly those who believe in it . . . [Power] is a myth which, if everybody believes in it, becomes to that extent self–validating. But it is still epistemological lunacy and leads inevitably to various sorts of disaster" (Bateson, 1972, pp. 486–487).

A more usual view is that power relationships become pathological only when they are overly rigid and the natural and inevitable demands for → **adaptability** in the course of the individual and → **family life cycle** can no longer be met. A specifically pathological form of power distribution occurs where there is a massive disturbance in → **self/ object differentiation** of each family member and when family members need, or firmly believe they need, each other in order to survive. In such pathological and pathogenic power situations, family members all feel equally dependent upon each other and yet all attempt to make the other family members dependent upon them. The result is a self–maintaining and self–perpetuating power struggle. A strategy that has been widely applied in such families, especially those in which there is a schizophrenic family member, is the therapeutic attempt to gain control and power over the definition of → **relationship** (Selvini-Palazzoli et al., 1978).

Bateson, G. *Steps to an ecology of mind*. New York: Ballantine Books, 1972.
Beckman-Brindley, S., & Tavormina, J. B. Power relationships in families: A social-exchange perspective. *Family Process 17:* 423–436, 1978.
Beer, S. *Decision and control*. New York: John Wiley & Sons, 1966.
Cartwright, D. A field theoretical conception of power. In D. Cartwright (Ed.), *Studies in social power*. Ann Arbor: University of Michigan Press, 1959, 183–220.
Cromwell, R. E., & Olson, D. H. (Eds.). *Power in families*. New York: John Wiley & Sons, 1975.
Dahl, R. The concept of power. *Behavioral Science 2:* 201–218, 1968.
Emerson, R. M. Power-dependence relations. *American Sociological Review 27:* 31–41, 1962.
Faller, K. Die Machtdimension der Familie und ihre Verwendung in der Therapie. *Familiendynamik 4:* 318–322, 1979.
Glick, I. D., & Haley, J. *Family therapy and research*. New York: Grune & Stratton, 1971.
Haley, J. An interactional description of schizophrenia. *Psychiatry 22:* 321–332, 1959.

268

Haley, J. *The power tactics of Jesus Christ and other essays.* New York: Grossman Publishers, 1969.

Haley, J. Development of a theory: A history of a research project. In C. E. Sluzki & D. C. Ransom (Eds.), *Double bind: The foundation of the communicational approach to the family.* New York: Grune & Stratton, 1976, 59–104.

Harsanyi, J. Measurement of social power in N-person reciprocal power situations. *Behavioral Science 7:* 81–91, 1962. (a)

Harsanyi, J. Measurement of social power, opportunity, costs and the theory of two-person bargaining games. *Behavioral Science 7:* 67–80, 1962. (b)

Hawley, A. Community power and urban renewal success. *American Journal of Sociology 68:* 422–431, 1963.

Hesse-Biber, S., & Williamson, J. Resource theory and power in families: Life cycle considerations. *Family Process 23:* 261–278, 1984.

Holm, K. Zum Begriff der Macht. *Kölner Zeitschrift für Soziologie und Sozialpsychologie 21:* 269–288, 1969.

Homans, G. C. Social behavior as exchange. *American Journal of Sociology 63:* 597–606, 1958.

Keeney, B. P. Not pragmatics, not aesthetics. *Family Process 21:* 429–434, 1982.

Lewin, K. Field theory and experiment in social psychology: Conceptual methods. *American Journal of Sociology 44:* 868–896, 1939.

March, J. The power of power. In D. Easton (Ed.), *Varieties of political theory.* Englewood Cliffs, N. J.: Prentice-Hall, 1966, 39–70.

Pollard, W., & Mitchell, T. Decision theory analysis of social power. *Psychological Bulletin 78:* 433–446, 1972.

Rappaport, A. F., & Harrell, J. A behavioral-exchange model for marital counseling. *Family Coordinator 21:* 203–213, 1972.

Riskin, J., & Faunce, E. E. An evaluative review of family interaction research. *Family Process 11:* 365–455, 1972.

Selvini-Palazzoli, M., Boscolo, L., Cecchin, G., & Prata, G. *Paradox and counterparadox: A new model in the therapy of the family in schizophrenic transaction* (translated by E. V. Burt). New York: Jason Aronson, 1978.

Simon, F. B. Die "Macht der Ohnmacht": Kommunikationstheoretische Überlegugen zur "emanzipatorischen" Therapie. *Psychiatrische Praxis 7:* 90–96, 1980.

Sprey, J. Family power structure: A critical comment. *Journal of Marriage and the Family 34:* 235–238, 1972.

Turk, J. L., & Bell, N. W. Measuring power in families. *Journal of Marriage and the Family 34:* 215–222, 1972.

Weeks, G., & Johnson, J. The power of powerlessness. *American Journal of Family Therapy 8:* 45–47, 1980.

Wolfe, D. Power and authority in the family. In D. Cartwright (Ed.), *Studies in social power.* Ann Arbor: University of Michigan Press, 1959, 99–114.

PRAGMATICS

Pragmatics [Greek *pragma*, action, deed] is an aspect of → **semiotics** that is especially important for family therapy. It investigates the relationship between sign, sign–giver, and sign–receiver.

Interpersonal communication, by means of which interactional partners influence each other's behavior, invariably occurs through an exchange of verbal or nonverbal signs. This interactional fact has been described and incorporated into family therapy by Ruesch and Bateson (1951), Bateson and his coworkers (Bateson, Jackson, Haley, & Weakland, 1956), and later by Watzlawick, Beavin, and Jackson (1967) (→ **communication theory,** → **epistemology,** → **syntax**).

Bateson, G., Jackson, D. D., Haley, J., & Weakland, J. H. Toward a theory of schizophrenia. *Behavioral Science 1:* 251–264, 1956.

Becker, E. *The birth and death of meaning: A perspective in psychiatry and anthropology.* Glencoe, Ill.: Free Press, 1962.

Hayakawa, S. I. *Language in thought and action.* New York: Harcourt, Brace & Co., 1949.

Morris, C. W. Foundations of the theory of signs. In O. Neurath, R. Carnap, & C. W. Morris (Eds.), *International encyclopedia of unified science, Vol. 1, No. 2.* Chicago: University of Chicago Press, 1938, 77–137.

Morris, C. W. *Signs, language and behavior.* New York: Prentice-Hall, 1946.

Ruesch, J., & Bateson, G. *Communication: The social matrix of psychiatry.* New York: W. W. Norton & Co., 1951.

Shands, H. G. *Semiotic approaches to psychiatry.* The Hague-Paris: Mouton, 1970.

Watzlawick, P., Beavin, J. H., & Jackson, D. D. *Pragmatics of human communication: A study of interactional patterns, pathologies and paradoxes.* New York: W. W. Norton & Co., 1967.

PRESCRIPTION

This term denotes a directive intervention whereby the therapist "prescribes" or directs a family or individual to behave in a specific way. Prescriptions are usually applied in the context of → **structural family therapy** and → **systemic therapy.**

As a rule, prescriptions are given as "homework" assignments between therapeutic sessions. A prescription is usually accompanied by a statement about the purpose of the directive; the statement also contains a → **reframing** of the prescribed behavior. If the therapist prescribes behavior that the family has avoided in the past, this behavior will then take on a new significance because it has been prescribed (→ **symptom prescription**). Prescriptions are often → **paradoxical interventions,** which serve to block or take to absurd lengths those problem–solving strategies that have become problems in themselves. The term "prescription" has been expanded to include not only homework assignments (such as family rituals) but also the therapist's interpretations of family interaction, which are communicated to the family at the conclusion of therapeutic sessions (→ **positive connotation**).

de Shazer, S. *Patterns of brief family therapy: An ecosystemic approach*. New York: Guilford Press, 1982.
Madanes, C. *Strategic family therapy*. San Francisco: Jossey-Bass, 1981
Minuchin, S. Structural family therapy. In G. Caplan (Ed.), *American handbook of psychiatry. Vol. II, Child and adolescent psychiatry, sociocultural and community psychiatry* (2nd ed.). New York: Basic Books, 1974, 178–192.
Selvini-Palazzoli, M., Boscolo, L., Cecchin, G., & Prata, G. *Paradox and counterparadox: A new model in the therapy of the family in schizophrenic transaction* (translated by E. V. Burt). New York: Jason Aronson, 1978.
Stierlin, H., Rücker-Embden, I., Wetzel, N., & Wirsching, M. *The first interview with the family* (translated by S. Tooze). New York: Brunner/Mazel, 1980.

* * * * * *

PROJECTIVE IDENTIFICATION

This term was introduced into psychoanalysis by Melanie Klein in 1946 to describe specific intrapsychic and interpersonal processes. It characterizes the way in which the individual projects undesired or highly desired aspects of the self onto others, and consequently identifies with these others. Klein considered this to be a defense process or mechanism. She observed how children attempted to control threatening instinctual drives by "recruiting" the mother to be the "container" of highly ambivalent needs, while at the same time identifying with the "container" at a relatively safe distance from their own ego. In further elaborations of this concept, it was seen as an important element of normal ego and personality development, as well as a form of "transpersonal defense" in interpersonal contexts. The latter aspect of projective identification is particularly important in psychoanalytically oriented family therapy and theory.

According to Thomas Ogden (1979), the process of projective identification can be separated into four phases: (1) the wish to shift or the fantasy of shifting highly desirable or undesirable aspects of the self onto another person; (2) feelings are induced in the projectee that correspond to the wishes or fantasies of the projector; (3) the projectee accepts and "processes" the projection; and (4) the original projector reaccepts or internalizes the "processed" projection. This definition shows that projective identification is not merely a transpersonal defense mechanism, but also a process that characterizes a number of nonpathological interpersonal interactions.

Whereas Melanie Klein viewed projective identification as a process of defense of control that the child initiates and directs onto one of its parents, most psychoanalytically oriented family therapists have viewed the parents as being the initiators of such transpersonal processes of defense or control. In the view of psychoanalytic researchers, the parents tend to be the ones who project their "narcissistic needs" onto the child (Richter, 1960, 1963) and/or delegate their children to fulfill these needs in various ways. Because of a diversity of opinion about the → **punctuation** of these processes, questions arose about the extent to which lineal (→ **lineality**) and circular (→ **circularity,** → **feedback**) processes were involved. A question was also raised about the role of real or alleged → **power** or dependence of the transactional partners in projection processes. If both partners are relatively similar in status (similarly powerful or similarly dependent), one speaks of a "trading of dissociations" (Wynne et al., 1958), that is, a form of reciprocal → **delegation** or → **collusion.** If the positions of power are unequal, the weaker, more dependent of the partners must necessarily adapt to the "stronger person's reality" (Stierlin, 1959).

Bowen (1978) has used the term *family projection process* in a special way that only partially overlaps with the concept of projective identification. Bowen regards this as "the basic process by which parental problems are projected to children. It is present in the full range of problems from the mildest to the most severe, such as hard–core schizophrenia and autism. The basic pattern involves a mother whose emotional system is more focused on children than on her husband and a father who is sensitive to his wife's anxiety and who supports her emotional involvement with the children. . . . The family projection process is universal in that it exists in all families to some degree. It alleviates the anxiety of undifferentiation in the present generation at the expense of the next generation. The same process by which the group functions better at the expense of one is present in all emotional systems" (pp. 204–205). Through the family projection process, the level of parental differentiation is passed onto the children, and the child may become a symptom bearer (→ **identified patient**) for the family.

Bowen, M. *Family therapy in clinical practice.* New York: Jason Aronson, 1978.
Grotstein, J. *Splitting and projective identification.* New York: Jason Aronson, 1981.
Klein, M. Notes on some schizoid mechanisms. *International Journal of Psychoanalysis 27:* 99–110, 1946.
Masterson, J. *New perspectives on psychotherapy of the borderline adult.* New York: Brunner/Mazel, 1978.
Masterson, J. *Countertransference and psychotherapeutic technique.* New York: Brunner/Mazel, 1983.
Ogden, T. On projective identification. *International Journal of Psycho-analysis 60:* 357–373, 1979.

Richter, H. E. Die narzisstischen Projektionen der Eltern auf das Kind. *Jahrbuch Psychoanalyse 1:* 62–81, 1960.

Richter, H. E. *Eltern, Kind und Neurose.* Stuttgart: Klett, 1963.

Sears, R. R., Rau, L., & Alpert, R. *Identification and child rearing.* Stanford: Stanford University Press, 1965.

Skynner, A. C. R. *Systems of family and marital psychotherapy.* New York: Brunner/Mazel, 1976.

Stierlin, H. The adaptation to the "stronger" person's reality. *Psychiatry 22:* 143–152, 1959.

Wynne, L. C., Ryckoff, I. M., Day, J., & Hirsch, S. I. Pseudo-mutuality in the family relations of schizophrenics. *Psychiatry 21:* 205–220, 1958.

Zinner, J. The implications of projective identification for marital interaction. In H. Grunebaum & J. Christ (Eds.), *Contemporary marriage: Structure, dynamics, and therapy.* Boston: Little, Brown & Co., 1976, 293–308.

Zinner, J., & Shapiro, R. Projective identification as a mode of perception and behaviour in families of adolescents. *International Journal of Psycho-analysis 53:* 523–530, 1972.

* * * * * *

PSEUDOMUTUALITY/ PSEUDOHOSTILITY

Wynne and his colleagues used these concepts to describe miscarried solutions to the human problem of striving both for relatedness and for identity. The predominant absorption in pseudomutual/pseudohostile relationships is to fit together (→ **binding**) at the expense of → **self/object differentiation** of the identities (→ **individuation**) of the persons in the relationship. Pseudomutuality and pseudohostility are → **family myths,** sustained by patterns of behavior, that deviation from fixed expectations is dangerous. The shared dread and avoidance of intrafamilial conflict or separation generates the facade of harmony of pseudomutuality; the fear of intimacy and closeness generates the persistent bickering (without genuine separation) of pseudohostility.

Wynne and his associates first observed these forms of relatedness in families with schizophrenic members, but similar phenomena in varying degrees of intensity are of widespread occurrence. In contrast to → **healthy/functional families,** these families display a rigid structure of role assignments (Ryckoff, Day, Wynne, 1959), any deviation from which provokes anxiety over unmanageable → **closeness/ distance.** As a result, spontaneity, zest, humor, and originality within the family context are experienced as threatening. In extreme instances, anything that conflicts with the established structure of the family role assignments must be blotted out. This results in a characteristic impermeability of perceived family boundaries with regard to the external environment (→ **rubber fence**). The only information that is allowed to penetrate into the family system is that which confirms the existing structure of pseudomutuality or pseudohostility.

What Wynne and his coworkers have posited as the interpersonal foundation of these family relational styles corresponds to a large extent with what other authors have described as → **fusion,** → **undifferentiated family ego mass,** and → **enmeshment.** These concepts concur with what, from a psychoanalytic perspective, is a disturbance of self/object differentiation or related individuation. These dysfunctional processes also are characterized by → **communication deviance** and disturbances in → **category formation.** (See also → **double bind,** → **mystification,** and → **boundaries.**)

Pseudomutuality also corresponds to the emotional overinvolvement component of → **expressed emotion,** and pseudohostility to the criticism component of that construct. Pseudohostility differs from Bateson's concept of → **schismogenesis,** which he originally described as *progressive* (escalating) differentiation leading to a breakdown of a relationship (Bateson, 1935, 1936). In the clinical observations reported by Wynne (1961), pseudohostility in one relationship in a family or in a therapeutic system is balanced by pseudomutuality in another relationship. Hence, the intactness of the system as a whole tends to be preserved for surprisingly long periods.

Bateson, G. Culture contact and schismogenesis. *Man 35:* 178–183 (article 199), 1935. (Reprinted in G. Bateson, *Steps to an ecology of mind.* New York: Ballantine Books, 1972, 61–72.)

Bateson, G. *Naven: A survey of the problems suggested by a composite picture of the culture of a New Guinea tribe drawn from three points of view* (1st ed.). Cambridge: Cambridge University Press, 1936. (2nd ed., Stanford: Stanford University Press, 1958.)

Ryckoff, I., Day, J., & Wynne, L. C. Maintenance of stereotyped roles in the families of schizophrenics. *American Medical Association Archives of General Psychiatry 1:* 93–98, 1959.

Wynne, L. C. The study of intrafamilial alignments and splits in exploratory family therapy. In N. Ackerman, F. L. Beatman, & S. N. Sherman (Eds.), *Exploring the base for family therapy.* New York: Family Service Association of America, 1961, 95–115.

Wynne, L. C. Communication disorders and the quest for relatedness in families of schizophrenics. *American Journal of Psychoanalysis 30:* 100–114, 1970.

Wynne, L. C. On the anguish and creative passions of not escaping double binds: A reformulation. In C. E. Sluzki & D. C. Ransom (Eds.), *Double bind: The foundations of the communicational approach to the family.* New York: Grune & Stratton, 1976, 243–250.

Wynne, L. C. The epigenesis of relational systems: A model for understanding family development. *Family Process 23:* 297–318, 1984.

Wynne, L. C., Ryckoff, I. M., Day, J., & Hirsch, S. I. Pseudo-mutuality in the family relations of schizophrenics. *Psychiatry 21:* 205–220, 1958.

* * * * * * *

PSYCHOANALYTICALLY ORIENTED FAMILY THERAPY

This term refers to schools of family therapy that attempt to integrate
psychoanalytic insights, concepts, and therapeutic procedures into family
therapy.

Sigmund Freud recognized, at least to some degree, the importance of
family relationships for the mental well–being (or otherwise) of his
patients. However, he mostly viewed family relationships in a rather
negative light. "No one who has any experience of the rifts which so
often divide a family," Freud stated in his *Introductory Lectures on
Psycho–Analysis* (1916–1917), "will, if he is an analyst, be surprised
to find that the patient's closest relatives sometimes betray less interest
in his recovering than in his remaining as he is" (p. 459). In his
"Recommendations to Physicians Practising Psycho–Analysis"
(1912), Freud stated: "As regards the treatment of their relatives, I
must confess myself utterly at a loss, and I have in general little faith in
any individual treatment of them" (p. 120). Freud's case history of
"Little Hans" (1909) contradicts his otherwise skeptical view of family
treatment. "Little Hans" was treated almost exclusively via Freud's
therapeutic influence with the parents. Freud did not, however,
consider the parents to be "involved" but, rather, saw them as having a
"co–therapeutic" function. In only one instance did Freud attempt
couples therapy, and with the couple who were to translate his works
into English—Alix and James Strachey (Stone, 1971, as quoted in
Broderick & Schrader, 1981).

A number of early psychoanalysts did, however, come into direct
contact with the families of their patients. (For a review of this, see
Broderick and Schrader, 1981.) This was particularly the case in the
areas of child therapy and child guidance, as well as in research in
developmental psychology. The earliest psychoanalytic family studies
were presented by Flügel in 1921 (see Bowen, 1975, p. 368). There also
existed early forms of family therapy, as mentioned by Richter (1974):
"Oberndorf appears to be the first person to have systematically
treated marital couples in a psychoanalytic manner ... which he
comprehensively described in the year 1932. A central topic of the
Psychoanalytic Congress in Lyon in 1936, was Family Neuroses and
Neurotic Families. Laforgue, Leuba and Aichhorn discussed in particular the pathological relationships between marital partners, as well as
between children and parents" (p. 123).

After the Second World War, family therapy quickly gained in
importance. In the development of this field, psychoanalytically
oriented and trained therapists played an important role. Among them
in the United States were: Nathan Ackerman, Donald Bloch, Ivan

Boszormenyi–Nagy, Murray Bowen, James Framo, Don Jackson, Theodore Lidz, Salvador Minuchin, Norman Paul, Fred Sander, Roger Shapiro, Samuel Slipp, Helm Stierlin, and Lyman Wynne. In England, → **object relations theory,** introduced by W. Ronald Fairbairn and further developed by Harry Guntrip and others, provided important impulses for psychoanalytically oriented family therapy. Among the representatives of the English movement were Arno Bentovin and A. C. Robin Skynner. Members of the Milan School in Italy, led by Mara Selvini–Palazzoli, also came to family therapy via psychoanalysis. In German–speaking countries, psychoanalytically oriented family therapy is represented by Horst Eberhard Richter, Eckart Sperling, Helm Stierlin, and Jürg Willi, although Stierlin has increasingly tended toward an integration of a systemic perspective into family therapy.

Contemporary French psychoanalysis appears to be the most consistent in its efforts to apply fundamental psychodynamic tenets and analytic techniques in the treatment of the family. In this treatment method, the family is viewed as a single patient; the unconscious fantasies, associations, and symptom production of the family as a whole are analyzed as a unit (Anzieu, 1975). The family's transference processes and the countertransference processes of the therapist are worked out in a manner analogous to that of individual and group psychoanalysis so as to break down the repetition compulsions with the family unit (Racamier, 1980).

Specific psychoanalytic contributions of importance in the development of family therapy are concepts such as ego function (→ **ego psychology),** → **inner objects,** → **self/object differentiation,** → **projective identification,** → **individuation,** and operational → **mourning.** Further, such concepts as → **delegation,** → **collusion,** and family-internal and family–external → **boundaries** are based on central psychoanalytic insights and/or constructs. In the light of such cross-fertilization of psychoanalysis and family theory and therapy, the question is posed again and again as to whether and how far the two approaches can be integrated in a comprehensive manner. More recently, Ciompi (1982) and Simon (1984) have made attempts in this direction. As desirable as such attempts are, they often turn out to be problematical. Essentially, this has to do with the fact that the differing scientific models attend to differing aspects of → **relational reality** and, thus, open up differing therapeutic perspectives. In psychoanalysis, for example, the central context is held to be the dyadic relationship.

Psychoanalytic theories, even today, are based extensively upon mechanistic models that are largely determined by a lineal (→ **lineality**) concept of causality. In contrast, in family therapy the typical observational setting is the family as a whole. Models of family therapy, therefore, are based extensively on the insights of → **cybernetics,** hence on a circular (→ **circularity**) concept of reality. This explains why the concepts of → **triangulation,** → **transference and countertransference,** and → **resistance** can have completely different connotations in the psychoanalytic context than they have in the framework of family therapy. It also explains why quite disparate views exist on the effectiveness of psychotherapy (→ **brief therapy**).

According to the psychoanalytic view, a protracted process of working through transference, countertransference, and resistance is required to obtain a profound and lasting restructuring of the personality. Systemic family therapists, however, are of the opinion that profound → **change** can be accomplished in relatively few therapeutic sessions. Finally, family therapists must ask whether and to what extent the improvement or the → **individuation** of the individual is desirable, or even possible, if it takes place without the improvement in and individuation of the other family members.

Everyday experience in family therapy has repeatedly shown that in work with not only those families with psychosomatically ill members, but also with families whose members present disorders of a psychotic, addictive, behavioral, neurotic, and borderline nature, efforts to support emancipation/individuation of the individual must take into consideration and promote the emancipation/individuation of all the family members (→ **symptom shift**). This explains the importance of the concept of → **multidirectional partiality** in family therapy. Further, it explains the importance attributed to the concepts of → **system** and → **context,** and of a concept of therapy in which the therapists consider themselves to be (among other things) "changers of systems" and "facilitators of family dialogue." This view is in obvious contrast to the psychoanalytic view that places the therapist essentially in a very specifically defined role as a partner in a dialogue.

Ackerman, N. W. *The psychodynamics of family life: Diagnosis and treatment of family relationships.* New York: Basic Books, 1958.

Ackerman, N. W. The psychoanalytic approach to the family. In J. H. Masserman (Ed.), *Individual and familial dynamics, Vol. II.* New York: Grune & Stratton, 1959, 105–121; also in D. Bloch & R. Simon (Eds.), *The strength of family therapy: Selected papers of Nathan W. Ackerman.* New York: Brunner/Mazel 1982, 250–259.

Ackerman, N. W. Prejudice and scapegoating in the family. In G. H. Zuk & I. Boszormenyi-Nagy (Eds.), *Family therapy and disturbed families.* Palo Alto: Science and Behavior Books, 1967, 48–57.

Anzieu, D. *Le groupe et l'inconscient.* Paris: Dunod, 1975.

Bentovim, A., Barnes, G. G., & Cooklin, A. (Eds.). *Family therapy: Complementary frameworks of theory and practice* (2 vols.). New York: Academic Press, 1982.

Bowen, M. Family therapy after twenty years. In D. X. Freedman & J. E. Dyrud (Eds.), *American handbook of psychiatry* (2nd ed.), *Vol. V: Treatment.* New York: Basic Books, 1975, 367–392.

Broderick, C. B., & Schrader, S. S. The history of professional marriage and family therapy. In A. S. Gurman & D. P. Kniskern (Eds.), *Handbook of family therapy.* New York: Brunner/Mazel, 1981, 5–35.

Ciompi, L. *Affektlogic. Über die Struktur der Psyche und ihre Entwicklung. Ein Beitrag zur Schizophrenieforschung.* Stuttgart: Klett-Cotta, 1982.

Fairbairn, W. *Psychoanalytic studies of the personality.* London: Tavistock Publications, 1952.

Framo, J. L. Rationale and techniques of intensive family therapy. In I. Boszormenyi-Nagy & J. L. Framo (Eds.), *Intensive family therapy: Theoretical and practical aspects.* New York: Harper & Row, 1965, 143–212.

Freud, S. [1909] Two case histories ("Little Hans" and the "Rat Man"). *The standard edition of the complete psychological works of Sigmund Freud. Vol. X.* London: Hogarth Press, 1955.

Freud, S. [1912] Recommendations to physicians practising psycho-analysis. *The standard edition of the complete psychological works of Sigmund Freud, Vol. XVII.* London: Hogarth Press, 1958, 109–120.

Freud, S. [1916–1917] Introductory lectures on psycho-analysis (Part III). The standard edition of the complete psychological works of Sigmund Freud, *Vol. XVI.* London: Hogarth Press, 1963.

Grotjahn, M. *Psychoanalysis and family neurosis.* New York: W. W. Norton & Co., 1960.

Guntrip, H. *Schizoid phenomena, object-relations and the self.* New York: International Universities Press, 1969.

Holmes, J. Psychoanalysis and family therapy: Freud's Dora case reconsidered. *Journal of Family Therapy 5:* 235–251, 1983.

Paul, N. L. The role of mourning and empathy in conjoint marital therapy. In G. H. Zuk & I. Boszormenyi-Nagy (Eds.), *Family therapy and disturbed families.* Palo Alto: Science and Behavior Books, 1967, 186–205.

Racamier, P. C. *Les schizophrènes.* Paris: Payot, 1980.

Richter, H. E. *The family as patient.* New York: Farrar, Strauss, & Giroux, 1974.

Sander, F. M. *Individual and family therapy: Toward an integration.* New York: Jason Aronson, 1979.

Schaffer, L., Wynne, L. C., Day, J., Ryckoff, I. M., & Halperin, A. On the nature and sources of the psychiatrist's experience with the family of the schizophrenic. *Psychiatry 25:* 32–45, 1962.

Shapiro, R. Adolescence and the psychology of the ego. *Psychiatry 26:* 77–87, 1963.

Shapiro, R. Action and family interaction in adolescence. In J. Marmor (Ed.), *Modern psychoanalysis.* New York: Basic Books, 1968, 454–475.

Simon, F. B. Der Prozess der Individuation: Über den Zusammenhang von Vernunft und Gefühlen. Göttingen: Vandenhoeck & Ruprecht, 1984.

Skynner, A. C. R. *One flesh: Separate persons.* London: Constable, 1976.

Slipp, S. *Object relations: A dynamic bridge between individual and family treatment.* New York: Jason Aronson, 1984.

Stierlin, H. Psychoanalytic approaches to schizophrenia in the light of a family model. *International Review of Psycho-analysis 1:* 169–179, 1974.

Stone, I. *The passions of the mind.* New York: Doubleday, 1971.

Willi, J. *Couples in collusion.* New York: Jason Aronson, 1982. (German edition: *Die Zweierbeziehung.* Reinbek bei Hamburg: Rowohlt Verlag, 1975.)

Willi, J. *Dynamics of couple therapy.* New York: Jason Aronson, 1984. (German

278

edition: *Therapie der Zweierbeziehung.* Reinbek bei Hamburg: Rowohlt Verlag, 1978.)
Wynne, L. C., Ryckoff, I. M., Day, J., & Hirsch, S. I. Pseudo-mutuality in the family relations of schizophrenics. *Psychiatry 21:* 205–220, 1958.

* * * * * *

PSYCHOHISTORY

Psychohistory represents a relatively new direction in historical research whereby political and social behavior are viewed as an expression of socialization processes and group fantasies as they have prevailed in particular cultural and historical eras.

Whereas traditional historians concentrate on "major events" such as wars, the founding and disintegration of nations, colonialization, and so forth, psychohistorians concern themselves with such questions as: What type of relationship did parents have with their children? How were children treated or mistreated? Which psychological processes and developmental tendencies came to light during a particular historical epoch?

Although psychohistorians are using similar research data, they tend to arrive at differing conclusions and theoretical models. For example, Ariès (1962) posits that the concept of "childhood" is an invention of the early modern era. Before this invention, so Ariès claims, there existed no noticeable difference between the status of a child and that of an adult. With the introduction of the concept of "childhood," a type of family was allegedly created that came to be characterized by more clearly delineated → **generational boundaries** and, in general, harsher methods of child rearing.

Lloyd deMause (1974), however, takes the stance that the farther one goes back in history, the harsher one finds the methods of child rearing to be. Therefore, deMause (pp. 51–54) posits six typical child–rearing models throughout the course of history:

1. The "infanticidal mode" is said to have existed from the beginning of human history until about the 4th century A.D. Children whom one did not consider "worthy" of being brought up into adulthood, because they were in some manner "defective," were killed. This had far–reaching emotional consequences for those children who were "allowed" to live; these children's dependence upon their parents was total, and the abuse by parents of a child's dependence was allegedly an everyday phenomenon.

2. The "abandonment mode" was supposedly in effect from the 4th until the 13th century. Parents believed that their children had souls. However, parents

projected onto their children their own bad and unacceptable wishes and strivings, thus making the children into dangerous creatures from whom parents felt they had to protect themselves. Therefore, they tended to send their children as far away as possible: to foster homes, to monasteries, or to be raised by servants.

3. The "ambivalent mode" may have determined the relationship between parents and their children from about the 14th to the 17th century. Although parents continued to project their own negative aspects onto their children, the children were finally allowed to take part in the parents' emotional life. Parents began to see it as their duty to "mold" their children (as if they were clay) in a certain culture–specific image.

4. DeMause believes that the "intrusive mode" became observable in the 18th century. It manifested itself in a strong tendency toward emotional closeness, in particular between mothers and children. Projection processes played a diminishing role in parent–child relations. Instead, parents attempted to tame, if not break, their child's spirit. It was felt to be necessary to control the child's internal life and to check its fears and desires. Parents prayed with their children and punished them harshly in order to achieve these ends. Obedience toward one's parents was the child's first commandment.

5. The so–called "socialization mode," which is said to have lasted from the 19th until the middle of the 20th century, aimed at helping the child to adapt to society and to control his or her impulses. Appropriate social functioning was considered to be the measure and goal of proper upbringing. Fathers began to be noticeably involved in the processes of child rearing.

6. The "helping mode" made its appearance about the middle of the 20th century. It was and is based on the assumption that a child knows better than its parents what is good for it at any particular point in its development. Thus, parents aim at helping the child reach its daily goals. At the same time, they tend to view themselves as their child's servants rather than as authority figures.

Each of these six modes corresponds to a "psycho–class," that is, a group within society that shares the same socialization processes and manifests similar personality structures. Also, members of various psycho–classes tend to share certain "group fantasies," thereby reflecting and creating a sort of collective (or national) identity. Hence, group fantasies encompass (and defend against) that which is collectively repressed, for example, a society's latent conflicts and problems, fears and secret wishes. Group fantasies can be brought to light with the help of deMause's technique of "fantasy analysis."

The importance that psychohistorians attach to particular socialization processes and/or group fantasies is also reflected in their studies of historical personalities such as Martin Luther, Mahatma Gandhi, Adolf Hitler, and so forth. Family therapists have a particular interest in the question of how various types of socialization experiences may relate to various forms of a → **relational reality** and types of family systems (→ **family typologies,** → **family sociology,** → **ethnicity and family therapy**).

Ariès, P. *Centuries of childhood: A social history of family life* (translated from the French by R. Baldick). New York: Alfred A. Knopf, 1962.
deMause, L. (Ed.). *The history of childhood.* New York: Psychohistory Press, 1974.
Erikson, E. H. *Young man Luther: A study in psychoanalysis and history.* New York: W. W. Norton & Co., 1958.
Erikson, E. H. *Gandhi's truth.* New York: W. W. Norton & Co., 1969.
Lasch, C. *Haven in a heartless world: The family besieged.* New York: Basic Books, 1977.
Lifton, R. J., & Olson, E. (Eds.). *Exploration in psychohistory:* New York: Simon & Schuster, 1974.
Stierlin, H. *Adolf Hitler: A family perspective.* New York: Psychohistory Press, 1976.

* * * * * *

PSYCHOLINGUISTICS/REPRESENTATIONAL SYSTEMS

This field of science concerns itself with the psychic preconditions of language as well as the linguistic influence on psychic structures and processes. The fundamental postulate of this approach is that the personal experiences in the individual's life history imprint themselves in the individual's subjective representational systems.

Psychic processes, in particular those of discursive thought, are extensively bound up with language and its structures. Human language, as a relatively digital medium of communication (→ **analogue/digital communication**), makes it both necessary and possible to translate an individual's perceptions about his or her internal and external worlds into a coded expressional medium. The manner and the conditions under which these translations take place are of great clinical and therapeutic interest (→ **code**). An understanding of these translation processes largely determines whether and to what extent therapists are able to enter into the subjective world of their clients, to hear "with a third ear," and, hence, to change the internal map of a client (→ **paradigm/model/map**).

From a psychoanalytic perspective, Lacan (1966, 1973) investigated certain affective processes in the light of insights gained in the field of linguistics. Lacan viewed the unconscious as being structured in a manner analogous to language and believed that it is the task of the analyst to "de–code" the manner and the "language" in which particular experiences are represented. Lacan's theoretical framework was that of → **structuralism** and → **semiotics.**

Bandler's and Grinder's experiments in these areas, beginning in 1975, and later with Delozier and Dilts, are of especial interest for family theory and the therapeutic models based upon it. Their work presents a method for analyzing the preferred perceptual modality (acoustic, visual, kinesthetic) of the individual and the way in which this preference is reflected in the individual's language. An understanding of the preferred perceptual medium allows the therapist to communicate better and more directly with a client. For example, a person who prefers a visual mode thinks and speaks accordingly, and will feel better understood by a therapist who also chooses this mode of communication. That which is subjectively and unconsciously transmitted in linguistic structures is not always identical to that which is consciously heard. In order to understand the rules of translation for both levels of consciousness, Bandler and Grinder investigated the methods of the hypnotherapist Milton Erickson (→ **hypnotherapy**). Their analysis was based on the theories of the linguist Noam Chomsky (1965, 1968). He postulated that every sentence of a natural language is structured differently in two nonidentical representation systems. The representational *form* in which the sentence is spoken (or, if written, how the sentence appears in print or script) is called "surface structure"; the representation of the *meaning* that a sentence has is called "deep structure." According to Chomsky, both structures are associated with each other in a specific manner. If, for example, a person says, "That window was broken," this sentence, as written here on the page, accords with a representation on the surface structure; on the level of deep structure, the sentence can be represented in the following manner: past (broken), someone, window, with something. This deep structure can be understood by anyone who speaks English in the following manner: (a) something happened in the past and (b) this event involved the following:

1. An action—the breaking—happened between:
   1a. an actor—a person or thing who carried out the act of breaking, represented here by "someone";
   1b. the object—a person or thing that was broken, represented in this instance by "window"; and
   1c. the instrument—a thing—that was used to break, represented in this instance by "something."

From the surface structure, a complex system of meaning that accords with the deep structure is derived by means of translation ("transformation") processes.

According to Bandler and Grinder (1975a), the mechanisms applied in the comprehension of sentences can also be applied in a therapeutic context. Sentences that represent therapeutic interventions (→ story telling) are structured in a manner in which particular subjective meanings are transmitted at the level of deep structure without being consciously perceived at the level of surface structure (p. 218). The therapist uses a sentence whose meaning appears relatively harmless on the level of surface structure; however, on the level of deep structure, it changes → punctuation, → reframing takes place, and the entire → epistemology of the patient is changed. Interventions of this sort can be constructed in three steps:

1. Choose the message the client should unconsciously understand.
2. Construct a sentence, or a series of sentences, or a story that expresses this message directly.
3. Replace all the nouns, in the sentence or story, that refer to the client and his or her present situation or problem with nouns that have no direct relevance for the client and his or her present situation and the problem related to it.

The general principle of this intervention strategy is that the patient should not be able consciously to recognize the meaning the sentence has; unconsciously, however, the client will apprehend the deep structure and use the message as a model to solve or evaluate the problem at hand. These techniques, which Erickson applied in hypnotherapy long before anyone made the effort to consider them from a theoretical perspective, were developed by Bandler and Grinder into a therapeutic method called → neurolinguistic programming. A caveat with regard to their theoretical concept is in order, however, because their theory is based extensively on Chomsky's work, which remains in dispute within the field of linguistics. Another objection must be raised with regard to the purely instrumental application of such techniques when the system of values that these techniques imply and to which they are oriented remains unreflected upon.

The investigations by Osgood, May, and Mison (1975) of the meaning content of certain affective concepts in twenty different languages are of great interest for family research. All the expressions investigated were statements about the three pairs of conceptual opposites "good/bad," "strong/weak," and "active/passive." Every person must develop a "world–view" and structure a "semantic space." The individual's emotional reactions receive their meaning largely within the dimensions covered by these three pairs of expressions. In particular, the issues involved in these dimensions have the greatest emotional impact on family life. Is the terrorization of the family by one family member an expression of "sickness" or "badness"? In one instance the family member's behavior is viewed as the "passive" suffering of a "weak" and ill person whose behavior cannot be judged on a moral plane. In another instance the family sees itself as being exposed to an "active," "strong," responsible malefactor. The attribution of "badness" has very different consequences for family interaction than does the attribution of "sickness."

Bandler, R., & Grinder, J. *Patterns of the hypnotic techniques of Milton H. Erickson, M. D., Vol. I.* Cupertino, Cal.: META Publications, 1975. (a)

Bandler, R., & Grinder, J. *The structure of magic, Vol. I.* Palo Alto: Science and Behavior Books, 1975. (b)

Bandler, R., & Grinder, J. *Frogs into princes.* Moab, Utah: Real People Press, 1979.

Bandler, R., & Grinder, J. *Reframing: Neurolinguistic programming and the transformation of meaning.* Moab, Utah: Real People Press, 1982.

Bandler, R., Grinder, J., & Satir, V. *Changing with families.* Palo Alto: Science and Behavior Books, 1976.

Brown, R. *Words and things.* Glencoe, Ill.: Free Press, 1958.

Brown, R. *Psycholinguistics: Selected papers.* New York: Free Press, 1970.

Chomsky, N. *Aspects of the theory of syntax.* Cambridge: Massachusetts Institute of Technology Press, 1965.

Chomsky, N. *Language and mind.* New York: Harcourt, Brace, Jovanovich, 1968.

Chomsky, N. *Rules and representations.* New York: Columbia University Press, 1980.

Dilts, R. B., Grinder, J., Bandler, R., Delozier, J., & Cameron-Bandler, J. *Neurolinguistic programming, Vol. I.* Cupertino, Cal.: META Publications, 1979.

Grinder, J., & Bandler, R. *The structure of magic, Vol. II.* Palo Alto: META Publications, 1976.

Grinder, J., & Bandler, R. *Trance-formations: Neuro-linguistic programming and the structure of hypnosis.* Moab, Utah: Real People Press, 1981.

Grinder, J., Delozier, J., & Bandler, R. *Patterns of the hypnotic techniques of Milton H. Erickson, M. D., Vol. II.* Cupertino, Cal.: META Publications, 1977.

Lacan, J. *Ecrits.* Paris: Editions du Seuil, 1966.

Lacan, J. *Les quartre concepts fondamenteaux de la psychoanalyse.* Paris: Seuil, 1973.

Lang, H. *Die Sprache und das Unbewusste.* Frankfurt: Suhrkamp, 1973.

Lenneberg, E. H. *Biological foundations of language.* New York: John Wiley & Sons, 1967.

Osgood, C., May, W., & Mison, M. *Cross-cultural universals of affective meaning.* Urbana, Ill.: University of Illinois Press, 1975.

Piatelli-Palmarini, M. (Ed.). *Language and learning: The debate between Jean Piaget and Noam Chomsky.* London: Routledge & Kegan Paul, 1980.

Rosen, V. H. Language and psychoanalysis. *International Journal of Psychoanalysis 50:* 113–116, 1969.

Simon, F. B. *Der Prozess der Individuation: Über den Zusammenhang von Vernunft und Gefühlen.* Göttingen: Vandenhoeck & Ruprecht, 1984.

* * * * * *

PUNCTUATION

Punctuation refers to the structuring and organization by an observer of a continuous sequence of events and behaviors. Two partners, for example, perceive and organize their ongoing interaction into various sequences, and each subjectively perceives different patterns of cause and effect, or different structures of interaction. Depending on whether the interactional process between A and B is seen from the perspective of A or B, it may seem as if A is reacting to B, or as if B is reacting to A. According to one punctuation, a wife nags because her husband withdraws from her; according to the other, the husband withdraws from his wife because she is constantly nagging him. The manner in which an ongoing communication process and/or interaction sequence is punctuated determines the meaning attributed to it and how each person's behavior will be evaluated, that is, who is responsible or "guilty," and how one decides to (re)act.

The term "punctuation" was introduced into research on family interaction by Bateson and Jackson (1964), following Whorf (1942) who developed the concept in the framework of his research on language. Watzlawick, Beavin, and Jackson (1967) explored the significance of the concept in greater detail. The question as to how interactional sequences are punctuated is central to family diagnosis and therapy. The individual family member's subjective punctuation of an interaction determines the meaning that he or she ascribes to his or her behavior as well as to the behavior of others. It also includes the → **context** that he or she marks off (→ **context marking**), particularly with regard to the interpretation of cause and effect. Furthermore, "ordering sequences in one way or another creates what, without undue exaggeration, may be called different realities" (Watzlawick, 1976). Thus, an understanding of punctuation can greatly facilitate the selection of therapeutic interventions (→ **reframing**).

Punctuation, as described here, represents a lineal (→ **lineality**) causal ordering of events, phenomena, and behaviors. This can partly be regarded as the expression and consequence of linguistic and/or grammatical constraints. As the foundations of one's own knowledge are rarely queried (→ **epistemology**), such cause–and–effect → **attributions** are likely to remain unquestioned; one's own behavior continues to be seen merely as a reaction to the behavior of an interactional partner. Changes in punctuations not only open up new ways of looking at a problem, but also provide new resources and solutions.

Bateson, G. *Steps to an ecology of mind.* New York: Ballantine Books, 1972.
Bateson, G., & Jackson, D. D. Some varieties of pathogenic organization. In D. McK. Rioch & E. A. Weinstein (Eds.), *Disorders of communication. Proceedings of the Association for Research in Nervous and Mental Disease, Research Publications, Vol. 42.* Baltimore: Williams & Wilkins Co., 1964, 279–290.

Bernal, G., & Golann, S. Couple interaction: A study of the punctuation process. *International Journal of Family Therapy 2:* 47–56, 1980.

Keeney, B. P. *Aesthetics of change.* New York: Guilford Press, 1983.

Shands, H. G. *The war with words.* The Hague-Paris: Mouton, 1971.

Simon, F. B. Präverbale Strukturen der Logik. *Psyche 36:* 139–170, 1982.

Watzlawick, P. *How real is real? Confusion, disinformation, communication.* New York: Random House, 1976.

Watzlawick, P., Beavin, J. H., & Jackson, D. D. *Pragmatics of human communication: A study of interactional patterns, pathologies and paradoxes.* New York: W. W. Norton & Co., 1967.

Watzlawick, P., & Weakland, J. H. (Eds.). *The interactional view.* New York: W. W. Norton & Co., 1977.

Watzlawick, P., Weakland, J. H., & Fisch, R. *Change: Principles of problem formation and problem resolution.* New York: W. W. Norton & Co., 1974.

Whorf, B. L. *Language, thought, and reality.* Cambridge: Massachusetts Institute of Technology Press, 1942.

* * * * * *

■ R ■

REDUNDANCY

Redundancy [Latin *redundare,* to overflow] refers to the repeated occurrence of particular events, phenomena, or behaviors.

The totality of redundancy, in other words, all those family behaviors that regularly repeat themselves, exhibits a → **structure,** i.e., a → **pattern** within the dimension of time. The observation of redundancies within family interaction makes it possible to recognize specific reciprocal relationships (→ **rules**) between interactional partners. For example, whenever A acts in a certain way, B responds in a certain way. This is not to be viewed as a causal chain in which A "causes" B to respond in that way, but, rather, as a linkage of behaviors in the context of a larger pattern or structure. However, in → **systems theory** and → **information theory,** the concept of redundancy is defined somewhat differently. Redundancy here refers to the total informational units of a message that do not alter the content of that message, and to the structures of a dynamic system that do not influence the functioning of the system as a whole. In this more narrowly defined sense, redundancy serves to reduce → **entropy** and to insure the specific function of information carriers (for example, the transmission of information by means of two channels) so that despite a disturbance in information transmission the receiver is still able to decipher the message.

Bateson, G. *Steps to an ecology of mind*. New York: Ballantine Books, 1972, pp. 399–425.

Jackson, D. D. The study of the family. *Family Process 4:* 1–20, 1965.

Watzlawick, P., & Beavin, J. H. Some formal aspects of communications. In P. Watzlawick & J. H. Weakland (Eds.), *The interactional view*. New York: W. W. Norton & Co., 1977, 56–68.

Watzlawick, P., Beavin, J. H., & Jackson, D. D. *Pragmatics of human communication: A study of interactional patterns, pathologies and paradoxes*. New York: W. W. Norton & Co., 1967.

* * * * * *

REFRAMING

This refers to a therapeutic strategy that effects an alteration in a client's or family's internal model of the world (→ **paradigm/ model/ map**). This model or "frame" directs behavior, feeling, and thinking. As such, it is comparable to the rules of a game or a → **code** that makes it possible to gather information and create patterns of meaning out of phenomenal events (see Goffman, 1974, p. 7). When reframing is effective, a change in behavior is to be expected.

Reframing interventions are consistently used in a wide variety of therapeutic approaches such as → **strategic therapy,** → **structural therapy,** → **communication therapy,** → **hypnotherapy,** and → **neurolinguistic programming.** Indeed, the question may be raised whether the effectiveness of *all* therapeutic processes, including those that emphasize "insight" and the "working out" of conflicts, are not ultimately due to the changing of internal maps. Among the interventions that aim at such changes, one can distinguish between deframing and reframing interventions (O'Hanlon, 1984). Also, such interventions may be viewed as a "softening up" or "hardening" of given → **punctuations** or boundaries between categories or perceptual sets (Omer, 1984). They can also entail a more direct, analytic interpretation, or a more indirect, "embedded" reframing (Berger, 1984; Kersey & Protinsky, 1984). (See also → **positive connotation,** → **binocular theory of change** → **paradoxical intervention,** and → **symptom prescription.**)

The concepts of framing and reframing also can be considered in terms of a → **hierarchy** of nested contexts. Hofstadter (1979) comments: "In frame language, one could say that mental representations of situations involve frames nested within each other. Each of the various ingredients of a situation has its own frame. . . . The theory of representing knowledge in frames relies on the idea that the world

287

consists of quasi–closed subsystems, each of which can serve as a context for others without being too disrupted, or creating too much disruption, in the process. . . . [A] frame contains knowledge of its limits of applicability, and heuristics for switching to other frames in case it has been stretched beyond its limits of tolerance. The nested structure of a frame gives you a way of 'zooming in' and looking at small details from as close up as you wish" (pp. 644–645).

Bandler, R., & Grinder, J. *Tranceformation.* Moab, Utah: Real People Press, 1981.
Bandler, R., & Grinder, J. *Reframing: Neurolinguistic programming and the transformation of meaning.* Moab, Utah: Real People Press, 1982.
Berger, M. Across the corpus callosum with Chris Columbus; or, how to put enough information into your left brain that when your right brain intuits, it does so intelligently. Some ideas for the learning of reframing. *Journal of Strategic and Systemic Therapies 3* (2): 22–28, 1984.
de Shazer, S. The confusion technique. *Family Therapy 2*: 23–30, 1975.
Goffman, E. *Frame analysis.* New York: Harper & Row, 1974.
Grunebaum, H., & Chasin, R. Relabeling and reframing reconsidered: The beneficial effects of a pathological label. *Family Process 17*: 449–455, 1978.
Haley, J. (Ed.). *Advanced techniques of hypnosis and therapy: The selected papers of Milton H. Erickson, M. D.* New York: Grune & Stratton, 1967.
Haley, J. *Uncommon therapy: The psychiatric techniques of Milton H. Erickson, M. D.: A casebook of an innovative psychiatrist's work in short-term therapy.* New York: W. W. Norton & Co., 1973.
Hofstadter, D. R. *Gödel, Escher, Bach: An eternal golden braid.* New York: Basic Books, 1979.
Kersey, B., & Protinsky, B. Reframing and embedded directives: A complementary intervention strategy. *Journal of Strategic and Systemic Therapies 3* (2): 17–20, 1984.
O'Hanlon, B. Framing intervention in therapy: Deframing and reframing. *Journal of Strategic and Systemic Therapies 3* (2): 1–4, 1984.
Omer, H. Frames and symptoms: Some implications for strategic therapy. *Journal of Strategic and Systemic Therapies 3* (2): 5–16, 1984.
Watzlawick, P., Weakland, J. H., & Fisch, R. *Change: Principles of problem formation and problem resolution.* New York: W. W. Norton & Co., 1974.

RELATIONAL BALANCE

Relational balances are a series of polarities that allow the characteristic problems and patterns of dyadic relationships to be brought into focus. Both partners contribute in different ways to these polarities. Important polarities in dyadic relationships include: moment–duration, difference–sameness, satisfaction–frustration, stimulation–stabilization, and closeness–distance.

According to Stierlin (1969, 1971), positive or negative → **mutuality** is determined by the way in which one copes with the tensions repeatedly created by such polarities. The concept of relational balance opens up perspectives on essential elements of dyadic relationships. In the framework of the systemic perspective, however, dyadic relationships are only parts of more extensive social systems (→ **individuation**).

The concept of relational balance, via which the movement of a relationship unfolds and takes shape, can be seen in connection with Hegel's paradigmatic description of the relationship between master and servant. Using a → **dialectical** approach, Hegel (1910) gives special predominance to three aspects of this relationship: desire-pleasure, work, and fear of death. The movement of the relationship can stagnate, which leads to a solidification of the positions of master and servant. The master has pleasure without the need to work; the servant has work without pleasure. Both miss out on important dimensions of growth, and both, within these roles, are cheated of a central human experience, the mastery of the fear of death.

Taking as an example the polarity moment–duration, it may be said that a momentary relationship becomes real only when its duration, limits, and finality are included in the definition of the relationship. Work on the relationship can be described as mastering its duration, which is at the same time a constant process of making each moment valuable. This type of activity is also a way of overcoming the fear of death.

Byng-Hall, J. Symptom bearer as marital distance regulator: Clinical implications. *Family Process 19:* 355–365, 1980.
Byng-Hall, J., & Campbell, D. Resolving conflicts in family distance regulation: An integrative approach. *Journal of Marital and Family Therapy 7:* 321–330, 1981.
Hegel, G. W. F. [1807] *The phenomenology of the mind, Vol. II.* London: Swann Sonnenschein, 1910.
Stierlin, H. *Conflict and reconciliation.* New York: Science House, 1969.
Stierlin, H. *Das Tun des Einen ist das Tun des Anderen.* Frankfurt: Suhrkamp, 1971.

* * * * * *

RELATIONAL ETHICS

It is the main proposition of → **contextual therapy** that human interaction is essentially guided by relational ethics. Ethics in this sense is not to be understood as a collection of moral values or guidelines determining what is "right" or "wrong," but rather as a search for → **justice** and fairness in human interaction. Accordingly, the functioning of a family depends on the long-term regulation or balancing of the credit and debit accounts (→ **ledger of merits**) between family members. In this process, the assets and claims accumulating over a number of generations play an essential role (→ **multigenerational perspective**). This balancing of the books must take into consideration the point of view of each family member and the feeling that one has done something for the family for which one has a right to be compensated. The therapeutic attitude that facilitates this is → **multidirectional partiality**, which also helps therapists not to impose their values upon the family.

The question of the ethics and values that govern interactions in family systems is characteristic of the therapeutic and theoretical work of Boszormenyi–Nagy. It is remarkable that the question of ethics and values in family interaction has been screened out by almost all other family therapy authors. This is especially surprising because judgmental processes are accorded a central role in systemic and cybernetic perspectives. To deny another person esteem, to devalue him or her, is all too often a reaction to the feeling of having done more for another person than one has received in return. The morality of a family is reflected in its communicational style, which can vividly display the conditions of mutual regard or disregard within the family. The feeling of → **self–esteem** that each family member must develop and maintain is, therefore, a function of the family's relational ethics.

The question of how a subjective or family → **epistemology** is constructed and how behavior is regulated accordingly cannot be answered without considering which criteria are employed in the judgment of what is "right" and "wrong." The → **punctuation** of interactions involves value judgments. What information is considered relevant or irrelevant, whether behaviors are → **dominant/ inferior,** and what standards are used to establish a → **hierarchy,** all involve evaluation. Thus, a cybernetic approach to family therapy requires a theory of intersubjective values (Simon, 1982). Boszormenyi–Nagy's work, influenced by Martin Buber in particular, can be credited with bringing into focus this essential perspective of human existence and family life. It is no coincidence that the terminology Boszormenyi–Nagy uses stems for the most part from the language of law and economics, which highlights his belief that these apparently dissociated spheres of sociopolitical life do meet and commingle in family life, and do determine the psychological reality of each individual. The fundamental claim to an eventual balancing of justice is, in Boszormenyi–Nagy's opinion, a basic factor of human existence. The foundation of his contextual therapy is his conviction that, alongside individual psychological mechanisms and transactional patterns, it is precisely the aspect of relational ethics that is decisive for successful therapy. A sense of responsibility for others has, in his opinion, existential significance for each individual. To facilitate the possibility of caring for others is the ethical goal of therapy.

Luhmann's sociological–systemic definition of "morality" differs from Boszormenyi–Nagy's more philosophical understanding of relational ethics. A quotation from Luhmann (1978) will illustrate how it is possible to integrate Boszormenyi–Nagy's concept into a systemic framework:

> The totality of the actually practiced *conditions* of mutual respect (*Achtung*) or disrespect (*Missachtung*) are the substance of the *morality* of a society.... Morality arises from implicit or explicit communication about respect, through the fact that such communication is possible when ego and alter–ego allow each other the opportunity to acquire respect, and signal to each other the accepted conditions under which this may be done, subsequently standardizing these conditions either implicitly or explicitly, subtly or drastically, concretely and situationally, uniquely or abstractly, and with or without consideration for the opinion of the other.... Morality is thus a coding process with the specific function of using conditions of respect to regulate communication about respect and thus provide a continual adjustment of the ego/alter–ego synthesis (p. 51).

Boszormenyi-Nagy, I. Intensive family therapy as process. In I. Boszormenyi-Nagy & J. L. Framo (Eds.), *Intensive family therapy: Theoretical and practical aspects.* New York: Harper & Row, 1965, 87–142. (a)

Boszormenyi-Nagy, I. A theory of relationships: Experience and transaction. In I. Boszormenyi-Nagy & J. L. Framo (Eds.), *Intensive family therapy: Theoretical and practical aspects.* New York: Harper & Row, 1965, 33–86. (b)

Boszormenyi-Nagy, I. From family therapy to a psychology of relationships: Fictions of the individual and fictions of the family. *Comprehensive Psychiatry 7:* 408–423, 1966.

Boszormenyi-Nagy, I. Relational modes and meaning. In G. H. Zuk & I. Boszormenyi-Nagy (Eds.), *Family therapy and disturbed families.* Palo Alto: Science and Behavior Books, 1967, 58–73.

Boszormenyi-Nagy, I. Ethical and practical implications of intergenerational family therapy. *Psychotherapy Psychosomatics 24:* 261–268, 1974.

Boszormenyi-Nagy, I. Mann und Frau: Verdienstkonten in den Geschlechtsrollen. *Familiendynamik 2:* 35–49, 1977.

Boszormenyi-Nagy, I., & Spark, G. M. *Invisible loyalties: Reciprocity in intergenerational family therapy.* New York: Harper & Row, 1973.

Buber, M. [1923] *I and thou.* New York: Scribner's, 1958.

Luhmann, N. Soziologie der Moral. In N. Luhmann & H. Pfürtner (Eds.). *Theorietechnik und Moral.* Frankfurt: Suhrkamp, 1978, 8–116.

MacGregor, R. Communicating values in family therapy. In G. H. Zuk & I. Boszormenyi-Nagy (Eds.), *Family therapy and disturbed families.* Palo Alto: Science and Behavior Books, 1967, 178–185.

Simon, F. B. Das verlorene Vertrauen und der Ruf nach Kontrolle: Systemtheoretische Aspekte der "Ausgrenzung." *Psychiatrische Praxis 9:* 59–63, 1982.

Simon, F. B. *Der Prozess der Individuation: Über den Zusammenhang von Vernunft und Gefühlen.* Göttingen: Vandenhoeck & Ruprecht, 1984.

Stierlin, H. *Conflict and reconciliation.* New York: Science House, 1969.

Stierlin, H. *Das Tun des Einen ist das Tun des Anderen.* Frankfurt: Suhrkamp, 1971.
Warner, S. M. Soft meaning and sincerity in the family system. *Family Process 22:* 523–535, 1983.

* * * * * *

RELATIONAL MODES/TRANSACTIONAL MODES/INTERACTIONAL MODES

All of these terms refer to typical modes of relationship between two or more partners, and/or family members. They include → **expelling,** → **binding,** and → **delegation.** These modes are especially exhibited in the processes of → **separating parents and adolescents.**

According to Stierlin, the modes of binding or expelling reflect the relative dominance of → **centripetal/centrifugal patterns.** The course of mutual detachment of the generations from each other will be determined essentially by the type and strength of these forces. If centripetal, binding forces turn out to be too strong, phase–adequate individuation and separation can be delayed. The child remains caught in the family ghetto, and the parents also miss out on important stages in their own → **individuation** and maturation. If centrifugal forces dominate, the individual as well as the → **family life cycle** manifest phase–inadequate expulsion or disattachment.

In the associations between generations, the relational modes thus function as covert organizational patterns underlying specific parent–child interactions. If the age–specific relational modes occur out of phase, too intensively, or in an inappropriate combination for the child, the development of the self suffers, as does the mutual process of detachment between parents and children. These relational modes thus reflect important contributions by parents and children toward this interpersonal process. They are effective in both a transitive as well as in a reciprocal manner. They are transitive in that they characterize the active formation of the growing adult–to–be who is still immature, dependent, and exposed to parental influence. This often takes place via concealed and subtle signals and sanctions. The child must inevitably conform to this "stronger reality." These relational modes are also reciprocal in that there is an exchange that affects both sides, in other words, a circular causality comes into effect. In these exchanges the children form and influence their parents as much as they are formed and influenced by them (→ **circularity,** → **relational reality**).

Beavers, W. R. *Psychotherapy and growth: A family systems perspective.* New York: Brunner/Mazel, 1977.

Boszormenyi-Nagy, I. Relational modes and meaning. In G. H. Zuk & I. Boszormenyi-Nagy (Eds.), *Family therapy and disturbed families.* Palo Alto: Science and Behavior Books, 1967, 58–73.

Stierlin, H. The adaptation to the "stronger" person's reality. *Psychiatry 22:* 143–152, 1959.

Stierlin, H. *Separating parents and adolescents: A perspective on running away, schizophrenia, and waywardness.* New York: Quadrangle, 1974.

Stierlin, H. *Psychoanalysis and family therapy: Selected papers.* New York: Jason Aronson, 1977.

Stierlin, H., Levi, L. D., & Savard, R. J. Centrifugal versus centripetal separation in adolescence: Two patterns and some of their implications. In S. C. Feinstein & P. Giovacchini (Eds.), *Adolescent psychiatry, Vol. II: Developmental and clinical studies.* New York: Basic Books, 1973, 211–239.

* * * * * *

RELATIONAL REALITY

For Bateson (1972), relational reality is a central concept. He posited that the *understanding* and *shaping* of relationships is the most central and enveloping human interest.

Stierlin (1959), following the example of Bateson, differentiates between "hard" and "soft" reality. Hard reality is that which is generally referred to as material, concrete, observable reality: stones that hurt if one is hit by them, streetcars that can run over one, etc. Soft reality is more difficult to elucidate and is most easily characterized as relational reality. It is dependent upon, created through, and sustained by perception, interpretation, emotion, and fantasy. It is created by, e.g., open or concealed opinions and expectations of spouses, parents, friends, and superiors, the → loyalty that binds one to certain people or groups, and the wishes, fantasies, and inhibitions that determine one's sexual behavior. One can also speak of psychic, empirical, social, interpersonal or interactional reality, or, as did Hegel, of the reality of the objective mind.

As used here, the concept of relation includes one's relationship to one's own body, internal experiences, and needs, as well as to one's relationship with other persons and social institutions. It must be said, however, that it is often difficult to differentiate between hard and soft reality. Both types of reality are filtered through subjective experience. Both are made accessible through perception and language, which is learned from and among other people. Hard reality perhaps can be defined as that upon which consensus can be reached without too much difficulty.

From the perspective of family therapy, the differentiation between hard and soft reality is useful. Soft reality is more a product of culture and, therefore, subject to historical change. It is thus predominantly a matter of constant intersubjective evaluation and confirmation of perceptions, mutual agreement about certain models, values, perspectives, and the sharing of a common focus of attention. In short, soft reality is a matter of negotiation, of dialogue, or of positive → **mutuality.**

Relational reality "softens" in proportion to the vagueness with which an interpersonal → **context** is delineated, and the tenacity with which the definition of → **relationship** is avoided. This type of softening is most pronounced in families with schizophrenic members. These families are characterized by a large measure of → **communication deviance,** → **mystification,** → **driving crazy,** and → **disconfirmation,** and it usually involves massive → **binding.**

Whereas the relational reality of families with schizophrenic elements ("schizo–present" families) is excessively softened, that of psychosomatic families (→ **family somatics**) tends to be excessively hard. Psychosomatic families tend to take on without question and to espouse without compromise a conventional view of the world. This view is considered to be the "hard facts of life." In psychosomatic families, there is also an excess of binding that blocks the possibility of → **individuation,** but in a way that is phenomenologically different from the softened reality of the schizo–present families.

The question of how soft or hard reality is, is related to the larger question of limits and possibilities of knowledge, in other words, to → **epistemology.** Epistemology has received increasing attention in the discussion of family therapy, especially as a result of Bateson's (1972) seminal work. There are also two schools of thought as to the softness of relational reality. In → **constructivism,** the softness of relational reality is stressed. Watzlawick (1976) insists that in human relationships, values, norms, etc., there exists no abiding, binding reality, but rather a multitude of differently construed realities. Dell (1981), on the other hand, takes the view that the nature of each perceiving, interacting organism defines the limits of what can become reality for that organism. He refers to the complicated relationship between epistemology and ontology, i.e., the connection and relations between the process of obtaining knowledge and the essence of being, as well as the formation of theory about both (→ **paradigm/model/map**).

Bateson, G. *Steps to an ecology of mind.* New York: Ballantine Books, 1972.
Bateson, G. *Mind and nature: A necessary unity.* New York: E. P. Dutton, 1979.

Dell, P. F. Researching the family theories of schizophrenia: An exercise in epistemological confusion. *Family Process 19:* 321–335, 1980.

Dell, P. F., & Goolishian, H. A. Order through fluctuation: An evolutionary epistemology for human systems. *Australian Journal of Family Therapy 2:* 175–184, 1981.

Stierlin, H. The adaptation to the "stronger" person's reality. *Psychiatry 22:* 143–152, 1959.

Stierlin, H. Die "Beziehungsrealität Schizophrener." *Psyche 35:* 49–65, 1981.

Warner, S. M. Soft meaning and sincerity in the family system. *Family Process 22:* 523–535, 1983.

Watzlawick, P. *How real is real? Confusion, disinformation, communication.* New York: Random House, 1976.

Wynne, L. C. The epigenesis of relational systems: A model for understanding family development. *Family Process 23:* 297–318, 1984.

$$* * * * * *$$

RELATIONAL STAGNATION

Relational stagnation is the rigidification of life patterns within the psyche of an individual and in his or her relations to others. In the frame of → **contextual therapy,** relational stagnation is considered to be a pathogenetic factor. It is also an aspect of → **relational ethics:** If responsibility for the present and future consequences of one's relational behavior is ignored, the possibility that certain interactional patterns will become fixed and carried over into the next generation is increased.

In contrast to an individual whose life is limited to the span of time between birth and death, family systems extend more or less limitlessly beyond the nuclear family into the sequence of the generations. In consideration of this, Boszormenyi–Nagy emphasized the importance of a → **multigenerational perspective** in therapy. The patterns of relationship that influence the emotions and behaviors of all family members in each generation must be altered where necessary to enable families to adapt to changing demands. Should a family be unable to meet such demands, it will become dysfunctional and have difficulty in childrearing. To facilitate adaptation, the accumulated → **ledger of merits,** family legacies, and ties of → **loyalty** over the generations must be taken into consideration. Relational stagnation occurs when a fine balance between adaptation and stabilization is not achieved or preserved, or if the ethical responsibility for one's own actions is not incorporated into one's relationships.

Boszormenyi-Nagy, I. The concept of schizophrenia from the perspective of family treatment. *Family Process 1:* 103–113, 1962.

Boszormenyi-Nagy, I. A theory of relationships: Experience and transaction. In I. Boszormenyi-Nagy & J. L. Framo (Eds.), *Intensive family therapy: Theoretical and practical aspects*. New York: Harper & Row, 1965, 33–86.
Boszormenyi-Nagy, I., & Spark, G. M. *Invisible loyalties: Reciprocity in intergenerational family therapy*. New York: Harper & Row, 1973.

$$* \quad * \quad * \quad * \quad * \quad *$$

RELATIONSHIP, DEFINITION OF

For many exponents of → **communication theory,** definition of relationship is a central concept in family theory and therapy. It describes how and to what extent relational partners achieve consensus about what is acceptable to each other in the relationship, in other words, the → **rules** that are valid for the relationship.

Haley (1959b) states that the definition of a relationship depends upon *who* is defining the relationship: "When one person communicates a message to another, he is maneuvering to define the relationship. The other person is thereby posed the problem of accepting or rejecting the relationship offered. He can let the message stand, thereby accepting the other person's definition, or counter with a maneuver defining it differently. He may also accept the other person's maneuver but qualify his acceptance with a message indicating that he is *letting* the other person get by with the maneuver" (p. 323).

In defining a relationship, the main question is whether it is to be regarded as symmetrical (→ **symmetry**) or complementary (→ **complementarity**). On many levels, however, → **communication** has content and relational aspects, each of which annotates the other. Thus, there are countless possibilities to refuse and avoid defining a relationship. Haley (p. 325) elucidates this by analyzing the formal features of a message to another person into four elements:

(1) I
(2) am saying something
(3) to you
(4) in this situation.

Haley adds that a "person can avoid defining his relationship by negating any or all of these four elements. He can (1) deny that *he* communicated something, (2) deny that something was communicated, (3) deny that it was communicated *to* the other person, or (4) deny the context in which it was communicated" (p. 325).

In Haley's opinion, the classical psychiatric symptoms of schizo-

296

phrenia can be understood to be the result of → **strategies** to avoid defining a relationship in order to maintain control over it: "The various and seemingly unconnected and bizarre symptoms of schizophrenia can be seen to have a central and rather simple nucleus. If one is determined to avoid defining his relationship, or avoid indicating what sort of behavior is to take place in a relationship, he can do so only by behaving in those ways which are describable as symptoms of schizophrenia" (p. 327). The varied forms of → **communication deviance** can be regarded as ways in which the failure to define relationships become manifest (Wynne, 1970). One can speak here of an excessive softening of → **relational reality** (Stierlin, 1959, 1981).

Selvini–Palazzoli and the Milan group of family therapists speak of "schizophrenic communication" as soon as a family member consistently avoids a definition of relationship. When this occurs, the tension with a family quickly reaches an intolerable level. The striving or → **game** for control in the relationship can end in a → **malign clinch.** To bring about a definition of relationship among family members, therapists employ strategies such as → **circular questioning,** → **paradoxical intervention,** and homework rituals, with the goal of promoting a definition of relationship. These → **prescriptions** are more difficult to apply, as well as more urgently needed, when there is → **binding.**

Boszormenyi-Nagy, I. A theory of relationships: Experience and transaction. In I. Boszormenyi-Nagy & J. L. Framo (Eds.), *Intensive family therapy: Theoretical and practical aspects.* New York: Harper & Row, 1965, 33–86.
Haley, J. The family of the schizophrenic: A model system. *Journal of Nervous and Mental Disease: 129:* 357–374, 1959. (a)
Haley, J. An interactional description of schizophrenia. *Psychiatry 22:* 321–332, 1959. (b)
Haley, J. Toward a theory of pathological systems. In G. H. Zuk & I. Boszormenyi-Nagy (Eds.), *Family therapy and disturbed families.* Palo Alto: Science and Behavior Books, 1967, 11–27.
Selvini-Palazzoli, M., Boscolo, L., Cecchin, G., & Prata, G. *Paradox and counterparadox: A new model in the therapy of the family in schizophrenic transaction* (translated by E. V. Burt). New York: Jason Aronson, 1978.
Selvini-Palazzoli, M., & Prata, G. A new method for therapy and research in the treatment of schizophrenic families. In H. Stierlin, L. C. Wynne, & M. Wirsching (Eds.), *Psychosocial intervention in schizophrenia: An international view.* Berlin: Springer-Verlag, 1983, 237–243.
Singer, M. T., & Wynne, L. C. Principles for scoring communication defects and deviances in parents of schizophrenics: Rorschach and TAT scoring manuals. *Psychiatry 29:* 260–288, 1966.
Stierlin, H. The adaptation to the "stronger" person's reality. *Psychiatry 22:* 143–152, 1959.
Stierlin, H. Die "Beziehungsrealität Schizophrener." *Psyche 35:* 49–65, 1981.
Watzlawick, P., Beavin, J. H., & Jackson, D. D. *Pragmatics of human communication: A study of interactional patterns, pathologies and paradoxes.* New York: W. W. Norton & Co., 1967.

Wynne, L. C. Communication disorders and the quest for relatedness in families of schizophrenics. *American Journal of Psychoanalysis 30:* 100–114, 1970.

* * * * * *

RESISTANCE

In the context of psychoanalysis, resistance consists of all forms of opposition by the patient to the analysis and the analyst. In family therapy, resistance refers to any aspect of the therapeutic system (including the family, the therapist, and the relevant context) that interferes with engagement in therapy or with the processes of therapeutic change.

Freud viewed resistance as impeding clarification of the patient's symptoms and hindering therapeutic progress. Initially, he attempted to subdue resistance by perseverance (the inverse of resistance). Later, he realized that analysis of resistance could unlock the repressed secrets of the patient's neurosis. Freud considered intra–analytic → **transference** a form of resistance and its interpretation a means of overcoming that resistance. In psychoanalysis, resistance encompasses those defense mechanisms that are activated during treatment when the patient's inner balance (of wishes and urges held in check by internal prohibitions) is endangered.

Anderson and Stewart (1983; see Chapter 1) have comprehensively reviewed the history of highly diverse views of resistance held by family therapists. A number of characteristic forms of resistance during family therapy, e.g., resistance to overdue development of related individuation have been described: joint avoidance and denial of existing conflicts (→ **collusion**); emotional fission of the family (→ **marital schism**); designation of a → **scapegoat;** various compensatory substitute mechanisms such as drug and alcohol abuse or sexual promiscuity; acting out; reversal of the parent and child roles (→ **parentification**); blurring of → **generational boundaries;** rigidification of → **roles;** dissolution of the family's organizational structure (→ **disengagement**); and the transference of family conflicts onto the community within which the family exists.

A family can also manifest its resistance toward therapy on a more blatant level by overt refusal or disinterest in participation in the therapeutic process, or by a covert lack of emotional involvement in the therapy session. Stanton and Todd (1981) have discussed the issue of "resistance" at the primary stage of recruiting and engaging families in family therapy. This often occurs when a rebellious adolescent, who is considered to be the "family problem," refuses to attend a family therapy session, or when a family or couple is referred for therapy by a medical, social, or legal institution, and is either overly fearful of the therapeutic process or completely skeptical about its usefulness. Resistance is also involved when an overly strong, bound–up family ($\rightarrow$ **binding**), for example, a family with a schizophrenic member, feels that the very idea of "family therapy" represents a threat to family unity, and the family then develops a unified front of resistance toward such therapy.

Anderson and Stewart (1983) have defined resistance in family therapy in broad systemic terms, not as located in the family but "as a property belonging to a therapeutic system, which can be expressed by the behavior of any part of that system. The therapeutic system includes family members, the therapist(s), and the agency or institution in which therapists practice. Resistances residing in different parts of the system are seen as operating in a synergetic and fluctuating manner, any or all of which can interfere with the successful initiation or completion of family therapy." Based on this view, families and therapists have "mutual responsibility in the process of facilitating change and overcoming resistance" (p. 37).

As an example of the therapist's contribution to resistance ("counterresistance") within the therapeutic system, Schaffer et al. (1962) described how the seemingly sensible efforts of family therapists to find meaning in a family's patterns of interaction will be at odds with the "culture" of families in which meaning is dreaded. The therapist's insistence on discovering meaning will polarize the therapist–family relationship and constitutes resistance to therapeutic change.

The way that family therapists deal with the various forms of resistance, whether by an individual or by the unified efforts of an entire family, depend both on the circumstances involved and on the theory and techniques of the therapist. In general, family therapists try simultaneously to maintain control of the situation and be flexible in their intervention strategies, yet at the same time to "go along" with the family's resistance, in other words, to avoid at all costs an escalation of resistance that would result from "resisting the resistance." In this respect, Erickson's $\rightarrow$ **hypnotherapy** (see Haley, 1973) has been of central importance. The diversity of approaches has varied from Ackerman (1962, 1966), who was explicitly confrontational and recommended "tickling the defenses" of the family, to de Shazer, who reframes "resistance" as the family's "unique ways of cooperating" (1982, p. vi) and speaks of the "death of resistance" (1984).

One must keep in mind that the concept of resistance is derived from the static–descriptive, mechanical concept of physical properties, such as Newton's Law (*"actio = reactio"*). This concept implies that the force of resistance must be equal to the force exerted. This concept, however, does not correspond to the → **cybernetic** view of resistance, which proceeds on the assumption that far–reaching → **change** in the individual and family can take place quickly and in a discontinuous manner (→ **brief therapy,** → **nonlinearity/step function**). Such considerations raise the question as to whether it is not more appropriate to view resistance from a perspective that gives greater importance to concepts such as → **game,** → **strategy,** and → **coherence.**

Ackerman, N. W. Family psychotherapy and psychoanalysis: The implications of difference. *Family Process 1:* 30–43, 1962.
Ackerman, N. W. *Treating the troubled family.* New York: Basic Books, 1966.
Anderson, C. M., & Stewart, S. *Mastering resistance: A practical guide to family therapy.* New York: Guilford Press, 1983.
Dell, P. F. Beyond homeostasis: Toward a concept of coherence. *Family Process 21:* 21–41, 1982.
de Shazer, S. *Patterns of brief family therapy: An ecosystemic approach.* New York: Guilford Press, 1982.
de Shazer, S. The death of resistance. *Family Process 23:* 11–17, 1984.
Fisch, R., Weakland, J. H., & Segal, L. *The tactics of change: Doing therapy briefly.* San Francisco: Jossey-Bass, 1982.
Gurman, A. S. (Ed.). *Questions and answers in the practice of family therapy.* New York: Brunner/Mazel, 1982.
Haley, J. *Uncommon therapy: The psychiatric techniques of Milton H. Erickson, M. D.: A casebook of an innovative psychiatrist's work in short-term therapy.* New York: W. W. Norton & Co., 1973.
Luther, G., & Loev, I. Resistance in marital therapy. *Journal of Marital and Family Therapy 7:* 475–480, 1981.
Schaffer, L., Wynne, L. C., Day, J., Ryckoff, I. M., & Halperin. A. On the nature and sources of the psychiatrist's experience with the family of the schizophrenic. *Psychiatry 25:* 32–45, 1962.
Stanton, M. D., & Todd, T. C. Engaging "resistant" families in treatment. *Family Process 20:* 261–293, 1981.
Watzlawick, P., Weakland, J. H., & Fisch, R. *Change: Principles of problem formation and problem resolution.* New York: W. W. Norton & Co., 1974.

* * * * * *

Revolving Slate

This concept, which Ivan Boszormenyi–Nagy applied in → **contextual therapy,** makes comprehensible how specific attitudes, expectations, and patterns of behavior of one generation of a family can be transferred to following generations.

The revolving slate phenomenon underlines the importance of invisible → **loyalty** and the significance of an unbalanced → **ledger of merits,** as well as the expectations (demands) that stem from the balance owing. A parentified child (→ **parentification**), for example, who has not been "reimbursed" for sacrifices made to the parents, will attempt to receive "recompense" (in a more or less covert manner) from his or her own children. These children will then have certain expectations with regard to their own offspring, and so forth. Certain parent–child interaction → **patterns** are thus carried over from generation to generation in a kind of self–destructive, vicious circle. This is an aspect of what Boszormenyi–Nagy and Spark (1973) describe as → **relational stagnation.** The revolving slate concept also makes various forms of → **delegation** more comprehensible.

Boszormenyi-Nagy, I., & Spark, G. M. *Invisible loyalties: Reciprocity in intergenerational family therapy.* New York: Harper & Row, 1973.

* * * * * *

RIGID TRIAD

This term refers to parent/child relational configurations in which the child is rigidly used to detour or deflect parental conflicts.

The term "rigid triad" was coined by Minuchin (1974) to describe three types of family structures in which "the boundary between the parental subsystem and the child becomes diffuse, and the boundary around the parents–child triad, which should be diffuse, becomes inappropriately rigid" (p. 102). In the first type of → **triangulation,** each parent attempts to gain support of the child in his or her conflict with the other spouse. The child is thereby exposed to conflicting → **loyalty.**

In the second type of rigid triad, one parent supports the child in a conflict between the child and the other parent; this has the effect of → **binding** the parent and the child into a rigid cross–generational coalition (→ **alliance/ alignment/ coalition**). In a triangulation of this type, the actual, underlying conflict between the two spouses is often barely recognizable as such. The strong bond between the child and its parental coalition partner can have serious consequences for the child's development, hindering the child in the necessary development of an autonomous identity (→ **separating parents and adolescents**).

The third type of rigid triad, → **detouring of conflicts,** occurs with either of two kinds of content. In the first instance, the child is defined (→ **attribution**) as "bad," and the parents are joined together in their efforts to control their offspring. In the second instance, they unite to protect a child who is viewed as sick or weak.

Hoffman. L. *Foundations of family therapy: A conceptual framework for systems change.* New York: Basic Books, 1981.
Minuchin, S. *Families and family therapy.* Cambridge: Harvard University Press, 1974.
Minuchin, S., Rosman, B. L., & Baker, L. *Psychosomatic families: Anorexia nervosa in context.* Cambridge: Harvard University Press, 1978.

* * * * * *

ROLES

Roles refer to the entirety of the expectations and norms that a group (for example, a family) has in regard to an individual's position and behavior within the group. A role is thus equivalent to the behavioral expectations that are directed toward an individual within a given situation or social → **context.**

Role Theory originated in the fields of social psychology and sociology (see Linton, 1945; Mead, 1934; Merton, 1949; Parsons, 1951; Thomas & Znaniecki, 1918) and was especially important in the early stages of the development of family therapy. Of particular importance was the work of Parsons, Bales, and associates (1955). Various family therapy theoreticians and clinicians subscribed to Parsons' and Bales's view of the family as a "social subsystem" in which particular members of the subsystem take certain roles in relation to one another (see Ackerman, 1951; Boszormenyi–Nagy, 1965; Lidz et al., 1957; Ryckoff et al., 1959; Spiegel, 1957; Wynne et al., 1958).

As early as 1942, Parsons wrote about the differentiation of roles in "kinship systems." More specifically, Parsons et al. (1955) described the structure of nuclear families as developing along two axes: an axis of → **power** and an axis of instrumental–versus–expressive function. Following this line of argument, the essential processes of family organization can be seen as the formation of → **hierarchy** and the attribution of either an "expressive" or an "instrumental" role within the subsystem.

In experimental studies of small, *ad hoc* groups, Bales and Slater (1955) concluded that, despite many obvious differences from families, a similarity between small groups and families was their tendency to develop, through the processes of social interaction, a differentiation of roles along the dimension of task (instrumental) role specialization versus socio–emotional role specialization. Once such specialization has occurred, allocation of power then takes place in order to deal with the problem of integration of the system. In a further effort toward generalization about role differentiation, Zelditch (1955) and Parsons et al. (1955) analyzed the available cross–cultural literature and concluded that role differentiation along the hierarchical axis of relative power and an instrumental–expressive axis is characteristic of nuclear families on a very broad cross–cultural basis. Indeed, they found that when leadership in nuclear families is not allocated along these dimensions, the family itself gives way; it does not develop new dimensions of role differentiation. However, they also noted that families do vary greatly across cultures in the context of role functioning and in who (for example, fathers versus mothers) assumes certain functions. Their point was that interaction within social systems seems to require that *somebody* takes roles along these dimensions.

In the United States in the 1950s, it was typical to assign to the father the role of being work– and goal–directed, while the mother was assigned the integrative and social–emotional role or task. The first family therapists were oriented toward this normative assignment. They tended to concentrate on pathological disorders in the structure of the family hierarchy such as occur, for example, in the role reversal involved in → **parentification.** It can hardly be denied that role differentiation does and must exist within social organizations; however, as has sometimes been overlooked, norms for the *content* of these roles cannot be established across different families. Currently, it appears to be more acceptable to see the existence of pathological effects where the role definitions have become overly rigid (regardless of content or who takes a particular role) as a result of prolonged or overdue developmental processes and the thwarting of necessary change.

The role relationship of the mother and the child, for example, changes as a result of reciprocal dependence and in relation to the family's → **coevolution** and coindividuation (→ **individuation**). This does not change the fact that the mother retains her status as mother and the child its status as child, despite the changing content of their *functional* roles. Hence, concepts of family therapy that seek to define the content of specific roles can only lay claim to validity within a specific period of time and in a particular culture.

Jackson (1965) sharply criticized the concept of role on the grounds that "a role encases the individual as a separate unit of study so that the *relations between* two or more individuals must necessarily be secondary phenomena" (p. 17). However, this criticism was based upon a use of the term contrary to that of authors such as those cited above. For example, Mead (1934), who was one of the first to give importance to the role concept in social science, explicitly emphasized that in role–taking each person "must be ready to take the attitude of everyone else" in an organized activity, and "these different roles must have a definite relationship to each other" (p. 151). Parsons (1951) and other sociologists made a further distinction between the "processual" aspects of "patterned interactive relationships," which he called *roles*, and the "positional" aspect—where the person is located in the social system relative to other persons—which he called *statuses* (p. 25), for example, mother, son, and so forth. Jackson, ignoring the traditional social science usage, loosely used the concept of role with a "positional" meaning and failed to recognize that even this "positional" aspect is always a function of individuals in a social context, never as an isolated, "separate unit."

Within the realm of family therapy, the sociopsychological concept of roles was further developed in particular by Richter (1963) who applied a psychoanalytically oriented framework to the study of roles: "By the role of the child . . . is meant here the structured entirety of the parents' unconscious expectational fantasies, in as far as they assign to the child the task of fulfilling a certain function[;] . . . . hence the role of the child is determined by the meaning the child receives in the context of the parents' attempt to resolve their own conflicts" (p. 73).

According to Richter, a generational role reversal takes place in families in which the child serves as a "substitute for the partner." Parents in this instance transfer impulses originally directed toward their own parents onto their children. In cases where a partner is missing or the relationship between the marital couple is severely disturbed, a child can function as a "spouse substitute." In a mother–son relationship, this can lead to "overprotection" or to an attitude of submissive wooing of the son by the mother. In a father–daughter relationship, this constellation leads to an incestuously tinged relationship.

If the child serves as a substitute for "an aspect" of the parent, the child can, because of its particular qualifications, serve as an "image of the parents." In this role, the child can be a substitute either for the parents' "ideal self" or for the "negative identity" of one of the parents. In the first instance, the parents seek in the child that which they always wanted to be; the child serves as a proxy for the parents' hopes of fulfilling their own thwarted striving toward success and recognition. By doing this, the child is pressed into balancing out the parents' low →	**self–esteem.** In negative identity processes, the nega-

tive aspects of self are transferred onto the child, in the role of →
scapegoat, by means of → **projective identification.**
Richter's concept of roles pointed the way to a → **multigenerational perspective** as well as to the complicated mechanisms of →
delegation. However, in Richter's theoretical outline of role structure,
the role of the child remains the focus of interest. Such a focus ignores,
or at least does not take into adequate consideration the essential
aspects of circular causality (→ **circularity**). If one wants to do justice
to the complexity of the concept of roles, one must take into consideration the dynamics of the complementary and/or reciprocal nature of
roles, and then view these in relation to the complementary needs of
individuals (Boszormenyi–Nagy, 1965).

Ackerman, N. W. "Social role" and total personality. *American Journal of Orthopsy-
chiatry 21:* 1–17, 1951.
Bales, R. F., & Slater, P. E. Role differentiation in small decision-making groups. In T.
Parsons, R. F. Bales, J. Olds, M. Zelditch, & P. E. Slater, *Family, socialization
and interaction process.* Glencoe, Ill.: Free Press, 1955, 259–306.
Boszormenyi-Nagy, I. Intensive family therapy as process. In I. Boszormenyi-Nagy &
J. L. Framo (Eds.), *Intensive family therapy: Theoretical and practical aspects.*
New York: Harper & Row, 1965, 87–142.
Frank, E., Anderson, C., & Rubinstein, D. Marital role ideals and perception of
marital role behavior in distressed and non-distressed couples. *Journal of Marital
and Family Therapy 6:* 55–64, 1980.
Jackson, D. D. The study of the family. *Family Process 4:* 1–20, 1965.
Lidz, T., Cornelison, A. R., Fleck, S., & Terry, D. The intrafamilial environment of
schizophrenic patients: II. Marital schism and marital skew. *American Journal of
Psychiatry 114:* 241–248, 1957.
Lidz, T., Fleck, S., & Cornelison, A. R. *Schizophrenia and the family.* New York:
International Universities Press, 1965.
Linton, R. *The cultural background of personality.* New York: D. Appleton-Century
Co., 1945.
Linton, R. Culture, society and the individual. *Journal of Abnormal and Social
Psychology 33:* 425–436, 1968.
Mead, G. H. *Mind, self, society.* Chicago: University of Chicago Press, 1934.
Merton, R. K. *Social theory and social structure: Toward the codification of theory
and research.* Glencoe, Ill.: Free Press, 1949.
Parsons, T. Age and sex in the social structure of the United States. *American
Sociological Review 7:* 604–616, 1942.
Parsons, T. *The social system.* Glencoe, Ill.: Free Press, 1951.
Parsons, T., Bales, R. F., Olds, J., Zelditch, M., & Slater, P. E. *Family, socialization
and interaction process.* Glencoe, Ill.: Free Press, 1955.
Parsons, T., & Fox, R. Illness, therapy and the modern urban American family.
Journal of Social Issues 8: 31–44, 1953.
Richter, H. E. *Eltern, Kind und Neurose.* Stuttgart: Klett, 1963.
Richter, H. E. *The family as patient.* New York: Farrar, Strauss, & Giroux, 1974.
Ryckoff, I., Day, J., & Wynne, L. C. Maintenance of stereotyped roles in the families
of schizophrenics. *American Medical Association Archives of General Psychiatry
1:* 93–98, 1959.

Selman, R. L. Taking another's perspective: Role-taking development in early childhood. *Child Development 42:* 1721–1734, 1971.

Spiegel, J. P. The resolution of role conflict within the family. *Psychiatry 20:* 1–16, 1957.

Spiegel, J. P. Cultural strain, family role patterns, and intrapsychic conflict. In J. G. Howells (Ed.), *Theory and practice of family psychiatry*. Edinburgh: Oliver & Boyd, 1968, 367–389.

Stierlin, H. "Role" und "Auftrag" in der Familientheorie und –therapie. *Familiendynamik 1:* 36–59, 1976.

Thomas, W. I., & Znaniecki, F. *The Polish peasant in Europe and America.* Chicago: University of Chicago Press, 1918.

Wynne, L. C., Ryckoff, I. M., Day, J., & Hirsch, S. I. Pseudo-mutuality in the family relations of schizophrenics. *Psychiatry 21:* 205–220, 1958.

Zelditch, M. Role differentiation in the nuclear family: A comparative study. In T. Parsons, R. F. Bales, J. Olds, M. Zelditch, & P. E. Slater, *Family, socialization and interaction process.* Glencoe, Ill.: Free Press, 1955, 307–351.

Zuk, G. H., & Rubinstein, D. A review of concepts in the study and treatment of families of schizophrenics. In I. Boszormenyi-Nagy & J. L. Framo (Eds.), *Intensive family therapy: Theoretical and practical aspects.* New York: Harper & Row, 1965, 1–31.

* * * * * *

RUBBER FENCE

Lyman Wynne introduced the term "rubber fence" to describe a characteristic process through which a family experiences itself, and is perceived by others, as if it were within an elastic boundary that helps the family members to maintain a sense of tolerable relatedness and to decrease the threat of divergence from within and intrusion from without.

According to Wynne, Ryckoff, Day, and Hirsch (1958), "when there is a continual effort in family relations to maintain → **pseudomutuality,** the family members try to act as if the family could be a truly self–sufficient social system" that provides protection against the dangers of both intrusions and departures (p. 211). However, efforts to maintain a behavioral boundary around a family cannot be sustained in living, growing systems such as families, which are subsystems that are inevitably participant in the larger society. To maintain the → **family myth** of self–sufficiency and harmonious relatedness, family members interpret and experience the family boundaries as continuous though unstable, stretching to incorporate those persons, experiences, and behaviors that fit and are complementary, and contracting to extrude those that cannot be ignored, seem threatening, or are noncomplementary (→ **complementarity**). Biological family members may thus be psychologically excluded and ostracized, sometimes by abandoning an → **identified patient** in a hospital (outside the "rubber fence"); nonfamily members, such as therapists, may be co–opted into the family system and its rules (within the "rubber fence"). With either extrusion or incorporation, new experiences act as "perturbations" to which the family accomodates without changing its organization (Maturana, 1978). This shared defense mechanism was first observed in families with a schizophrenic member, but similar phenomena, with varying degrees of intensity, subsequently have been noted in other families and in other enduring relational systems. These processes are manifestations of a disturbed relationship between the individual, the family, and the social environment (→ **relational reality**), and are associated with impaired potentiality toward → **coevolution**, → **individuation**, → **morphogenesis**, and → **mutuality**.

Maturana, H. R. Biology of language: The epistemology of reality. In G. A. Miller & E. Lenneberg (Eds.), *Psychology and biology of language and thought*. New York: Academic Press, 1978.

Wynne, L. C. Communication disorders and the quest for relatedness in the families of schizophrenics. *American Journal of Psychoanalysis 30:* 100–114, 1970.

Wynne, L. C. The epigenesis of relational systems: A model for understanding family development. *Family Process 23:* 297–318, 1984.

Wynne, L. C., Ryckoff, I. M., Day, J., & Hirsch, S. I. Pseudo-mutuality in the family relations of schizophrenics. *Psychiatry 21:* 205–220, 1958.

* * * * * *

RULE/FAMILY RULE

As defined by Jackson (1965b), rules are "relationship agreements" that "prescribe and limit the individuals' behaviors over a wide variety of *content* areas, organizing their interaction into a reasonably stable system" (p. 9). Because families interact in repetitious sequences, rules highlight → **redundancy** in family patterns.

Jackson (1965b) stated that "the family is a *rule–governed system:* that its members behave among themselves in an organized, repetitive manner and that this patterning of behaviors can be abstracted as a governing principle of family life" (p. 6). The way in which family rules are formulated is shaped by the → **epistemology** of the observer or family member who punctuates (→ **punctuation**) the family sequences. In other words, rules are "as if" descriptions by an observer, and not a fixed "reality" (Dell, 1982).

Rules derived from observation of family behavior may express such things as: "In this family the members behave as if one must be strong and helpful *or* sick and needy, but they cannot be both, even at different times"; or "This family behaves as if disagreement is life–threatening and the appearance of harmony must be preserved at all costs" (the rule of → **pseudomutuality**). Dell (1982) has noted that it is an epistemological error to think of families as behaving for a systemic purpose, e.g., "the daughter is sacrificing herself in order to protect the family." Such a formulation would be dualistic because it suggests that the "rule" exists outside of the family and causes family dysfunction. A more systemic rule formulation would specify that an observer is punctuating the sequence—*as if* the daughter is sacrificing herself—in a manner that fits with specific behaviors of other family members.

Jackson referred to family relationship rules as *norms,* which are inferred from observation of interaction and constitute a kind of family homeostatic (→ **homeostasis**) setting or baseline. Values presumably exist prior to the occurrence of specific behavioral patterns from which family rules and norms are inferred. Like rules, values provide guidelines for behavior, but are held by individuals, while family rules are systemic features of interaction. A specific rule identified by Jackson (1965a) is the marital "quid pro quo," a metaphorical "bargain" arising out of the active process of working out the marital relationship.

Family members ordinarily cannot formulate the rules inferred about them by an observer, or do so in quite different terms. Family rules appear to function as if they were implicit, unwritten laws. When they are made explicit, they are disrupted. In → **systemic therapy,** a family's rules are often prescribed to be carried out as a ritual (→ **paradoxical intervention**), whereupon this behavioral pattern evaporates (Selvini–Palazzoli, et al., 1978). Ford (1983) has proposed the alternative strategy of constructing a context that will generate the counter–rule to the rule that the family seems to have been following. Ford and Herrick (1974) have applied Jackson's concept of family rules to family assessment data. They make a distinction between "small" rules and "large" rules, which have the quality of a family life style or → **paradigm.** They identified five such rules: "children come first"; "two against the world"; "share and share alike"; "every man for himself"; and "until death do us part." This set of rules has served as the basis for a → **family typology** (Ford & Herrick, 1982).

Formally speaking, family rules contribute to the definition of → **relationship** and often specify whether the relationship is complementary or symmetrical (→ **complementarity,** → **symmetry**). It is possible to observe whether the family's system of rules serves to sustain → **stability** and → **coherence** via homeostasis, or whether → **coevolution**

308

and the → **individuation** of family members is possible. Other family rules may have to do with the type and extent of achieved or expected → **mutuality** (→ **harmonizing**, → **disconfirmation**), the keeping of → **family secrets**, and, most importantly, the maintenance of → **family myths.**

Bodin, A. M. The interactional view: Family therapy approaches of the Mental Research Institute. In A. S. Gurman & D. P. Kniskern (Eds.), *Handbook of family therapy.* New York: Brunner/Mazel, 1981, 267–309.
Dell, P. F. Beyond homeostasis: Toward a concept of coherence. *Family Process 21:* 21–41, 1982.
Ford, F. R. Rules: The invisible family. *Family Process 22:* 135–145, 1983.
Ford, F. R., & Herrick, J. Family rules/Family life styles. *American Journal of Orthopsychiatry 44:* 61–69, 1974.
Ford, F. R., & Herrick, J. A typology of families/Five family systems. *Australian Journal of Family Therapy 3:* 71–81, 1982.
Haley, J. Toward a theory of pathological systems. In G. H. Zuk & I. Boszormenyi-Nagy (Eds.), *Family therapy and disturbed families.* Palo Alto: Science and Behavior Books, 1967, 11–27.
Jackson, D. D. Family rules: The marital quid pro quo. *Archives of General Psychiatry 12:* 589–594, 1965. (a)
Jackson, D. D. The study of the family. *Family Process 4:* 1–20, 1965. (b)
Paterson, T. The family rule concept in the theory of family therapy. *Australian Journal of Family Therapy 1:* 129–137, 1980.
Riskin, J. Methodology for studying family interaction. *Archives of General Psychiatry 8:* 343–348, 1963.
Selvini-Palazzoli, M., Boscolo, L., Cecchin, G., & Prata, G. A ritualized prescription in family therapy: Odd days and even days. *Journal of Marriage and Family Counseling 4:* 3–9, 1978.
Watzlawick, P., & Beavin, J. H. Some formal aspects of communications. In P. Watzlawick & J. H. Weakland (Eds.), *The interactional view.* New York: W. W. Norton & Co., 1977, 56–68.
Watzlawick, P., Beavin, J. H., & Jackson, D. D. *Pragmatics of human communication: A study of interactional patterns, pathologies and paradoxes.* New York: W. W. Norton & Co., 1967.

* * * * * *

■ **S** ■

SCAPEGOAT

As applied in family theory and therapy, this biblical metaphor refers to a situation in which parents attempt to resolve a conflict between themselves by seeking and/or exaggerating problems in another family member. As a rule, the person "recruited" to be the scapegoat is a child.

Certain parents project their interpersonal tensions and conflicts onto their children in order to harmonize the discord in their marital relationships (→ **triangulation**, → **detouring of conflicts**). In this lineal (→ **lineality**) view of the causal schema of behaviors, the parents become the guilty parties and the child the passive victim. Therapists who use intervention strategies solely based on lineal models of causality run the risk of overlooking the systemic nature of family dynamics (→ **circularity**, → **multidirectional partiality**, → **neutrality**, → **justice**, → **power**, → **delegation**).

Ackerman, N. W. *Treating the troubled family*. New York: Basic Books, 1966.

Ackerman, N. W. Prejudice and scapegoating in the family. In G. H. Zuk & I. Boszormenyi-Nagy (Eds.), *Family therapy and disturbed families*. Palo Alto: Science and Behavior Books, 1967, 48–57.

Paul, N. L., & Bloom, J. Multiple family therapy: Secrets and scapegoating in family crisis. *International Journal of Group Psychotherapy 20:* 37–47, 1970.

Vogel, E. F., & Bell, N. W. The emotionally disturbed child as the family scapegoat. In E. F. Vogel & N. W. Bell (Eds.), *The family*. Glencoe, Ill.: Free Press, 1960, 412–427.

Watzlawick, P., Beavin, J., Sikorski, L., & Mecia, B. Protection and scapegoating in pathological families. *Family Process 9:* 27–39, 1970.

* * * * * *

SCHISMOGENESIS

Schismogenesis [Greek *schisma*, a division; *genesis*, origin, generation] is a category system introduced into the field of cultural anthropology (ethnology) by Gregory Bateson in 1935 and 1936 to describe the "process of differentiation in the norms of individual behaviour resulting from cumulative interaction between individuals" (1936, p. 175).

In 1935, Bateson described schismogenesis as follows:

The possibilities of differentiation of groups are by no means infinite, but fall clearly into two categories (a) cases in which the relationship is chiefly symmetrical, *e.g.*, in the differentiation of moieties, clans, villages and the nations of Europe; and (b) cases in which the relationship is *complementary, e.g.*, in the differentiation of social strata, classes, castes, age grades, and, in some cases, the cultural differentiation between the sexes. Both these types of differentiation contain dynamic elements, such that when certain restraining factors are removed the differentiation or split between the groups increases progressively toward either breakdown or new equilibrium. (pp. 67–68)

Family theory and therapy subsequently took over this system of categories to characterize important familial and clinical patterns of relationship (Jackson, 1959). In a complementary (→ **complementari-ty**) relationship, the submissive and dominant behaviors of the two interactional partners differ but fit together (→ **collusion**); in a symmetrical (→ **symmetry**) relationship, the behaviors of the two (or more) partners oscillate into an escalation of the behaviors and of the "stakes" involved, much as in an arms race.

In Bateson's first formulation (1935), schismogenesis, either symmetrical or complementary, leads "ultimately to hostility and the breakdown of the whole system" (p. 68). He also described a third category of relationships that he called reciprocal: "[I]n every single instance the behavior is asymmetrical, but symmetry is regained over a large number of instances. . . . The reciprocal pattern . . . is compensated and balanced within itself and therefore does not tend toward schismogenesis" (p. 69). Jackson (1959) regarded such relationships as "mature" and used the term "parallel" rather than reciprocal when there are "frequent complementary and symmetric crossovers" (p. 127).

In a 1958 Epilogue, published with a reprinting of his 1936 book *Naven,* Bateson stated that his earlier effort to account for the "presumed dynamic equilibrium of the system" by a balance between symmetrical and complementary processes was "at best an unsatisfactory explanation, since it assumed that two variables will, *by coincidence,* have equal and opposite values" (p. 287). Between the first and second editions of *Naven,* Bateson had become participant in the development of the theories of → **cybernetics** and → **feedback** systems. Using the concepts of self–corrective circuits and → **circular causality,** Bateson reviewed his earlier field data from New Guinea and found that an excess of symmetrical rivalry triggered complementary rituals, and conversely. He concluded that "this oscillation between the symmetrical and the complementary" prevented the social disintegration that had been predicted by his earlier lineal view of schismogenesis (in which only a coincidental balance could prevent breakdown) (p. 291).

Further, Bateson considered "random" events that may be "introduced into the very signals upon which the system depends for its self–corrective characteristics" (p. 300). When a system is disrupted by a nontrivial, random event, "death" of the system may occur—as was predicted in the earlier concept of schismogenesis. In 1958, Bateson hypothesized that, alternatively, *discontinuous* change may take place, with the creation of a new system, typologically more complex than the original (→ **fluctuation, dissipative structures**).

Bateson, G. Culture contact and schismogenesis. *Man 35:* 178–183 (article 199), 1935. Reprinted in G. Bateson, *Steps to an ecology of mind.* New York: Ballantine Books, 1972, 61–72.

Bateson, G. *Naven: A survey of the problems suggested by a composite picture of the culture of a New Guinea tribe drawn from three points of view* (1st ed.). Cambridge: Cambridge University Press, 1936. (Second edition, Stanford: Stanford University Press, 1958.)

Bateson, G. *Steps to an ecology of mind.* New York: Ballantine Books, 1972.

Jackson, D. D. Family interaction, family homeostasis and some implications for conjoint family psychotherapy. In J. H. Masserman (Ed.), *Individual and familial dynamics.* New York: Grune & Stratton, 1959, 122–141.

* * * * * *

"SCHIZOPHRENOGENIC" MOTHER

This term designates a mother who is not capable of drawing a clear boundary between herself and her child or of differentiating between her own needs and emotions and those of her child.

The concept "schizophrenogenic mother" belongs to the early stages of the development of family therapy, and is very much bound to a lineal (→ **lineality**) concept of causality; it is a concept that needs to be viewed in a critical light today. The concept was coined by Fromm–Reichmann (1948) as a result of her observations, in psychoanalytic therapy, that specific aspects of the dyadic mother–child relationship can result in a failure of the child to develop an integrated personality. Mothers who are overly involved in the lives of their children, who intrude and intervene, who overprotect and constantly control the lives of their children, are likely to thwart the autonomous and integrated development of their children's → **identity.** Such mothers often feel unfulfilled or incomplete as women, and make it apparent to their children that life without them would be meaningless. The children of such mothers thus grow up with the feeling that it is their duty to provide a "meaning in life" for their mothers. To separate from mother would mean mother's death; it also would mean (or so these children imagine) their own destruction. The early childhood stage of belief in one's own omnipotence is thus carried on into adolescence. When the children of these mothers attempt to separate they often decompensate psychotically. The → **individuation** process has been disturbed because the mother–child relationship does not fit, develop, and change with the changing demands of the individual and → **family life cycle.**

In the development of family theory and therapy, the concept of the schizophrenogenic mother has had both positive and negative aspects. The concept did throw light on interactional patterns; it allowed one to view the relationship form as pathological, instead of regarding schizophrenia as an idiosyncratic attempt at conflict resolution by an individual. This was a step in the direction of going beyond the limitations of individual–oriented psychology. However, it also seduced early family therapists into thinking in terms of lineal causality, and in implicitly holding the mother to be "guilty" of the child's psychosis. The concept of circular causality (→ **circularity**) had yet to be introduced into the analysis of interactional structures. The question had not yet been raised about the extent to which even a neonate could be viewed as an active interactional partner, nor had the notion of a → **multigenerational perspective** emerged in the examination of family structures.

The exclusive consideration of the mother–child relationship left the father very much an "outsider" within the family system. The father was seen as being "too weak" to have a corrective influence upon the highly disturbed → **self/object differentiation** of the mother, and thus unable to help the child in the establishment of interpersonal → **boundaries.** It was not taken into consideration at that time that a closely binding mother and child relationship can have a function of its own within the parental subsystem (→ **triangulation**).

What the concept of schizophrenogenic mother did introduce, and what had been hitherto disregarded, was the consideration that the development of the affective and cognitive structures of the child are largely determined by the interactional conditions to which the child is exposed. Even when the child is viewed as determining to some extent the reality of the parent's existence, the fact remains that the → **power** that the parents have over the child is greater than that which the child has over the parents, given the purely physiological advantage the parents have in being more autonomous (→ **autonomy**) than the child. The parents are hence in a position to determine the → **relational reality** of the child to a large degree.

The concept of the schizophrenogenic mother, however, had unfortunate effects on therapeutic interventions. Caught up in the concept of lineal causality, early family therapists viewed the child as the innocent victim while the mother (later, the family) was arraigned as the pathogenic "cause" of the child's psychosis. Given this view of the mother as the "evil–doer," early therapists (consciously or unconsciously) saw the goal of therapy as being the separation of the child from the mother. This simplistic attitude was shared by the more naive elements of the social psychiatry and antipsychiatry movements. Taking a stand for the interests of the patient led to the notion that parents were something between devils and monsters. More recently, an opposite, but still lineal view has been taken by parent advocacy groups who dismiss *any* participant contribution of family life and emphasize biologic causation exclusively. However, any type of therapy that espouses either of these views does not do justice to the complexity of biologic factors, to the "normal" ambivalence of family relationships, and to the active partnership of the patient in making the decision not to separate from the family (→ **separating parents and adolescents**) by refusing to become an autonomous individual, and by remaining actively caught up in the web of the family → **game.** The therapist who attempts to restructure such a constellation must be in a position to maintain an attitude of → **multidirectional partiality** and/or → **neutrality** toward the family system.

Alanen, Y. The mothers of schizophrenic patients. *Acta Psychiatrica et Neurologica Scandanavica, Suppl. 124,* 1958.
Beavers, W. R., Blumberg, S., Timken, K. R., & Weiner, M. F. Communication patterns of mothers of schizophrenics. *Family Process 4:* 95–104, 1965.
Cheek, F. E. The "schizophrenogenic mother" in word and deed. *Family Process 3:* 155–177, 1964.
Fromm-Reichmann, F. Notes on the development of treatment of schizophrenics by psychoanalytic psychotherapy. *Psychiatry 11:* 263–273, 1948.
Fromm-Reichmann, F. Notes on the mother role in the family group. In D. M. Bullard & E. V. Weigert (Eds.), *Psychoanalysis and psychotherapy: Selected papers of Frieda Fromm-Reichmann.* Chicago: University of Chicago Press, 1959, 290–305.
Mark, J. The attitudes of the mothers of male schizophrenics toward child behavior. *Journal of Abnormal and Social Psychology 48:* 185–189, 1953.
Searles, H. F. Positive feelings in the relationship between the schizophrenic and his mother. *International Journal of Psycho-analysis 39:* 569–586, 1958.
Stierlin, H. The adaptation to the "stronger" person's reality. *Psychiatry 22:* 143–152, 1959.
Tietze, T. A study of mothers of schizophrenic patients. *Psychiatry 12:* 55–65, 1949.
Weakland, J. H., & Fry, W. F. Letters of mothers of schizophrenics. *American Journal of Orthopsychiatry 32:* 604–623, 1962.

* * * * * *

SCRIPT

Script refers to the plan or "scenario" according to which each individual designs his or her own life.

The concept of script and script analysis originated in "transactional analysis" (Berne, 1972; English, 1976; Steiner, 1966). Alfred Adler had earlier developed similar ideas in his "individual psychology," in which he described and analyzed how individuals develop a "life–style" or a "life–plan" that is dependent upon the interactional processes the individual had experienced as a child (see Ansbacher & Ansbacher, 1972).

314

Even small children reach certain conclusions about themselves—
what sort of relationships one has or should have, and what one feels
about these relationships or thinks one should feel. This is an aspect of
one's model of the world that encompasses not only one's view of the
past and the present but also extends into one's conception of the future
(→ **paradigm/model/map**). Identification with the heroes or anti-
heroes of stories and fairytales allows one to draft a life script, a script
in which one's perceptions and feelings about the present are described,
as well as a notion of one's future destiny. The essential factors of
family interaction (→ **expelling**, → **binding**, → **delegation**) can thus be
arranged to form an ordered whole. An individual's life script is not
merely a production of interactional processes; it also influences these
processes and works in the sense of a "self–fulfilling prophecy" (→
identity/self–definition, → **self–reference**).

Ansbacher, H. L., & Ansbacher, R. R. *The individual psychology of Alfred Adler: A
    systematic presentation in selections from his writings.* New York: Basic Books,
    1972.
Berne, E. *What do you say after you say hello?* New York: Grove Press, 1972.
English, F. *Transaktionale Analyse und Skriptanalyse: Aufsätze und Vorträge.*
    Hamburg: Altmann, 1976.
Steiner, C. M. A script checklist. *Transactional Analysis Bulletin 5:* 133–135, 1966.

SELF–ESTEEM

In reference to the question of how and to what extent an individual
develops the feeling of self–worth or worthlessness, individual psychology
and family therapy find themselves on common ground. The emphasis
in → **ego psychology** is on an individual's developing and maintaining a
feeling of self–esteem in order to survive. How this happens depends on
intrapsychic evaluation processes (from a psychoanalytic viewpoint these
are seen as an aspect of the "ideal self" or "superego") and standards, as
well as on interactions and, in particular, on familial processes having to
do with negotiation of acknowledgment. The latter is of central interest
for family theory and practice.

Satir (1972) demonstrated that the value persons place on themselves
depends to a great extent on the value that close family members have
granted them. Self–esteem is thus regulated by mechanisms of mutual
appreciation and depreciation. The standards for evaluating one's own
worth are developed in the family of origin and are later transferred to
other relational contexts. Most behaviors and personal strategies

315

become more easily comprehensible when it is understood that every individual needs a certain degree of self–esteem in order to survive. If an individual is incapable of developing a stable sense of self–esteem, the question arises as to which family–internal relationship and communication patterns reinforce the individual's feelings of worthlessness, and how these can be changed. However, the family is not solely responsible for an individual's self–esteem; job success and social acceptance are also essential in the development and the maintenance of self–respect. Further, an individual's → **autonomy** will depend on the degree to which he or she is able to maintain a feeling of self–esteem even in the absence of external validation. A therapist can positively influence the self–esteem of one or more persons by intervening in their social interaction and by changing the standards that an individual uses to evaluate the self (→ **paradigm/model/map**). This can be done most effectively by intervention strategies such as → **positive connotation,** → **reframing,** and → **symptom prescription.**

Becker, E. *The birth and death of meaning: A perspective in psychiatry and anthropology.* Glencoe, Ill.: Free Press, 1962.
Laing, R. D. *The divided self.* London: Tavistock Publications, 1960.
Laing, R. D. *The self and others: Further studies in sanity and madness.* London: Tavistock Publications, 1969.
Mead, G. H. *Mind, self, and society.* Chicago, University of Chicago Press, 1934.
Satir, V. *Conjoint family therapy: A guide to theory and technique.* Palo Alto: Science and Behavior Books, 1964.
Satir, V. Symptomatology: A family production. Its relevance to psychotherapy. In J. G. Howells (Ed.), *Theory and practice of family psychiatry.* Edinburgh: Oliver & Boyd, 1968, 663–670.
Satir, V. *Peoplemaking.* Palo Alto: Science and Behavior Books, 1972.
Satir, V. Self-esteem, mate selection, and different–ness. In R. J. Green & J. L. Framo (Eds.), *Family therapy: Major contributions.* New York: International Universities Press, 1981, 237–261.
Stierlin, H. Shame and guilt in family relations: Theoretical and clinical aspects. *Archives of General Psychiatry 30:* 381–389, 1974.
Sullivan, H. S. *Conceptions of modern psychiatry: The first William Alanson White Memorial Lectures* (2nd ed.). New York: W. W. Norton & Co., 1953. (a)
Sullivan, H. S. *The interpersonal theory of psychiatry.* New York: W. W. Norton & Co., 1953. (b)

* * * * * *

SELF/OBJECT DIFFERENTIATION

This concept was mainly developed and applied by authors with a psychoanalytic orientation. The concept implies that each individual should in the course of his or her development formulate a concept of self that is differentiated from the identity of other individuals and is autonomous in itself. Here "self" is defined as the set of all ideas and perceptions of one's own being as they are developed in the course of individual development and are then more or less integrated into and perceived as a functional whole (→ **identity**).

This concept assumes that a newly born child is faced with the task of discriminating perceptually (→ **punctuation**) between that which belongs to itself and that which belongs to others in the context of a family–wide network, but especially in the context of the mother–child interaction. Inadequate differentiation between self and object exhibits itself either in the tendency toward fusion with the object or the inability to form a relationship to the object. The process of progressive differentiation between self and object thus goes hand in hand with the process of related → **individuation.** Within the context of these processes, family–specific → **rules** determine what kind of definition of self will be negotiated, e.g., where an individual's self and the power it has begins and where it ends. Accordingly, there exists in family theory and therapy a wide range of opinions about the acceptable or forbidden types of self/object differentiation (→ **centripetal/centrifugal patterns,** → **enmeshment,** → **undifferentiated family ego mass,** → **fusion,** → **pseudomutuality/pseudohostility**).

Family therapy, psychoanalysis, and cognitive psychology all ask: How do self and object become differentiated in the course of individual and family development? Psychoanalytically oriented authors view this question from within the framework of → **ego psychology,** the psychology of self, and the various concepts about narcissistic personality disorders. These theories, however, run the risk of viewing "ego" or "self" as an entity in isolation from interaction with others, that is, from the relationships within which a self and ego must develop and survive. This view inevitably leads to a lineal view of causality (→ **lineality**).

Various psychoanalytically oriented researchers in the field of developmental psychology have described in particular the reciprocal interactions between mother and child, and also the child's ability to differentiate self and object (Mahler; 1975; Spitz, 1954; Winnicott, 1965; Wynne, 1984). To varying degrees, these authors do justice to the circularity of interactional processes. Studies of the cognitive development of the child, carried out for the most part by Piaget (1970), suggest that the development of a child's concept of self is largely determined by the type of family interaction to which the child is exposed. Recently, Ciompi (1982) has attempted an integration of the psychoanalytic theory of object relations and the precepts of cognitive theory (→ **affect logic**). Kegan (1979) also draws upon

Piaget's work, and his stages of self/object differentiation are analogous to Piaget's stages of cognitive development.

Self/object differentiation may also be viewed as an aspect of social cognition. Selman (1980) outlined the following stages:

1. The object is perceived from an egocentric perspective.
2. Identification with the object becomes possible. The individual develops the ability to view himself or herself from the perspective of the other.
3. Only in this third stage is one able to view the relationship between self and object from the perspective of a neutral observer.

In family therapy, the systematic confrontation with the perception of the other is an essential aspect of the therapeutic process because it leads to the improvement of self/object differentiation of the individual family members. In this respect, → **systemic therapy** is the most stringent in its striving, by means of → **circular questioning,** toward the external–perspective plane.

Anonymous. Toward the differentiation of a self in one's own family. In J. Framo (Ed.), *Family interaction: A dialogue between family researchers and family therapists.* New York: Springer Publishing Co., 1972, 111–166.

Arieti, S. *The intrapsychic self: Feeling, cognition, and creativity in health and mental illness.* New York: Basic Books, 1967.

Bowen, M. A family concept of schizophrenia. In D. D. Jackson (Ed.), *The etiology of schizophrenia.* New York: Basic Books, 1960, 346–372.

Ciompi, L. *Affektlogik. Über die Struktur der Psyche und ihre Entwicklung. Ein Beitrag zur Schizophrenieforschung.* Stuttgart: Klett-Cotta, 1982.

Fogarty, T. F. System concepts and the dimensions of self. In P. J. Guerin (Ed.), *Family therapy: Theory and practice.* New York: Gardner Press, 1976, 144–153.

Guntrip, H. *Schizoid phenomena, object-relations and the self.* New York: International Universities Press, 1969.

Hartmann, H. *Essays on ego psychology.* New York: International Universities Press, 1964.

Jacobson, E. The self and the object world. *Psychoanalytic Study of the Child 9:* 75–127, 1954.

Kagan, J., & Moss, H. A. *Birth to maturity: A study in psychological development.* New York: John Wiley & Sons, 1962.

Karpel, M. A. Individuation: From fusion to dialogue. *Family Process 15:* 65–82, 1976.

Kegan, R. *The evolving self: Problem and process in human development.* Cambridge: Harvard University Press, 1979.

Kernberg, O. F. *Object relations theory and clinical psychoanalysis.* New York: Jason Aronson, 1976.

Kohut, H. *The analysis of the self. A systematic approach to the psychoanalytic treatment of narcissistic personality disorders.* New York: International Universities Press, 1971.

Kohut, H. *The restoration of the self.* New York: International Universities Press, 1977.

318

Mahler, M. *On human symbiosis and the vicissitudes of individuation. Vol. I, Infantile psychosis.* New York: International Universities Press, 1968.
Mahler, M. S., Pine, F., & Bergman, A. *The psychological birth of the human infant: Symbiosis and individuation.* New York: Basic Books, 1975.
Piaget, J. *Genetic epistemology* (translated by E. Duckworth). New York: Columbia University Press, 1970.
Selman, R. L. *The growth of interpersonal understanding: Developmental and clinical analyses.* New York: Academic Press, 1980.
Simon, F. B. *Der Prozess der Individuation: Über den Zusammenhang von Vernunft und Gefühlen.* Göttingen: Vandenhoeck & Ruprecht, 1984.
Spitz, R. A. Genèse des premières relations objectales. *Revue Française de Psychoanalyse 28,* 1954.
Spitz, R. A. *No and yes: On the genesis of human communication.* New York: International Universities Press, 1957.
Spitz, R. *A genetic field theory of ego formation: Its implications for pathology.* New York: International Universities Press, 1959.
Spitz, R. *The first year of life: A psychoanalytic study of normal and deviant development of object relations.* New York: International Universities Press, 1965.
Sullivan, H. S. *Conceptions of modern psychiatry: The first William Alanson White Memorial Lectures* (2nd ed.). New York: W. W. Norton & Co., 1953. (a)
Sullivan, H. S. *The interpersonal theory of psychiatry.* New York: W. W. Norton & Co., 1953. (b)
Winnicott, D. W. Transitional objects and transitional phenomena. In D. W. Winnicott, *Collected papers: Through paediatrics to psycho-analysis.* New York: Basic Books, 1958, 229–242.
Winnicott, D. W. *The maturational processes and the facilitating environment.* New York: International Universities Press, 1965.
Wynne, L. C. The epigenesis of relational systems: A model for understanding family development. *Family Process 23:* 297–318, 1984.

* * * * * *

SELF–ORGANIZATION/AUTOPOIESIS

These terms refer to the ability of systems to change their structures under conditions of changes in the environment, usually achieving a higher level of complexity in the process and thereby potentiating their chances of survival. Structural changes of this order both maintain the → **stability** of the system and provide the impetus for the development of more complex organizational forms (→ **coevolution**). The concept of self–organization is usually used as a generic term that includes the concepts of self–repairing systems, learning systems, and self–reproducing systems. Such systems include living organisms as well as families, social groups, and societies. The essential aspects of this self–organization is a striving for balance in a constantly changing environment; but this is only possible if the system constantly remains able to create the elements that constitute it.

In considering the concept of self–organization, if one did not take into account the contextual environment of the system, one would be left with the mere observation of balancing processes. In a stable, closed ecological system (→ **ecology**), → **feedback** processes will maintain certain parameters, disturbances are offset (→ **homeostasis**), and → **learning** is unnecessary. No new information accrues, no demand for change is made upon the system, and its structure remains static.

Processes of self–organization that meet the above criteria can be found in inanimate nature. In the field of physics, Haken (1984) speaks of synergetics as a science of ordered, self–organized, collective behaviors bound to certain general principles. In the field of chemistry, Prigogine has emphasized the importance of so–called "dissipative structures" whereby "order is formed through fluctuation"; this concept is used to describe characteristics of certain conditions of systems leading to new and relatively autonomous structures (→ **fluctuation**) (Dell & Goolishian, 1981; Prigogine, 1976; Prigogine & Stengers, 1984).

In the consideration of life processes, one is dealing with open, not closed, systems. The environment is never static and is constantly changing. As changes in the environment influence the life conditions of such open systems (for example, organisms or families), the system must change its original structure. An open system requires the ability to learn and to develop new structures in order to insure a certain degree of continuity and self–preservation in an environment that is in a constant state of flux and change.

Maturana and Varela used the term "autopoiesis" to depict processes preserving the integrity of a system (Maturana & Varela, 1980; Varela, Maturana, & Uribe, 1974). The preservation and evolution of a system thus depends on the system's ability to change. Autopoietic systems have the ability to reproduce their own elements, thereby maintaining the system's unity and → **coherence**. These systems are thus self–referent (→ **self–reference**) or recursive. The application of the concept of autopoiesis to family therapy suggests itself when one begins to regard interactional and behavioral rules as evolutionary systems. Consequently, mechanisms that have maintained family forms and structures over the course of generations may be considered to be autopoietic. However, the discussion of these natural science concepts in the family therapy literature has been confusing and controversial. (See, for instance, articles in the March and December, 1982 issues of the journal *Family Process*.)

As a start toward conceptual clarity, it must be stated that cybernetic models are neutral with regard to the dimension of time. This means that they only depict specific logical structures. In the *observation* of these logical structures, however, the existence of such phenomena as → **circularity** or self–reference can be established. When one observes sequences *within* the dimension of time, the nonreversibility of processes is highlighted. From this perspective, a behavior is incapable of referring back to itself (→ **lineality**). Because all equilibrium models and concepts of homeostasis are neutral with regard to the dimension of time, they can never provide a complete description of natural life processes. If one loses sight of this fact, one inevitably runs the risk of applying the concepts of equilibrium and homeostasis in an inappropriately reductionistic and concretized manner, and of overlooking the fact that time sequences are not temporally reversible in reality. A system that has become unbalanced and attempts to regain its equilibrium changes itself, hence changes the conditions of its environment; this in turn changes the system, which in turn changes the environment, and so on *ad infinitum*. Therefore, one may never assume that the environment remains constant.

Concepts such as the balance of structures, feedback loops, and the principle of circularity, nevertheless, do illustrate in a relatively exact manner how a system (an individual or a family) attempts to achieve and sustain a state of balance. These concepts elucidate a dynamic process comparable to a man who stumbles and then must continue running in order not to lose his balance. The creation of new structures in a state removed from an energetic balance, such as Prigogine describes with his concept of "dissipative structure," accords with that which Ashby (1952) described as the phenomenon of second–order → **change**. On the level of structure, → **morphogenesis** and → **morphostasis** are equivalent to such second– and first–order changes. Whether first– or second–order change is necessary depends on the developmental speed of the entire ecological system that is caught up in the process of coevolution. The ability of a system to survive, that is, the system's ability to maintain itself as a coherent unity, is determined to a great extent by its ability to learn, i.e., to change its internal logical organization. Systems that rigidly attempt to hold onto once–successful balancing mechanisms become dysfunctional. Self–organization thus demands a logically higher level of balancing behavior, i.e., the ability to establish again and again a balance between stability and change (→ **rules**, related → **individuation**, → **relational balance**).

Ashby, W. R. *Design for a brain*. London: Chapman & Hall, 1952.
Davies, P. C. W. *The runaway universe*. New York: Penguin Books, 1980.
Dell, P. F. Beyond homeostasis: Toward a concept of coherence. *Family Process 21:* 21–41, 1982.
Dell, P. F., & Goolishian, H. A. Order through fluctuation: An evolutionary epistemology for human systems. *Australian Journal of Family Therapy 2:* 175–184, 1981.

Haken, H. *The signs of structure synergetics.* New York: Van–Nostrand Reinhold, 1984.

Jantsch, E. *The self-organizing universe.* Elmsford, N. Y.: Pergamon Press, 1980.

Luhmann, N. Autopoiesis, Handlung und kommunikative Verständigung. *Zeitschrift für Soziologie 11:* 366–379, 1982.

Maruyama, M. Morphogenesis and morphostasis. *Methods 12:* 251–296, 1960.

Maturana, H. R. The organization of the living: A theory of the living organization. *International Journal of Man-Machine Studies 7:* 313–332, 1975.

Maturana, H. R., & Varela, F. J. *Autopoiesis and cognition: The realization of living.* Boston: Reidel, 1980.

Nicolis, G., & Prigogine, I. *Self-organization in nonequilibrium systems: From dissipative structures to order through fluctuations.* New York: John Wiley & Sons, 1977.

Prigogine, I. Irreversibility as a symmetry breaking factor. *Nature 248:* 67–71, 1973.

Prigogine, I. Order through fluctuation: Self-organization and social system. In E. Jantsch & C. Waddington (Eds.), *Evolution and consciousness: Human systems in transition.* Reading, Mass.: Addison-Wesley, 1976, 93–133.

Prigogine, I., & Stengers, I. *Order out of chaos: Man's new dialogue with nature.* New York: Bantam Books, 1984.

Speer, D. C. Family systems: Morphostasis and morphogenesis, or "Is homeostasis enough?". *Family Process 9:* 259–278, 1970.

Varela, F. J., Maturana, H. R., & Uribe, R. Autopoiesis: The organization of living systems, its characterization and model. *Biosystems 5:* 187–196, 1974.

Zeleny, M. (Ed.). *Autopoiesis, dissipative structures, and spontaneous social orders.* Boulder, Col.: Westview, 1980.

Zeleny, M. (Ed.). *Autopoiesis: A theory of living organization.* Amsterdam: Elsevier, 1981.

* * * * * *

SELF–REFERENCE

This refers to the possibility of making statements, by means of language or other sign systems, that refer back to the statement being made or to the maker of the statement. Processes and structures that "work back" upon themselves are in general considered to be self–referent. This applies to all systems in which → **feedback** and → **self–organization/ autopoiesis** processes play a role.

As human thought, emotion, and interpersonal communication are bound to the use of sign systems, self–reference is possible in intrapsychic and interpersonal processes. Here certain nonlineal (→ **lineality**) sequences of causality or causal concepts come into play. Perceptions, expectations, and theories of behavior rebound back onto those involved. These perceptions, expectations, and theories of behavior determine how the individual behaves, whether certain expectations

322

are met or not, and whether certain theories are validated or falsified. Examples of this are: Oedipus, whose fate was the fulfillment of a prophecy; the client undergoing psychoanalytic treatment who has read some psychoanalytic literature; the revolutionary who views the world through the lens of Marxist theory. The effect of these processes may be that certain beliefs, fears, and expectations do come to pass (self–fulfilling prophecy) or do not (self-denying prophecy). Both of these processes run counter to traditional lineal–causal thinking.

In the area of interpersonal communication, problems arise when a self–referent statement leads to a paradox. An example of this is the paradox of Epimenides the Cretan who said: "Cretans are always liars." The paradox of this self–referent statement stems from a mixing of → **logical types.** Other problematic, self–referent situations arise when two persons are engaged in reaching an agreement about their relationship to each other. The attempt to arrive at a "clarification of relationship" is also part of the relationship. In such a situation there is a risk of mixing up logical types if both interactional partners are unwilling or unable to "view their relationship from the outside."

The lithograph by M.C. Escher on page 216a of this volume illustrates the process of self–reference. Within the context of a dyadic relationship, each partner "draws" to a certain extent his or her picture of the other. This "drawing," however, is a part of the whole picture, which represents the relationship of the two hands to each other. Such a relationship only becomes clear when one views the picture from an outside perspective, and this is very likely the reason why the presence of a third party (a child, a therapist, a lover) can ease matters in a conflict between a couple. When the therapist becomes the third party in a conflict situation, an "outside" or objective perspective is assured to a certain extent (→ **couples therapy,** definition of a → **relationship**).

Bateson, G. *Mind and nature: A necessary unity.* New York: E. P. Dutton, 1979.
Cronen, V. E., Johnson, K. M., & Lannamann, J. W. Paradoxes, double binds, and reflexive loops: An alternative theoretical perspective. *Family Process 21:* 91–112, 1982.
Maturana, H. R., & Varela, F. J. *Autopoiesis and cognition: The realization of living.* Boston: Reidel, 1980.
Morin, E. *La méthode. I: La nature de la nature.* Paris: Seuil, 1977.
Varela, F. J. A calculus for self-reference. *International Journal of General Systems 2:* 5–24, 1975.

* * * * * *

SEMANTICS

Semantics [Greek *sema*, sign] is a science, within the field of → **semiotics,** concerned with the relations between signs and their meanings.

Semantics forms one of the foundations of → **communication theory.** It studies how verbal and nonverbal signs are exchanged, and the relationship between signs and their meanings. These aspects are of interest especially to family therapists who adopt the tenets of → **communication therapy** (→ **pragmatics,** → **syntax,** → **psycholinguistics).**

Carnap, R. *Introduction to semantics.* Cambridge: Harvard University Press, 1959.
Hayakawa, S. I. *Language in thought and action.* New York: Harcourt, Brace, & Co., 1949.
Korzybski, A. *Science and sanity.* Chicago: International Non-Aristotelian Library, 1933.
Morris, C. W. Foundations of the theory of signs. In O. Neurath, R. Carnap, & C. W. Morris (Eds.), *International encyclopedia of unified science, Vol. 1, No. 2.* Chicago: University of Chicago Press, 1938, 77–137.
Morris, C. W. *Signs, language and behavior.* New York: Prentice-Hall, 1946.
Peirce, C. S. *Collected papers* (6 vols.). Cambridge: Harvard University Press, 1931–1935.
Sapir, E. In D. G. Mandelbaum (Ed.), *Selected writings of Edward Sapir in language, culture, and personality.* Berkeley: University of California Press, 1949.
Shands, H. G. *The war with words.* The Hague-Paris: Mouton, 1971.
Ullmann, S. *The principles of semantics.* Oxford: Blackwell, 1951.
Vygotsky, L. S. *Thought and language* (translated by E. Hanfmann & G. Vakar). Cambridge: Massachusetts Institute of Technology Press, 1962.
Werner, H., & Kaplan, B. *Symbol formation: An organismic-developmental approach to language and the expression of thought.* New York: John Wiley & Sons, 1963.
Whorf, B. L. *Language, thought, and reality.* Cambridge: Massachusetts Institute of Technology Press, 1942.

* * * * * *

SEMIOTICS

Semiotics [Greek *sema*, a mark, a sign] is the general science of signs (for example, language signs) and their use. According to Morris (1938, 1946), semiotics consists of three approaches: (1) the syntactic approach, which concerns itself with the relationship between sign and sign—for example, the relationship between words, sentence structure, etc. (→ **syntax**); (2) the semantic approach, which concerns itself with the relationship between a person's name and the person himself or herself (→ **semantics**); and (3) the pragmatic approach, which investigates the relationship between a sign, its sender, and the receiver of the sign (→ **pragmatics**).

In communication processes, every condition, every event, and every form that a system shows can have the character of a sign. This is not, however, an objective characteristic of the system, but depends on someone seeing and interpreting the event or condition, i.e., ascribing a meaning to that event or condition. Different types of signs possess different ranges of meaning (→ **analogue/ digital communication**).

The general principles of sign use and processing are the foundation of → **communication theory** and → **information theory.** In order to function, human systems depend on the exchange and processing of signs; hence, semiotics has had a substantial, albeit indirect, influence on the development of family theory and method. Processes that are related to the differentiation of sign and signified object are of great interest for family therapists. A map is not a territory and menus are not there to be eaten. A confusion between sign and signified object can be the effect of or result in → **communication deviance,** such as is frequently found in families with a schizophrenic member (→ **structuralism**).

The insights of semiotics represent a part of the foundations of → **cybernetics.** Almost all psychological theories (and psychoanalysis in particular) attach a great deal of importance to questions of symbol formation and symbol processing. However, because the definition of "symbol" or "symbolization" has become a matter for much confusion (see Kreitler, 1965; Lorenzer, 1972), there is an advantage in applying the original, standardized definitions of linguistics (see Rosen, 1969).

Carnap, R. *Introduction to semantics.* Cambridge: Harvard University Press, 1959.
Hayakawa, S. I. *Language in thought and action.* New York: Harcourt, Brace, & Co., 1949.
Korzybski, A. *Science and sanity.* Chicago: International Non-Aristotelian Library, 1933.
Kreitler, S. *Symbolschöpfung und Symbolerfassung.* München: Reinhardt, 1965.
Lorenzer, A. *Kritik des psychoanalytischen Symbolbegriffs* (2nd ed.). Frankfurt: Suhrkamp, 1972.
Morris, C. W. Foundations of the theory of signs. In O. Neurath, R. Carnap, & C. W. Morris (Eds.), *International encyclopedia of unified science, Vol. 1, No. 2.* Chicago: University of Chicago Press, 1938, 77–137.
Morris, C. W. *Signs, language and behavior.* New York: Prentice-Hall, 1946.
Peirce, C. S. *Collected papers* (6 vols.). Cambridge: Harvard University Press, 1931–1935.
Rosen, V. H. Language and psychoanalysis. *International Journal of Psycho-analysis 50:* 113–116, 1969.
Shands, H. G. *Semiotic approaches to psychiatry.* The Hague-Paris: Mouton, 1970.

Shands, H. G. *The war with words.* The Hague-Paris: Mouton, 1971.
Uexküll, T. von. Signs, symbols, and systems. In S. Chatman, U. Eco, & M. Klinkenberg (Eds.), A semiotic landscape. Berlin: Hawthorn, 1979, 487–492.
Uexküll, T. von. Semiotics and medicine. *Semiotica 38:* 205–215, 1982.

* * * * * *

SEPARATING PARENTS AND ADOLESCENTS

Intergenerational conflicts typically come to a head with the appearance of the emerging, relative autonomy in adolescents and their detachment from their parents. Strictly speaking, this is less a separation than a bid for new hierarchical positions within the family, including new rights and duties as well as a new → **relational balance,** with the attendant possibility of new degrees and forms of related → **individuation** for each family member. This reciprocal process is marked by changes in the life cycle of the individual as well as changes in the → **family life cycle.**

The process of mutual separation and the negotiation of new positions within the family structure often take a dramatic course and manifest themselves in the interplay and predominance of transactional modes such as → **binding,** → **expelling,** and → **delegation.** When the binding mode predominates, the adolescent remains caught in the family ghetto. The relational → **roles** and → **rules** that stress family → **loyalty** and → **cohesion** do so at the cost of the child's autonomy and individuation. Such families are referred to as "binding" and/or "bound–up" families. Experience in family therapy shows that such families often have psychosomatic (especially anorexic) and psychotic adolescents. Also, many teenagers with school problems, school phobias, and substance abuse are inclined to be strongly bound up with their families and/or to be bound delegates of their parents. In contrast, families with neglected or delinquent children, or children subject to other types of psychosomatic ailments, tend to be from predominantly expelling families. However, both bound–up and expelled children often exhibit similar developmental deficits and disturbances that hinder their establishing an → **identity** of their own.

An understanding of the parents in their midlife situation is of particular importance for effective therapeutic judgment and intervention in the separation process. The growing independence of the children forces the parents to organize their lives differently and to redefine their marital relationship so as to establish a new relational balance. This process is more difficult when the parents see their *raison d'être* in the raising of their children. It is equally difficult when parents feel that they themselves have missed out on an adventurous and emotionally intense adolescence. In this case, parents often need their children as delegates, as proxies to compensate for this sense of deprivation. The separation of adolescents from their parents is more likely to succeed if the parents can either go through a process of grieving or catch up on some of the carefree and intensive life experiences that they believe they were denied as teenagers.

As far as the adolescents are concerned, the more that they derive their sense of importance and → **self-esteem** from their role as parental delegates, the more difficult it will be for them to separate from their families. The separation process between the generations usually involves a multigenerational dynamic in which at least three generations are involved. Successful or unsuccessful separation of the present generation is very often adumbrated by the separation processes undergone by preceding generations. Therapeutically, it is often of great value in dealing with disturbed teenagers and their families to introduce the theme of parent–grandparent relations into therapy (→ **multigenerational perspective**). In fact, this can be indispensable in the case of severe separation disturbances such as those involving schizophrenic transactions.

Blos, P. *The adolescent passage: Developmental issues:* New York: International Universities Press, 1979.

Erikson, E. H. The problem of ego identity. *Journal of the American Psychoanalytic Association 4:* 56–121, 1956.

Erikson, E. H. Identity and the life cycle: Selected paper. *Psychological Issues, Monograph No. 1,* 1959.

Haley, J. *Leaving home: The therapy of disturbed young people.* New York: McGraw-Hill, 1980.

Kagan, J., & Moss, H. A. *Birth to maturity: A study in psychological development.* New York: John Wiley & Sons, 1962.

Kegan, R. *The evolving self: Problem and process in human development.* Cambridge: Harvard University Press, 1979.

Shapiro, R. Adolescence and the psychology of the ego. *Psychiatry 26:* 77–87, 1963.

Shapiro, R. Action and family interaction in adolescence. In J. Marmor (Ed.), *Modern psychoanalysis.* New York: Basic Books, 1968, 454–475.

Stierlin, H. *Separating parents and adolescents: A perspective on running away, schizophrenia, and waywardness.* New York: Quadrangle, 1974.

Stierlin, H. *Delegation und Familie.* Frankfurt: Suhrkamp, 1978.

* * * * * *

SEX THERAPY

This is a problem–oriented, predominantly directive and educational form
of couples therapy aimed at resolving sexual dysfunctions.

Although many family and couples therapists do not view sexual
problems as having precedence over other types of problems, there has
been an increase in the development of specialized methods for the
treatment of sexual dysfunctioning. Whereas psychoanalytic theories
assume that sexual disorders stem from individual development and
life experiences, in particular, disturbances during the so–called Oedipal phase, sex therapy today orients itself to the more purely scientific
research of Masters and Johnson (1970), with its emphasis on the
physiological foundations of human sexuality.

Sexuality is an area of marked personal vulnerability in which
defense mechanisms are especially prominent (see Kaplan, 1974).
Thus, the goals of sex therapy are based on a concept of "normal" or
"healthy" sexuality. However, normative concepts fluctuate according
to culture, social class, and historical eras. In present–day Western,
industrial societies, → self–esteem and the enjoyment of life depend to
a considerable extent upon a satisfactory sex life, which seems to be
most successful when the wishes of both partners as to frequency and
types of sexual practices correspond. This will involve both partners'
ability to recognize and accept their own and each other's body image
and physical needs, and the ability to communicate openly about
sexual matters in an atmosphere of mutual trust.

Sex therapy has never had a unified theoretical basis. Its methods
and theories are eclectic, and this makes the construction of unified,
psychologically sound diagnostic systems difficult. The simplest
method appears to be the orientation toward purely physical symptoms. Kaplan (1974, 1977) differentiates between three types of sexual
disorders: disorders of sexual desire, disorders of excitement, and
disorders of orgasm. Sex therapists further distinguish between "primary" and "secondary" sexual disorders, and between "absolute" and
"situational" disorders. Primary disorders are those that have existed
from the onset of the individual's sexual life; secondary disorders
develop later. Situational disorders only occur in specific situations;
absolute disorders develop quite early and are independent of situational circumstances. Besides partial or complete individual therapy,
the methods of sex therapy also extend to group therapy and, in
particular, couples therapy in its more restricted sense.

In general, one can differentiate between three stages of therapy:

1. Stage one consists of a phase of clarification and the establishment of contact and mutual trust between the couple and the therapist, including an elucidation of the couple's personal and sexual history, the clarification and outlining of the problem constellation, and, based on this, the establishment of therapeutic goals. Part of the process involves a consensus that the initiative for change must come from the clients themselves.
2. Stage two is oriented toward change. An attempt is made by means of behavioral therapy (e.g., sensate focus exercises) to reduce fear and to help the couple gain insight into the interactional patterns that are problematic for them. Information, clarification, sexual education, lessening of the pressure to "perform," and the training of sexual techniques are all aspects of this stage.
3. The third stage attempts to prepare the clients for what they can expect in the future, i.e., to enable them to deal with future sexual problems without the aid of therapy. The therapists help the clients to develop realistic goals for the future and to clarify how much further change is desirable and attainable.

Many systemic–oriented therapists object to therapy forms that focus solely on sexual problems. A survey of the literature on sex therapy shows that the multifaceted aspects of interpersonal relationships all play a part in the therapeutic situation, and that sexual dysfunctionality cannot be viewed as simply a "technical" problem divorced from the context of other areas of the couple's relationship. Sexuality is certainly an area of central importance for the individual; it is the cornerstone of a couple's intimate relationship and the area in which problems of closeness and distance are experienced most vividly. These aspects of relationship, however, influence not only the couple's sexual life but also the entirety of their relationship and functioning as individuals (→ **relational balance**).

Heiman, J. R., LoPiccolo, L., & LoPiccolo, J. The treatment of sexual dysfunction. In A. S. Gurman & D. P. Kniskern (Eds.), *Handbook of family therapy.* New York: Brunner/Mazel, 1981, 592–627.
Kaplan, H. S. *The new sex therapy: Active treatment of sexual dysfunctions.* New York: Brunner/Mazel, 1974.
Kaplan, H. S. Hypoactive sexual desire. *Journal of Sex and Marital Therapy 3:* 3–9, 1977.
Kaplan, H. S. *Disorders of sexual desire and other new concepts and techniques in sex therapy.* New York: Brunner/Mazel, 1979.
Kaplan, H. S. *The evaluation of sexual disorders: Psychological and medical aspects.* New York: Brunner/Mazel, 1983.
Leiblum, S., & Pervin, L. (Eds.). *Principles and practice of sex therapy.* Tavistock Publications, 1980.
LoPiccolo, J., & LoPiccolo, L. *Handbook of sex therapy.* New York: Plenum Press, 1978.
Masters, W. H., & Johnson, V. E. *Human sexual inadequacy.* Boston: Little Brown & Co., 1970.

* * * * * *

SOCIOLINGUISTICS

Sociolinguistics, an area of research within the fields of sociology and anthropology, investigates the relation between patterns of perception and language and sociocultural context.

Of particular interest for family therapy is the work of Basil Bernstein (1971) and Marie Douglas (1970, 1982) in this field. According to Bernstein, there are two fundamental categories of language that can be differentiated in linguistic and sociological terms. The first is characteristic of social contexts in which the interactional partners share the same fundamental concepts. In this instance, every statement made serves to confirm a perceived social order and social cohesion. The second category appears in social contexts in which the speakers are not aware of or do not share each other's fundamental assumptions. According to Bernstein, there also exist two corresponding types of linguistic → **codes:** (1) a restricted code that limits speakers to a few, rigidly organized, syntactical alternatives and (2) an elaborate code that allows speakers to choose from a multitude of possibilities those alternatives that best suit their purpose. Both types of codes develop in different social contexts, among which the often class–specific context of family relationships is of particular importance.

Stimulated in part by Bernstein's research, the anthropologist Douglas (1970) developed concepts to differentiate further between social systems and structures of language and/or perception. She investigated the interaction of individuals particularly with regard to two social dimensions which she called "grid" and "group": "One (the first dimension of grid) is order, classification, the symbolic system. The other (the dimension of group) is pressure, the experience of having no option but to consent to the overwhelming demands of other people" (p. 81). Using these categories, she and the researchers who followed her were able to determine and compare typical patterns of perception and communication in a number of sociological microcosms and macrocosms.

Like other fields of sociological research (→ **ethnomethodology**), sociolinguistic research is of importance for family theory and therapy. This research not only gives insight into the social context of the family and other interpersonal relationships but also points up central problems that arise in the processes of negotiation and validation of → **relational reality** between interactional partners. As a whole, sociolinguistics throws light on historical, cultural, and social conditions of our structures of perception and knowledge (→ **paradigm/ model/ map,** → **epistemology,** → **semiotics,** → **syntax,** → **constructivism**).

Bernstein, B. *Class, codes and control, Vol. I: Theoretical study towards a sociology of language.* London: Routledge & Kegan Paul, 1971.
Bernstein, B., & Henderson, D. Social class differences in the relevance of language to socialization. *Sociology 3:* 1–20, 1969.
Douglas, M. *Natural symbols.* New York: Vintage Press, 1970.
Douglas, M. *Essays in the sociology of perception.* London: Routledge & Kegan Paul, 1982.
Hymes, D. *Foundations in sociolinguistics.* Philadelphia: University of Pennsylvania Press, 1974.
Sapir, E. In D. G. Mandelbaum (Ed.), *Selected writings of Edward Sapir in language, culture, and personality.* Berkeley: University of California Press, 1949.
Whorf, B. L. *Language, thought, and reality.* Cambridge: Massachusetts Institute of Technology Press, 1942.

* * * * * *

STABILITY

This term refers to the ability of a dynamic system to reestablish equilibrium after perturbations have been triggered by interaction with the environment.

The concept of stability needs to be considered carefully in comparison with the concepts of → **homeostasis,** → **change, first and second order,** → **adaptability,** → **autonomy,** → **resistance,** and → **coherence.** Bateson (1979) stated that a living system achieves stability and escapes enduring changes "either by correcting change or changing itself to meet the change or by incorporating continued change into its own being" (103). Stability and change, in Bateson's view, always should be described in context, with each component characterized according to logical typing of what "changes" and what "stays the same." Dell (1985) objects to this formulation:

By choosing to explain the behavior of things in terms of context, Bateson is led to describe objects and organisms in terms of surviving versus changing. This is an obsever's *punctuation* of the interaction. More important, however, Bateson portrayed stability or survival as an *active* opposing of change via resisting, correcting, adapting, or incorporating. To punctuate the interaction in such a fashion is to commit the "fallacy of resistance" (Dell, 1982) which assumes that environmental events *ought* to change a system and, if they do not change the system, that the system's stability must be *explained*—via notions of resistance, homeostasis, correcting, adapting, incorporating, and so on. (p. 20)

Certain essential features of adaptability and of the development of dynamic systems (organisms, families, etc.) can be expressed within the framework of a concept of stability. Adaptability in this instance implies the capacity to make a transition to states of higher stability, and an ability to balance an ever increasing complexity of environmental conditions. This process is achieved through → **trial and error.** The simplest of the mechanisms that foster stability is the → **feedback loop,** which enables a specific parameter to be held at a steady level. A more complex form of stability has been described by Ashby (1952) as "ultrastability," which obtains under the following conditions:

1. when the system is stable or can maintain stability in relation to a specific set of environmental disturbances; and
2. when the system, which has been further destabilized by environmental disturbances with which it cannot cope, chooses from its repertoire of behaviors those that eventually lead to a restabilizing of the system.

Hence, the system must possess a number of behaviors and the ability to choose between these behaviors as well as the ability to "jump" from one behavior type to another. Mathematically speaking, the system must possess a parameter that has the characteristics of a step function (Klaus & Liebscher, 1979) (→ **nonlinearity/ step function).**

An even more advanced type of stability is represented by so–called "multistability," which is present when a system is formed by the linkage of ultrastable subsystems that are able to exist independently of one another. In this way, change can be kept limited. Only when subsystems can react autonomously to encroaching disturbances can the system prevent the alteration of all the elements of the system or subsystem by encroaching, destabilizing factors. The formation of such → **boundaries,** which are based on the relative autonomy of the subsystems (for example, individuals in a family system), insures the stability of the system as a whole. From the perspective of → **information theory,** this means that through the process of boundary formation, information that could have a destabilizing effect upon the system as a whole can be eliminated. These then are differences that no longer "make a difference" for the system as a whole.

All these concepts of stability must take account of the fact that stability, of whatever type, is merely relative. The boundaries of the system in its environment can only be defined relative to the system's own coherence. Accordingly, stability is merely a model that allows one to discriminate a system from its environment. In reality, environment and system represent a single, indivisible ecological system (→ **ecology/ ecosystem**) whose subsystems are constantly influencing each other (→ **holism**). All this occurs over a time span (→ **diachronic/ synchronic**) within which the environment is in a steady state of change, although the rate of change varies. The model that best does justice to these complex processes is that of → **coevolution.**

Given these considerations, the stability of a family unit should never be seen as being static. Even in the form of stability that has been given the label of homeostasis, the stability that is attained is actually a dynamic equilibrium in which continuous change occurs yet *relatively* uniform conditions prevail. Family stability is a type of metastability that constantly strives toward a balance between established (old) and necessary (new) structures. A set of family → **rules,** for example, that states that children aged 12 or 23 can be treated in the same way as when they were three, is thus not a stable system. It is a rigid system and an expression of a disturbance in the family's adaptability that inevitably will lead to dysfunctionality, the formation of symptoms, and the dissolution of the family as an evolutionary unit encompassing a number of generations.

Ashby, W. R. *Design for a brain.* London: Chapman & Hall, 1952.
Ashby, W. R. *An introduction to cybernetics.* London: Methuen, 1956.
Bateson, G. *Mind and nature: A necessary unity.* New York: E. P. Dutton, 1979.
Dell, P. F. Beyond homeostasis: Toward a concept of coherence. *Family Process 21:* 21–41, 1982.
Dell, P. F. Understanding Bateson and Maturana: Toward a biological foundation for the social sciences. *Journal of Marital and Family Therapy 11:* 1–20, 1985.
Goodwin, B. C. Biological stability. In C. H. Waddington (Ed.), *Towards a theoretical biology, Vol. 3: Drafts.* Edinburgh: Edinburgh University Press, 1970, 1–17.
Hoffman, L. *Foundations of family therapy: A conceptual framework for systems change.* New York: Basic Books, 1981.
Klaus, G., & Liebscher, H. *Wörterbuch der Kybernetik* (4th revised ed.). Frankfurt: Fischer, 1979.
Maturana, H. R., & Varela, F. J. *Autopoiesis and cognition: The realization of living.* Boston: Reidel, 1980.
May, R. M. *Stability and complexity in model ecosystems.* Princeton, N. J.: Princeton University Press, 1973.

* * * * * *

STEPFAMILIES/ BLENDED FAMILIES

Divorce, and the consequent re–formation of partnerships whereby a father or a mother is replaced by a stepfather or stepmother, is an increasingly frequent phenomenon. Because the absent parent continues to play a parental, albeit limited role, and continues to claim certain rights with regard to the newly formed family, the children are often exposed to a conflict of → **loyalties.** The stepfather or stepmother, with the latter's decidedly negative role in folklore and fairy tales, is placed in a difficult position. The multiplicity of roles in blended families can lead to confusion, distress, and family disorganization.

Empirical investigations have confirmed that stepfamilies function differently from so–called "normal families" (→ **healthy/ functional families**). The central problem is the concurrent existence of the original family and the "new" family. Whereas the history shared by the original family continues to manifest itself in some form (the children particularly being an "embodiment" of the original relationship), the new stepfamily has no common tradition. The problems posed by lack of continuity are further reinforced by attempts to achieve the status of an ideal, "normal" family and, hence, a tendency to deny the difficulties posed by unrealistically high expectations of self and others.

The children's problems are a result of often insufficiently mourned–for losses, divided loyalties, feelings of guilt because of the parents' divorce, and the difficulty of being "at home" in two households, in a binuclear family. The absent parent remains present in the child's fantasy, and as an idealized figure or a bogey in the new family constellation.

The clarification of the complex roles, expectations, and relationship problems that ensue between parents, stepparents, and stepchildren, and between stepchildren and their new brothers and sisters, are the central task of family therapy with blended families. The goals of therapy are the alleviation of guilt, the clarification of the ties of loyalty, and the formation and the support of realistic forms of family organization. The transition from → **divorce therapy** to therapy with blended families is often a continuous one.

Clingenpeel, W. G., Ievoli, R., & Brand, E. Structural complexity and the quality of stepfather-stepchild relationships. *Family Process 23:* 547–560, 1984.
Krähenbühl, V., Jellouschek, H., Kohaus-Jellouschek, M., & Weber, R. Stieffamilien: Struktur, Entwicklung, Therapie. *Familiendynamik 9:* 2–18, 1984.
Morawetz, A., & Walker, G. *Brief therapy with single-parent families.* New York: Brunner/Mazel, 1984.
Perkins, T. F., & Kahan, J. P. An empirical comparison of natural-father and stepfather family systems. *Family Process 18:* 175–183, 1979.
Sager, C., Brown, H., Crohn, H., Engel, T., Rodstein, E., & Walker, L. *Treating the remarried family.* New York: Brunner/Mazel, 1983.
Visher, E. B., & Visher, J. S. *Stepfamilies: A guide to working with stepparents and stepchildren.* New York: Brunner/Mazel, 1979.
Walker, L., Brown, H., Crohn, H., Rodstein, E., Zeisel, E., & Sager, C. J. An annotated bibliography of the remarried, the living together, and their children. *Family Process 18:* 193–212, 1979.

* * * * * *

STORY TELLING

The telling of stories is a therapeutic strategy within the framework of → **communication therapy,** → **hypnotherapy,** and → **neurolinguistic programming.** Bateson (1979) called a story a "pattern in time." Should the → **pattern** of this story correspond to the client's or family's model of the world, it becomes highly relevant for interpersonal relationships and thus allows for an interpretation and/or → **reframing** of the family's or client's internal map (→ **paradigm/ model/ map**). Optimally, a story as → **metaphor** presents the client with the possibility of identifying with the actors of the story, of expanding his or her view of the problem, and of introducing new perspectives for its solution.

Therapy is to a large extent the reconstruction of the individual's or family's → **epistemology.** This epistemological basis influences the individual's life → **script,** which is largely made up of "stories." Bateson posited that people as a rule think in stories because stories reduce the complexity of the world by bringing → **diachronic/ synchronic** structures together in a pattern in time. The nonreversibility of time, a fundamental characteristic of each individual's experience of the world, and the simultaneity of interactional processes are especially highlighted in story telling.

Within the framework of therapy, stories can be used to establish a bond of mutual trust between patient and therapist. Stories can also be used diagnostically because they are made up of a number of elements that can be used as projective techniques. A therapist can gain information about the client's model of the world by assessing the client's reaction to particular aspects of a story, observing which parts of the story capture the client's attention, and taking into account how the client understands the story. Stories can also be used to illustrate the connection between relationships, to suggest solutions to problems, to help the client toward self-knowledge by means of symbols, to implant new ideas, or to give directions. The processes of interpretation and reframing that take place through the telling of stories touch upon both cognitive and affective aspects of experience, elucidating and presenting them in their interactional and scenic context. The various layers of meaning in a story allow the client to independently choose a personal interpretation of the story. This helps to keep → **resistance** at a minimum because the client does not feel threatened on a conscious level (see Zeig, 1980, pp. 4–26) (→ **psycholinguistics**).

Auerswald, E. H. Thinking about thinking in family therapy. *Family Process 24:* 1–12, 1985.

Bandler, R., & Grinder, J. *Patterns of the hypnotic techniques of Milton H. Erickson, M. D., Vol. I.* Cupertino, Cal.: META Publications, 1975. (a)

Bandler, R., & Grinder, J. *The structure of magic, Vol. I.* Palo Alto: Science and Behavior Books, 1975. (b)

Bandler, R., & Grinder, J. *Tranceformation.* Moab, Utah: Real People Press, 1981.

Bandler, R., & Grinder, J. *Reframing: Neurolinguistic programming and the transformation of meaning.* Moab, Utah: Real People Press, 1982.

Bateson, G. *Mind and nature: A necessary unity.* New York: E. P. Dutton, 1979.

Cade, B. Some uses of metaphor. *Australian Journal of Family Therapy 3:* 135–140, 1982.

Erickson, M. H., & Rossi, E. *Hypnotherapy: An exploratory casebook.* New York: Irvington, 1979.

Erickson, M. H., Rossi, E., & Rossi, S. *Hypnotic realities: The induction of clinical hypnosis and forms of indirect suggestion.* New York: Irvington, 1976.

Gordon, D. *Therapeutic metaphors: Helping others through the looking glass.* Cupertino, Cal.: META Publications, 1978.

Grinder, J., & Bandler, R. *The structure of magic, Vol. II.* Palo Alto: META Publications, 1976.

Grinder, J., Delozier, J., & Bandler, R. *Patterns of the hypnotic techniques of Milton H. Erickson, M. D., Vol. II.* Cupertino, Cal.: META Publications, 1977.

Lankton, S. *Practical magic: The clinical applications of neuro-linguistic programming.* Cupertino, Cal.: META Publications, 1979.

Zeig, J. (Ed.). *A teaching seminar with Milton H. Erickson.* New York: Brunner/Mazel, 1980.

Zeig, J. *Ericksonian approaches to hypnosis and psychotherapy.* New York: Brunner/Mazel, 1982.

* * * * * *

STRATEGIC THERAPY

This directive form of therapy is consistent with the principles of → **cybernetics.** Family problems are seen as being the expression of dysfunctional organizational patterns such as blurred → **generational boundaries,** the pathological formation of triangles (→ **triangulation**), confusions in the family → **hierarchy,** as well as disturbances of adaptation in the context of the → **family life cycle.** The therapist begins by negotiating the goals of therapy with the family and then proceeds to develop a → **strategy** for achieving these goals.

Like → **systemic therapy,** strategic therapy can be viewed as a derivation of → **communication therapy.** Both of these approaches are based on cybernetic → **system** and → **feedback** theories, and are closely related to → **information theory** and the theory of → **games;** in both, diagnostic and therapeutic emphasis is placed on the functional aspect of symptoms for the family and the individual. Despite these similarities, systemic and strategic approaches do have differences, which has led to numerous attempts at clarifying how the two approaches can or cannot be integrated. (See, for example, the *Journal of Strategic and Systemic Therapies 3*, No. 3 and No. 4, 1984.)

Strategic therapists constantly ask: "How does the symptom serve to uphold family → **homeostasis?**" "How is the symptom being used to help the family master a → **crisis** in the context of the family life cycle?" "How and why does the presence of the symptom fail to solve the problem?" "How can the symptom be replaced by a new and more effective solution to the problem?" Because it is not possible to determine the function or significance of a symptom on the level of the individual alone, the problems of the → **identified patient** have to be understood and changed within the → **context** of the family system. Hence, the goals of strategic therapy are to change the sequences, the rules, and the meaning of family interaction.

Strategic therapy typically takes place in a series of stages. In the initial stage, the therapist, using positioning strategies, establishes contact with the family and gathers information as to why the family has sought therapy. The therapist accepts the family's view of the problem, even if this includes the idea that the identified patient is the real problem and, "The rest of us are just fine." From this initial information, the therapist in conjunction with the family works out the definition of the therapeutic goals. The therapist asks each member of the family in concrete terms what his or her minimum goal in therapy is, and how would each of them recognize that this goal had been achieved (Weakland, Fisch, Watzlawick, & Bodin, 1974). Staying as close to the behavioral level as possible (who does what and when), the therapist attempts to discern the problematic aspects of the family's interactional → **rules** and yet to avoid enmeshment in a power struggle with the family.

In the next stage of therapy, the therapist often employs highly directive intervention methods. These methods are therapeutically *and* diagnostically valuable in that they enable the therapist to gain insight into the family's organizational structure, problem–solving strategies, and flexibility, by observing the family's reaction to the directive interventions. The therapist then attempts to change the family's interpretative schemata and patterns of communication, and, in particular, through methods of → **reframing,** → **positive connotation** of symptoms, prescribing strategies, and → **paradoxical interventions,** to remove blocks that hinder the family's development.

Although many strategic therapists work alone, a growing number prefers teamwork and observation through a one–way mirror. This preference stems from the realization that during therapy a new, more or less coherent system is created between the therapist and the family, and the therapist who works directly with the family has more difficulty in maintaining an objective view of the new system of which he or she is a part.

Strategic therapists vary as to the length and number of sessions they believe are adequate; some report as many as forty weekly sessions. There does, however, appear to be a clear trend toward → **brief therapy,** and many strategic therapists doubt the efficacy of anything over ten or fifteen sessions (see Zuk, 1975). The intervals between sessions are usually shorter than those in → **systemic therapy** (Milan models), although many strategic therapists seem to favor intervals of more than a week, or a variable interval—briefer at the beginning of therapy and longer in later stages (→ **frequency of sessions**).

A strategic model of therapy assumes that change can be brought about in the system by change in any single element of that system. From this point of view, it appears possible to conduct family therapy by working with individual members only, "family therapy without a family" so to speak (Watzlawick & Coyne, 1979). In such an approach, however, it is especially important to view the patient's problem in the light of its relevance to the relationship system (generally the family system) and not merely in its relevance to the patient as an individual.

There are many situations in which strategic therapy seems indicated. The literature speaks of treatment success in a large number of problem areas: psychosocial, psychiatric, and psychosomatic problems, to mention just a few. (For a survey of the literature on the subject of treatment applicability, see Stanton, 1981b, pp. 368–369.)

Fisch, R., Weakland, J. H., & Segal, L. *The tactics of change: Doing therapy briefly.* San Francisco: Jossey-Bass, 1982.

Haley, J. *Strategies of psychotherapy.* New York: Grune & Stratton, 1963.

Haley, J. *Uncommon therapy: The psychiatric techniques of Milton H. Erickson, M. D.: A casebook of an innovative psychiatrist's work in short-term therapy.* New York: W. W. Norton & Co., 1973.

Haley, J. *Problem-solving therapy.* San Francisco: Jossey-Bass, 1976.

Haley, J. *Ordeal therapy.* San Francisco: Jossey-Bass, 1984.

MacKinnon, L. Contrasting strategic and Milan therapies. *Family Process 22:* 425–441, 1983.

Madanes, C. *Strategic family therapy.* San Francisco: Jossey-Bass, 1981.

Madanes, C. *Behind the one-way mirror: Advances in the practice of strategic therapy.* San Francisco: Jossey-Bass, 1984.

Madanes, C., & Haley, J. Dimensions of family therapy. *Journal of Nervous and Mental Disease 165:* 88–98, 1977.

Mazza, J. Symptom utilization in strategic therapy. *Family Process 23:* 487–500, 1984.

Papp, P. The Greek chorus and other techniques of paradoxical therapy. *Family Process 19:* 45–57, 1980.

338

Papp, P. *The process of change.* New York: Guilford Press, 1983.

Rabkin, R. *Strategic psychotherapy: Brief and symptomatic treatment.* New York: Basic Books, 1977.

Rabkin, R. The midgame in strategic therapy. *International Journal of Family Therapy 2:* 159–168, 1980.

Stanton, M. D. Family therapy: Systems approaches. In G. P. Sholevar, R. M. Benson, & B. J. Blinder (Eds.), *Emotional disorders in children and adolescents: Medical and psychological approaches to treatment.* New York: SP Medical and Scientific Books, 1980, 159–179.

Stanton, M. D. An integrated structural/strategic approach to family therapy. *Journal of Marital and Family Therapy 7:* 427–439, 1981. (a)

Stanton, M. D. Marital therapy from a structural/strategic viewpoint. In G. P. Sholevar (Ed.), *The handbook of marriage and marital therapy.* New York: SP Medical and Scientific Books, 1981, 303–334. (b)

Stanton, M. D. Strategic approaches to family therapy. In A. S. Gurman & D. P. Kniskern (Eds.), *Handbook of family therapy.* New York: Brunner/Mazel, 1981, 361–402. (c)

Stanton, M. D. Fusion, compression, diversion, and the workings of paradox: A theory of therapeutic/systemic change. *Family Process 23:* 135–167, 1984.

Watzlawick, P., & Coyne, J. Depression following stroke: Brief, problem-focused family treatment. *Family Process 19:* 13–18, 1979.

Watzlawick, P., Weakland, J. H., & Fisch, R. *Change: Principles of problems formation and problem resolution.* New York: W. W. Norton & Co., 1974.

Weakland, J. H., Fisch, R., Watzlawick, P., & Bodin, A. M. Brief therapy: Focused problem resolution. *Family Process 13:* 141–168, 1974.

Zuk, G. H. *Process and practice in family therapy.* Haverford, Pa.: Psychiatry and Behavior Science Books, 1975.

* * * * * *

STRATEGY

Strategy is a plan of action, a *modus operandi* in more or less predictable situations that allows one to make decisions likely to facilitate reaching a specific goal.

The concept of strategy, as used in everyday language, has been more precisely defined in → **game** theory. Neumann and Morgenstern (1944) have suggested that every game player does not make a decision as to how to move a piece only when it becomes necessary to do so but, rather, that the player has worked out beforehand how he or she will proceed in any given situation. If one assumes that every individual wishes to reach certain goals and/or satisfy certain needs, then any interactional → **context** may be seen as a game in which the interactional partners (for example, the members of a family) attempt to score "points." It follows that family → **rules** are then the rules of a game.

The manner in which the individual manages to get his or her needs met is a strategic, behavior plan that covers every imaginable situation. However, the rules of a family system are subject to change as dictated by the demands of a family–wide → **coevolution** and → **individuation.** A strategy used by a preschooler to achieve his or her ends is usually not very successful for an adult. Insistence on the continued use of inappropriate strategies generally means that the family system is rigid, and very likely pathological. In order to apply therapeutically effective, strategic methods, the therapist needs to develop a long–term, goal–oriented plan that is scrupulously "attuned" to the particular game the family or client is playing (→ **strategic therapy,** → **systemic therapy**).

Haley, J. *Strategies of psychotherapy.* New York: Grune & Stratton, 1963.
Klaus, G., & Liebscher, H. *Wörterbuch der Kybernetik* (4th revised ed.) Frankfurt: Fischer, 1979.
Neumann, J. von, & Morgenstern, O. *Theory of games and economic behavior.* Princeton, N. J.: Princeton University Press, 1944.
Watzlawick, P., Beavin, J. H., & Jackson, D. D. *Pragmatics of human communication: A study of interactional patterns, pathologies and paradoxes.* New York: W. W. Norton & Co., 1967.

* * * * * *

STRUCTURAL FAMILY THERAPY

This directive method of family therapy was developed by Minuchin and his associates. It is based upon a normative concept of a → **healthy family.** Particular emphasis is placed upon the → **boundaries** between family subsystems and the establishment and maintenance of a clear → **hierarchy** based on parental competence to decide all matters that relate to the family.

A structurally oriented therapist sees the first task as the assessment of dysfunctional structures in the family, such as blurring of boundaries, confusion in the family hierarchy, and the existence of rigid, patho-logical coalitions (→ **triangulation,** → **rigid triad**). Further, it is generally believed to be essential that the therapist "join" (→ **joining**) the family, which means to attune oneself to the manner in which the family thinks, speaks, and feels. The therapist often imitates the family's style (in mimesis) and takes up the family's images, expecta-tions, and metaphors. The therapist may "track" the family interaction by allowing, or even encouraging family patterns to unfold naturally before intervening overtly.

The therapist then uses a variety of techniques to restructure diffuse or rigid boundaries of the family as a whole and its subsystems, thereby enabling the development of new and more effective problem–solving strategies and correcting patterns of → **enmeshment** and → **disengagement.** For example, the therapist may unveil and activate unresolved and/or covert family conflicts. Often the structural therapist engages in "unbalancing"—at least temporarily throwing his or her influence behind a less dominant member or subsystem—in order to promote a shift to a more functional family structure. Also, the therapist may draw attention to family structures that manifest themselves in the family's seating arrangement during the session by deliberately changing the seating arrangement. In general, the therapist wants the family members to practice new ways of relating together through → **enactment** within the actual session. Whenever possible, the therapists supports the leadership of the parents and seeks to break up dysfunctional, cross–generational structures in which the children take on aspects of parental roles. In so doing, the therapist, at least temporarily, assumes a dominant, hierarchical position in regard to the family and is thus able to intervene in the family system. After the family has completed therapy, the therapist remains in some sense present in the family's fantasy and, hence, may continue as a therapeutic factor in the family system.

Aponte, H. Underorganization in the poor family. In P. J. Guerin (Ed.), *Family therapy: Theory and practice.* New York: Gardner Press, 1976, 432–448.

Aponte, H., & VanDeusen, J. Structural family therapy. In A. S. Gurman & D. P. Kniskern (Eds.), *Handbook of family therapy.* New York: Brunner/Mazel, 1981, 310–360.

Keeney, B. P., & Ross, J. M. *Mind in therapy: Constructing systemic family therapies.* New York: Basic Books, 1985.

Minuchin, S. *Families and family therapy.* Cambridge: Harvard University Press, 1974. (a)

Minuchin, S. Structural family therapy. In G. Caplan (Ed.), *American handbook of psychiatry. Vol. II, Child and adolescent psychiatry, sociocultural and community psychiatry* (2nd ed.). New York: Basic Books, 1974, 178–192. (b)

Minuchin, S., & Barcai, A. Therapeutically induced family crisis. In C. J. Sager & H. S. Kaplan (Eds.), *Progress in group and family therapy.* New York: Brunner/Mazel, 1972, 322–329.

Minuchin, S., & Fishman, H. C. *Family therapy techniques.* Cambridge: Harvard University Press, 1981.

Minuchin, S., Montalvo, B. G., Guerney, B., Rosman, B. L., & Schumer, F. *Families of the slums: An exploration of their structure and treatment.* New York: Basic Books, 1967.

Minuchin, S., Rosman, B. L., & Baker, L. *Psychosomatic families: Anorexia nervosa in context.* Cambridge: Harvard University Press, 1978.

Stanton, M. D. Family therapy: Systems approaches. In G. P. Sholevar, R. M. Benson, & B. J. Blinder (Eds.), *Emotional disorders in children and adolescents: Medical and psychological approaches to treatment.* New York: SP Medical and Scientific Books, 1980, 159–179.

* * * * * *

STRUCTURALISM

Structuralism is a mode of research that assumes that social behaviors and cultural products can be described and investigated as if they were a language and a communication → **code.** Those behaviors that are explicitly allowed, forbidden, or prescribed in a social system are thought to be traceable to the abstract system of rules (unconscious algebra) upon which they are based. In particular, the internal logic of rituals and myths that determine the daily living, thinking, and feeling in a social system can be elucidated.

Although the structuralist approach coincides to a great extent with that of systems theory (→ **system**), very few family therapists consider themselves to be structuralists. The reason for this is very likely that structuralist thought is a product of French–speaking countries and systemic theory is largely a product of Anglo–American culture. Ferdinand de Saussure, considered to be the founder of structuralism, analyzed languages with the help of the method described above. Distinguishing between language as a system and language as it actually manifests itself, he attempted to discover the system of rules implicit in language (de Saussure, 1916). This approach was further developed in the field of linguistics (Chomsky, 1957, 1965, 1968; Jakobson, 1971). Such research, initially concerned only with the phenomena of language, eventually expanded into → **semiotics** and its subareas of → **syntax,** → **semantics,** and → **pragmatics.**

Claude Lévi–Strauss was the founder of the structuralist approach to cultural anthropology. His work illustrates the close relationship between systemic and structuralist thought, and makes extensive use of the findings of → **cybernetics** and → **game** theory. Within the context of developmental psychology, Piaget (1968, 1970) remained faithful to the precepts of structuralist thought in his investigation of genetic epistemology. In the area of psychoanalysis, Lacan (1966, 1973) used the structuralist method to reinterpret the basic structure of Sigmund Freud's theories (see Lang, 1973, 1980) (→ **psycholinguistics**).

342

Structuralism and family theory both have a fundamental interest in the development and formation of structures, in the relationship of these to the functioning of a system, in the developmental rules of a system, and, above all, in the relationship between interactional structures and the structures of knowledge (→ **epistemology**). One possible criticism of some proponents of structuralism is that they tend to view structures as concrete entities and ignore important aspects of change and development inherent in systems.

Chomsky, N. *Syntactic structures.* The Hague: Mouton & Co., 1957.
Chomsky, N. *Aspects of the theory of syntax.* Cambridge: Massachusetts Institute of Technology Press, 1965.
Chomsky, N. *Language and mind.* New York: Harcourt, Brace, Jovanovich, 1968.
de Saussure, F. *Course in general linguistics.* New York: Philosophical Library, 1916.
Jakobson, R. *Selected writings* (2 vols.). The Hague: Mouton, 1971.
Lacan, J. *Ecrits.* Paris: Editions du Seuil, 1966.
Lacan, J. *Les quarte concepts fondamenteaux de la psychoanalyse.* Paris: Seuil, 1973.
Lang, H. *Die Sprache und das Unbewusste.* Frankfurt: Suhrkamp, 1973.
Lang, H. Freud—ein Strukturalist? *Psyche 34:* 865–884, 1980.
Lévi-Strauss, C. *Structural anthropology.* New York: Basic Books, 1963.
Lévi-Strauss, C. *The savage mind* (translated from the French, *La pensée sauvage,* by G. Weidenfeld and Nicolson Ltd., 1962). Chicago: University of Chicago Press, 1966.
Piaget, J. *Le structuralisme.* Paris: Presses Universitaires de France, 1968.
Piaget, J. *Genetic epistemology* (translated by E. Duckworth). New York: Columbia University Press, 1970.
Siomopoulos, V. *The structure of psychopathological experience.* New York: Brunner/Mazel, 1983.

* * * * * *

STRUCTURE/FUNCTION/PROCESS

These related concepts express different ways of viewing natural processes.

Within the framework of → **cybernetics,** the concept of *structure* describes the entirety of the relationships between the elements of a dynamic system. Two elements may be regarded as being linked when the "exit" of one element provides for the "entrance" of the other, or a change in one is followed by a change in the other, all of which means that → **information** is being transferred. If the entirety of these linkages is designated as a structure, one cannot describe it in terms of a static process but, rather, in terms of → **diachronic/synchronic** relations. Furthermore, only on the basis of the recurrence of specific patterns of interaction and of a → **redundancy** of behavior processes can one make any inferences about the → **rules** and, hence, the structure of a given system. Because such *processes* are repetitive sequences in the dimension of time, one must guard against the concept of structure being a static entity. The direction and regulation of these processes are not random, but are determined by their *function* in a given context. One can elucidate the reciprocal relationship between structure and function by asking: "What purpose does a specific structure serve?" and "With which structure can a function best be fulfilled?"

All animate and inanimate phenomena in the world appear as events in the continua of space and time. Everything that can be said about these phenomena is related to the observer's experience of these phenomena. Hence, while descriptions are never objective, they do say something about the observer and about the conditions under which the observation is being made. Russell (1969) noted that the raw material of our experience consists "of events," which we "come to believe" are permanent "bodies" (p. 129). Every perception, whether scientific or of an ordinary, everyday nature, thus creates a structure; in other words, dynamic processes are "translated" into static processes (see Simon, 1984). Models are constructed that suggest that the world is composed of *things* (→ **paradigm/model/map**).

What all of this means for family therapy and theory is that the family represents a dynamic web of events whose structure and rules of behavior are not to be regarded as complete in themselves but, rather, must be viewed in terms of their function for each individual family member as well as for the family as a whole. Hence, the structure of a family is never static or unchangeable; if a structure does not change, this merely means that it does not need to change at the moment. Therapy, as a process of restructuring, demands and strives toward an alteration of the conditions and/or functions that maintain the structure of a dysfunctional system.

Each family possesses a certain amount of → **autonomy** vis-à-vis its environment, and a family's → **adaptability** is oriented toward the family's internal model of the world. Dysfunctional behavior can thus be regarded as a disturbance of the developmental processes via which a normal system is capable of changing its environment and the environment is capable of changing the system. An interruption of these circular processes may express itself in a tendency toward rigidity in the family's map of the world, as well as a blockage of necessary → **coevolution** and → **individuation.** Under these circumstances, the task of therapy becomes the removal of these blocks to development. This can only take place by altering the relationship between symbolic representation of the family's view of the world and its regulating behavior. As long as a particular view of the world is confirmed in all activities of the family or system, there exists no reason for the system to change its structure.

In principle, there are two methods of restructuring a system. The first works via corrective experience and reflection, by means of which an internal model can be changed (as happens, for example, in psychoanalysis). In the second method, one attempts to influence directly unconscious structures, the affective and cognitive mechanisms that determine the structure of the model (→ epistemology, → reframing). This is the method applied in → communication therapy, → strategic therapy, → systemic therapy, → hynotherapy, and → neurolinguistic programming. If family or psychic structures are considered to be nonstatic, demonstrating specific functions that can be confirmed or challenged as they interact with the environment, then a number of the concepts of psychoanalysis can be seen as being compatible with those of systemic family therapy (see Ciompi, 1982).

Ciompi, L. *Affektlogic. Über die Struktur der Psyche und ihre Entwicklung. Ein Beitrag zur Schizophrenieforschung.* Stuttgart: Klett-Cotta, 1982.

Garcia-Shelton, L. M., & Brody, H. Family structure and development. In R. B. Taylor (Ed.), *Fundamentals of family medicine* (2nd ed.). Berlin: Springer-Verlag, 1983, 8–21.

Levant, R. Diagnostic perspectives on the family: Process, structural and historical contextual models. *American Journal of Family Therapy 11*: 3–10, 1983.

Parsons, T., Bales, R. F., Olds, J., Zelditch, M., & Slater, P. E. *Family socialization and interaction process.* Glencoe, Ill.: Free Press, 1955.

Rapaport, D. (Ed.). *Organization and pathology of thought.* New York: Columbia University Press, 1951.

Russell, B. *The ABC of relativity* (3rd ed.). London: George Allen & Unwin, 1969.

Simon, F. B., *Der Prozess der Individuation: Über den Zusammenhang von Vernunft und Gefühlen.* Göttingen: Vandenhoeck & Ruprecht, 1984.

Taylor, W. R. Research on family interaction I: Static and dynamic models. *Family Process 9*: 221–232, 1970.

* * * * * *

SYMBOLIC–EXPERIENTIAL FAMILY THERAPY

This form of growth–oriented therapy (→ growth therapy), espoused by Carl Whitaker, employs directive methods although it is oriented to psychoanalytic concepts. New experiences are conveyed to the family on the level of symbolic–primary processes.

This type of therapy has derived its approach largely from child analysis and play therapy. Social adaptation to the normative structures of society is not a goal of symbolic–experiential therapy. Its goals are to create a feeling of togetherness between family members, to establish a sense of personal freedom, to promote individual and collective creativity, and to achieve acceptance of the idea that personal "craziness" can be viewed as a positive resource. In order to achieve these goals, the therapists of this school may heighten existing stress within the family. For example, they will define an individual family member's symptoms as being the problem of the system as a whole, or they will attempt to create "family patriotism," i.e., something on the order of a family "team spirit." Another method is to clarify how the family's relationship to the members of their extended family, to earlier generations, to the community, to their social environment, and to their culture, affects the family's → **relational reality.** Like most family therapists, regardless of their theoretical affiliations, symbolic–experiential therapists attempt to encourage the demarcation of generations, i.e., to clarify and structure the → **boundaries** between them. At the same time they attempt to teach the family members how to play together. By means of **games,** rigid role structures can be made more flexible, and, within clearly defined limits (→ **context marking**), the roles of the others may be "tried on for size," hence promoting individual and family development.

As a rule, two cotherapists form a team. They attempt to forge a bond with the family (→ **joining**) and then to maintain a flexible distance to the family. The therapist's interventions are often playful, humorous, and at times even take on a form of self–caricature. The therapist thus endeavors to demonstrate on a symbolic level that → **family myths,** above all the myth of individuality, are only true in a restricted sense, that every "truth" can be viewed from another perspective and, hence, that every family tragedy may contain elements of a theater of the absurd.

In a manner similar to analytical child therapy, there is no attempt to induce change by means of conscious reflection and insight into family processes but, rather, by means of playful, symbolic interactions that create new experiences for the family. All this serves the purpose of attaining a higher level of related → **individuation.** The choice of interventions is explicitly influenced by both → **transference and countertransference** relations. Unlike psychoanalysis, the therapeutic attitude is not (relative) abstinence but → **multidirectional partiality.** The therapist is encouraged to bring countertransference reactions into the therapeutic session in an appropriate manner and, if the situation allows, as a species of → **metacommunication.**

Whitaker believes that trust in the creative power of the therapist's unconscious is more important than training in specific therapeutic techniques. He believes that the therapist's intuitive, creative sense is able to find the most suitable intervention for any situation that could arise in the therapeutic session. The form of therapy described above corresponds closely to the healing-through-encounter → **model of family therapy.**

Keith, D. V., & Whitaker, C. A. Add craziness and stir: Psychotherapy with a psychoticgenic family. In M. Andolfi & I. Zwerling (Eds.), *Dimensions of family therapy.* New York: Guilford Press, 1980, 139–160.
Keith, D. V., & Whitaker, C. A. Play therapy: A paradigm for work with families. *Journal of Marital and Family Therapy 7:* 243–254, 1981.
Napier, A. Y., & Whitaker, C. A. *The family crucible.* New York: Harper & Row, 1978.
Neill, J. R., & Kniskern, D. P. *From psyche to system: The evolving therapy of Carl Whitaker.* New York: Guilford Press, 1982.
Whitaker, C. A. Psychotherapy of the absurd: With a special emphasis on the psychotherapy of aggression. *Family Process 14:* 1–16, 1975.
Whitaker, C. A., & Keith, D. V. Family therapy as symbolic experience. *International Journal of Family Psychiatry 1:* 197–208, 1980.
Whitaker, C. A., & Keith, D. V. Symbolic-experiential family therapy. In A. S. Gurman & D. P. Kniskern (Eds.), *Handbook of family therapy.* New York: Brunner/Mazel, 1981, 187–225.

* * * * * *

SYMMETRY

Symmetry [Greek *syn,* of like measure, like, same; *metron,* measure] designates a pattern of relationship that is based on a striving toward equality and the minimization of differences between partners.

The term symmetry was introduced into interactional research, along with the term → **complementarity,** by Bateson (1936). In his research among the indigenous population of New Guinea, Bateson discovered that social differentiation follows two patterns: either the differences between two individuals or groups are emphasized or their similarities are emphasized. Bateson called this differentiation process → **schismogenesis.** According to Bateson's formulation in *Naven,* human relationships in general can be seen as differentiating through either complementary or symmetrical processes.

Family and systemic therapists have a particular interest in symmetrical relationships in which neither of the two interactional partners is able to agree to being on the "same level"; when two interactional partners each strive to maintain the → **dominant** position in the relationship, a "symmetrical escalation" results, a struggle in which each partner attempts to be "a little more equal" than the other. The mutual feeling of being secure only in the dominant role is characteristic not only of the armaments race between nations but also of marital → **power** struggles. An advanced state of symmetrical escalation is the → **malign clinch,** which can result in the family relational pattern of → **marital schism** (Lidz, Cornelison, Fleck, & Terry, 1957). In a nonescalating symmetric relationship, partners are able to meet in an attitude of positive → **mutuality,** trust, and respect, and are also able to confirm each other's definitions of "I" and "Thou."

Bateson, G. *Naven: A survey of the problems suggested by a composite picture of the culture of a New Guinea tribe drawn from three points of view.* Cambridge: Cambridge University Press, 1936.

Jackson, D. D. Family interaction, family homeostasis and some implications for conjoint family psychotherapy. In J. H. Masserman (Ed.), *Individual and familial dynamics.* New York: Grune & Stratton, 1959, 122–141.

Lidz, T., Cornelison, A. R., Fleck, S., & Terry, D. The intrafamilial environment of schizophrenic patients: II. Marital schism and marital skew. *American Journal of Psychiatry 114:* 241–248, 1957.

Sluzki, C. E., & Beavin, J. Symmetry and complementarity: An operational definition and a typology of dyads. In P. Watzlawick & J. H. Weakland (Eds.), *The interactional view.* New York: W. W. Norton & Co., 1977.

Watzlawick, P. Wesen und Formen menschlicher Beziehungen. In H.–G. Gadamer & P. Vogler (Eds.), *Neue Anthropologie, Vol. 7.* Stuttgart: Thieme, 1975, 103–131.

Watzlawick, P., Beavin, J. H., & Jackson, D. D. *Pragmatics of human communication: A study of interactional patterns, pathologies and paradoxes.* New York: W. W. Norton & Co., 1967.

* * * * * *

SYMPTOM PRESCRIPTION

Symptom prescription is a → **paradoxical intervention** in that it runs counter to the → **epistemology** of the symptom–bearer and his or her interactional partners.

The therapist prescribes to the family or the individual patient that they should continue to do exactly that which they have considered to be "symptomatic" or "sick." Prescribing the symptom means that both its → **context** and the family interaction pattern will be changed. This intervention belongs to the repertoire of → **communication therapy,** i.e., → **strategic therapy** and → **systemic therapy.** It is based on a → **cybernetic** concept of the function of symptoms in family systems, according to which, symptoms have a communicative function within human relationships. Within a given cultural, subcultural, or family context, symptoms represent a form of language. They have specific meanings and their own grammar. Rules exist as to how members of the group are expected to react toward the symptom. If, for example, persons appear to be depressed and forlorn, this usually instigates attempts by others to comfort and cheer them up.

Out of these and other → **rules** of behavior, → **feedback loops** are developed, and these create the conditions under which symptoms become stabilized. Thus, symptoms will take on specific functions that they did not have when they first originated in the interactional system. If one views a symptom merely as something negative, a manifestation of a dysfunctional system to be gotten rid of as quickly as possible, one loses sight of the symptom's positive, "functional" aspects. Depressive behavior, for example, allows interactional partners to create and maintain a type of interpersonal context in which the depressed partner is "cared for" and the other partner does the caring.

When therapists prescribe symptoms, they give a → **positive connotation** to and place the adaptability aspects of symptoms at the center of attention. This → **reframing** of the symptom's meaning makes it impossible for the family and the individual to maintain their previous interpretation of the symptom's meaning. With the introduction of new information, the old rules regarding who is supposed to react to what and in which way are challenged. Behavior is inevitably changed. Because a prescribed symptom never "spontaneously" reappears, it can be said to be under conscious control. Hence, the often held premise that a "symptom–bearer" is not able to change a symptom is invalid. A symptom that can be "caused" can also be "caused to disappear." If a person continues to exhibit a symptom when he or she can control its occurrence, then one must conclude that the symptom–bearer wishes, consciously or unconsciously, to keep the symptom. An active or passive attitude toward the symptom on the part of the symptom–bearer reflects his or her self–image and degree of → **autonomy.**

Andolfi, M. Prescribing the families' own dysfunctional rules as a therapeutic strategy. *Journal of Marital and Family Therapy 6:* 29–36, 1980.

Frankl, V. E. Paradoxical intention: A logotherapeutic technique. *American Journal of Psychotherapy 14:* 520–535, 1960.

Haley, J. *Strategies of psychotherapy.* New York: Grune & Stratton, 1963.

Papp, P. The Greek chorus and other techniques of paradoxical therapy. *Family Process 19:* 45–57, 1980.

Raskin, D. E., & Klein, Z. E. Losing a symptom through keeping it: A review of paradoxical treatment techniques and rationale. *Archives of General Psychiatry* *33:* 548–555, 1976.

Selvini-Palazzoli, M., Boscolo, L., Cecchin, G., & Prata, G. *Paradox and counter-paradox: A new model in the therapy of the family in schizophrenic transaction* (translated by E. V. Burt). New York: Jason Aronson, 1978.

Watzlawick, P., Weakland, J. H., & Fisch, R. *Change: Principles of problem formation and problem resolution.* New York: W. W. Norton & Co., 1974.

* * * * * *

SYMPTOM SHIFT/SYMPTOM FORMATION

Within the perspective of family therapy, symptoms, whether physical, psychic, or behavioral, are seen as having an individual as well as a family–wide meaning and/or function. The more that a symptom serves a family–wide function, the greater is the likelihood that, in a static family structure, the disappearance or change in the symptoms of one family member will lead to symptom formation in other family members.

As early as the late 1950s and early 1960s, general practitioners noticed that symptoms could be "passed around" between family members (Kellner, 1963). For example, if a daughter regained an interest in life and work, the mother then showed signs of depression; if a teen–age son "kicked" the drug habit, the father began to drink, and so forth. This type of family–wide symptom (ex)change and shift has been explained in various, often very similar ways. Ackerman (1956) pointed to the "interlocking pathology" in family relationships. Boszormenyi–Nagy and Spark (1973) described the appearance and disappearance of symptomatic behavior from a → **multigenerational perspective** as being, among other things, the consequence and the expression of hidden → **loyalty.** Watzlawick and his associates (Watzlawick, Weakland, & Fisch, 1974) emphasized that the phenomenon of "passing around" symptoms or symptom shift is to be expected when a second–order → **change** is due but has not yet taken place. According to Stierlin (1978), important → **delegations** can be carried out by various members of a family, including that of taking on a symptom. Of central importance here is the concept of → **binding.** The existence of a strong bond prevents attainment of an adequate level of related → **individuation** within the family. When a bound symptom–bearer attempts to escape the family, the pressure is put upon another family member to take up the "relay stick" and to develop substitute symptoms.

All of these formulations accord with an observation made by Schöttler (1981) in the context of his analysis of severely ill, psychosomatic patients: "Towards the end of the second and during the beginning of the third phase of treatment, after about two to three years of treatment, the main psychosomatic symptoms of the patients tend to disappear. . . . At this point one often observes that large numbers of the members of the patient's family become seriously ill. In the beginning it is usually the mother of the patient, followed then by the patient's father, siblings and the patient's spouse. This is especially noteworthy in that all of these patients except one lived apart from their families of origin since the beginning of therapy" (p. 131). The phenomenon of symptom shift or symptom change described above raises a number of difficult questions about the adequacy, efficiency, and the evaluation criteria of procedures used in individually oriented therapy and/or its "success" in any given case.

Ackerman, N. W. Interlocking pathology in family relations. In S. Rado & G. Daniels (Eds.), *Changing concepts of psychoanalytic medicine*. New York: Grune & Stratton, 1956, 135–150; also in D. Block & R. Simon (Eds.), *The strength of family therapy: Selected papers of Nathan W. Ackerman*. New York: Brunner/Mazel, 1982, 174–184.

Boszormenyi-Nagy, I., & Spark, G. M. *Invisible loyalties: Reciprocity in intergenerational family therapy*. New York: Harper & Row, 1973.

Jackson, D. D. Family practice: A comprehenisve medical approach. *Family Process* 7: 338–344, 1966.

Kellner, R. *Family ill health: An investigation in general practice*. New York: Charles C. Thomas & Sons, 1963.

Schöttler, C. Zur Behandlungstechnik bei psychosomatische schwer gestörten Patienten. *Psyche 35:* 111–141, 1981.

Stierlin, H. *Delegation und Familie*. Frankfurt: Suhrkamp, 1978.

Watzlawick, P., Weakland, J. H., & Fisch, R. *Change: Principles of problem formation and problem resolution*. New York: W. W. Norton & Co., 1974.

* * * * * *

SYNERGETICS

Synergetics [Greek *syn,* with, together; *ergon,* work] is a field of scientific endeavor concerned with "how things work together." It addresses especially the question of how structures evolve and organize themselves (→ self-organization). At the same time, it tries to elucidate and formulate the general principles that govern such organizational processes, whether in animate or inanimate nature. Accordingly, synergetics can be defined as the science of ordered, self-organizing, collective behaviors. As such, it offers models of how individuals behave while they interact with each other.

The science of synergetics was pioneered by the theoretical physicist Herman Haken who became interested in processes of self–organization while doing research on laser rays. The concepts that developed out of this work appear to have relevance for the psychosocial domain in general and family therapy research in particular. According to synergetics, all processes of self–organization become intelligible once we assume that numerous interacting subsystems create "a kind of invisible ordering hand" through which they let themselves be "enslaved." Haken speaks of an "order parameter" that governs the behavior of the individual parts (or subsystems) even though it is created through the very interaction of the individual parts. For example, language serves as an order parameter whose rules have to be observed by all those who want to communicate with each other via language. These rules, however, are in themselves the result of processes of verbal communication; they are created, maintained, and altered by the very process of communication. If a system's order parameter changes, its interactional patterns will also change. When several parameters compete with each other, there will result among them a struggle for survival. The system may lose its → **equilibrium** and its → **stability.** It may undergo a → **crisis,** may dissolve into chaos, or develop new structures out of chaos (→ **chaos theory**).

In the realm of human communication processes, → **context marking** may be viewed as such a parameter. Accordingly, any unclarities about context markings (→ **logical types,** → **double bind**) may lead to loss of equilibrium, to crises, or to chaotic interactional patterns. This has special significance for a theory of schizophrenia. Also, any paradigm that serves to structure perception and cognition (→ **paradigm/model/map**) may be viewed as an order parameter that enslaves "the behaviors of a system" (be this a scientific community, a work group, or a family). Like Ilya Prigogine in his theory of "dissipative structures," Haken posits that → **fluctuations** in a system's behavior may compete with each other and may lead to changes in the system's overall structure. One may say that the individual parts in open systems are constantly testing out new interactional patterns and that, in this testing, they are following principles that govern evolution. These principles also determine which patterns will finally prevail (→ **coevolution**). In contrast to closed systems in which disorder (→ **entropy**) increases when they are left undisturbed, open systems (according to synergetics) will constantly develop new order structures (→ **individuation**).

Haken, H. (Ed.). *Synergetics: Cooperative phenomena in multi-component systems.* Stuttgart: Teubner 1973.
Haken, H. *Synergetics: An introduction. Nonequilibrium phase transitions in physics, chemistry and biology* (2nd ed.). Berlin: Springer-Verlag, 1978.
Haken, H. (Ed.). *Pattern formation and pattern recognition.* Berlin: Springer-Verlag, 1979.
Haken, H. (Ed.). *Dynamics of synergetic systems.* Berlin: Springer-Verlag, 1980.
Haken, M. *The signs of structure synergetics.* New York: Van–Nostrand Reinhold, 1984.
Pacault, A., & Vidal, C. (Eds.). *Synergetic: Far from equilibrium.* Berlin: Springer-Verlag, 1978.
Prigogine, I. Time, structures, and fluctuations. *Science 201:* 777–785, 1978.

* * * * * *

SYNTAX/SYNTACTICS

As a part of → **semiotics,** syntax theory concerns itself with the relation between signs. The term syntax [Greek *suntassein,* to arrange in order] designates the set of all formal rules valid for a language or system of signs. The syntax of a language or sign system determines how particular signs may be linked together and how the relation between the signs of the system may be defined. Thus, it determines the structure of the sign system.

All communication processes are bound to the processing of signs; therefore, the structure of the sign system automatically segues into the process of communication. The relation between structure and process, however, is dialectic and reciprocal (→ **structure/function/ process**). Because perceptions through which all knowledge becomes possible are coded and stored in the form of signs, questions regarding the nature of our knowledge (→ **epistemology**) are closely related to inquiry into syntax underlying the model of the world under examination (→ **paradigm/model/map**). Questions such as these are also a concern of → **psycholinguistics.** Family theory and therapy are finding the study of this field increasingly relevant (→ **communication therapy,** → **pragmatics,** → **semantics**).

Bandler, R., & Grinder, J. *The structure of magic, Vol. I.* Palo Alto: Science and Behavior Books, 1975.
Chomsky, N. *Aspects of the theory of syntax.* Cambridge: Massachusetts Institute of Technology Press, 1965.
Chomsky, N. *Language and mind.* New York: Harcourt, Brace, Jovanovich, 1968.
Grinder, J., & Bandler, R. *The structure of magic, Vol. II.* Palo Alto: META Publications, 1976.

Morris, C. W. Foundations of the theory of signs. In O. Neurath, R. Carnap, & C. W. Morris (Eds.), *International encyclopedia of unified science, Vol. I, No. 2.* Chicago: University of Chicago Press, 1938, 77–137.
Morris, C. W. *Signs, language and behavior.* New York: Prentice-Hall, 1946.

* * * * * *

SYSTEM/SYSTEMS THEORY

The most general definition of system [Greek *systema*, a composite thing] is the ordered composition of (material or mental) elements into a unified whole. The various fields of systems research concentrate on differing aspects or perspectives of the elements and systems. General systems theory, like → **cybernetics,** concerns itself with the functions and structural rules valid for all systems, irrespective of their material constitution. The premises of systems theory are based on the insight that a system as a whole is qualitatively different, and "behaves" differently, from the sum of the system's individual elements. In the framework of family therapy, the application of the term "system" is identical to its application in the field of cybernetics. This concept takes account of system features like → **feedback,** the processing and storage of → **information,** → **adaptability,** the ability for → **self-organization,** and the development of → **strategies** for the system's own behavior.

The cybernetic theory of systems provides an abstract framework for the observation of dynamic structures. Its foundations lie in → **control theory,** whose rules were found to have validity outside the realm of mechanical systems where the theory originated. The field of biology in particular proved to exhibit a number of controlling structures. Biological and societal systems, however, are a great deal more complex than mechanical systems. This complexity could only be handled with the aid of abstract mathematical methods, for the most part through set theory approaches. An abstract concept of structure, as developed by Kleene (1956), can be applied to all varieties of phenomena. According to Kleene, a system of objects is a non–empty set, a class or domain (a number of such sets) of objects between which certain relationships exist (see Klaus & Liebscher, 1979, p. 806).

An abstract system concept of this type allows one to view all unities that are isomorphic (→ **isomorphism**) as if they were one and the same system. The entirety of the relationships of such a system is as a rule described as the system's → **structure.** The application of the concepts of systemic theory is a form of → **abstraction,** in other words, the application of a model. The various insights of systems theory have not as yet been conclusively formed into a unified theory, although attempts have been made to develop a "general system theory" (see Bertalanffy, 1950, 1968).

Buckley (1967) also tried to describe the evolution and principles of a general systems theory. In his view, different premises are involved in the description of different systems levels, such as mechanical, organismic, and sociocultural system levels. These levels are hierarchically ordered: Sociocultural systems subsume biological and mechanical ones, but not vice versa. Using Buckley's principles, Fraser (1984) and Duncan (1984) have developed certain therapeutic implications of this view of systems.

The essential difference between theoretical systems models and real processes is the partly random determination of real systems. Further, natural systems as a rule are part of a larger → **context** that usually cannot be grasped in its entirety; hence, the behavior of such a system is not completely predictable. Natural systems are always parts of larger systems whose elements determine the → **stability** of the system in the frame of a reciprocal → **coevolution.** Important epistemological conclusions deriving from systems theory (→ **epistemology**) include those concerning the circular (→ **circularity**) nature of a number of causal processes.

In the light of the above, every unity, regardless of the material composition of its elements, can be viewed as a system. This results in a → **hierarchy** of systems, depending on what is viewed as a "whole" and what is regarded as a "part." Traditionally, psychology has viewed the individual as a unity, and the individual's developmental features and processes have been considered to be a part of this unity. Within the framework of family therapy and theory, the individual is viewed as being a part of the larger system of the family. This view changes the models used to explain an individual's behavior. This wider framework does not view behavior as being independent of environmental conditions and as the product of intrapsychic processes, but as the result of the interplay of reciprocal processes between interactional partners. "Individual" and "family" are seen as systems of differing → **logical types.** The behavior of the family as a whole is determined by the rules of communication and interaction applicable in the family system, as well as by the structure of the family itself, in other words, by the type of reciprocal relations that exist between the members of the family.

What is to be designated as a system, i.e., where the boundaries between system and environment are to be drawn, is a question of definition. The same applies to the distinction between "open" and "closed" systems. The → **boundaries** of "closed" systems do not allow → **information** to penetrate into the system. Such closed systems are largely incapable of adapting to changes in the environment (→

adaptability). Examples of this are those families that have erected a → **rubber fence** between themselves and their social environment, allowing in only information that confirms the family's view of the world. "Open" systems have the ability to change their internal structure by incorporating new information into the system (→ **entropy/negentropy**).

It should be mentioned that other ideas have been put forward regarding the nature of "closed" systems. Keeney (1983), for example, views the family as a "closed organizational system" that attempts to maintain its organizational unity in the face of "disturbances" from the environnment. For practical purposes, in family therapy it is of little consequence whether the therapist's intervention is regarded as leading to a structural change in the family system via introduction of information into an "open informational system" or via "disturbance" of a "closed organizational system."

In family diagnostics it has been found useful to differentiate between family subsystems (parents, sibling, etc.). Within the framework of the subsystems, interactional rules apply that are not valid for the family system as a whole. Parents interact differently toward one another than they do toward their children, and siblings have a set of interactional rules that do not apply to the parents. If the boundaries between subsystems are not clearly defined, this often has far–reaching and pathological consequences for the family as a unit (→ **generational boundaries**, → **perverse triangle**, → **parentification**, → **alliance/coalition/alignment**). There are no general rules for determining which subsystem is to be viewed as relevant for therapy, or which individual family members should be included in therapy. Practical considerations usually will determine whether one makes the circle of participants large or small. The most important determining factor is presumably the degree of mutual → **binding** between individual family members.

Bertalanffy, L. von. *Modern theories of development.* London: Oxford University Press, 1933.

Bertalanffy, L. von. The theory of open systems in physics and biology. *Science 3:* 23–29, 1950.

Bertalanffy, L. von. *General systems theory.* New York: George Braziller, 1968.

Buckley, W. *Sociology and modern systems theory.* Englewood Cliffs, N.J.: Prentice-Hall, 1967.

Buckley, W. (Ed.). *Modern systems research for the behavioral scientist: A sourcebook.* Chicago: Aldine Publishing Co., 1968.

Duncan, B. L. Adopting the construct of functionality when it facilitates system change: A method of selective integration. *Journal of Strategic and Systemic Therapies 3* (3): 60–65, 1984.

Emery, F. E. (Ed.). *Systems thinking: Selected readings.* Harmondsworth, England: Penguin Books, 1969.

356

Engel, G. L. The need for a new medical model: A challenge for biomedicine. *Science 196:* 129–136, 1977.

Engel, G. L. The clinical application of the biopsychosocial model. *American Journal of Psychiatry 137:* 535–544, 1980.

Fraser, J. S. Process level integration: Corrective vision for a binocular view. *Journal of Strategic and Systemic Therapies 3* (3): 43–57, 1984.

Gray, W., Duhl, F., & Rizzo, N. *General systems theory and psychiatry.* Boston: Little, Brown & Co., 1969.

Hill, R. Modern systems theory and the family: A confrontation. *Social Science Information 10:* 7–26, 1971.

Keeney, B. P. What is an epistemology of family therapy? *Family Process 21:* 153–168, 1982

Keeney, B. P. *Aesthetics of change.* New York: Guilford Press, 1983.

Klaus, G., & Liebscher, H. *Wörterbuch der Kybernetik* (4th revised ed.). Frankfurt: Fischer, 1979.

Kleene, S. C. Representation of events in nerve nets and finite automata. In C. E. Shannon & J. McCarthy (Eds.), *Automata studies.* Princeton, N.J.: Princeton University Press, 1956, 3–41.

Koehler, W. Closed and open systems. In F. E. Emery (Ed.), *Systems thinking.* Harmondsworth, England: Penguin Books, 1974, 59–69.

Maturana, H. R. The organization of the living: A theory of the living organization. *International Journal of Man-Machine Studies 7:* 313–332, 1975.

Maturana, H. R., & Varela, F. J. *Autopoiesis and cognition: The realization of living.* Boston: Reidel, 1980.

Miller, J. G. Living systems: The group. *Behavioral Science 16:* 302–398, 1971.

Miller, J. G. *Living systems.* New York: McGraw-Hill, 1978.

Stanton, M. D. Fusion, compression, diversion, and the workings of paradox: A theory of therapeutic/systemic change. *Family Process 23:* 135–167, 1984.

Varela, F. J., Maturana, H. R., & Uribe, R. Autopoiesis: The organization of living systems, its characterization and model. *Biosystems 5:* 187–196, 1974.

* * * * * *

SYSTEMIC THERAPY

This term systemic therapy often is used to refer to the Milan model of family therapy, but also is frequently used with a much wider meaning—interchangeably with the term "systems therapy"—by family therapists who apply principles of → **systems theory** in their work. The Milan model of family therapy consistently uses a → **cybernetic** concept regarding family relationships. A special interview technique, → **circular questioning,** allows the formation and verification/falsification of dynamic hypotheses about the interactional bases and functions of family problems. The therapist assumes a metaposition vis-à-vis the family system by maintaining an attitude of → **neutrality.**

The diversity of family therapists who practice "systemic therapies" can be quickly understood by perusal of contributors to the new publication, *Journal of Strategic and Systemic Therapies,* and by the grouping of models under the heading of "systems therapy approaches" in the *Handbook of Family Therapy* (Gurman & Kniskern, 1981).

The Milan Model of systemic therapy was developed by Selvini–Palazzoli and her coworkers (1978, 1980a). More recently, the original Milan team has divided and adopted approaches that differ (Pirrotta, 1984). The Milan models are based on the work of Bateson (1972) as well as on → **communication theory** as developed by Watzlawick and his associates (Watzlawick, Beavin, & Jackson, 1967; Watzlawick, Weakland, & Fisch, 1974). In these models, the family is viewed as a self–organizing, cybernetic system in which all the elements are linked to one another, and the presenting problem of the family fulfills a specific function for the family system. The social context—for example, the referring institution, the doctors, and the therapeutic team itself—are considered as potentially important elements of the system and, hence, are included in the therapeutic considerations with regard to the family.

Therapy begins with the formulation of hypotheses regarding the reasons why the family is seeking aid from this particular therapeutic institution, the expectations the family has toward the institution, the goals the family hopes to accomplish in the therapy, and the way all of the foregoing relate to the internal structure of the family and/or the presenting problem. These initial hypotheses are examined, confirmed, or revised through the process of circular questioning. In the process, the therapuetic team attempts to establish an idea of the family's → **epistemology** of itself, and to change it if necessary. The precondition for success is the → **neutrality** of the therapeutic team; the team must maintain its metaposition vis–à–vis the family's patterns of interaction. The maintenance of this metaposition is facilitated by using a special treatment setting: Part of the team works directly with the family while the other part observes the interface of team and family from behind a one–way mirror. This procedure makes it more difficult for the family to tempt the therapeutic team into joining in the family interactional system.

From the outset, the hierarchically dominant, "expert" role of the therapeutic team is made clear to the family. The insistence on this dominant position enables the therapeutic team to introduce information into the family system, to create and legitimize new possibilities for behavior through strategies of → **reframing** and → **symptom prescription,** and to evaluate the behavior of individual family members in a manner that contradicts the family's epistemology of itself (→ **positive connotation**). By means of these intervention strategies, the therapeutic team aims to create second–order → **change** in the family system. In accord with this goal, the initiative, the activity, and the responsibility for change or for non–change in family behavior is restored to the family itself. Because systemic therapy uses relatively long intervals between sessions (→ **frequency of sessions**), this gives the family time to change between sessions. On the average, a course of systemic therapy consists of not more than ten sessions, as in **brief therapy,** and often uses → **teamwork/cotherapy.**

"Link therapy," developed by Judith Landau, (1981, 1982) is a systemic form of working with one person rather than the whole system. A transitional map is drawn, illustrating the structure, patterns, and processes of the family through time, and, using this map as a guide, a nonsymptomatic member is selected who is comfortable in connecting with all parts of the system. He or she is trained and coached to be therapist to his or her own family system.

Bateson, G. *Steps to an ecology of mind.* New York: Ballantine Books, 1972.

Gurman, A. S., & Kniskern, D. P. (Eds.). *Handbook of family therapy.* New York: Brunner/Mazel, 1981.

Keeney, B. P., & Ross, J. M. *Mind in therapy: Constructing systemic family therapies.* New York: Basic Books, 1985.

Landau, J. Link therapy as a family therapy technique for transitional extended families. *Psychotherapeia 7:* 382–390, 1981.

Landau, J. Therapy with families in cultural transition. In M. McGoldrick, J. K. Pearce, & J. Giordano (Eds.), *Ethnicity and family therapy.* New York: Guilford Press, 1982, 552–572.

MacKinnon, L. Contrasting strategic and Milan therapies. *Family Process 22:* 425–441, 1983.

Penn, P. Circular questioning. *Family Process 21:* 267–280, 1982.

Pirrotta, S. Milan revisited: A comparison of the two Milan schools. *Journal of Strategic and Systemic Therapies 3* (4): 3–15, 1984.

Selvini-Palazzoli, M. *Self-starvation: From individual to family therapy in the treatment of anorexia nervosa.* New York: Jason Aronson, 1978.

Selvini-Palazzoli, M. Why a long interval between sessions? The therapeutic control of the family-therapist suprasystem. In M. Andolfi & I. Zwerling (Eds.), *Dimensions of family therapy.* New York: Guilford Press, 1980, 161–169.

Selvini-Palazzoli. The problem of the sibling as the referring person. *Journal of Marital and Family Therapy 11:* 21–34, 1985.

Selvini-Palazzoli, M., Boscolo, L., Cecchin, G., & Prata, G. *Paradox and counter-paradox: A new model in the therapy of the family in schizophrenic transaction* (translated by E. V. Burt). New York: Jason Aronson, 1978.

Selvini-Palazzoli, M., Boscolo, L., Cecchin, G., & Prata, G. De erste Sitzung einer systemischen Familientherapie. *Familiendynamik 2:* 197–207, 1977.

Selvini-Palazzoli, M., Boscolo, L., Cecchin, G., & Prata, G. Hypothesizing-circularity-neutrality: Three guidelines for the conductor of the session. *Family Process 19:* 3–12, 1980. (a)

Selvini-Palazzoli, M., Boscolo, L., Cecchin, G., & Prata, G. The problem of the referring person. *Journal of Marital and Family Therapy 6:* 3–9, 1980. (b)

Selvini-Palazzoli, M., & Prata, G. Snares in family therapy. *Journal of Martial and Family Therapy 8:* 443–450, 1982.

Selvini-Palazzoli, M., & Prata, G. A new method for therapy and research in the treatment of schizophrenic families. In H. Stierlin, L. C. Wynne, & M. Wirsching (Eds.), *Psychosocial intervention in schizophrenia: An international view.* Berlin: Springer-Verlag, 1983, 237–243.

Stanton, M. D. Family therapy: Systems approaches. In G. P. Sholevar, R. M. Benson, & B. J. Blinder (Eds.), *Emotional disorders in children and adolescents: Medical and psychological approaches to treatment.* New York: SP Medical and Scientific Books, 1980, 159–179.

Tomm, K. One perspective on the Milan systemic approach: Part I. Overview of development, theory and practice. *Journal of Marital and Family Therapy 10:* 113–125, 1984. (a)

Tomm, K. One perspective on the Milan systemic approach: Part II. Description of session format, interviewing style and interventions. *Journal of Marital and Family Therapy 10:* 253–271, 1984. (b)

Watzlawick, P., Beavin, J. H., & Jackson, D. D. *Pragmatics of human communication: A study of interactional patterns, pathologies and paradoxes.* New York: W. W. Norton & Co., 1967.

Watzlawick, P., Weakland, J. H., & Fisch, R. *Change: Principles of problem formation and problem resolution.* New York: W. W. Norton & Co., 1974.

* * * * * *

■ T ■

TEAMWORK/COTHERAPY

Teamwork has proven to be particularly effective in family therapy. There are three reasons for this: First, in the course of family therapy, it is exceedingly difficult for one person to perceive and process all the information that presents itself; second, supervision and observation of the interaction between therapist and family is a great deal easier when part of the team can observe from behind a one–way mirror; third, cotherapists or team members can more easily and flexibly take complementary roles that highlight intrafamilial differences and thereby can facilitate change.

A central problem for family therapists of all persuasions is the processing of the flood of information that emerges in a family therapy session. A solution to this problem is the cotherapy approach. How this will function depends upon the intervention methods used. Psychoanalytically oriented family therapists favor such therapy as a means of stimulating and controlling transference processes (e.g., by using a male and a female therapist). In the experiential–symbolic model of

Whitaker (Whitaker, 1978; Whitaker & Keith, 1981), cotherapy frees up a therapist to be more innovative and to use fantasy more freely than if he or she were alone without a colleague to "rescue" and provide support (Whitaker, 1975). Heterosexual cotherapy teams are often recommended to engender trust and minimize → **triangulation** in therapy with conflicted, especially divorcing or divorced, couples.

Proponents of → **systemic therapy,** → **strategic therapy,** and → **brief therapy** have often chosen to divide the therapeutic team into two or more groups; one part of the team works directly with the family, and another part of the team observes the therapist–family interaction from behind a one–way mirror. Although the therapists working directly with the family will try to be objective and neutral in their evaluation of the family, this is always a difficult task; exposed to transference and countertransference processes, the therapist almost always becomes involved in family interaction, that is, becomes a part of the "family system." Those team members who observe this interaction from behind a one–way mirror are in a better position to determine which of the observed processes are specific to the family and which have to do with the therapist's interaction with the family.

There are no firmly established rules as to how teamwork is to proceed. For those therapists who are accustomed to working alone, teamwork is often bothersome; such therapists feel that they are being controlled and restricted in their therapeutic methods. When the members of a therapeutic team have some experience in working together, and are able to do so in a noncompetitive atmosphere of trust, the strains of therapy can be greatly eased, and the potential for the processing of information and the introduction of appropriate strategies is substantially improved. Moreover, certain intervention strategies that have been derived from the theory of family therapy can hardly be successfully applied when there is only one therapist; such strategies include → **crisis family therapy,** → **network therapy,** and → **multiple family therapy.**

In recent years a number of innovative uses of a team approach have been introduced in the family and marital therapy field. A creative use of therapeutic teamwork is the "Pick–a–Dali Circus" approach of Landau and Stanton (1983) in which a team of several persons may be in the same room with the family. Members of the team overtly identify with different family coalitions and positions on a given issue. One team member usually serves as "identified therapist" and is joined with the family or the → **identified patient.** Using → **metaphors** and position statements, the team members expand the various positions of the family members, often pushing them to extreme poles, introducing new options, and facilitating change in the family system. Another approach, described by Sheinberg (1985) is to enact a debate among team members, who then present to the family a dilemma that is a strategically constructed isomorph (→ **isomorphism**) of the family situation.

In addition to using team and cotherapy methods in teaching, supervision, and consultation, advocates believe that these approaches produce more rapid and efficient results. However, no studies of cost–effectiveness that takes into account the number of personnel used have yet been reported.

Breunlin, D. C., & Cade, B. Intervening in family systems with observer messages. *Journal of Marital and Family Therapy 7:* 453–460, 1981.

Cornwell, M., & Pearson, R. Cotherapy teams and one-way screen in family therapy practice and training. *Family Process 20:* 199–209, 1981.

de Shazer, S. *Patterns of brief family therapy: An ecosystemic approach.* New York: Guilford Press, 1982.

Landau, J., & Stanton, M. D. Aspects of supervision with the "Pick-a-Dali Circus" Method. *Journal of Strategic and Systemic Therapies 2:* 31–39, 1983.

Montalvo, B. Aspects of live supervision. *Family Process 12:* 343–359, 1973.

Napier, A. Y., & Whitaker, C. A. *The family crucible.* New York, Harper & Row, 1978.

Papp, P. *The process of change.* New York: Guilford Press, 1983.

Penn, P., & Sheinberg, M. Is there therapy after consultation? A consultation map in five steps. In L. C. Wynne, S. H. McDaniel, & T. T. Weber (Eds.), *The family therapist as systems consultant.* New York: Guilford Press, in press.

Selvini-Palazzoli, M., Boscolo, L., Cecchin, G., & Prata, G. *Paradox and counterparadox: A new model in the therapy of the family in schizophrenic transaction* (translated by E. V. Burt). New York: Jason Aronson, 1978.

Sheinberg, M. The debate: A strategic technique. *Family Process 24:* 259–271, 1985.

Stierlin, H., Rücker-Embden, I., Wetzel, N., & Wirsching, M. *The first interview with the family* (translated by S. Tooze). New York: Brunner/Mazel, 1980.

Whiffen, R., & Byng-Hall, J. (Eds.). *Family therapy supervision: Recent developments in practice.* New York: Grune & Stratton, 1982.

Whitaker, C. A. Co-therapy of chronic schizophrenia. In M. Berger (Ed.), *Beyond the double bind: Communication and family systems, theories and techniques with schizophrenics.* New York: Brunner/Mazel, 1978, 155–175.

Whitaker, C. A., & Keith, D. V. Symbolic-experiential family therapy. In A. S. Gurman & D. P. Kniskern (Eds.), *Handbook of family therapy.* New York: Brunner/Mazel, 1981, 187–225.

* * * * * *

TRANSFERENCE AND COUNTERTRANSFERENCE IN FAMILY THERAPY

In introducing the concepts of transference and countertransference, Freud (1905, 1912) drew upon experience in psychoanalysis, in which human relationships were perceived in a new way. Derived from observations in the dyadic interactional setting of psychoanalysis, these concepts change and expand if applied to observations in the setting of family therapy. Minimally, it becomes necessary to differentiate between *transfamilial* and *intrafamilial* transference.

Transfamilial transference phenomena occur when patterns of behavior, fantasies, attitudes, expectations, and the like, which were established in early and intense relationships with members of the individual's family of origin, in particular with the parents, are transferred in an inappropriate manner onto persons who are not members of the family system. Transference processes directed toward the analyst or therapist are examples of transfamilial transference processes, and were long considered to be the only therapeutically relevant type of transference phenomena.

Intrafamilial transference processes occur when transference phenomena are inappropriately directed toward members of the same family system. As a rule, at least two generations of the family are involved. For this reason, one could also speak of "transgenerational transference processes." In family therapy, it is possible to differentiate between two axes of intrafamilial transference: those directed by the parents onto the child, and those directed by the child onto its parents. In the former, the child becomes the target of parental fantasies, attributions, and perceptions, which may appear to rob the child of a personal → **identity.** In such circumstances, the child is often parentified (→ **parentification**). Transference thus plays a part in → **delegation** processes.

When the direction of the transference process is reversed, the child directs the transference toward the parents. A typical example of this is when the child–become–adult continues to direct infantile attitudes, perceptions, and conflicts onto the parents. The parents are thus inappropriately perceived as fantasy–distorted persecutors of childhood or as idealized objects of adulation. In short, the child continues in adulthood to view its parents through the eyes of its childhood experience, and remains unable to differentiate between its fantasies about the parents and the way the parents really are now. This indicates a lack of related → **individuation.**

Family therapists must take account of both forms of transference. All in all, however, intrafamilial transference processes tend to be the most decisive. This means that, in contrast to the dyadic, analytic context, the therapist will be less concerned with the development of complex transference and countertransference processes in regard to his or her own person, and more concerned to understand and exploit the dynamics of intrafamilial transference. Strategies of → **neutrality** and → **multidirectional partiality** help to offset the development of such processes. If such processes become too intense, however, placing a → **positive connotation** on them will insure that they will have a largely positive effect within the therapeutic process. Within context described above, the concept of countertransference gains an expanded and, in some ways, novel significance. It can now be applied to a therapist's attitudes, perceptions, and "blind spots" that hinder his or her attempts to maintain a fair, neutral, and evenly empathic attitude toward the whole family. As a rule, the countertransference problems that therapists have will often be bound up with experiences and unresolved conflicts within their own family of origin (→ **multigenerational perspective**). Hence, a working out of conflicts stemming from one's own experience of earlier family life takes on the same status that training analysis has for neophyte psychoanalysts.

Canavaro, A. Transference and countertransference in family therapy. *International Journal of Family Psychiatry 1:* 249–262, 1980.
Ferenczi, S. Introjection and transference. In S. Ferenczi, *Contributions to psychoanalysis* (translated by E. Jones). New York, Basic Books, 1950.
Freud, S. [1905] Fragment of an analysis of a case of hysteria. *The standard edition of the complete psychological works of Sigmund Freud, Vol. VII.* London: Hogarth Press, 1953, 7–122.
Freud, S. [1912] The dynamics of transference. *The standard edition of the complete psychological works of Sigmund Freud, Vol. XII.* London: Hogarth Press, 1958, 97–108.
Jackson, D. D. Transference revisited. *Journal of Nervous and Mental Disease 137:* 363–371.
Schaffer, L., Wynne, L. C., Day, J., Ryckoff, I. M., & Halperin, A. On the nature and sources of the psychiatrist's experience with the family of the schizophrenic. *Psychiatry 25:* 32–45, 1962.
Stierlin, H. Familientherapeutische Aspekte der Übertragung und Gegunübertragung. *Familiendynamik 2:* 182–197, 1977.

* * * * * *

TRIAL–AND–ERROR METHOD

This is a heuristic procedure that allows a system in an unknown evironment to seek out behavioral alterations in order to insure its adaptation and continuation. The trial–and–error method is a principle that structures the behavior of individuals and families (→ **self–organization, → coevolution**).

The structures of knowledge (→ **epistemology**) develop largely through trial–and–error methods. In order to survive, an individual must satisfy specific needs and seek out and experiment with the best methods to achieve this end. Only those behaviors that lead to this goal in an effective manner are retained. It is for this reason that Ashby (1956) found the term "hunt and stick" more appropriate to describe this phenomenon than "trial and error."

The processes by which a system (an individual or a family) establishes its behavioral repertoire, that is, the development of its survival → **strategy** and adequate → **structure,** is not preordained but, rather, is largely determined by chance. The prerequisite for the application of the trial–and–error method is the existence of → **feedback** processes. Only then is → **learning** possible.

Ashby, W. R. *Design for a brain.* London: Chapman & Hall, 1952.
Ashby, W. R. *An introduction to cybernetics.* London: Methuen, 1956.
Bateson, G. *Steps to an ecology of mind.* New York: Ballantine Books, 1972.
Klaus, G., & Liebscher, H. *Wörterbuch der Kybernetik* (4th revised ed.). Frankfurt: Fischer, 1979.

* * * * * *

TRIANGULATION

Triangulation refers to the expansion of a conflict–ridden, dyadic relationship in order to include a third person (child, therapist, etc), which results either in a "covering–up" or a "defusing" of the conflict.

Partners in conflict may be faced with the dilemma that either one of them wins and the other loses, or that the relationship may fall apart. In such circumstances, a solution to the dilemma may be the inclusion of a third person. The loser in a conflict can compensate for defeat by entering into a covert or overt bond with a third party and thereby reestablishing the balance of the dyadic relationship (→ **perverse triangle**). Conflict also can be avoided if the third party, usually a child, provides a problem (→ **scapegoat**) or is delegated (→ **delegation**) to produce problematic behavior.

Minuchin (1974) described the various forms of pathological triangle structures under the concept of → **rigid triad.** He emphasizes triangulation in which overtly or covertly conflicted parents attempt to win the sympathy and support of their child at the cost of their spouse's relationship to the child. This places the child in an intense conflict of → **loyalty.** Minuchin also describes triangles that serve as a → **detouring of conflicts.**

Bowen (1976) described the "triangle, a three–person emotional configuration," as the "basic building block of any emotional system, whether it is in the family or any other group" (pp. 75–76). This viewpoint differs from the psychoanalytic emphasis on dyadic constellations. The shifting emotional forces within the triangle can be regarded as a special case of the changing configurations in social systems associated with → **alliance/alignment/coalition** and with alienation and splits.

Weakland (1960) comprehensively described three–party interaction in families in relation to → **double bind,** → **marital skew,** → **pseudomutuality,** and the Stanton and Schwartz (1954) hypothesis (three–party institutional situations in which patient disturbance occurs when the patient is the subject of covert or overt staff disagreement).

Besides these pathological forms of triangulation, Bowen (1976) and Zuk (1981) have described therapuetically effective forms of triangulation. In these instances, the therapist relieves the triangulated child by entering into the triangle. Zuk uses the strategy of entering into different coalitions and acting as a "go–between" in order to challenge and change the structure of the system.

Bowen, M. Theory in the practice of psychotherapy. In P. J. Guerin (Ed.), *Family therapy: Theory and practice.* New York: Gardner Press, 1976, 42–90.

Bowen, M. *Family therapy in clinical practice.* New York: Jason Aronson, 1978.

Haley, J. Toward a theory of pathological systems. In G. H. Zuk & I. Boszormenyi-Nagy (Eds.), *Family therapy and disturbed families.* Palo Alto: Science and Behavior Books, 1967, 11–27.

Hoffman, L. *Foundations of family therapy: A conceptual framework for systems change.* New York: Basic Books, 1981.

Jackson, D. D. The eternal triangle: An interview with Don D. Jackson, M. D. In J. Haley & L. Hoffman (Eds.), *Techniques of family therapy.* New York: Basic Books, 1967, 174–264.

Lidz, T., Cornelison, A. R., Fleck, S., & Terry, D. The intrafamilial environment of schizophrenic patients: II. Marital schism and marital skew. *American Journal of Psychiatry 114:* 241–248, 1957.

Minuchin, S. *Families and family therapy.* Cambridge: Harvard University Press, 1974.

Minuchin, S., Rosman, B. L., & Baker, L. *Psychosomatic families: Anorexia nervosa in context.* Cambridge: Harvard University Press, 1978.

Stanton, A. H., & Schwartz, M. S. *The mental hospital. A study of institutional participation in psychiatric illness and treatment.* New York: Basic Books, 1954.

Weakland, J. H. The "double-bind" hypothesis of schizophrenia and three-party interaction. In D. D. Jackson (Ed.), *The etiology of schizophrenia.* New York: Basic Books, 1950, 373–388.

Wynne, L. C., Ryckoff, I. M., Day, J., & Hirsch, S. I. Pseudo-mutuality in the family relations of schizophrenics. *Psychiatry 21:* 205–220, 1958.

Zuk, G. H. *Family therapy: A triadic-based approach* (revised ed.). New York: Human Sciences Press, 1981.

* * * * * *

■ U ■

Undifferentiated Family Ego Mass/ Emotional Stuck-Togetherness/ Lack of Differentiation

Undifferentiated family ego mass is a concept introduced by Murray Bowen to describe "a conglomerate emotional oneness that exists in all levels of intensity" (1966, p. 355). "On one level each family member is an individual, but on a deeper level, the central family group is as one" (1961, p. 45).

The concept implies a specific type of → **individuation** disorder. Some sibling family members "are able to achieve almost complete differentiation from the family while others achieve less. The one who becomes the psychotic is an example of one who achieves little differentiation" and is not treated by the others as if he or she could possibly be autonomous (Bowen, 1961, p. 45). Bowen notes that he uses the term " 'emotional process' to describe the emotional responsiveness by which one family member responds automatically to the emotional state of another, without either being consciously aware of the process" (1960, p. 368). The level of involvement of any one family member in the family ego mass depends on the intensity of the emotional process and the functional relationship of the individual to the central "mass" at that moment.

Psychoanalytically speaking, there exists no perceivable differentiation between self and object, and an individual's identity is suppressed in the interests of avoiding collective conflict (→ **self/ object differentiation, → object relations theory**). Bowen and his followers have increasingly used the term "lack of differentiation of self" to refer to these phenomena. Similar or identical states are described by the concepts of → **pseudomutuality, → enmeshment,** and → **intersubjective fusion.**

Anonymous. Toward the differentiation of a self in one's own family. In J. Framo (Ed.), *Family interaction: A dialogue between family researchers and family therapists.* New York: Springer Publishing Co., 1972, 111–166.

Bowen, M. Family relationships in schizophrenia. In A. Auerback (Ed.), *Schizophrenia.* New York: Ronald Press, 1959, 147–148.

Bowen, M. A family concept of schizophrenia. In D. D. Jackson (Ed.), *The etiology of schizophrenia.* New York: Basic Books, 1960, 346–372.

Bowen, M. The family as the unit of study and treatment. *American Journal of Orthopsychiatry 31:* 40–60, 1961.

Bowen, M. The use of family theory in clinical practice. *Comprehensive Psychiatry 7:* 345–374, 1966.

Bowen, M. Theory in the practice of psychotherapy. In P. J. Guerin (Ed.), *Family therapy: Theory and practice.* New York: Gardner Press, 1976, 42–90.

Bowen, M. *Family therapy in clinical practice.* New York: Jason Aronson, 1978.

Kerr, M. E. Family systems: Theory and therapy. In A. S. Gurman & D. P. Kniskern (Eds.), *Handbook of family therapy.* New York: Brunner/Mazel, 1981, 226–264.

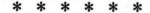

AUTHOR INDEX

374

378

SUBJECT INDEX